SACRED HORSES

Jonathan Maslow

SACRED HORSES

The Memoirs of

a Turkmen

Cowboy

RANDOM HOUSE

NEW YORK

Copyright © 1994 by Jonathan Maslow
Map copyright © 1994 by Anita Karl and Jim Kemp
All rights reserved under International and Pan-American Copyright
Conventions. Published in the United States by Random
House, Inc., New York, and simultaneously in Canada by
Random House of Canada Limited, Toronto.

Library of Congress Cataloging-in-Publication Data
Maslow, Jonathan Evan.
Sacred horses: the memoirs of a Turkmen cowboy/Jonathan Maslow.
p. cm.
"Published in the United States by Random House, Inc.,
New York and simultaneously in Canada by Random House
of Canada Limited, Toronto"—CIP t.p. verso.
Includes bibliographical references and index.
ISBN 0-679-40875-4
1. Turkmenistan—Description and travel. 2. Maslow, Jonathan
Evan—Journeys—Turkmenistan. 3. Horses—Turkmenistan. I. Title.
DK934.M37   1994   915.8'5048—dc20   93-11382

Manufactured in the United States of America
Book design by J. K. Lambert
24689753
First Edition

FOR LILIYA

I do not portray being; I portray passing.

—*Michel de Montaigne*

Fill up your time, to escape nostalgia and regret,
and travel the earth, for perhaps it is your heaven.

—*Sinbad the Sailor*

Acknowledgments

The making of this book over several years would have been impossible without the support and assistance of many individuals and institutions, only some of whom are named within its pages. Therefore, I would like to acknowledge and thank my silent partners in this endeavor: The John Simon Guggenheim Foundation, for initially funding my study of the Russian language; my Russian teachers Svetlana Guo Hong Xu, Lilian Giverts, Mark and Marina Maymind, and my dear Professor Merle Barker of Rutgers University/Camden; my equestrian guru, Ilona Uj-helyi, and my riding philosopher and companion, Professor Betsy Bowden of Rutgers University/Camden; my wonderful Cape May County librarians Marie Jones, Tom Leonard, and Robert Geddis, who have never refused me a single query or request for materials, no matter how arcane or outlandish; my colleagues at the Louisiana Scholars College in Natchitoches, Louisiana, where I started and finished writing this book; and Northwestern State University, which gave me a temporary home while writing.

I would also like to thank new friends made during this project, whose advice and encouragement helped enormously: Victor and Galina Fet; Phil and Margot Case; my fellow delegation members from Albuquerque, Sally Alice Thompson and Professor Greg Gleason of the University of New Mexico; and Steven Weeks, for holding down the fort.

Heartfelt thanks go, too, to my editor at Random House, my rock, always there with the right answers to my most ridiculous questions, and to my agent, Kathy Robbins, along with her user-friendly staff.

For their able assistance in the photographing and filming of the Akhal-Teke horses, I must express my deep appreciation to my old friend Eddie Marritz for all his camera help; Moira Ratchford, who survived the expedition to Turkmenistan with flying colors; Peter Rolufs for his help in putting together the filming kit; Charles Cox for his fantastic faithfulness to the documentary project; Dina Levitt and Claire Downey for their professional succor to a fly-by-night filmmaker; and Peter Blum of Technisphere and Bob Manners of Camera Stop for technical assistance beyond the call. Finally, a posthumous salute to my dear friend Marion Zunz, who helped me shape my journeys to Central Asia, saw me off at the airport, and who never failed to believe in me for a single second. Hail and farewell: We will travel together on that distant shore.

Contents

Acknowledgments *xi*

Map *xiv*

  I.   Sofarawayistan *1*

 II.   The Delegation *29*

III.   In the Shadow of Bucephalus *215*

IV.   Afterword *329*

Selected Bibliography *335*

Index *339*

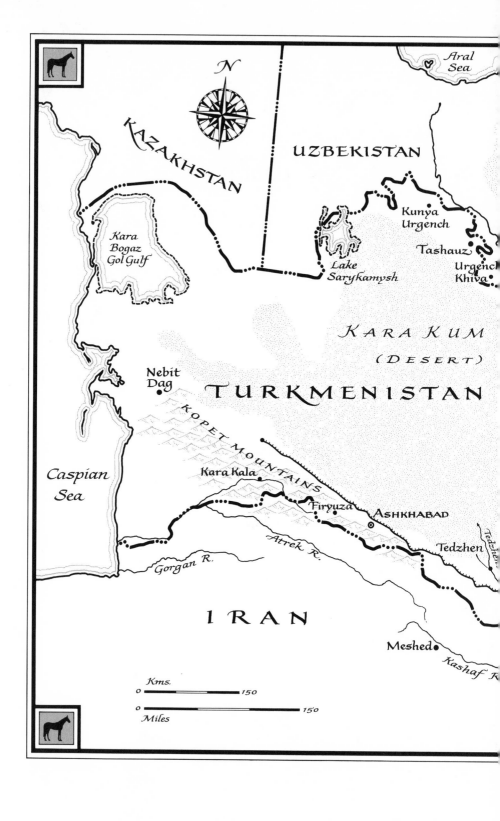

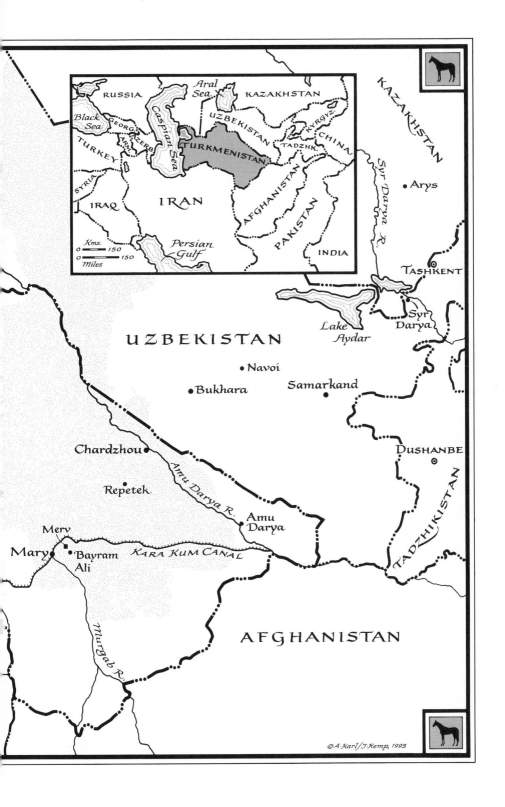

PART I

Sofarawayistan

The earliest story I heard about myself featured equus. I must have been two years old at the time, or at most three—walking, but through a completely novel world. I was being taken for a stroll by my favorite uncle, Max, in Prospect Park, in Brooklyn, where he lived and I sometimes visited. Along the way, we came upon an old-fashioned horse-drawn tinker's wagon, the last of which were still clopping the streets of the outer boroughs of New York City in the early 1950s. Short and thick, swaybacked, sprung-kneed, cock-ankled, galled, cankered, matted, mangy, and every kind of colored, the horse that stood before the cart was what Uncle Max would later describe as the epitome of the "woebegone steed."

"You stood there looking at that woebegone steed," Uncle Max would say, "and, oh, you would have thought it was the most beautiful horse in the entire world. You just stood there in awe, with your mouth open and your eyes wide. All you could say was, 'Horse . . . horse . . .' That old woebegone steed looked like it was on its way to the glue factory. But you would have thought it was Alexander's horse Bucephalus!"

I think many people feel this same powerful, mystical attraction the first time they cast their eyes on horses. Most probably get over it; I never did. Uncle Max was a high school history teacher who knew how to light a flame under his students. He tied my boyish fascination with horses to chess, knights, chivalry, barbarians, and the Middle Ages. It was from him I first heard the names Alexander the Great and Genghis

Khan. Another year when I went to visit him in New York, he took me to the great hall of medieval armor at the Metropolitan Museum of Art, where each poised phantom knight in his sun-drenched suit of chain mail and wondrously wrought plate armor is mounted on a life-size statue of a puissant medieval charger in full chivalric regalia. The second story I ever heard about myself was how I dragged my cousin Abby by the hand up under the legs of one of the horses to check out the genitalia.

There came next a religious devotion to television cowboys, particularly to my personal saint, Hopalong Cassidy—a slightly portly middle-aged graying hero, who rode a snow-white quarter horse with a beautiful flowing mane on a silver-studded saddle—whom I desperately wanted to be my father. His sidekick was Gabby Hayes, a comic frontier character actor with the slow rural wit of Sancho Panza. Each episode promised a climactic chase at full gallop. I have called it a religious experience, but perhaps ethical is better because it was through television cowboys that many boys of my generation learned our semblant sense of right and wrong. My early ideas of virtue were intimately tied up with riding horses.

Then, laid up in the hospital with a broken wing in the rambunctious summer of my sixth year, I refused to stop crying until my parents brought to the children's ward a complete metal model set of Camelot—the castle, not the movie—with a hundred toy knights and a hundred toy chargers.

From this moment on, I lived at King Arthur's Round Table. I actually practiced walking pigeon-toed and bowlegged, as if I spent all my days hugging the sides of my steed. When I thought no one was looking at the dinner table (which was often, because our family ate at different times due to work schedules), I would imitate medieval table manners, tearing a hunk of meat off with my teeth and tossing the bone to the family Airedale; when caught, I was immediately ordered to leave the great dining hall of the castle, which had in the meantime reverted to our own modest suburban kitchen.

I learned to read with one and only one purpose in mind: to consume again and again the tales of Lancelot and Galahad, Sir Gawain and Sir Kay, and, of course, the Redcrosse Knight (cool name!). I scrutinized the illustrations of charging and jousting in literally scores of old volumes of those tales, as well as the illustrations of Lady Godiva, who was sometimes shown riding a black horse in her pale-white buff. I took one

4

copy after another of the Arthurian legends out of the public library, and at the truly foolish age of eight started carrying a wooden sword and cardboard shield. All I wanted for Christmas was a scratchy white wool sweater with a red cross on it. This Arthurian mania went on for several years and was not, I see now, easy for my parents to cope with. Is it any wonder a psychiatrist I once consulted concluded I had a "white knight" complex—the overwhelming need to rescue women from dire straits and win their love?

The only real freedom the knights errant had was the freedom of movement, attained with their horses. It was this same freedom I came to treasure above all others: that liberty to be here and gone, to roam the world like a nomad.

They say most girls lose their passion for horses when they discover boys. I'm not a girl and I didn't lose anything. Instead of losing my passionate identification with horses, it only got stronger as I grew older. I went to work after college at a Vermont horse farm near a New Hampshire track. My menial duties were to turn the horses out to pasture in the morning (they were trotters), muck out the stalls, spread new wood chips down, spread the manure out in the pasture with a tractor, get the horses back into their stalls by dark, and feed them before leaving. Once a week I would go down to the local sawmill with Miss Phoebe, the young woman who owned the farm, and shovel a ton of wood chips down from the mill attic through a chute into her pickup truck. The rest of the time I mended fences with her aged father. I earned a whole dollar and a half an hour, plus one square meat-and-potatoes midday meal. I was as happy as a little shepherd boy, and from this time decided I would throw in my lot with country people, and reside in rural areas where horses are prevalent.

Miss Phoebe was all business. She came out to work in the crisp Vermont mornings in knee boots and riding breeches, her glossy black hair tied back in a ponytail. She didn't bother with gloves or ear muffs. Her skin was like bleached leather. She would spend the mornings exercising horses with the sulky up and down the country road. In the afternoon she was busy either trailering horses to the track or getting new boarders. Under her hand even strung-out Thoroughbred stallions eventually became pliant. Although my job involved no riding, from being around her I picked up a serious attitude and calm disposition when dealing with horses. I never saw her lose her temper, even if she was stepped on. I also got my first glimpse of that romantic notion at the root of all horsemanship: that human and animal can work together as a team, blending mind and muscle in a perfectable union, to accomplish something as useful as transport, as beautiful as a high, fast trot, as thrilling as a race over seven furlongs.

A huge mountaineering pack stuffed with bedroll, clothes, and gear for an undetermined length of stay in the semiarid wastes of Central Asia. High black riding boots, bootjacks, and breeches. A hundred dollars' worth of Bic pens, Marlboro cigarettes, lipstick, mascara, chewing gum, balloons, baseball cards, pocket calculators, rubber balls, condoms, aspirins, fifty-nine-cent perfumes, a couple dozen pairs of cheap panty hose—in short, trade gifts for every man, woman, and child in the Republic of Turkmenistan. A money belt worn around my waist containing five hundred dollars in one-dollar bills, perhaps equally useful for emergency airfare or bribes. A camera bag with two 35 mm. bodies, three lenses, a Polaroid instant with extra film, and fifty rolls of color slide film. A pannier with maps of Central Asia, a pocket atlas of the then Soviet Union, notebook, Russian dictionary, a Russian grammar I'd concocted myself, documents, and several creative letters of introduction I had also composed and thought might come in handy.

These and a big gray cowboy hat, to prove I was indisputably American under any circumstance, were what I was carrying when I hooked up with Mrs. Sally Alice Thompson in Kennedy Airport for the long outbound trip to Turkmenistan. She was a retired schoolteacher and citizen-diplomat, a kindly, gray-haired woman with a beatific, auntly expression, wearing a trench coat with a lot of miles on it and sensible shoes, leading a small valise and video camera on a set of collapsible wheels. How brave, I thought, for a woman her age to go traipsing off to Turkmenistan, a place that does not even appear on most maps of the USSR and has no communications with the West. We flew to Frankfurt, where we shared a four-dollar pint of orange juice in the glitzy terminal for transit passengers, then boarded a Lufthansa flight for Moscow. It was mid-April, and as the jet began its descent, one could see rivers thawing below. A cold sunny haze drifted over great jagged chunks of ice—not white and blue ice, but strangely brown and gray, as if haggard, fatigued, and fouled.

Since the domestic flight from Moscow to Ashkhabad, the Turkmen capital, was not departing till the next morning, we had to spend the night in the Soviet capital. I had no particular wish to visit Moscow for one day in a state of jet lag, forming the kind of superficial impression that passes for expert testimony back home, so I decided to regard this delay as nothing more than a linguistic opportunity to try out my newly learned Russian. I imagined myself as a participant in an "arrival in Moscow" dialogue of the kind contained in every Russian language textbook—"Hello. I'm so pleased to meet you. My name is . . ."

"You are foreigner?"

"I am an American tourist."

"Tourist? That is good joke. You look like foreign spy. What is your object here in Soviet Union?"

"Sightseeing. Could you please show me your military installations, nuclear facilities, and the private homes of your political leadership?"

For the first time I can remember in my adult life, I did not make a single entry in my notebook.

Sally Alice had arranged home hospitality for us through an international hosting organization to which she belonged. The apartment was located by the outer bank of the Moscow River in one of the city's infamously anonymous drab housing complexes. It belonged to a sad-eyed theatrical singer named Marina and her musician-boyfriend Volodya, childlike in his innocence. The apartment was full of tomato and cabbage seedlings in paper cups for the couple was tenaciously taking advantage of one of the perestroika reforms: renting a garden plot for one ruble to grow vegetables. With the arrival of Professor Greg Gleason, an academic expert on Central Asia who had already been in Moscow for a month doing research at the Soviet Academy of Sciences, our little American delegation to Turkmenistan was complete.

We were up at 4:30 A.M. for the long taxi ride to the airport, transiting in the half-light of dawn a city that seemed more shadow than substance. The roads were already clogged with dark gnarly military trucks, tankers, heavy equipment, and Jeeps. Icy rain mixed with diesel exhaust spewed smog over the highway. Then the city fell away, and we drove through miles and miles of groves thick with white birches. The trees stood magnificently straight and silent, like noble witnesses to a sorrowful Slavic saga.

There are words in every language that convey meaning by their sound alone; the name of Domodedovo Airport is among them. It was a world-class house of the dead, fit only for the transport of corpses. The main terminal was more crowded than a New York subway train at rush hour, and the people milling or struggling to get through seemed even angrier than New Yorkers. Amid the sleet, slop, and squalor of the floor, large families of unknown ethnic origin were sleeping in heaps on their luggage. As soon as we entered, we joined this writhing mass of humanity, and there was no longer any way to know where we were being taken, much less direct ourselves.

After being pushed and shoved to the other side of the terminal, we confronted nothing more than a confusing series of closed and draped office doors with no signs. Fortunately, Greg had been out to Domodedovo to get ticket information several days earlier and knew where to turn. We entered a smaller glassed-in area with an Aeroflot desk and a souvenir stand. At the check-in counter, one woman was handling tickets, while another was accepting baggage. Although separated by only three feet, they spoke to each other over a public address system. I was intently practicing my Russian verbs of motion, trying to make the place go away.

"*Ya u-letayu.*" "I am flying away." "*Ya budu prilechat'.*" "I will land [somewhere else]." "*Ya lechu.*" "I am leaving in an airplane [but I will come back]."

We were directed to buy our tickets at the tiny window of a cramped office that seemed to emit only duotone gray, like a newspaper photograph. Greg, whose Russian was by far the most fluent of the three of us, stepped up and began, "Excuse me, I would like—"

"And I don't like," the woman official inside snapped back. She immediately rose from her seat and left the office.

"Wow—testy," Greg said with a smile. Short and good-looking in his sporty golf cap and professorial tweed sport jacket, he also looked unmistakably foreign. His good humor made him seem all the more unrepentantly so. On the flight to Frankfurt, Sally Alice had told me the story of how she had met Professor Gleason. Shortly after she initiated the Sister Cities contacts between Albuquerque, New Mexico, and Ashkhabad that had led to our trip, a local anti-Communist had objected to the Albuquerque city council on the grounds that there had been a prison camp in Turkmenistan under Stalin. Professor Gleason had written a letter to the newspaper pointing out that the Turkmen were a poor and powerless ethnic minority in a marginal backwater of the Soviet empire, and very eager to meet people from the United States and other parts of the world. They could hardly be blamed for Stalin's crimes against humanity; in fact, they had suffered themselves.

Greg said, "She'll come back in a few minutes and I'll give her what they call here a 'little gift,' and then she'll become much more tractable and sell us the tickets."

There had been some discussion about our being able to purchase tickets for rubles once we were in country, but today this was clearly not in the cards. For a two-dollar bribe each, we were sold Moscow–Ashkhabad tickets for sixty dollars in hard currency. Then two luggage lackeys led us down an outside back staircase to a waiting school bus, which drove us and about fifty others around one wing of the terminal to another separate waiting area—another cattle yard without chairs or benches.

It was still a few minutes before the airport café opened. I was famished from not having had anything substantial since we had arrived the day before. Also, I doubted that in this country there could be such a thing as a breakfast flight, so I was prepared for some "defensive" eating, in case nothing should appear later on. Remembering my family's credos—"Always eat before you go to a stranger's house at mealtime" and "Always stick something in your pocket to eat down the road"—I muscled in with the opening surge as soon as the café doors were unlocked—only to find that the customers were being served plates of loathsome skinned, steamed, slimy greenish frankfurters, which I could no more eat than the putrid carcass of road-killed crow. But then I found some lovely fresh-baked raisin biscuits and glasses of tea with sugar lumps, and was happy for the first time since landing. How easily people adapt to want and deprivation: The road to a human's ideological loyalty is through the alimentary canal.

The passengers were hurried onto a proper shuttle bus, then driven two hundred feet to yet another waiting room, where military security X-rayed and hand inspected our carry-on luggage. The white Ilyushin jets were all impressively lined up outside wing to wing across the tarmac. At last they rolled the boarding stairs up to our aircraft. The rain was petering out. I was antsy to get going; anything would be better than another hour at Domodedovo.

In crudely oversimplified terms, the geography of the former Soviet Union is divided into two parts. In the north are vast forests known as taigas, broken by the Ural Mountains, but basically extending east to the Siberian Arctic. In the south the steppes of Eurasia stretch from Ukraine to Manchuria, some thirty-five hundred miles of wide-open semiarid grasslands and deserts linking the European and Asian landmasses. The steppes of Central Asia are among the most remote, unknown, least assimilated, and physically forbidding regions of the extinct Soviet empire. Summer in the steppes is blazing hot and bone dry, with normal daily temperatures reaching 105°F. Winter is windy and cold, with temperatures dropping to −59°F. The steppes are completely treeless except for riparian woods. In the Russia of the czars, those who had to travel them would set off in a horse-drawn droshky, simply following the direction in a straight line, no geographical obstacles to detour them and no roads necessary. The mind can hardly embrace the empty longing of Anton Chekhov's description of the steppes: "Sultry heat in summer, in winter frost and snowstorms, terrible nights in autumn when nothing is to be seen but darkness and nothing is to be heard but the senseless angry howling wind, and, worst of all, alone, alone for the whole of life."

Humans have used the Central Asian steppes as pasture for horses, sheep, camels, and goats since at least 3000 B.C., and it was from this same region that horse-mounted nomads terrified and decimated the settled ancient worlds of China and Europe. The nomads of the Eurasian steppes, whose depredations followed almost exactly the distribution pattern of the wild Eurasian horse, were a major influence on the Russian national character, which is traditionally viewed by Russians as the product of the long life-and-death struggle between forest and steppe. The Russians draw their national myth from the aggrieved notion that they were set back many centuries in the development of civilization by shielding Europe from the steppes barbarians, and then delayed several centuries more under the bitter Mongol yoke. As a Russian prince told the Marquis de Custine at the start of his Russian travels in 1839: "Russia today is scarcely four hundred years removed from the invasion of the barbarians, whereas the West was subjected to the same crisis fourteen centuries ago. A civilization a thousand years older puts an immeasurable distance between the morals of nations. . . . Since the invasion of the Mongolians, the Slavs, until that time one of the freest peoples of the world, have become slaves—first of the conquerors and afterwards of their own princes. . . . Think at each step you take in this land of Asiatic people that the influence of chivalry and Catholicism has been missed by the Russians."

Yet as the "Mother Earth" of Russian folk myth, the soil and sky without limit, as well as the crossroads of the old East–West and North–South trade routes, connecting East and West like a great sea without water, the Eurasian steppes have always effected a strong pull on the Russian soul. "You, too, are an exile," wrote Mikhail Lermontov. "You wail for your wide spacious steppes! There you had room to unfurl your cold wings."

The steppes pulled on my restless soul, too. In 1988, when the reforms taking place in the USSR gave promise of making freedom of travel possible for foreigners, an ardent desire and crazy idea burned in my head: to cross the steppes at a steady trot, with only the treeless plain, the horizon, and Chekhov's "baked lilac sky" before me. I had just turned forty, the biblical halfway point in life, and found myself divorced and without children—in other words, a biologically superfluous male, footloose, and still afflicted with a pulsating wanderlust. The German cognate for the English word "wander" is *bewandert*, which originally meant skilled and proficient, associating travel with learning and education. What little proficiency and few skills I had developed in the first half of life had come about mainly through the heurism of travel. Temperamentally impatient, I had learned to let days on the road unfold at their own pace. I never sought in foreign travel a cure for, or escape from, the frustrations of modern life, only the psychological stamina to put up with those frustrations.

So much of the supposedly exciting life of the world traveler consists of sheer waste of time and boredom: This contradiction alone, whether discovered anew in a tropical forest or at O'Hare Airport, taught me to be on guard for the ways all apparent human realities succumb, upon analysis, to quite different inner realities. I had spent much time by myself in countries where I had no one to rely on. It was not self-reliance I sought or developed, but its very opposite: the necessity, as a matter of self-preservation, to emerge from my individualist Western shell and find companionship with animals, trees, winds, rain, and landscapes. Spending time with inarticulate people, I had learned to observe in silence. Moreover, my travels had shown me in a visceral way the great discovery of physics that time and space are not separate and opposed realms, but a continuum. To travel through the world is to travel through history, whatever fossils of the human past may cross our path.

But more than anything, I wanted to visit the plains where horses were first domesticated, husbanded, and ridden. I was eager to count the mammals and the flowers of spring, and to find the storied nomads. Even if none still existed, I wanted to see their lands, their animals, and to hear at close hand tales of them. I let intuition and dreams lead me on. Writers are becoming, willy-nilly, the anthropologists of our time while young anthropologists increasingly avoid traditional or "primitive" cultures in favor of studying the effects of fast-food restaurants on family life in Atlanta—thereby avoiding the difficulties of travel, arranging absences from academic positions, and learning languages. The societies on the margin of the developed world are being abandoned to gumptious journalists and dreamy scribblers. It is anthropology on the cheap and, what's more, bad anthropology, for writers always have their own agendas, and make no pretense to objectivity. We love a good story more than the most prized fact.

Readers should beware: It is the very extinction of traditional cultures all over the world that has driven trained anthropologists away from their study and drawn writers to them. They symbolize something many writers believe about our own society, for writers are rarely on good terms with it, while anthropologists have been largely neutralized by the decent and sensible world of tenure, grants, and the statistically measurable. Going and almost gone are the white-maned romantics, the eccentric ladies in safari suits, anthropologists who would disappear to study the peyote cult somewhere unreachable in Mexico, or archaeologists who would dig for years on end in remote Syria. About all that is left of that generation, aside from their books and museum collections, are

Indiana Jones movies. In other words, with the increasing infiltration of writers into the far-flung realms of human society, anthropology is returning to the worst aspects of nineteenth-century amateurism.

Though I thought at the outset that such a journey across the steppes was highly unlikely, I could still take pleasure in the prodigious planning and preparation—particularly with finally undertaking in middle age to become a competent horseman, and with trying to learn the Russian language. In addition, in 1988, I knew very little about the horses of the Central Asian steppes.

The Eurasian steppes are almost indisputably the place where humans first domesticated, bred, and eventually mounted horses as well as one of the places where *Equus caballus* flourished as a wild species. The exact date of the horse's domestication is unknown, but by the third millennium B.C., steppe herdsmen were likely keeping mares for food and milk, leaving them in season where wild stallions would cover, or mate with, them. Everything learned from paleontology and archaeology tends to confirm the idea that a wild blood horse continued to exist in Central Asia long after domestication. According to Soviet mammalogist W. O. Witt, it had "outstanding speed and endurance, (was) high on the leg, with a dished face, and highly developed nervous system."

With the invention by the Central Asian nomads of the harness and stiff saddle, steppe peoples were ready for a life of long migrations and constant mounted warfare over pasturage and water. They were highly mobile cavalry archers—the scourge of ancient warfare—and traveled with their herds in front of them so that each man might create the scarifying effect of fifty. When the Scythians swept across the steppes in the seventh century B.C., they already were the ancient world's most infamous warriors. Herodotus said of them, "Their country is the back of a horse." By that time, they were gelding colts for use as pure riding horses. These Central Asian light cavalry-type horses became far and away the most famous horses of the ancient world, sought after by Chinese emperors, Mongol khans, and Persian sultans. When Herodotus described the Persian empire's military resources led by King Xerxes into Greece in 480 B.C., the Arabs were expressly distinguished as riding camels, not horses, while the Central Asian tribes contributing horse cavalry were those who gave their names to these anciently renowned breeds: Turanian, Bactrian, Median, and Parthian horses. Eventually, they acquired the name Turkoman horse, from the Turkoman tribes who were the most recent nomads to occupy the extreme southwestern

Asian dry steppes and deserts. This classical area of fine horse breeding is located in the former Soviet Republic of Turkmenistan.

About one year after I began to plan my journey across the steppes, I came across an article on Turkmenistan in a Soviet magazine. It described a Socialist republic in the Kara Kum Desert with a population of "former nomads" now practicing settled agriculture with the help of water from the eleven-hundred-kilometer Kara Kum Canal, a monumental Soviet engineering project diverting water from the Amu Darya River. The Amu Darya had been known in ancient times as the Oxus and was the limit of the known world until Alexander's march through barbarian Asia. The intriguing term "former nomads" seemed to go along with the article's coy admission that tampering with nature on such a grand scale as diverting the Amu Darya River was the principal reason the Aral Sea was drying up, creating new desert and salinated wastelands. What is a former nomad anyway? I wondered. Did it mean a people granted sufficient pasturelands that they were no longer forced to migrate and conflict with their neighbors, or a people denied all rights to herds and pasturelands, thus cut off from their traditional livelihood and culture? Perhaps it was some combination of the two, but the article did not say, and the term itself smacked of the ruthless process by which "civilization" was imposed on peoples by more technologically advanced societies for profits and political ends.

Much to my surprise and excitement, however, the article went on to say that Turkoman horses were still bred there, refined further as the Akhal-Teke breed. Consulting *The Encyclopedia of the Horse,* I found the Akhal-Teke described, in unflattering terms, as "a small, lean, wiry, obstinate horse," albeit with a handsome and unique golden-colored coat possessing a "brilliant metallic sheen." Cryptic coloring and camouflage for life on the golden steppes? Akhal-Tekes, I further learned, are among the world's toughest breeds. They were employed in a famous marathon trek in 1935 from Ashkhabad—the marvelously named capital of Turkmenistan—to Moscow, some 2,500 miles, during which the horses crossed 225 miles of the Kara Kum Desert bounding the steppes on the north in three days with no water whatsoever.

When the Soviet curators of the fine exhibition "Nomads of the Eurasian Steppes" at the National Museum of Natural History in Washington agreed that Turkmenistan was the best place to go if I hoped to find horses, ex-nomads, and ride through the Eurasian steppes, I began to focus on that little-known and remote corner of the world called the

Soviet Republic of Turkmenistan—where, the Soviet ethnologists warned, I ought to bring a truckload of provisions since there was nothing at all to eat. In this matter, however, they proved incorrect. When I finally got to Turkmenistan, all the people did was eat. I have never seen more food in my life.

For the next two years I tried in every way imaginable to visit the Central Asian Soviet Republic of Turkmenistan. Before perestroika and glasnost, travel to the region had been *streng verboten* (strictly forbidden) to foreigners. For one thing, it was a Muslim area. More important, it shared frontiers with Iran to the southwest and Afghanistan to the southeast. In short, it was a zone of formidable Stalinist paranoia, and later, when a Turkmen friend took me for a Saturday afternoon drive through miles and miles of desert pockmarked with KGB listening posts, Red Army patrol towers, barbed-wire fences, and fields of Erector set military installations, I saw how fear and mistrust could decorate and desolate a desert landscape. In the 1980s, with war raging in Afghanistan, political scientists commonly referred to Central Asia as the "soft Moslem underbelly" of the Soviet empire, and boldly prophesied the possible breakup of the Soviet Union along religious lines sometime in the twenty-first century. Which once again shows how alarmingly wrong political scientists can be.

Still, despite the new openness that began in 1985 with Mikhail Gorbachev's ascent to power, getting to the Kara Kum Desert proved no simple matter. Prospective foreign visitors had to go through a byzantine bureaucratic process. Before the Soviet embassy in Washington would grant a visa, an official invitation to the Soviet Republic of Turkmenistan had to be obtained—except that the Soviet authorities would not help obtain the invitation. "We can be of no assistance. We can provide no information" was the canned answer the embassy officer dished out. That was all.

Nor, I discovered, was there any way of communicating directly with Turkmenistan; therefore, no method of soliciting the invitation document on my own. The Soviet magazine article on Turkmenistan had mentioned an Akhal-Teke stud farm in Ashkhabad, but there turned out to be no direct telephone links from the West to Ashkhabad. Calls from the United States were routed through Moscow, then supposedly to Tashkent, in the Central Asian republic of Uzbekistan. There all telephonic communications died, like a river vanishing into the desert. Listening to the line ring for half hours at a time, I imagined that last telephone pole in Uzbekistan standing like Christ's cross in a windy void, a mane of lines dangling raggedly down, rattling in the sirocco: alone! alone till the end of time! In any event, the operators in Tashkent never answered. Allah only knows if there *are* telephone operators in Tashkent.

I launched letters into vacuous space, the envelopes addressed in reverse order—country first, name last—in the old Russian postal custom. When no replies arrived in a year's time, I was sure they had never been delivered—*also* an old Russian postal custom. Perhaps even now, in a completely transformed USSR, my letters are lying, written in bad Russian, at the bottom of a pile on the desk of a low-level KGB officer in Moscow. If he ever opens them, I hope he sees the ridiculous humor in them.

Month after month I made telephone calls to private American exchange organizations, foundations, universities, scientific institutes, writers' and journalists' associations, geographical societies—anyone I thought might know something about Turkmenistan, or have contacts among the Turkmens. All useless. Even organizations wholly dedicated to Soviet–American relations hadn't a clue.

"Turkmenistan?" I heard the question mark in the voice many times. Then head scratching, uncrinkling of maps. "You mean Kazakhstan?"

"No. Turkmenistan."

"Tadzhikistan?"

"No."

"Kirghizstan?"

"Never mind."

Now isn't that just the way it is? I asked myself. Here we are, charging full tilt into the Information Age, celebrating planetary shrinkage and the growth of the global village, with all our dandy computer networks and satellite uplinks, the whole damn solar system supposedly on our remote-control devices, and then there is Turkmenistan—better known, in fact, to Marco Polo in the thirteenth century.

What is called Turkmenistan today then lay along the northern route of the Great Silk Road, which the Polos traversed on their way to Cathay to discover spaghetti and to trade with the Chinese. As caravan merchants, the Polos knew these lands well enough. They once spent several years in nearby Bukhara, waiting out a war. Marco Polo mentions the "Turcomans" on the very first page of his memoirs: "a primitive people, speaking a barbarous language," he curtly summed them up. But the Venetians praised their "good Turcoman horses," and said they wove the most beautiful carpets in the whole world.

Before Genghis Khan and his Golden Horde pulverized the territory to lifeless dust in 1219, the area of much of modern-day Turkmenistan was known as Khwarizm. Or Khwârazm. Or Khwarezm, which is milder on the throat and tongue. Or just Chorasmia, as the ancient Greeks called it.

The Mongols' intention was to obliterate Muslim civilization, which had flourished in Khwarizm since the Arabian conquest at the beginning of the eighth century. The Arab geographers of Islam's fabulous bloom described southwest Asia in lyrical details from firsthand knowledge. Ibn Battutah compared the Chorasmian capital Urgench to "the perturbing sea," because there were so many people bustling about in its bazaars and streets.

Long before the Mohammedans spread the Word of Allah on horseback, however, the same Chorasmia lay athwart the path of Alexander the Great on his otherwise whirlwind march across the world. The horse-mounted tribesmen of Chorasmia, Parthia, Sogdiana, Hyrcania, Margiana (sometimes known collectively as the Sacae) put up such a fierce guerrilla-style resistance to Alexander's phalanxes—the first highly mobile light cavalry the Greeks, or any Europeans, had ever encountered—that no chronicler of ancient times failed to speak of them. Arrian, in the *Anabasis of Alexander,* written in about 150 A.D., told the story of Pharasmanes, king of the Chorasmians, who, in submitting his tribe to Alexander's power, offered to personally conduct the king through Chorasmian dominions to the land of the Amazons, bordering Chorasmia, a tribe of woman warriors who fought with javelins and short bows from the backs of their tall, swift horses. It is said the Amazon queen came to Alexander with a proposition of sexual union, maintaining that the child would be proclaimed a god at birth.

As winter followed autumn, and autumn followed summer, making no noticeable progress toward actually obtaining travel documents to Turkmenistan, I delved into Strabo, dabbled in Quintus Curtius Rufus, and daydreamed around the *Histories* of Herodotus, written several generations before Alexander and a lot less certain of what was fact and what was fantasy in "hither Asia." Not a single ancient writer, however, Muslim or pagan, failed to mention the stupendous quality of the region's riding horses. Herodotus said they were sacred among the Persians. Xenophon, the Greek historian who wrote *Treatise on Horsemanship,* the first book still extant on horses, tells the story of a Sacae horseman at the equestrian contests celebrating the Persian Cyrus the Great's capture of Babylon, who left the others at the starting line and finished the race half the length of the hippodrome ahead of the pack. Then the Sacaen presented his horse to one of Cyrus's companions as a gift. For this reason, some say the Sacae were never really vassals of Persia, but rather considered as allies.

Such tales only made me want to go to Turkmenistan all the more.

So absorbed did I become in my private campaign to go to the steppes of Central Asia that I almost failed to notice that my knowledge of the Russian language was actually advancing. After two years of sweat and toil, it had gone from less than zero to merely pathetic. I could now express myself almost as well as a Russian two-year-old. Make no mistake: I had no illusions I could become fluent in Russian. Such a hard language would take years of study and practice to speak competently, and such a labor would be better done by a younger linguist than I. No, I had entered Johns Hopkins University's summer immersion program in Russian with the much more modest hope of accomplishing simple conversations, particularly asking and comprehending travel directions. One has a strong disinclination to be always dependent on guides and interpreters, and I have long felt that traveling through a foreign country with no clue to its language is like making love to a complete stranger—exciting but, in the end, meaningless.

Johns Hopkins's summer Russian institute was run like a slave labor camp, which was fine with me. Five days a week, my six classmates and I were tortured through three hours of class, slapped around three hours of language lab, then subjected to six hours of punishing written homework. In short, one ate, breathed, and slept Russian—though as for sleep, there wasn't much time. Only an orderly masochist could have delighted in the smell of sweat coming off that mental *gymkhana*.

Russian, I soon discovered, is a language with an immense iron superstructure of grammar upon which are welded thousands of rules. It is like an office complex from hell, built to house an infernal lingual bureaucracy. Not only are there rules to boggle the mind, but each rule has perhaps four hundred, or slightly more, exceptions. This makes Russian seem like a language at war with itself, and at first one is astonished that such a language has produced some of the world's most emotionally deep literature—the poems of Pushkin, the prose of Tolstoy, Turgenev, Pasternak. There is no present tense of the verb "to be." Therefore, you cannot say, "I am," "you are," or even "we are." There is no direct way of saying "I have." You must say instead the equivalent of "There is by me." No direct way of saying "I like." You say, "To me it is pleasing." No direct way of saying "I'm thirsty"; instead you must say, "I want to drink." There is no word for "thirsty" in Russian.

By the same token, if it's nasty syntax you're after, Russian is made for you: Double negatives are encouraged ("I don't need no help in Russian because it don't matter none to me"). Every noun has twelve cases, six singular and six plural. Impersonal constructions make it hard to know who's doing what to whom. Most fun of all, Russian verbs are chosen not only to describe action, but also various "aspects" of the action (such as whether the action was completed, happened more than once, or was successful in outcome). Taking these verbal aspects into account means there have to be many more verbs in Russian than in English—or for that matter, in any Romance language since we all have tenses, not "aspects." Russian needs perhaps four or five times as many verbs. This is why the average American has three thousand words in his everyday vocabulary, while the typical Russian has about seven thousand.

Then there are plain nonsense rules, like this one, from our textbook: "In Russian, nouns which denote inanimate objects may be masculine, feminine, or neuter." Why would anyone feel a need to give inanimate objects a gender other than neutral?

Here is an entry from my journal indicating how confused and discouraged I was in those first few weeks at Johns Hopkins:

Tuesday. June 21. Total loss of confidence. Learning Russian akin to brainwashing. First must destroy the personality, replace with text-book dialogues. Tear down to build up. New alphabet, new pronunciations, new vocabulary, heavy grammar, plus two ways of writing (handwritten and printed Russian are markedly different). Among classmates, four have previously failed Russian at their home universities, here trying to make up. One guy failed it twice. All beginning to think like Gulag prisoners. Total identification with our instructor/ interrogator Svetlana. She is half Chinese–half Russian, from Shanghai. Former national children's swim champion of the People's Republic. Both parents Russian language professors before Chinese Cultural Revolution, when they lost their jobs, and were forced to change their family name to words meaning, "Not Sufficiently Red." Svetlana, 20 or 21, looks like proud peasant girl on package of "Red Dawn" brand rice. Her teaching method is Confucian: drill, drill, drill, and more drill. "Repetition is the Mother of Understanding," she told us. Forced marches through barely known grammatical territory. This could be her slogan: "The mind must sweat before the tongue grows strong!" I stare at her moving lips 3 hours a day. Svetlana, standing in front of the blackboard, pounding her fist into her open palm when one of us gives wrong answer. Svetlana, her hand over her book over her heart.

It was at about this time that our class began to study what are called in Russian *glagoly dvizhenia*—the so-called verbs of motion. These verbs of motion are a family of verbs, all involved in various kinds of movement—walking, going by vehicle, swimming, and flying, to name four of the basics. These verbs, of which there are only several dozen in the Russian language, have their own special rules of syntax and usage. The main rule is to use different verbs to represent two of the fundamental aspects of motion—that is, one-way travel and round trip, regular, or habitual movement. If you are heading for the doctor's office on foot, for example, you would use the unidirectional verb of motion that describes walking there: *idti*. But if you are on the way back, or if you are going to come back, or if you expect that you will come back—or even if you *usually* come back—then you must use an entirely different verb: *khodit'*.

One night I dreamed: I come out of a building, and my pickup truck is gone. My wife has driven it away because she's jealous of Svetlana. I must use the unidirectional verb of motion in the dream to describe her driving away because it is unlikely she will return with the pickup, even in a dream. Then I meet Svetlana. She is wearing a black Speedo bathing suit with a red sash that says MISS WORLD COMMUNISM, and she is driving a red Miata sportscar. Now I use the multidirectional verb of motion, cleverly figuring that she drives her car habitually.

Svetlana offers me a ride: "*Sadites, pazhaluista.*" "Sit, please."

We drive off (multidirectional verb of motion here, because I don't know where we're going). But before one minutenik has passed, the car suddenly lurches forward, the tires leave the ground, and we're flying! We are flying in Svetlana's sportscar. We are flying in the car because it is clear what has occurred: I am confusing my verbs of motion.

"*Nelzya!*" commands Svetlana. "Not permitted!"

But what can I do? We are careening and bumping around the sky, directly over a sea of emerald green grass and trees. I put my head back in case the passenger seat ejects, and close my eyes (unidirectional) until finally I remember that it's "*yekhat'*," not "*letat'*," that is called for. The Miata puts its nose down, and plunges toward Earth (unidirectional). Fortunately for me, the act of landing after flying does not require a verb of motion (though flying per se does). Just in the nick of time, the car comes in for a crash landing, narrowly missing several schoolchildren on a playground.

From this moment on, I became infatuated with the Russian verbs of motion, and from this time forward, influenced through the weird power of the subconscious mind, learning Russian became fun—a kind of mental travel game I was sure would be exercised on real terrain some-day soon. After all, the verbs of motion are a specialized sector of the Russian language, developed specifically for all who would venture out in the Russian-speaking world. It's true that Russian can sometimes seem like a language made up by some people in wild animal skins standing around a campfire at night on the outskirts of Yekhupetz. At the same time, sitting in front of a television has no directional aspect. Nor does shopping at the mall. In Russian, you have actually got to move before you decide which verb of motion to use.

My riding skills improved at a more even pace. In fact, my equestrian education was going extremely well under the wondrous tutelage of riding instructor Ilona Ujhelyi. Her teaching methods not only helped me acquire the correct seating, form, and aids—the use of the legs and hands—but also helped me define my passion for horses. Speaking of the downward transition from canter to trot we'd been practicing, Ilona said, "If I simply told you to move down to a trot, you would have a mental image of slowing, and you would use your aids to accomplish that image. That is why, instead, I say to 'move forward into the trot.' Now you have a new image of keeping your leg on the horse, and simply resisting with your hands and back. It is going to make a much smoother, more unified transition when you think 'forward.' It's always forward progress that you want to imagine. Remember that the defini-tion of good horsemanship is not impeding the horse's forward move-ment."

I was struck then with the Oriental nature of riding: the importance of the correct mental image; the brain translating the image into action; the way of channeling forward energy in different ways. I was aware of the fact that, as a Hungarian, Ilona shared a common ancestry with the Central Asian nomadic warriors who rode into Eastern Europe, and I hoped that her way of synthesizing contemplation with athletic discipline gave me an insight into the world's oldest equestrian cultures. Not knowing what conditions I would find if I ever got there, I started a regimen of riding three afternoons a week, working up to walking, trotting, and cantering, around an enclosed pasture for two hours without stopping. As my stamina increased, so did my concentration.

In the wintry depths of the following January, 1991, I hit pay dirt. A delegation of "citizen diplomats" was going to Ashkhabad in mid-April under the auspices of the International Sister Cities program, which pairs American cities with foreign cities for cultural exchanges and trade development. Because of their desert geographies, Ashkhabad had been paired with Albuquerque, New Mexico. The delegation was being led by Sally Alice Thompson. After I explained my curiosity about Turkmen horses to her on the telephone, she had me call the delegation's only other member, Greg Gleason. Neither one had any objection to my tagging along with their demidelegation as ex officio reporter, photographer, and baggage handler. Nor did they oppose my plan to try to extend the two-week invitation issued for the delegation by the city soviet of Ashkhabad, in case I should find the opportunity to stay and travel on.

"We'll all be basically on our own once we get there," Sally Alice said. Her voice had a slow, craggy matter-of-factness that was the foundation of a dry wit I liked immediately. She continued, "You know, I led a delegation of fifteen of us from Albuquerque last year. When we got to the airport in Ashkhabad everyone went off with their host families. It wasn't till we'd split up that I realized no one knew anyone else's telephone number. Things aren't well organized in Ashkhabad. I didn't see some of them till we got to the airport to go home two weeks later." She paused a second, then burst out laughing.

Although I generally try to steer clear of representing anyone but myself, this sounded sufficiently informal, and there was no way I was going to turn down this rare chance. So I became a voluntary member of the citizens' diplomatic delegation to Ashkhabad, representing, of all places, Albuquerque, New Mexico—a city some two thousand miles from my home on the Jersey shore, and to which I have never been.

While boarding, Professor Gleason mentioned to me that a fellow standing behind us had told him he was going to Ashkhabad to buy horses. I dropped back in line and started to talk to Alexei, a Bulgarian who spoke English very slowly, but not badly. He said it was his second trip to Turkmenistan, and he hoped to buy forty Akhal-Teke horses, but not from the Komsomol-run stud farm, he made clear at once. He wouldn't do business with the Communists; he had no use for them. He had his own Turkmen contacts who wanted to make their own horse trades with Eastern Europe. Alex, as he preferred to be called, was a former steeplechase jockey with receding black hair and distrustful hawkish features, and was dressed for a morning jog in nylon running pants, running shoes, and a brightly striped nylon windbreaker over a T-shirt. As soon as we took off on the half-empty flight, I changed seats to find out more from him.

"I am the businessman," said Alex. "This my company." He handed me his business card, Bulgarian on one side, Russian on the other.

I glanced at the Russian side. "VICOM. Is that who you're buying the Akhal-Teke horses for?"

"No," said Alex. "For BEREKAKS IMPEKS."

"What's that?"

"That my company."

"I thought you said VICOM was your company."

"No. I work for the VICOM. I am regional director the resort hotel on Black Seashore. You know Black Seashore?"

"Never."

"Is most beautiful. I invite you. I have the fifty horse in my stables there."

"So that's BEREKAKS IMPEKS?"

"No. BEREKAKS IMPEKS associate company with the BEVIKO."

"The what?"

"The BEVIKO is Soviet–Bulgarian joint enterprise with the BEREKAKS IMPEKS, buy the forty horse for the VICOM. You understand?"

"Oh, sure."

"Is the private enterprise."

"Why didn't you say so at the beginning?"

Alex continued, "In August, I make first auction Akhal-Teke horse there in my home, Kavarna."

"What will they be sold for? For what use?"

"For the dressage, the long-distance racing, and the steeplechase. You know Akhal-Teke horse?"

"Not yet."

Clouds of reverence, ambition, and suspicion crossed Alex's face. His black eyebrows knit together conspiratorially, and he lowered his tone.

"Please, I tell you. These horse you will never forget. There is no such horse in world like these horse. When you see Akhal-Teke horse, you are see something very wonderful. Not usual. This is desert horse. They raise their head so high, to smell the danger long way off. From baby they run always in deep sands, they make the very high step, very beautiful for the dressage. I believe no horse in the world can beat these horse in steeplechase. The coat shine like the gold."

Alex was obviously determined to become the missionary to the West of Akhal-Teke horses. He spoke of little else. He told me that prior to now Turkmen had to sell all their three-year-olds for five hundred rubles to the trading firm that controlled the Moscow auction (in Soviet times, the ruble was paired one for one with the dollar). At auction, the Akhal-Tekes went for several thousand dollars, and the Turkmen never saw a kopeck of the profits. Most of their horses ended up in the private stables of party bosses and high-ranking military officers. Krushchev had presented one to the Queen of England as a gift.

Alex outlined his plans for taking forty Akhal-Tekes out of the country. He said he was in partnership with some very rich Turkmen—two brothers named Guvanch and Bigench Djumaev. They owned fourteen *kolkhozi* (farms) that produced horses, karakul sheep, camels, and honey. They would help him arrange all the documentation and transport. He thought they might rent a prop plane to fly the horses three thousand kilometers to Bulgaria since shipping uncrated horses near the whine of jet engines was too dangerous. However they shipped them, Alex intended to take two Turkmen trainers with him back to Bulgaria to work with the horses. No one could ever know these horses better than Turkmen, who work with them twenty-four hours a day and sleep in the stables with them. The main hitch, he said, was the *"preparat."* After thirty years of continuously spraying herbicides over the cotton plantations of Turkmenistan, the Soviets had succeeded in completely poisoning the land. Now animals and people were "going crazy," and Alex was worried that the horses would also be affected. He was going to try to ship blood samples back for testing in a Bulgarian lab, since he didn't trust a Soviet one.

"You have the camera, yes?" Alex asked.

"Yes."

"Okay, I show you then. Tomorrow you meet with me. To me have the car. We drive together into desert. You will make the photography of the most good Akhal-Teke horse in Turkmenistan."

I was about to explain to Alex the Texas proverb about leaving the dance with those that brung you—in this case, the Albuquerque delegation—when suddenly from the rear of the cabin came the delectable aroma of frying chicken. There was no mistaking it. It wasn't some prepackaged, microwaved, reconstituted poultry product, either; it was a real, down-home chicken fry. I could actually hear the sizzle of the fat. My mood improved wondrously as I imagined a nice potato salad and coleslaw on the side. Surely if Aeroflot had chickens they would also have potatoes and cabbage.

"Catch you later," I told Alex and promptly returned to my assigned seat between Gleason and Sally Alice, guessing that the humorless totalitarian stewardesses would never serve a meal to a hooligan who had left his assigned position. Nevertheless, I was feeling more kindly about Soviet service now that I saw a real meal in my immediate future. I even started rehearsing my dinner-table Russian: "To me is pleasing the leg. It is necessary the fork and knife. Is this the salad of potatoes? Tasty, very tasty!"

But as my craven Western hedonism reached fever pitch, the Aeroflot hostesses wheeled a cart of covered fried chicken platters up to the crew's cabin and then served the passengers a plastic cup of black tea, a lump of sugar in a railroad-train wrapper, and one plain, hard cookie. This was the passengers' allotment. Fried chicken was only for the heroes of socialist labor up in the cockpit.

Sally Alice bit into her cookie with a crunch I was sure must have damaged her front teeth. She was cheerful as a trooper, though we had been traveling now for forty hours. "Don't worry," she said. "You'll see more food in Ashkhabad than you ever have in your whole life."

"Really? I could use a square meal."

"Sometimes I think the real reason the Turkmen invite foreign guests," she said, "is so they can all go round to each other's houses and eat and drink for free. They'll probably give you a whole sheep for lunch today."

"I like a good leg of mutton. Is that the way it was the last time?"

"Golly, yes. This big chief of the Turkmen Friendship Society—they're the official hosts of our delegation—is named Djura. He invited me to one banquet after another. I guess Muslims aren't supposed to drink, but it certainly didn't stop him."

PART II

The Delegation

As the jet made its descent to Ashkhabad the sky was clear. On one side of the aircraft were flat sands all the way to the northern horizon, pocked in April with chalky green tufts of spring vegetation. On the other side the sheer rock faces of the Kopet-Dag Mountains climbed seven thousand feet high in forbidding steel gray, black, and deepest crimson. On top, where the USSR bordered Iran, were snowcaps, blindingly bright beneath the morning sun. It was a stark, discontinuous geography, the desert hemmed in by the mountains as if by an enormous prison wall. Perhaps there is no place on Earth where you can see so clearly the line between tectonic plates of the planet's crust. Or perhaps the Soviets had decided to store the Iron Curtain here until it was required again.

As we rolled across the tarmac of Ashkhabad Airport the Aeroflot hostess welcomed the passengers to Turkmenistan and told us not to leave our seats. We didn't. She announced there were many distinctive touristic facilities available in the capital of the Turkmen Soviet Republic: two hotels, restaurants, fountains, parks, a library, the great Kara Kum Canal!

The plane came to a full stop, the passengers still sitting until told to leave. I got up and started gathering my camera bag and Sally Alice's video camera from the overhead compartment. One of the hostesses immediately moved in. Using the formal imperative mood, she ordered me to sit down. It would not be my last crime or misdemeanor in the Republic of Turkmenistan, and I remember thinking: I'm really here, in the land of command and obedience.

We waited for the flight crew to leave the plane first. The Russian sense of courtesy and hierarchy are the same thing. I glanced back and Alex gave me a knowing nod, as if this were the trump argument for escaping the world of delegations and officialdom. As soon as the crew was out, the passengers all fled for the exit.

Out on the tarmac, two heavy iron gates opened before our bedraggled little delegation. I half expected to see a desert tableau of sand dunes, date palms, camels, and men reclining on beautiful rugs smoking interesting herbs through a hookah. Instead, the reception party awaiting us beyond the gates consisted of a sinister knot of men in dark suits, black leather jackets, and dark sunglasses. We were about to be either arrested or assassinated. One of them came forward to present Sally Alice with a big bouquet of red, white, and pink carnations. He boomed out in English, "Welcome to Ashkhabad, our friend Alice-a Thompson-a! We await you with great expectation!"

"Hello, Djura," Sally Alice said with a minimum of enthusiasm. The reception party swarmed over us.

"Ahh, you Gleason," the same man said to me. "Ha-ha-ha-ha! Welcome Ashkhabad, Gleason! I am Djura Semedov, director Turkmen Friendship Society. I am biiiiig man here. Very, very big! You come with Alice-a Thompson-a. She is our great friend! How you feel now? You feel okay?"

"I'm Maslow, not Gleason." I shook his hand: It felt like a little pillow with feathers inside.

"Yes, I know!" he cried. "You feel okay, cowboy from New Mexico, Gleason. Ha-ha-ha-ha!"

The others in the reception committee laughed, too, and he slapped high fives with them. His face was not as round as a Mongol's, not as open as a Slav's, not as fine as a Persian's, nor as pale as a Chinese. In short, he was Korean. Striped tie, playboy sunglasses, big mole, small white fangs; he handled himself like a PR man touting an execution, trying to make the event seem upbeat. Chastising myself for making snap judgments, I took an instant and spontaneous loathing to him.

"Now I introduce other members Turkmen Friendship Society," said Djura. "First my son M——. He biiig man in training. Ha-ha-ha-ha!"

"Ha-ha-ha-ha!" the others chorused, including the son, a big goof in an ill-fitting suit, more Middle Eastern looking than his father.

"This your host, Dr. Sh——," Djura said to me, and recited a name with so many syllables and back-to-back consonants that I despaired of remembering it as soon as I heard it. I shook hands with a plain little man of perhaps fifty in thick eyeglasses, like Harry Truman in a brown wrapper. He spoke no English at all. Djura went on, "Dr. Sh— biig doctor here, head medical institute. Have beautiful young daughter fix you when sick. Ha-ha-ha-ha!"

The doctor laughed and they slapped high fives again. Was this a traditional Turkmen greeting, shamelessly stolen by American athletes, or had they copied it from American sports events on television? I wondered. Whatever, it occurred to me the poor doctor had laughed without the slightest idea that Djura had joked about his daughter.

The introductions went on and on: the deputy mayor, the assistant minister of heavy machine production, a newspaper photographer without a camera, some old goat who had won the Order of Lenin. I glanced around. All other activity in the area had come to a halt. People were crowded around to see the foreigners. Women in brightly colored head shawls and men in long robes and black sheepskin hats were watching our reception, eyes wide with dull curiosity mixed with awe. Over in a corner behind the gates I spotted Alex the Bulgarian. He was with a solidly built Turkmen in his late thirties whose broad Mongolian face and sharp little nose had a look of intelligence and dignity mixed with mischief and irony. While Djura continued, I slipped out of the ring and crossed the few feet separating us.

"Alex"—I grabbed his sleeve—"I will definitely call you tomorrow. Positively. Where can I reach you?"

"This my colleague, Guvanch Djumaev." He introduced us.

I summoned up my language skills and tried to say in Russian that Alex had told me about him, and to express my great interest in Akhal-Teke horses. Djumaev folded his arms and listened, nodding with the hint of a smile. I could feel his shrewd eyes assessing me in my blue jeans and cowboy hat. Then, giving me his business card, he replied politely but formally that he would be at my service.

Over the course of the next weeks and months Guvanch proved as good as his word. Whatever I wanted to do, wherever I wanted to go, Guvanch would arrange it. That initial politeness would turn first into a fast friendship, then into an intense fraternity, deeper than any relationship an American and a Turkmen could ever have dreamed. Once when Guvanch had already become my trusted host and guide through the many byzantine intricacies of Turkmen society, I asked him why he had seemed so amused that first morning when Alex introduced us at the airport. Guvanch shrugged and said in his offhand manner, "Because the whole Turkmen KGB was there to meet your delegation."

They stuffed us into an assortment of dented sedans lined up at the curb, and we drove off toward our hosts' dwellings for lunch. The doctor, whose name I still didn't know, took the wheel of a dusty green sedan. In the backseat was a young, fair-haired Russian in a black leather jacket, a former Tass journalist and current teacher of English introduced as Sasha Reebok—an easy name to remember, just like the running shoes. The caravan from the airport soon dispersed, and we tore along broad, straight, treeless avenues full of potholes and bumps, past mangled metal factory buildings where small herds of sheep, camels, and goats grazed the weeds growing round them. It was a kind of Marxian tableau in reverse: industrial socialism returning to the nomadic past. Missing was the Age of Reason.

I couldn't tell whether the factories were under construction, closed down, abandoned, or still operating in this state of disorder. Perhaps some were in one mode, some in others. However, as we continued through the city I saw more and more of Ashkhabad in this same unfinished state—somewhere between a construction site and a junk-yard. Mammoth modern buildings with ugly, repetitive metal façades; so-called modern sculptures, unrecognizable heaps of twisted metal; a park with a dozen concrete walks like the spokes of a wheel, but no trees or flowers. In the distance, in front of the forbidding Kopet-Dag Mountains bordering Iran, what looked like an entirely new city of concrete high-rise apartments was going up. Sasha said it had been under construction for seven years. I wished it another seven. The construction cranes grouped around the complex looked like a herd of dragons browsing on concrete broccoli. Despite the heavy traffic of cars, fuming buses, and old-fashioned yellow trolleycars, the roadsides streamed with pedestrians and their animals. Groups of women in long blue dresses with distinctive, brightly colored, beautifully patterned yokes and head-pieces walked with shopping bags slung over their shoulders or large circular loaves of flat bread in their arms. Sasha Reebok said the head-pieces signified their tribe or clan.

"Those are Teke," he said, pointing out a green headpiece. "It's the majority tribe."

"The Turkmen have five tribes," the doctor said, perking up. "It is the famous opening line from Turkmen national poet Makhtymkuli. Lenin Avenue has now been renamed in his honor."

"Really? I'd love to read some of his work." Soviet ethnographic sources on Turkmenistan left the distinct impression that the nomadic desert dwellers of Turkmenistan had no written literature.

"I can show you!" The doctor made a quick series of complicated turns, taking us down a prettier avenue shaded with trees and past a leafy city park. "There!" He pointed proudly to a bronze statue in the park as we sped by without slowing down. "That's Makhtymkuli! Turkmen national poet!" The great father of Turkmen letters was dressed in flowing robes and turban, reclining on his pedestal with a large book curled in his forearm like a leg of lamb.

The city was as extensive as it was without interest; it took forty minutes to cross to the doctor's neighborhood. Ashkhabad seemed to have an impressive number of statues and billboards of Comrade Lenin. It was also lavishly supplied with fountains, a wonderful consideration in the desert, although most of them were not operating. Again we began passing the same construction-site junkyards, both residential and indus-trial. Stores? Not a single one. On the contrary, there were only clump after clump of high-rise apartment houses, in pastel blue, green, and pink. Except for the pretension of modernity, I could not understand why anyone would build fifteen-story buildings in the middle of the desert; it's not as though they lacked real estate.

The longer we drove the less favorable my impression became of the Turkmen capital. A strong wind kicked up immense sand devils. Blotted out by the swirling sand, brigades of old women bent over puny whisk brooms swept the curbs; they would have accomplished as much by putting their lips together and blowing. In a vacant lot strewn with rubble men holding pails and jars were lined up before a beer wagon. In its barrenness, Ashkhabad reminded me of downtown Managua,

Nicaragua, which was destroyed in an earthquake and never rebuilt, the downtown consisting of block after ghostly block of weedy ruins of buildings. Sure enough, when I asked, Sasha Reebok confirmed my impression. Ashkhabad, too, had been devastated by an earthquake in 1948. Only the railroad station and the Communist party headquarters had survived the impact. Nobody knew the exact death toll.

The doctor lived in what is called a *microrayon* (subdivision) of older two-story apartment houses formed around a central sandlot on the edge of town. From the outside it appeared much like an American postwar public housing development in, say, Miami, or Houston—functional in design, dysfunctional in repair. From the state of the unpatched plaster, it could have been twenty years old or more.

I had been told or read somewhere that the Soviets had undertaken to "civilize" Asian nomads by making them live in apartment houses instead of their traditional felt-covered tents. Inside the doctor's ground-floor apartment I saw that you can take the nomad out of the tent, but you can't take the tent out of the nomad.

The floors were spread and the walls were hung with Oriental carpets. The bedding was rolled up and stored in a chest during the day, and everyone scrupulously removed their shoes before entering. The Muslim separation of women and men was loosely enforced, the women staying more or less in the kitchen and an enclosed patio; the men occupying the dining room–living room. There was Turkmen plumbing—a small porcelain bathtub, a toilet that flushed weakly, and a sink with the pipes detached under the drain. It was not the worst sanitation I had ever seen, but they stored the garbage in the unvented bathroom, making for a ripe miasma. I washed up, feeling guilty, as only an American could, that the wastewater was plummeting straight down to the floor, and I came out to the dining room to meet the family before lunch.

The elder son, Dovran, was a medical student; the younger son, Serdar, a pimply teenager in high school. They were singularly free of fun and laughter. There were a brother-in-law and a sister-in-law, who turned out, on closer questioning, to actually be cousins. They were all in Western clothes. The doctor apologized for his wife's absence; she, too, was a doctor, on duty at the hospital.

The next moment the doctor's daughter slipped in barefoot to serve green tea and hard candies. Her name was either Gulya or Yedesh (later I would hear her called by both names). As she set the tea tray down before her father, my eyes took in an exotic-looking young woman robed in bright yellow floor-length silk. She had brilliant dark eyes inside sloping pointed lids heavily lined with kohl; pouting, secretive lips; and hennaed hair that gave off illusory purple highlights. When I noticed she wasn't being introduced, I struck a cheap blow for women the world over and stood up and introduced myself. Carried away, I then asked if there was anything I could do to help serve the meal. The girl giggled and fled the room immediately.

The doctor poured the first cup of tea, and returned it to the pot three times, a Turkmen custom. I found the tea wonderfully hot and soothing after the long journey. Then the men were served dinner. Sally Alice was right—they had indeed slaughtered a sheep in honor of my arrival. They had hung it up and slit its throat in front of the apartment that very morning. It came to the table first in a greasy broth, next as the filling in steamed dumplings much like ravioli (though the Italians, I thought, do it better), and finally in bits of meat mixed with rice as pilaf, or *plov*. The vegetables consisted of a few sprigs of parsley, several radishes, and green onions on a small plate. Turkmen do not concern themselves with the seven food groups.

It was all going to be very ceremonious and polite, I thought, until the doctor stood up and opened a bottle of vodka. I had traveled halfway around the globe, my body hadn't adjusted to the time difference, much less the water, and drinking on an empty stomach was the last thing I felt like doing. Besides, I hoped to keep my few wits about me. In short, I simply wasn't in the mood to drink vodka, but when I tried to politely refuse, my Russian failed me and I ended up saying stupidly, "I don't drink."

At this, the doctor nearly fell to the floor, looking utterly confused. He turned to Sasha Reebok and said something in Turkmen, which has a pleasant guttural sound. Remembering what Sally Alice had said about Turkmen using the occasion of her previous visit to drink and eat, I wondered if the doctor had been issued this bottle especially because of our arrival. You might procure a sheep in Ashkhabad with money, but I hadn't seen any liquor stores on the way in from the airport—only that file of tortured men waiting for beer in the raw sun. Perhaps the doctor worried that if word got back to the Turkmen Friendship Society that his foreign guest had refused drink, no more vodka would be issued him. More likely, it occurred to me, I was breaking some desert custom.

"Friend Jon," Sasha Reebok turned to me looking concerned, "won't you drink with us?"

"No, thanks." I was going to play it out to see what happened.

"You are perhaps feeling ill? We want to drink to your arrival."

I said, "I simply don't choose to drink. You've heard of choice, haven't you?"

Apparently thinking Sasha had straightened it out, the doctor poured me a huge double shot of vodka and set it before me. This stiffened my neck considerably. I wished to be a good member of the Albuquerque delegation, as well as a good guest, but I had no intention of giving in to blatant social pressure. If it came to it, I was prepared to call a cab and check into a hotel. (How foolishly little I then understood about being a "foreign guest" in the land of command and obedience! Soon enough I would begin to realize that the line between guest and hostage became vague under the dread sun of the Kara Kum.)

I raised my voice to Sasha. "Look, tell him I can't drink. Tell him it's against my religion—oh, tell him I'm an alcoholic! A drunk! He's a doctor; he'll understand. You all can go ahead and drink without me. I don't mind. I won't be offended, believe me. I can drink something soft—soda or juice or something."

Sasha spoke in Turkmen. The doctor pushed his thick glasses back up his nose, but took the news with grace. To divert attention, I took out my journal and pen and said, "By the way, Sasha, could you please spell the doctor's name for me? I'd like to be able to pronounce it properly."

This did the trick, both averting any further unpleasantness and establishing my right to ask questions and make notes without giving offense. When Yedesh brought in a pitcher of delicious "*compot*," made of grapes steeped in sugar water, I knew I had mastered the situation. I accepted my host's toast, and toasted him back. The doctor's name was Shikhmurad—not so hard, really, after you practice it twenty or thirty times.

Lunch resumed. With Sasha there to interpret for me, I slipped easily into the stream of question-and-answer, letting the conversation drift like a canoe on a calm bayou, dipping my paddle in from time to time with a question just to keep it going. After three or four shots of vodka, Dr. Shikhmurad got very companionable, and was soon telling me his life story. He was of the Geoklen, a minority Turkmen tribe, and had been born in a *kibitka,* a tent in the desert. He was only one year old when the big earthquake destroyed Ashkhabad. He didn't remember the big tremor, but when it was all over, those nomads still living in the desert survived, while the Turkmen who had been settled in the city by

Stalin suffered heavy family losses. No figures had ever been released, but it was said that 150,000 Turkmen had perished in the calamity. Afterward, Shikhmurad came to the city, received his medical education, met his wife, and joined the Communist party. She, too, had been raised in the country, but came from a village in the mountains. She was from another tribe. Dr. Shikhmurad became the director of the medical institute where they trained nurses and had 200 people working under him. After the earthquake, Stalin had repopulated Ashkhabad with people from all over the Soviet Union, so that for a generation Turkmen were a minority in their own capital. But Turkmen, the doctor said, liked big families—eleven, twelve, or more children were not uncommon—so their population soon overtook the others.

As lunch was ending, the cousins and sons excused themselves from the table. Yedesh served another pot of green tea, and we sat munching chocolates with gooey centers. The girl brought in her own lunch plate and sat in the far corner, our eyes not meeting. Sasha Reebok lit up one of the Marlboros from a pack I had given him, and said his parents, Jews from Ukraine, had emigrated to Turkmenistan in the years following the earthquake. His father was an engineer.

"Did they come voluntarily or were they forced by the authorities?" I asked.

"You cannot understand how it was in the Soviet Union in those days, Jon—is it all right I call you Jon?" he asked. "When you received your graduation from university, they offered you a place to work, wherever they required people. My father and mother were young and full of ideals about building socialism. They thought there was more opportunity here, and the desert climate was healthy."

"Is it still?"

"We have recently had a big environmental scandal here, you know." He grinned, evidently relishing the chance to speak with an American. "A lead article in the newspaper *Komsomolskaya Pravda* exposed the terrible state of children's health in Turkmen republic. It said the infant mortality rate here is the highest in the USSR because of pesticides contaminating the drinking water. The article—how do you say—turned Turkmenia on the ear?"

"On *its* ear," I corrected him.

"Yes, on its ear. You know, I would like very much to learn American slang."

"I can help you," I said, "but I want something from you, too."

"You are the honored guest here. Just ask."

"I want your help. There are many things here I want to see and do. I am especially interested in Akhal-Teke horses. I want to get outside the city and go into the desert. I want to see the nature reserves. I don't want to sit around Ashkhabad for two weeks and then go home and say I've seen Turkmenistan. You could help me interpret, and you know the ropes around here."

"The ropes?"

"That's good American slang for 'You know your way around here.' How to get places; how to arrange things."

"Ah, yes, I see." He waved his cigarette. "The ropes! But didn't they tell you, Jon? Tomorrow morning there will be a meeting at Turkmen Friendship Society with your delegation. You can present your plan then."

"Hmm," I mused, keeping my own counsel. "You'll be there?"

"Yes, yes, I promise. I will help you."

"Okay. The first thing I want is a map of Ashkhabad and the vicinity."

"I will try to get it for you, Jon," Sasha said. "Now maybe you will rest? They will make a dinner tonight here in your honor. They will fry the meat in the sheep fat. It is Turkmen national dish."

"Yum," I said. Then I asked the doctor in Russian if Turkmen cuisine included horse meat.

"Not at all," he said. At the mention of horses his eyes brightened. "Turkmen love horses more than anything in the world. When I was a boy in the desert, our horse was part of the family. You will never find a Turkmen eating a horse. The Kazakhis eat horse. The Uzbekis drink mare's milk. But a Turkmen? Never."

I retired for a rest in the back bedroom they had assigned me. The room possessed the only bed in the house, deliciously made up with clean sheets. I removed the limp clothes I had been wearing since New York and fell instantaneously into a deep, dreamless nap. When I woke, it was pitch black out. I lay for a moment, listening to the sparse night sounds—the whining engines of distant traffic, a few dogs barking. Through the thin wall separating me from the dining room, I could hear the men partying, laughing loudly, and drunkenly reciting English phrases:

"I am going home."

"I am going home because I have a business."

"I am going home because I have a lot of things to do."

And then the unmistakable booming voice of Djura Semedov: "I am biiiig man! Ha-ha-ha-ha!"

They all laughed, and there was a slapping of palms. I decided they could hold a dinner in my honor without me, turned over, and went back to sleep.

The next day the confusion began early. It now transpired that Dr. Shikhmurad had driven in from the airport yesterday in a borrowed car. His own car had been under repair for several months. There were no spare parts to be had in Ashkhabad—the result, he claimed, of perestroika. There were also no mechanics or garages. The man who owned the borrowed car was supposed to come by the doctor's place at 7:30, a full two and a half hours before the time our meeting was supposed to start. When he hadn't come by 8:45, Dr. Shikhmurad panicked and went off to borrow someone else's vehicle to get us to the Turkmen Friendship Society center.

I was served breakfast alone in the dining room by Gulya; her mother was still on duty at the hospital. My appetite was restored by a good night's sleep, so I ate one of the warmed-up meat dumplings from yesterday's lunch with a mild pepper sauce, two hardboiled eggs, and several pieces of the dry hard flat bread I had seen women carrying in the streets, washing it all down with repeated doses of the addictively delicious hot green tea. When I was finished, I carried the dishes back into the kitchen myself, if only to catch a glimpse of Gulya, whom I had established was nineteen. When I entered the kitchen to put the dishes in the sink, I could see her through the open doorway to the narrow front patio. She had a little mat on the floor, where she could lie down and keep watch out the open windows. From there she could see the neighbors going in and out, the children playing, perhaps the seasons changing, the world going by, her own circumscribed life passing away. She was curled up on her mat like a little dog, staring into space, smoothing her auburn hair. When she became aware of me, she did not move, but made a low sound in the back of her throat, a sound I had never heard before, like a moan and a sigh mixed with simple acknowledgment of another's presence. It was a sound of heart-wrenching human recognition. Something about that strange sound made me realize I was probably just as exotic to her as she was to me, and it gave me my first insight into what it might mean to pass one's life in a place so cut off from any sense of being able to grab life by the tail and shake it, to know one's life as an endless series of exactly similar days, serving exactly similar meals to exactly similar men—whether fathers, brothers, husbands—then lying down on your mat to see the exact same view out the window.

The meeting was scheduled for ten. At 9:50, Dr. Shikhmurad ran desperately into the house and hurried me outside. He had brought one of his students with an old green Moskvich sedan, built on a Fiat body. As soon as we were all seated inside, it refused to start. Click. Click. Click. It wouldn't even turn over. Dr. Shikhmurad threw up his hands and got out again to push. He was a lean, wiry man, and couldn't budge the vehicle in the soft sand. But when I got out to help, he became flustered, and adamantly asked me to get back inside the passenger seat in the front. I got the idea that the help of a foreign guest was not permitted. It didn't bother me in the least to be late for the meeting, but I could see beads of anxious sweat on my host's nose and felt sorry for him.

"Why don't we grab a taxi?" I said, trying to be helpful.

This only made matters worse. It was as if I had insulted his hospitality—again. He collected several men from the apartment complex, and while I sat there adding to the weight, they pushed backward and forward, until finally managing to start the car in reverse. The student revved the engine and Dr. Shikhmurad quickly jumped back inside. At last we were off. It was ten past ten.

"Fast, fast," said Dr. Shikhmurad, adding, as if to himself, "all is in order."

We raced downtown to a gated whitewashed two-story stucco building set back from one of the tree-lined avenues across from the city park, only to learn that the meeting had been pushed back an hour. No one had bothered to inform us. We were forty minutes early. It was just this kind of time wasted that I hate about being part of a delegation, but I was determined on my first full day in Turkmenistan to be patient and not let anything bother me. I remembered my riding instructor Ilona's drilling into me the importance for the horseman of "attitude," the mental part of riding. "Head up, eyes ahead, maintain your walk attitude," she would say. "Communicate with your horse first with your mental attitude, then your seat, then your legs, and only last with your hands. If you want to go left, think left first. Your horse will pick up your mental signal. Then reinforce the command with your aids." This approach, she said, made the difference between riding *on* a horse and riding a horse.

As with horses, so with humans: I had decided to approach our official meeting with a firm, confident, unflustered composure—a walk attitude. I was glad I hadn't drunk the vodka yesterday and had no hangover to deal with. I was wearing my attitude, too, in the form of a fresh white starched dress shirt and silk tie, and carrying my camera bag in case I wanted to leave: No one ever stops a photographer when he wants to leave someplace, only when he wants to enter.

Completely cool, I even started whistling the first bars of the overture to *La Bohème* as we ascended the staircase to the offices on the second floor. But Dr. Shikhmurad stopped me on the staircase, and with his own composure wrecked from the morning's stresses, he pleaded with me not to whistle inside the building. "It is bad, malevolent, and summons the evil eye," he said sternly. "And please don't whistle in my home, I ask you!"

"Okay, okay. No harm intended. I won't whistle, I promise." It puzzled me that a physician, head of a medical institute—a Communist at that—should be so concerned about the evil eye. Scratch a dialectical materialist, find a superstitious pagan.

Upstairs, Dr. Shikhmurad left me at the office of the Turkmen Friendship Society. He had to check in at his institute, but said he would be back to pick me up after the meeting. I told him that would not be necessary; I could take a cab if he would give me his address, but I could tell by the way he stiffened and raised his eyebrows that this was absolutely out of the question.

"I will be here with the car at twelve-thirty," he repeated. "We'll have lunch at my house. I will bring the car—"

"I heard you the first time," I interrupted. It was a real mania with him.

The office of the Turkmen Friendship Society was in the corner of the second-floor landing, flanked on one side by the local office of the Soviet

Ministry of Foreign Affairs and on the other by the Tass News Agency office, where an old-fashioned newswire machine clacked away. So much for direct people-to-people contacts; so much for citizen-diplomats of the kind our delegation was supposed to represent. Sally Alice was up against professionals here, there was little doubt. What could you make of a place that had professional citizens, where people were paid to organize friendship to foreigners?

When I knocked, Djura Semedov opened the door, showing me into his office. He was in shirtsleeves and loose tie; maybe he had once seen a Dewar's ad in an American magazine. "Djura Semedov. Age: 40-something. Profession: Big Man. Latest Achievement: hosting important foreign guests." His face had the blank look of a perched hawk surveying the ground for prey.

"Maslov, good morning!" he said. "Welcome Turkmen Friendship Society office. You have slept veery veery well, right? You slept through dinner party in your honor."

"Good morning. Yes, thanks, I slept fine. I'm afraid I was very tired from the long trip."

"You must drink vodka, Maslov. Russians teach Turkmen to drink vodka. Now Turkmen custom. Dr. Shikhmurad think you don't like him! Vodka good for international friendship. Ha-ha-ha-ha!"

The narrow corner room had space only for Djura's large desk, empty except for the telephone, a metal locker, and eight or ten chairs lined along the wall immediately in front of the desk. A rich sunlight dappled by vine leaves outside streamed pleasantly through the window. It was only now that I recognized the old goat from the reception party yesterday. He was sitting with a worn attaché case on his lap. With tremendous effort he dragged his aged carcass to his feet to greet me.

Djura introduced him as Mr. Ataev. "Veteran World War Two, people's deputy, member Turkmen Academy Arts and Sciences, president Turkmen Writers Union, vice president Turkmen Friendship Society . . ."

And party hack, by all odds, I thought, trying to meet the man's vague, averted eyes. Djura assured me that Mr. Ataev had written many well-known novels, but it was hard to believe that he could write an interesting postcard. His bald cranium looked like it would be more useful for driving nails. Djura said, "Mr. Ataev known whole world over. Have many many contacts with foreigners."

Mr. Ataev said, "My very big friend, Turkmen doctor, live in Upper Montclair, New York."

"Upper Montclair is in New Jersey," I corrected him. "I'm from New Jersey."

"You know Upper Montclair? Perhaps you know my friend there, Dr. Sershharshmaxyaxshinkh . . ."

"I'm afraid I don't know your friend."

"Upper Montclair is near Albuquerque, yes?" Mr. Ataev was a little confused.

Djura broke in forcefully. "You talk Mr. Ataev now, Maslov. Learn many many things Turkmen culture. He biiiig famous writer here. Ask him any question. You look like Turkmen cowboy today, Maslov. Ha-ha-ha-ha!" Then he left the room.

From his attaché case Mr. Ataev pulled out a tattered paperback book he said he was translating from English into Russian. It was titled *The Turkmen in the Age of Imperialism: A Study of the Turkmen People and Their Incorporation into the Russian Empire.*

Thumbing through the table of contents, I noticed that the central chapter was devoted to the battle of Geok Tepe, when the Russians defeated the Turkmen in 1879, leading to Turkmenistan's "incorporation" into the Russian empire. "Mr. Ataev, I am most interested in the history of the Turkmen people, which is completely unknown in the West. Perhaps you could please tell me something about the Russian conquest of the Turkmen. For example, what happened at the battle of Geok Tepe?"

Mr. Ataev pretended he hadn't heard me and tried to change the subject to oil and gas development.

"Getting back to the battle of Geok Tepe," I insisted, "I would especially like to know the part that cavalry played in the Turkmen–Russian warfare of the pre-Soviet period. For example, did the Turkmen ride Akhal-Tekes?"

At this Mr. Ataev prised the book out of my hands as if I had asked for the launch codes of the Turkmen nuclear arsenal. He rammed the volume back into his briefcase and snapped the lock shut, all the while mumbling about the number of oil rigs and the volume of natural gas production. He was obviously reciting from a prepared script, and I had the clear impression that an actual exchange of information wasn't part of his exalted concept of "international friendship" or "contacts with foreigners."

In the summer language course in political Russian I had taken at Johns Hopkins I had come across the frequently used term *offitsialnoye litso,* or "official face." At the time the concept had stumped me. It seemed to mean more than our concept of "spokesperson." Diplomats, bureaucrats, many types of government officials were called this. Now I realized exactly what it meant: a person reduced to an official mouthpiece, at first perhaps with thoughts and feelings of his own, but later on, growing into the role, a cipher programmed to deliver the party line under any and all circumstances until finally becoming a one-dimensional frontman cleansed of all personal opinion and individualism. In short, not simply a mask, but a mask with no real face behind it.

It was useless to speak further with the old goat. I left the office and went across the landing, slipping quietly into the conference room. I was alone in the austere, high-ceilinged room. It had been prepared for our delegation with tea service, bottles of mineral water, and glasses, but someone had left a map of the Turkmen republic on the long table. I searched for Geok Tepe, and found it only about forty kilometers northwest of Ashkhabad, at the edge of the Kopet-Dag Mountains. With this, I sat down to make a few notes in the remaining minutes until our meeting began. My notes read:

April 16. What is Geok Tepe? Did all the Turkmen fight together, or only certain tribes? Who were the Russian troops? Cossack cavalry? How do the Turkmen feel about the long dominance of the Russians in Central Asia? How has Russian and Soviet hegemony influenced horse breeding?

It was about this time that Djura came into the conference room. When he saw the map and me writing over it, his whole body tensed and he said, "What you do now, Maslov?"

"I'm studying the geography of Turkmenistan," I said innocently, knowing full well by his grim and steely puss that any map approaching accuracy must be considered a top-secret document.

"Who gave map?"

"Oh," I said, "Mr. Ataev did. We were discussing oil and gas development."

No one alive could follow all the nooks, niches, and nuances in the historical relations between the Russians and the Turkmen tribes that have led to the present sorry state of cultural mongrelization. No one alive would want to. In the several years of waiting to travel, I had amassed whatever written materials exist on Turkmenistan, especially old travel memoirs, but had purposely not read them in order to see things with somewhat fresh eyes. Nevertheless, later, in an act of pitiless intellectual vengeance on the official faces, I was at least able to satisfy my curiosity about the battle of Geok Tepe with a little help from the 1882 account of the British traveler Edmund O'Donovan. O'Donovan just "happened" to be only a few kilometers from Geok Tepe when the Russians inflicted the coup de grâce to Turkmen independence in 1879, and watched the entire encounter through field glasses from a rise in the Kopet-Dag foothills. O'Donovan identifies himself as "special correspondent" of the *London Daily News,* but reading between the lines of his travels, it is pretty clear he was a British spy. A good one, by all odds: First he cozied up to the Russian military leadership and traveled with their expeditionary forces as they crossed the Caspian Sea from Baku. Then he managed to cross the lines and win the trust of the Teke chieftain Makdum Kuli Khan, the loser in the conflict.

At the time, the British were closely monitoring czarist Russia's advance into Central Asia from their imperial outposts in India and Afghanistan, which borders Turkmenistan in the south, across the Hindu Kush. The Russians had been slowly incorporating the area then known as Turkestan as the final act of an almost sacred mission to control the entire empire of their former Mongol masters. Russian— really Muscovy—expansion had been more or less continuous ever since the great Asian warrior Tamerlane had attacked and defeated Toktamysh's Golden Horde in 1391, thereby allowing the self-styled Czar Ivan III to renounce Muscovy allegiance to the Tartars. His son, Ivan the Terrible, went from repudiation to aggressive action, initiating Russia's four-hundred-year drive into the nomadic heartlands.

With the breakup of the Mongol empire, the numerous Turkic tribes of the steppes reemerged from under the Mongol yoke to fight each other and resume their constant attempts to plunder and despoil their neighbors. The Turkmen were apparently unremitting in this regard, and the Tekes were the worst of all. Their chief occupation consisted of making *chappows,* or plundering raids, for cattle, horses, and slaves on anyone within range of their swift, durable horses. Every Teke tribesman kept at least one horse for this purpose, and was always armed with a scimitar and rifle. When they weren't raiding on their own account, the Teke hired themselves out to the local khans as mercenaries, and received payment according to the number of flayed heads of the khan's enemies they delivered to his feet. There was one reward set for bringing in eight heads, another for ten heads, and still another for twenty heads. For delivering forty heads, you received a silk robe with gold threads.

O'Donovan notes that the settled agriculture practiced in the region resembled a kind of military-farming cultural complex, where the peasants went into the fields every day armed to the teeth to fend off raiders. Every village pasture, wheat, or barley field had a brick tower with a wall and mounted guards kept watch for the approach of raiders. At the first signs of a *chappow* party approaching, they herded their animals under the wall and went up into the tower to defend themselves. In modern terms such an economy emphasized redistribution over productivity, with results Reaganauts could have predicted: The Turkmenistan that O'Donovan describes was a decimated land of abandoned irrigation systems, cities and towns in ruin, and a declining, impoverished population.

This ceaseless internecine hostility, of course, made the Russian conquest far easier than it would have been had the nomads united. The Russians could even justifiably call it "pacification." O'Donovan relates, for instance, that when the Russian forces reached the eastern shores of the Caspian Sea, they found two Turkmen tribes, the Yamuts and the Tekes, allied to resist them. But as soon as the Russians defeated the Yamuts, they showed the utmost eagerness to serve the Russian invaders against their Teke brethren. Two thousand irregular Yamut cavalry signed up, delighted at the chance the Russian invasion provided for paying off old scores against their traditional enemies. "Private feuds," says O'Donovan, "are at all times more powerful among the nomads than even national interests."

In the Turkmen tongue "*geok*" originally meant "the color of the sky." Today it more commonly means "blue" or "green," the desert people making no great distinction between colors that are, after all, more significant to littoral types. *Tepe* is an earth mound. Turkmenistan is heavily pockmarked with such mounds, either by the natural drifting of sand or by sand's covering over some abandoned brickwork. As far as O'Donovan could tell, the *tepe* in question was indeed a sand-buried ruin of an older village, while the *geok* supposedly referred to the cerulean color of the *tepe* when seen from a distance. To O'Donovan it looked yellowish-orange. In any case, as he points out, the battle didn't take place at Geok Tepe, but at a Russian-built fortress called Yengi Sheher four or five miles away, where the entire population of fifty thousand to sixty thousand Teke *kibitkas* covered the ground within the rectangular brick walls.

On January 9, 1879, the whole Teke cavalry force made a lightning sortie against the Russian entrenchments thrown up in front of the gates of the fortress about a thousand yards away. However, the Teke plans had been compromised and the Russians were ready. Only two breech-loading field pieces and several prisoners fell into the hands of the besieged Tekes, who did not know how to use the former and cut the throats of the latter. Russian reinforcements, rushed to the front, set up their field pieces two thousand yards from the town, and shelled it continuously for twelve days.

Meanwhile, a large body of Teke cavalry left its stronghold to act as a reserve. It was then, as O'Donovan tells the tale, that the old Turkmen habit of rustling and banditry entered the picture. The khan of Kuchan, "thinking the moment a favourable one for doing a stroke of business on his own account, while the Tekes were occupied with the defense of their stronghold, sent out a *chappow* of a hundred horsemen to seize whatever grain, cattle, or horses, they could find in the outlying Turco-man [sic] villages." The Teke reserve cavalry turned its attention to ambushing the Kuchan raiders. This was the type of fighting at which the nomads were really expert, and not a single man of the Kuchan escaped alive. However, with the Teke forces divided, and the Russians entrenched around Yengi Sheher with artillery, short work was made of the siege.

O'Donovan deemed it unsafe to cross open ground, where he could have been taken by either Russian scouting parties or Teke cavalry, so he kept to the slopes of the mountain chain, towering six thousand feet over the Teke plain about twelve miles from Geok Tepe. On January 24, a heavy cannonade commenced against the northwestern and southeastern portions of the town. O'Donovan went on, "I could plainly see, by the smoke of the guns and the movements of the combatants, that the attack had begun in earnest, and I watched its results with intense anxiety." The Russians concentrated their assault line against the southern wall of the fortifications, and after a desperate conflict it became clear that they had mined the gate and broken through. Further resistance by the wild Tekes was hopeless. A crowd of horsemen began to ride in confusion from the other side of the town, and spread in flight over the plain. The Russians made no effort to pursue them. Immediately afterward "a mass of fugitives of every class showed that the town was being abandoned by its inhabitants," streaming with their cattle and effects toward the Persian frontier. "The Turcoman fortress had fallen, and all was over with the Akhal Tekes."

With the fall of Turkmenistan, the Russian conquest of Central Asia was complete. The first order of business was completion of the great Central Asian railroad, connecting St. Petersburg and Moscow with such faraway cities as Tashkent and Samarkand. With the railroad came Russian merchants, and then Russian colonists, spreading into the lands last united by Genghis Khan in the thirteenth century. With the Russian colonists came not just the will to conquer and exploit, but also the equally human spirit of inquiry, fostered originally by Peter the Great's decree that all archaeological and ethnographic artifacts were to be collected for his Museum of Anthropology and Ethnology in Petersburg.

In the whole area from the Caspian Sea to the Altai Mountains of Mongolia, the Russians found hundreds of sparsely populated tribes who spoke related Turkish dialects and had quite similar ways of life. They were pastoralists, who barely cultivated the mean steppe soils, but kept sheep, goats, horses, camels, and cattle. In most cases, no matter what they herded, the social and economic fabric of their lives was woven around the horse, and their herding was done on horseback. Their horses were kept without fences in a more or less wild state approximating the original equine herd behavior before domestication. Control over the stallion was exercised through the mares, which were sometimes kept hobbled near tents. At other times it was the stallion that was tethered while the herder mounted a bell mare to lead the herd. A major difference from horses in the wild state was that colts were usually kept in a separate pack, sold, raised for meat, or castrated for riding. Geldings were accorded a special place of pride among the Central Asian nomads, ridden exclusively by the rich or powerful members of their society—the khans, their chief warriors, and traders with large herds. It had long ago been discovered on the Eurasian steppes that castrating stallions produced the most tractable and, therefore, desirable riding horses, with the powerful physique and instincts of the stallion but without that bothersome sex.

A unique cultural attitude toward the horse and riding it epitomized the peoples of the region. Horses were considered the single unit of wealth, and spiritual taboos about equus survived all across Central Asia. Among the Yakuts of the Siberian plateau, it was forbidden to strike a horse, and considered a crime even to speak roughly to one. The German-Russian ethnologist Wilhelm Radloff found in his studies of the Kirghiz steppe that among the Kirghiz mounted nomads, striking another man's horse or making insults against it were considered the same as striking or offending the man. Throughout Central Asia, marriage dowries and criminal fines were commonly calculated in so many head of horses. Although milking rather than raising meat was the principal concern of pastoral nomads, they revered horse meat, usually served only on ceremonial occasions. Similar reverence was also shown to mare's milk and the dairy products derived from it. *Kumis*—fermented mare's milk—was to the Central Asian like red table wine to the French. A serious offense was committed by anyone who failed to set a bowl of *kumis* before a stranger.

Among all these nomadic peoples, herding followed a similar pattern, the motivation for which is echoed in an ancient Kirghiz proverb: "Summer is like heaven; winter is like hell." Eurasian nomadism was seasonal, determined by how natural conditions affected the availability of forage and water. In his introduction to the catalog accompanying the 1989 U.S.–Soviet exhibition "Nomads of the Eurasian Steppes," Dr. Vladimir Basilov described how several Central Asian cultures fit into this pattern. The Kazakhs, for instance, migrated with their livestock as much as fifteen hundred kilometers to the milder south before winter, then headed back north to spring pastures. The Kirghiz and other nomads living near mountains migrated vertically, taking their animals up to higher elevations in summer to take advantage of alpine grazing, then bringing them down in winter to the open steppe, when snow covered the mountain forage. Mongolian herdsmen did the opposite, moving their livestock where there was adequate water near rivers and lakes on the steppe in summer, then taking them up into the mountains in winter, where they melted the snow for water. In the Altai Mountains, where sufficient forage is found throughout winter, migrations rarely exceeded ten kilometers.

The Russian ethnographers who followed, or in some cases accompanied, the czarist armies and Russian colonists began to distinguish a continuum of nomadism. The Turkmen, occupying the desert between the Caspian and Aral seas, kept sheep but not cattle, and lived as close to literally nomadic as possible. Constantly on the move, looking for forage and water for their sheep, or else sand dunes to protect their livestock from the howling winter winds, the Turkmen tribes had no fixed winter quarters. East of the Aral Sea, in present-day Uzbekistan, Kazakhstan, and Kirghizstan, families usually owned private winter grazing areas. Instead of constantly moving in search of open pasture to feed their herds, they shifted between permanent winter and summer camps. In the Altai and Sayan mountains, the area of present-day Tuva and Mongolia, herders moved only at intervals of several years, when the accumulation of waste made new camps necessary; technically, they could not be considered nomadic at all.

The term nomadism, therefore, described a tremendous range of pastoral activities. No matter what the specifics, however, these tribes were united by the fact that they spent practically their entire lives mounted. They contemptuously looked down on any other kind of transport, especially walking, and by the time a herdsman reached middle age, his legs were so bowed from years in the saddle that he was only able to walk awkwardly and with difficulty. To say that Eurasian nomads were generally better riders than Europeans is a given. What matters more is that the Eurasian nomads practiced, in protean form, the same style of horsemanship later adopted in the West.

The Central Asian rider used a stiff boat-shaped saddle, built on a wooden tree rising to high arches front and back, covered with hide, and padded with deer hair. With the high posts to brace the rider front and back, he sits nestled deep in the saddle. This was the basic design that would be adopted by the medieval knights of Europe, the Spanish *hidalgos* (noblemen), and ultimately in the American West. Not surprisingly, Central Asian nomads did not rise to the trot. There was, though, a fundamental difference between the way the nomads rode and the equitation of the armored knights. The latter rode straight-legged, with their legs thrust forward on long stirrup leathers attached to a stirrup bar at the front of the saddle, and the knight's seat braced against the cantle. This rear inclination put the knight in a secure position to sustain the shattering impact of a lance charge without falling. The Central Asian horseman used shorter leathers attached to a stirrup bar placed nearer the middle of the saddle flap. This brought the heel and hip into line, thrusting the seat and pelvis forward. He rode with the leg bent at the knee, hugging the horse's side with the whole inside of the leg, and this forward position favored speed and balance over security. As my instructor Ilona would say, the medieval knight rode *on* the horse, whereas the Central Asian, with full leg contact and forward seat, rode the horse. Anyone who rides will recognize this Central Asian forward seat and bent leg as the precursor of our modern riding style, employed for equestrian sports from dressage to jumping and cross country. It was probably first learned in Europe from the Hungarians, who had Central Asian Hunnish roots, and it really took hold during the Renaissance, when medieval chivalric tactics on heavy chargers finally gave way to the light cavalry style and school riding on finer horses.

Although the Central Asian nomads were patriarchal cultures characterized by male dominance and hierarchical clan structures, survivals of matriarchy and group marriage were sometimes present. Herodotus had first described this practice among the barbarian Scythians: When a father died, his sons married their widowed mothers; when a brother died, his siblings married their widowed sisters-in-law. On the steppes of Eurasia, women rode, sometimes owned horses, and shared herding duties. By the nineteenth century, however, there were no reliable accounts from Central Asia of women warriors. Apparently, the legendary Amazon women, who arrived at Alexander's camp with a frank proposition from their queen, had not managed to carry on their line. For this loss we may blame Alexander personally. Instead of joining the bare-breasted women warriors in matrimony to his Greeks, as he did in many other cases when alliances were useful, Alexander feared for their safety among his rapacious troops, and sent them home with a note telling the queen he would come get her with child as soon as he had some free time. In the event, of course, he was too busy conquering the world, and never got around to it.

By eleven o'clock Sally Alice and Greg arrived, and the long-awaited meeting began: green tea and candies, and a lengthy harangue by Djura Semedov on the Turkmen hope that the Albuquerque–Ashkhabad Sister City relationship could be "broadered" and "deepen" by our delegation's visit. He was showing off his English to the Turkmen and Russians lined up across the table and on both ends. His English wasn't terrible, only ludicrous; I caught Sasha Reebok's eye on the other side of the room and winked derisively. When he broke out in a broad grin, I felt I had made a friend, which may have been a first at the Turkmen Friendship Society.

While Djura boomed on, I took the opportunity to regard Sasha more closely. All I knew about him was that he was thirty-two, married with a young son, and a former Tass reporter. He had told me that when he found out that another journalist was coming to Ashkhabad, he had asked to be my host, but they had refused because he had a cold-water flat without a telephone. He smoked and drank vodka, and his English was exceptionally good for someone who had never been out of the Soviet Union. I knew he was Jewish, although his broad face, slight features, fair complexion, and stocky build were about as Slavic as they come. Then I remembered his saying yesterday that he wanted to learn American slang, which struck me as odd. What use would a Jewish guy in Turkmenistan have for fluency in English? Maybe it was nothing more than the desire to break the tedium of life with an occasional opportunity to meet foreign delegations—or perhaps it was something else. In his red shirt and black leather jacket, his sunglasses resting on his head, he certainly looked the part of a small-town KGB agent, but his sense of humor showed intelligence, and our common professional backgrounds made me want to know him. I was aware from Djura's pointed comments about drinking with Dr. Shikhmurad that someone had reported my behavior, and I hoped it wasn't Sasha. Anyway, what did I have to hide? What did *they* have to hide? Why had Djura been so visibly upset when he found me with the map? Was it any different from the German map of Turkmenistan I had in my bags back at Dr. Shikhmurad's house?

Djura was finishing. "So you come here, our great friend, Alice-a Thomson-a, enjoy our Turkmen hospitality. You eat with us! You drink with us! You stay in our house! You are in our hearts!" But it had an accusatory edge, as if he were slyly trying to make her feel indebted to him.

When he was done, Sally Alice remained seated in her old trench coat and said simply, "It's really wonderful to be here with you all again. I really hope we can both get something out of this visit. I'm very excited about visiting the school, so we can set up a satellite link between your students and ours in Albuquerque so they can study weather and geography together. Also, I'm going to videotape the concert your Ashkhabad symphony will give on April 1st of our New Mexico composer John Robb's music. I should tell you that his family in Albuquerque is thrilled about this concert. I'm very much looking forward to the concert myself. And please explain to your people that I don't have much good news about the carpets they left with me to sell. I sold one to friends, but I haven't been able to sell any of the others. Guess I'm not much of a rug seller."

As Djura translated into Russian, the phalanx of Turkmen officials in shiny business suits across the table from us frowned and scowled. When Sally Alice finished, they talked back and forth among themselves in rapid Turkmen. Then Djura said, "And invitations? You bring invitations, Alice-a Thomson-a?"

"What invitations do you mean, Djura?" asked Sally Alice. She looked at him with the naïveté of Mrs. McGoo.

"Invitations to bring Turkmen folk ensemble, Turkmen crafts exhibition, to Albuquerque, America. Your mayor make us this invitation."

"Oh, gosh, Djura," she said. "I don't think the mayor was serious about that. He sometimes says things he doesn't mean, like all politicians."

The official faces didn't like this at all. Apparently, they had been busily acquiring the necessary documents for the folk ensemble and selecting the delegation that would go to America with the crafts exhibition. I had no doubt this delegation would include most of the gentlemen across the table, led by Djura Semedov, Big Man Turkmen Friendship Society. I got the strong impression that the invitations were the main reason they had invited our delegation.

One of the honchos now started browbeating Sally Alice through Djura. Hadn't she brought definite plans, dates, documents, written agreements to sign? Wasn't the mayor of Albuquerque as good as his word? What was the hitch? The Sister City program had to be mutual, et cetera, et cetera.

Greg Gleason put his face in his hands as I quietly drank green tea and watched. Sally Alice held her own. She tried to explain that American mayors sometimes indulge in the rhetoric of friendship, when international relations are about the farthest thing from their actual political interests. The supposed invitation had been an empty gesture of goodwill, perhaps concocted on the spot during a reception the mayor had attended unwillingly. By the next day he had probably forgotten all about the Turkmen folk ensemble.

The pitiful hangdog expressions on the official faces made the remainder of the meeting unpleasant. Djura asked all three of us to tell them what we hoped to accomplish during our stay in Ashkhabad. While Greg wowed them with his Russian, I went over to Sasha Reebok, pulled him outside the conference room, and asked if he would call the Bulgarian for me. "Tell him I'll meet him tomorrow morning anywhere he says."

"Who is this, Jon?" Sasha asked.

"I met him on the flight from Moscow. He's a horse dealer; he's offered to show me some Akhal-Tekes. You're welcome to come along. In fact, I'd appreciate it."

"Akhal-Tekes? This would be very interesting for me. I have not seen them myself."

"But you grew up here."

"Yes, yes, I am from Ashkhabad."

"Let me introduce you to your own country."

Finally Sasha agreed, and I went back inside. When my turn came, I kept it simple and brief. I mentioned my interest in Turkmen horses, and said I would like to visit the Komsomol stud farm. If possible, I would also like to visit the republic's nature reserves to photograph desert landscapes and observe the wildlife.

"Komsomol stud no problem," Djura replied. "We arrange tour. What else?"

"The nature reserves," I repeated. "*Zapovedniki.*"

Now Djura was more evasive. I would have to meet with officials from the state conservation committee of the Ministry of Forestry—an odd ministry to have in the desert, I thought. But at this point I was willing to throw Djura a small bone as a test to see if the Turkmen Friendship Society would actually help me with contacts for onward travel. Out of caution, however, I did not mention my hope of extending my visa, much less my dream of crossing the Kara Kum and the steppes beyond it. I wanted to get the lay of the land first and meet some horsemen and biologists. I noticed that the others were following a similar course. Sally Alice had said she would like to visit the children's hospital, without mentioning the five hundred medical syringes we had brought as a gift, perhaps not wanting them to fall into the wrong hands. Professor Gleason, who knew his way around Soviet bureaucracies better than either of us, also played it close to the vest, mentioning his wish to meet with political scientists and legal specialists, but not mentioning a conference in the United States on Central Asian water issues that he was planning. He had told me earlier there would be several invitations for Turkmen to attend.

As our little presentation ended, Sasha Reebok came back into the conference room and whispered to me that Alex the Bulgarian would pick us up the following morning at Dr. Shikhmurad's *microrayon;* it was all set.

I decided not to tell Dr. Shikhmurad about this. Then if Djura found out, I could be certain who the informant was. Though the meeting ended in a sour key for the Turkmen, it had turned out quite satisfactory for at least one American delegate.

That afternoon I went to find several field biologists I had an introduction to through Victor Fet. Fet is a Russian field biologist specializing in scorpions and spiders who now lives in New Orleans. I had met him on the telephone; he was one of the hundreds of calls I had made the year before, looking for some way to get an invitation to Turkmenistan. It turned out that Victor and his wife, Galina, a botanist specializing in rare plants, had worked for twelve years in the nature reserves of Turkmenistan before emigrating to the United States. Although he couldn't help me secure an invitation, I had several long and fruitful conversations with him by phone before taking off, and he had sent me the names of several of his former colleagues. Victor also had a warning for me: "If you want to have an interesting trip, try to get out to the nature reserves. They are wild, fantastic places. Go to Repetek in the Kara Kum Desert. Go up into the Kopet-Dag Mountains. There at Kara Kala you can see the great garden of wild Asian varieties of fruits and grains made by Vavilov, the geneticist liquidated by Stalin. The only problem is that they may still not let a foreigner go to some of these places on the frontiers with Iran and Afghanistan. You must try very hard; otherwise you will sit on a carpet with the men and drink green tea for two weeks. But you will have no trouble finding horses. Turkmenia is still untouched. If you want to ride, you only have to say, 'Bring me a horse!'"

Instead, I was now riding around in still another borrowed car, looking for Victor's colleague Dr. Gennadi Kuznetsov. This car belonged to Dr. Shikhmurad's cousin Mahmut, a traffic cop with a thin black mustache. I felt safe in this car. I got in the front, laid my camera bag on the floor, and set a pack of Marlboros on the dash. Mahmut's eyes danced; he liked me.

Sasha Reebok and Dr. Shikhmurad, who insisted on accompanying the foreign guest, got in the back. In the middle of the afternoon, the dust and sand swept through Ashkhabad like a plague. No one was working but the dust brigades. Women and children sat huddled on the ground, their heads swathed in silk veils to keep out the sand. We passed a statue of Lenin, who was getting his historical comeuppance with sand in his face. Then the wind died, and the Kopet-Dag Mountains seemed to have moved closer. The wild blue peaks emerged from the sandstorm, jagged like dragon's teeth, so close that I felt I could reach out and touch them. The sky was cloudless and bristling blue. You could never reach heaven from the Kara Kum; the sky was too high.

Mahmut turned on the radio and Turkmen music played as we headed out Makhtymkuli Avenue. The singer's wailing voice seemed to swirl and sway crazily in time to the dust devils. His high pitch and hoarse cries seemed to fit the heat of an afternoon well over a hundred degrees. It was a plaintive voice that came from five hundred years away, out of the common grave of a whole tribe, buried with their horses. A dry Asian voice that cursed the earth and sang that life is only suffering. Lonely wanderers in the cosmos, the Turkmen would never make a melody of their homeland. At last, I thought, I really have reached Central Asia.

When we got a few kilometers out of town to the address of the national park station where Kuznetsov was supposed to have his office, workers were sitting outside under some trees. The head man told us Kuznetsov no longer worked there.

I asked to use the phone since Victor Fet had been good enough to provide me with a number for the Turkmen Society for the Conservation of Nature, where I planned to go next to inquire about Kuznetsov.

The head man said, "There's a phone inside, but it doesn't work."

"Is there a public phone around?"

"No."

"Well, where's the closest phone I can use?"

"There isn't one."

"Well, do you know where Kuznetsov works now?"

"No," said the head man. "In April, he could be out in the field somewhere."

"Maybe I could reach him at home. Do you have a phone book I could use?"

"A book of the telephone?" the head man looked puzzled.

"We do not have such things here, Jon," said Sasha.

No working phone, no public phones, no phone books. How the devil do these people communicate? Then I saw how silly my question was. Under the façade of roads and concrete structures, official-sounding agencies, and men in suits was another Turkmenistan, silent and uncommunicative. Why would the Soviet state want to allow people to communicate and exchange information? Remembering all the times I'd tried to reach Turkmenistan from the States, I became gloomy at the prospect that it might prove almost as difficult to reach anyone from inside Turkmenistan.

We all got back into Mahmut's beat-up car, turned around, and headed back toward town. I was in danger of losing my "walk" attitude. I wanted to come up out of the saddle and jog out of the city. I wanted to sleep out in the mountains under the Asian stars. It was, surprisingly, Dr. Shikhmurad who came up with the idea of going downtown to the Kalinin Institute of Agriculture. He thought the Turkmen Society for the Conservation of Nature was headquartered there. I appreciated the way he pitched in to help solve the problem, and decided my host was a good-hearted soul even if he informed on me to Djura. I was beginning to see that the wolf and the sheep could reach a modus operandi here in Turkmenistan. I was also beginning to feel guilty about taking my host away from his work for the day. He had been running around borrowing cars since 8:00 A.M. He was the head of the medical institute where they trained two hundred nurses for the birthing hospital; surely he had more important things to do. He could just as easily have not come up with his suggestion that we try the agriculture institute.

Mahmut swept up the circular driveway and deposited us on the front steps of a dignified neoclassical building with a statue out front of Mikhail Kalinin, one of Lenin's compatriots. Mahmut lit up a Marlboro, turned up the radio, and said he would wait outside, like a professional chauffeur. When a cowboy hat, a black leather jacket, and a little man in thick glasses suddenly appeared in the lobby, the students must have thought it was a raid. They started running in four directions as well as up the stairs. Finally they calmed down enough to direct us to the second floor, where a Professor Ovez Sopiev rose from his desk and strode forward to welcome us.

Professor Sopiev had the elegant upright posture and slow graceful movements of a crane. He was a tall, dark, cerebral Turkmen ornithologist in his early sixties, with kind eyes, gray hair, and an intelligent face, sad around the edges. When Dr. Shikhmurad told him who I was and why I had come, Sopiev set his eyes on mine and shook hands long and warmly. He said, "I have met your eyes before in our country."

In Russian it sounded very pretty, if not poetic, and I was touched. "You are right," I said. "I am of Russian–Jewish descent. You won't be able to tell from the bad way I speak Russian, but my grandfather was born in Ukraine."

"Why have you come to me without an appointment?" asked Sopiev with a slight smile. "All my life I have been waiting for an American to walk into my office and say he was interested in our natural history."

"That's precisely why I have arrived without an appointment," I said, and Sopiev laughed heartily. I explained that I was looking for Dr. Kuznetsov or Dr. Atamuradov, with a letter of introduction from my Russian biologist friend, Victor Fet, that I was *very* interested in the natural history of Turkmenistan, and that I had hoped Kuznetsov or Atamuradov might help me extend my visa and visit the *zapovedniki*. A traveler must use his eyes, his wits, and his instincts; Professor Sopiev's sincerity swept ceremony before it.

Unfortunately, he replied, they were both in the field. Spring in the desert lasted only four to six weeks, during which most plants bloomed and animals gave birth to young. Although it was the most interesting time for a foreigner to explore the country, it was also the most difficult time to arrange travel since most researchers went into the field to work. In Atamuradov's absence, Sopiev himself was acting director of the Society for the Conservation of Nature, an older organization revived under perestroika reforms. "Please sit down; we will have some green tea now and discuss these matters."

I had noticed a wall poster of a photograph of a horse's head with the words "Akhal-Teke, Turkmenia" written under it hanging on the wall of Sopiev's office above his desk. The white horse had a long, slightly concave, stately head, and large flaring nostrils. I asked him about it.

"Turkmenistan produces four domestic animals unique in the world," said the professor: "the Akhal-Teke horse, the Astrakhan sheep, the Bactrian camel, and the Ovcharki dog. That stallion in the photograph was taken from Turkmenistan to Moscow and sold to the American millionaire oilman Armand Hammer. They say he had over a hundred Akhal-Tekes in a stable in Moscow and was preparing to ship them to the United States when he died. That stallion is now owned by the Konnozavod, the stud farm in Moscow."

Just then tea was served. More green tea. I was going to float away on a river of green tea if I didn't find a urinal soon. I went down to the basement, Sasha Reebok accompanying me. In the men's room they had two urinals in separate rooms. One was for the students, the other for the faculty. Other than the signs, they were both exactly alike and smelled exactly the same. I stepped up to the students' urinal since it was closer, and Sasha used the faculty *pissoir*. When we got back to Sopiev's office, Dr. Shikhmurad had left to check in at his institute, which was apparently nearby. In a few minutes, I had my maps, letters of introduction, and documents spread all over the professor's little work table. I had gone to the trouble of bringing a typed list of the nature reserves, along with an elaborate letter of introduction from my editor, also composed by myself, which read in part, "A hundred warm greetings and a thousand best wishes to the people of the Turkmen Soviet Socialist Republic! From New York City in the United States of America we send our hearty hello and hopes for communication, peace, and friendship between our peoples."

We went over the list of *zapovedniki*; Professor Sopiev meticulously corrected my Russian spelling. I had laid out a tour of nature reserves in a progressively eastern direction, hoping that I might get to the Amu Darya River on the border with Uzbekistan and somehow continue east across the hungry steppes. But Sopiev said that with so many nature reserves, I could hardly expect to visit all of them in two weeks. He suggested I try a two-track approach, visiting a few *zapovedniki* under his guidance, while trying to extend my visa here in Ashkhabad.

I had a short list in mind as a fallback position. It included Repetek, the world's only Institute of the Desert, where they supposedly study the process of desertification; Kara Kala, in the Kopet-Dag Mountains, which I knew from Victor could be reached on horseback; and Badkhyz, in the remote foothills of the Hindu Kush, where one of the last surviving herds of the Central Asian wild ass, the onager, lives far from any roads.

"Badkhyz is in the border zone with Afghanistan, and Kara Kala in the border zone with Iran," Sopiev said. "It used to be very difficult for foreigners to visit the border zone, but nowadays, under perestroika, it might be possible."

"Do you yourself go into the field?" I asked him.

"Yes, but usually in December. I go bird watching to study migration at that time of the year, but there's another reason I go in that month."

He took from his bookshelves a volume he had written on traditional Turkmen falconry to show me. It turned out Professor Sopiev was a leading authority on the subject. He had not only written on it, but had also brought one of the few practicing Turkmen falconers to an international anthropology conference on the tradition of falconry in Central Asia. "The falconers start hunting in December," he explained. "A trained hawk costs twice the price of a good horse. The hawk hunts only with a dog. The dogs are called Turkmen Tazy. They are very fast and sleek, and like the Rhodesian ridgeback, they have no bark. The dogs flush and run the hares before the hawk is released by the falconer to attack. It's the same hare as in your southwestern deserts in Arizona and New Mexico."

At first Sopiev said they didn't use horses. I found that strange, but later on in the conversation it developed that horses had become so rare, hard to come by, and expensive that the Turkmen falconers had given up and now hunted on foot with their bird and dog.

"What happened to make horses so rare?" I asked him.

"Many of our Akhal-Teke horses were killed without thought, even slaughtered and eaten. It was a terrible calamity for the Turkmen—and for the world, which hardly knows about it. Someday the horse breeders of the West will want to go back to the original genetic material that produced the Thoroughbred to strengthen the blood lines, the way agronomists do with food crops. We believe the Akhal-Teke are, as our academician Bilonogov put it, the last drops of pure blood that brought forth all the racehorses of the world."

Sopiev was forthright and matter-of-fact, but I sat for a moment in doubting silence. Was it possible that the Akhal-Teke was the progenitor of the modern racehorse? I found this no easier to accept than the idea that the Turkmen horses had been slaughtered for food, especially given

Dr. Shikhmurad's highly charged statement that a Turkmen would never kill his horse, no matter what, never eat the animal he so loved. It was my first indication that Turkmen horses had not remained outside the influences of the USSR's three quarters of a century of total politics.

"That was in the time of Stalin," Sopiev said. "We have only started to speak about these things in the last few years."

"By 'these things' you mean that the Turkmen were forced under Stalin to slaughter the thing they loved best in the world?"

Professor Sopiev was silent, perhaps embarrassed by my directness.

I went on. "Can you show me any documentary evidence linking Akhal-Tekes to the English Thoroughbred?"

Professor Sopiev remained charming, but demurred. "I can see you are a serious person with sound goals," he said. "I would like to help you in whatever small way I can, but you must not expect to do everything in one minute here. This is not the West. You must go slowly. You must go through proper channels. You will need a special permit to go into the border zone. You will need a letter from the head of the Turkmen Friendship Society to the director of the agricultural institute. You may need other documents as well. It will require patience and calm; otherwise, you will get nowhere."

We woke up Mahmut, who was asleep slumped over the wheel of the car under some trees in the driveway of the agricultural institute. I got in the front and said, "Sasha, how about a drink?"

"A drink, Jon?" he said. "I don't understand. You are thirsty?"

"No, no, no, no, no. I mean, let's go to a bar or café and I'll buy you a drink. It's after five o'clock."

"A bar?" he said. "But there are no bars in Ashkhabad."

"There are hotels in Ashkhabad. We passed one on the way here. The Turkmenistan Hotel. Surely the hotel has a café."

"But you are not registered at this hotel, Jon."

"What difference does that make? They'll sell an American in a cowboy hat a drink. I guarantee it."

Sasha got sweaty and anxious. He lit a Marlboro and said, "Anyway, Jon, I should tell you, we are due at the Turkmen Friendship Society. There is a musical recital put on by conservatory students in your honor, followed by a reception with English-language students."

"You're kidding. Why wasn't I told about it?"

Now he looked as though he had failed me. He cringed like a dog that had stolen the Sunday roast off the kitchen counter and was waiting for a beating.

"Well," I said, "I'll buy you a drink after the reception. You've been extremely helpful to me today, Sasha. I want you to know how appreciative I am. It's been enjoyable working with you."

"I, too, have found today most . . . interesting."

We cruised back to the Turkmen Friendship Society headquarters, the last place I wanted to be. Professor Gleason was already there when we arrived, accompanied by his host, a newspaper photographer named Gennadi with soft runny eyes, and a young brunette Turkmen woman, an economist Gleason said he was interviewing.

"What are you interviewing her about?" I asked him.

"Nothing heavy yet," he reported with admirable suavity. "And how's it going for you so far?"

"Not too bad. I insulted my host by not drinking vodka yesterday, and today Djura got furious because I was looking at a map of Turkmenistan. But tomorrow I'm supposed to go to look at horses with the Bulgarian from the flight from Moscow. What's the story with this guy Djura?"

"Yeah, is he a creep or what," agreed the professor. "He's certainly the biggest asshole I've met in Ashkhabad."

"Is he dangerous?"

"Look, the worst they can do now is ask you to leave the country," he said. "But I wouldn't worry; that would be very bad form. These guys get a lot of points for hosting foreigners. The last thing they want is a scandal."

Sally Alice came late. She weaved up the staircase, and several men went to her assistance. She was still wearing her old trench coat and sensible shoes, but she did look the worse for wear. She said to me, "Golly, once you go to one of these Turkmen's houses as a guest, you never get away. They just want you to eat and drink more!"

They seated us quickly in three stuffed armchairs on the second-floor landing. The first pieces were traditional Turkmen music played on the dutar—a fretless two-stringed instrument about the size of a mandolin, but strummed in a droning manner, not unlike an Indian sitar. The male singing was so harsh and whining that you couldn't hear yourself think. Then two women in formal Western gowns played lovely romantic pieces on the piano, classical melodies based on Turkmen folk themes. I liked it so much that I promptly dozed off.

We went into the conference room for the reception. The English students, all non-Turkmen women, were waiting for us. The table was set for tea, with plates of coffee cake some one of them had probably made. While tea was served, the table gradually split up into three groups, each around an American. The women around me were middle-aged and wore too much makeup. After all the Russian-language classes I had been in, without, however, mastering half the grammar, I didn't mind walking them through an oral exercise.

"My name is Jonathan. What is your name?"

"Marina . . . Tanya . . . Nadya."

"I'm very glad to meet you. How long have you studied English?"

"Eight year . . . six year . . . one, uhhhh . . ."

"Year?"

"Yez, wan ear."

"I live in America. Where do you live? Are you married? What are you doing tonight after the reception?"

Down at the other end of the table, I noticed Professor Gleason holding forth in a similar manner. The woman economist had disappeared; instead, he had five or six pretty young women around him who were looking at him with stars in their eyes. Some guys have all the luck. In the meantime, I reflected, I hadn't done too badly on my first full day in Turkmenistan. I had a date to meet Alex the Bulgarian, which might lead to something more interesting than this sort of event. And I had Professor Sopiev on my side, a potentially invaluable ally with his formal manners and Oriental counsel. He had obviously been much taken with me. In my mind's eye danced the enticing idea that maybe I had unwittingly landed in the Thoroughbred's ancestral homeland. I knew that at least one of the foundation stallions of the English Thoroughbred was indeed a horse known as the Byerley Turk, though I had no idea then what "Turk" meant in this context. England certainly was fighting in Turkey in the sixteenth and seventeenth centuries when Thorough breeding began and the Ottoman Empire certainly had many cavalry horses.

"Tomorrow, ten A.M., Maslov," a voice boomed over my shoulder. "You will meet with assistant to mayor of Ashkhabad. Ten A.M. tomorrow morning."

I looked up from the English lesson. "Djura Semedov, as I live and breathe!"

"Tomorrow, ten A.M. You will meet with assistant to mayor of Ashkhabad."

"Sorry, Djura. No can do. I have a previous appointment."

He went rigid. "You will come to meeting tomorrow at ten o'clock, Maslov."

I said, "I'm sorry, Djura, but I have an appointment I can't break."

"Where you go appointment?"

"I'm going to see some horses."

"Komsomol stud?"

"No. Somewhere else."

"How you make appointment?"

"By telephone, believe it or not."

"Where you phone from? You phone from Dr. Shikhmurad's house?"

I didn't like his line of questioning. "What difference does it make?"

I didn't tell him it was the phone in his office.

"You will come to the meeting with assistant to mayor of Ashkhabad," he insisted again. "Tomorrow at ten A.M. be at Turkmen Friendship Society."

"That's impossible," I said. "I'm a writer, not a diplomat. I don't have anything to do with getting your invitations to Albuquerque, and if you want me to come to one of your get-togethers here, let me know ahead of time and I'll put it on my schedule. I'm tired of your springing events on me when I have other things to do here."

"You will come to meeting, Friendship Society, ten o'clock tomorrow morning!"

I laughed and tossed my head like a green horse showing an inexperienced rider who's boss, but said nothing more, and shortly thereafter the reception broke up early, about 7:00. From the way the women scattered, I suspected they needed to get home to make dinner. Everyone left by the grand staircase that led down to the double entrance doors and the portico outside. The good news was that we were leaving;

the bad news was that I still had to ask Djura about acquiring the permit Professor Sopiev had described. He was standing on the portico, saying good-bye to Sally Alice with his hands cradling hers.

"Alice-a Thomson-a, you our biiiig, very good friend! Thank you, you come to Ashkhabad. Go now to host house. I join you tonight there. We make Ashkhabadi picnic. Ha-ha-ha-ha!"

Some children lurking about the portico presented Sally Alice with a bouquet of handsome blue irises, and she got into the backseat of a black Volga, a much tonier car than the wrecks I had been riding around in all day. As the solid sedan descended the drive, Djura and I stood on the portico together, waving good-bye like the first couple outside the White House. I showed him the list of nature reserves I wanted to visit, all typed in Russian on the letterhead of a friendly Boston public-television station, and asked him to write a letter to the head of the agricultural institute so I could obtain the permit.

"We talk about this tomorrow morning at meeting," he tried to put me off.

"I told you I can't attend that meeting, Djura."

At this he waved his arms at me furiously. "I must leave now!" he barked. "My driver's wife in hospital."

"Nothing serious, I hope."

"Have baby," he said.

"Well, when can I talk to you about this? Tomorrow's Wednesday. I'm busy. How about first thing Thursday morning?"

"Yes. Thursday. You come Turkmen Friendship Society any time!"

I went "home" to Dr. Shikhmurad's apartment. He wasn't around, but his wife, Yenye, had finally gotten off work. She was a plump pleasant woman with a friendly wrinkled face like a dried melon that had turned brown, tied around with a green Teke head cloth. She and the children were watching an ice hockey game on the television in the dining room. The Soviet Union was playing Canada. It seemed ironic to see a game played on ice here, where the temperatures daily topped one hundred, but Yenye said she loved sports on television, especially when the Soviet Union won. They rose from their chairs and cheered when the Soviets scored a goal.

I went in and stretched out on the bed in the dark, gazing out the window beyond a street lamp to the few stars in the lucid black sky. The world felt flat and treeless in Turkmenistan. How small, naked, and alone man feels in such a place, where no forest meets savannah. There was no place to hide here because everything had been wiped away. History itself had been like a geologic cataclysm. The accumulation of human strata over eons had been eroded silently; the task of reconstruction and analysis seemed hopeless before such muteness. Yet somewhere near here, in times before recorded history, wild stallions must have roamed the desert night, covering the mares let out by their herders in season. Perhaps men must geld their wildness if they are to move forward in this world. The walk attitude of Ilona Ujhelyi had won a battle against the Stalinist bureaucrat Djura Semedov, but it was only the first battle. I went to sleep early, sure there would be many more.

Ancient Turkmen proverb: A man may choose his friends, but Allah chooses his enemies.

How lucky I was, then, to choose Guvanch Djumaev. When I arrived the next morning with the Bulgarian, Guvanch received me in his office with the traditional "Salaam Aleikham" greeting and two-handed shake. He offered me the seat of the favored guest, on his right hand. While we waited for tea to be served, he conducted business in the traditional Central Asian fashion, known as the *divan*, which I was to come to know and admire, if not quite enjoy. At the head of Guvanch's desk, making a *T* with it, was a long table with a dozen or so chairs. Everyone who had business that morning with Guvanch sat around the table at the same time. There was Alex, who had horse business. Two weathered fishermen from the Caspian Sea, who had fishing to discuss. A fat Armenian was there negotiating a cotton deal. A partner was working on the wording of a contract. So it went—clients, partners, employees, guests, friends. Guvanch dealt with them all at once and one at a time. No one shouted; no one tried to press his case forward out of turn. The atmosphere was Oriental and respectful. I could imagine the *divan* taking place in a yurt with the men lying on rugs. On Guvanch's desk, under glass, was a printed listing of the telephone numbers of every government agency in the republic. This in itself was impressive. He had recently had a Bulgarian phone system installed and was already mastering the modern art of pushing buttons and talking on two lines at once.

Guvanch was a consummate Central Asian executive, in the literal meaning of that term: one who executes. He responded to a dozen different problems with a cool, decisive air, though the towel placed under his elbows to catch the sweat showed how hard he was working. He could turn his undivided attention on a dime. He kept up a pace like a steady trot, dealing with one matter after another. He wasted no time on pleasantries over the phone; instead, he shouted orders or questions, sometimes in Russian, sometimes in Turkmen, then cut the conversation short. As he talked to someone at the table, his eyes perused documents, which he signed while he spoke on the phone. Sometimes he would stop to think for fifteen or twenty seconds before making a decision. Then he looked almost Mongolian, with his thin eyes set far apart, and his short, sharp beak. It came as a surprise to learn he had been in business for only a few months. It came as no surprise to find out he had formerly been the general secretary of Ashkhabad's Komsomol organization, one of the most responsible political jobs in the republic.

Guvanch had quit Komsomol only eight months before, and was now director of a private cooperative he had formed in a joint venture with the Bulgarians. This was the famous BEVIKO Alex had mentioned on the plane. The cooperative was dealing in horses, sheep, cotton, fruits, vegetables, honey, and fish, though I don't think this list is complete. They also operated a printing plant. The cooperative had apple orchards a few kilometers outside of town, and was negotiating with foreign investors to start processing apple juice in a new factory. With Bulgarian partners on the Black Sea, they were also getting into tourism, already running a plane and bus tour to Bulgaria and Turkey. Guvanch had recently made his first cotton sale to a Canadian company whose president had come to Ashkhabad; he was interested, but cautious, about doing more business with the West.

From what I could gather, it seemed the BEVIKO cooperative was building a small private commercial empire with Guvanch Djumaev at the helm. In his seedy ground-floor office suite—an area that might have housed an air-conditioning repair business or maybe a small freight handler in the United States—Guvanch Djumaev reached out from the *divan* to the world like an enlightened Asian pasha in his palace court. His activity conquered the lascivious inertia of the desert. His decisions turned a sandy waste into a sea for caravans. His pointed finger chased the very cobras away from the sands of the old silk route.

There is nothing romantic about running a shop or pushing papers in an anonymous office tower, but commerce has its adventure. It was trade that linked nations and civilized men, bringing them together for another purpose than war. Commerce distills luck from action. It judges the quality of things. Only commerce requires men to become citizens of the world. It follows the pattern of the seasons. The raw scent of earthly products hangs about commerce; it is about the here and the now of life. As I watched Guvanch, I couldn't help remembering that the prophet Mohammed was himself a successful trader whose long commercial career began as a caravan conductor for the rich widow Khadija, whom he married. Wasn't it on the caravan road that the prophet first learned about Christianity from an itinerant monk? This has conferred upon the trading profession an elevated dignity in Muslim culture that still endures. By tradition, Mohammed is supposed to have described traders as "the couriers of the world and the trusty servants of God upon Earth," held them as exemplars of the devout life, and accorded them a position in Muslim hierarchy ranking beside the martyrs of the faith. In the Muslim Day of Judgment, the honest merchant will sit in the shadow of God's throne.

I soon jumped into the *divan*, chatting with Guvanch between his other petitioners. With Sasha Reebok's help, we discussed the economic situation in the Turkmen republic. Guvanch explained that prior to perestroika, Moscow treated Turkmenistan like a colony, buying raw agricultural, mineral, and petroleum products at low prices fixed by the Soviet state in its own interest. Now the Turkmen were trying to obtain technology and equipment so that they themselves might profit from the processing of their own rich raw materials.

The Bulgarian got very impatient with this abstract talk, and broke in. "Excuse, please," he said to me, "but this man Guvanch is not only the businessman. He is the horseman. He know the horse here most good of the people. This man led Turkmen riders on Akhal-Teke horse from Ashkhabad to the Moskva. Many thousand kilometers they ride across Kara Kum Desert, across Russia, to the Moskva. You should ask to him of this marathon."

Horses hadn't been mentioned at all so far, so I did ask, and learned something even more amazing about my new acquaintance. In 1988, fifty-three years after a group of Turkmen horsemen rode to Moscow in eighty-eight days in the famous marathon I had read about, Guvanch Djumaev had conceived of riding the Ashkhabad–Moscow marathon over again with a group of Turkmen ranging in age from eighteen to sixty-four years old. No one had ridden across the Kara Kum Desert in half a century. Their motives were fourfold, he said. From a scientific point of view, they wanted to find out how the endurance of the present-day Akhal-Teke stacked up against the Turkmen horses of yesteryear, and to measure feeding and watering requirements on a forty-six-hundred-kilometer ride. From the cultural standpoint, Djumaev hoped to revive the equestrian traditions of the Turkmen nomads, in eclipse since the time of Stalin. From a sporting interest, what equestrian would not have wanted to make such a ride? It was the sporting adventure of ten lifetimes, an event your grandchildren's grandchildren would hear stories about. They were also aware that long-distance equestrian racing had been accepted as a new Olympic event. From a purely business interest, the publicity generated by such an unusual event could be useful at a time when commercial power was becoming more decentralized, and Turkmenistan had the opportunity to retake control of its own horse-breeding industry. Perhaps some oil-rich sheik would hear about the Turkmen's horses, and buy himself an Olympics team.

Without prodding, Guvanch pulled out his scrapbook and began showing me the record of the great ride. It was strangely like looking at pictures of my own dream. A newspaper journalist from Moscow had ridden with them, making color photographs and filing several stories along the way. The Turkmen rode in their traditional costume: loose riding pants, black knee boots, red-and-yellow silk robes, and huge white sheepskin hats. They looked wonderfully authoritative on their English saddles. In the first ten days they had crossed the bleak sands of the Kara Kum in temperatures that reached 65 degrees centigrade (149°F). It was so hot that they rode from 4 A.M. until 9 A.M., then again from 5 P.M. until 10 P.M., feeding and watering the horses at 11 P.M., and only sleeping themselves from midnight to 3:30 A.M. In this way they made seventy-five kilometers a day with three- to four-year-old Akhal-Teke stallions. They couldn't ride more tractable geldings because none are available in Turkmenistan: So few Akhal-Teke studs are left—between one hundred and one hundred fifty—that all stallions are left intact.

Soon Guvanch's marathon stories swept the *divan* up and away on a magic carpet ride. All other business ceased for a while. "The night was always the most dangerous time," he said. "We could not see where our horses' feet were falling. Many different kinds of snakes hunt at night in the desert. Horses are deathly afraid of snakes. Sometimes one horse would suddenly take off at a full gallop, you couldn't stop him, and we would know there had been a snake underfoot. Once a large cobra coiled up a horse's leg. There was nothing anyone could do; we thought the horse would certainly be bitten and die. But the horse stood absolutely still, didn't move a muscle, and eventually the cobra slithered down and went away. But another cobra bit one of our riders on the big toe when he was asleep and had his boots off. The cobra's venom is deadly unless the antidote is administered instantly. Fortunately we had a doctor with us, who went right over to the man and injected the antivenom. He survived, but couldn't ride for a few days. Altogether we lost only one horse, but unfortunately it was a fine Akhal-Teke stallion with champion blood lines. Its heart gave out. It probably wasn't properly conditioned for the stress. It just lay down, and thirty seconds later it was dead.

"One night after we had dismounted," he continued, "we tethered the horses and ate our bread with salt and tea. Then we went to sleep on the ground. In the night, a terrible sandstorm blew across the desert. We were caught on the ground, and simply had to cover our heads, as if in a strafing attack. The wind was so intense it carried off everything. Everything! The saddles blew away, the horses' rations, our personal gear. In a few minutes it passed by, and when we looked up, everything was gone, including the horses. They ended up in all different locations in the desert. It took us till the end of the next day to find all of them again. It was lucky we didn't lose any of the animals that night.

"Another time in the desert," he said, "we were trotting along— usually we rode a fast trot, which the Akhal-Tekes can maintain for hours even in the hottest temperatures. Suddenly, one of the stallions in the lead caught the scent of something and ran away with a young rider. It was a feral mare out in the desert."

"An Akhal-Teke?" I inquired.

"We think so, yes. It looked very much like an Akhal-Teke mare. Well, the young boy riding him couldn't control the stallion. No one could in a situation like that. The stallion mated with the feral mare there in the desert, with the boy on his back. We were only fortunate he didn't get crushed. Then it got really dangerous. When the other stallions caught up, they all started to fight over the mare. With us mounted. It was all we could do to stop them from killing each other."

Eventually they reached Russia at the northern limit of the Kara Kum, where the land turned to arable steppe. It was August and cool, and they picked wild huckleberries and wild cherries for their meal. Peasants ran from the fields to present their procession with flowers and bread. In the towns, they were feted by local officials; children paraded with them; ethnic groups danced in their honor. They crossed the Moscow River into the Soviet capital in a chilling autumn rain, and Guvanch was received in his Turkmen costume by the Moscow city soviet, where he gave a speech and was awarded the key to the city, the first Turkmen ever so honored. He made the front page of several Moscow newspapers, and the Turkmen's arrival was reported on the evening news program that went out to the entire Soviet Union.

All of this was told with a touch of appropriate physical swagger, leavened by self-deprecating humor. When I asked Guvanch if he rode much now, he patted his small but lively paunch, and said, "I would like to, but I have little time right now. I lost twelve kilos on the *probeg* [marathon] from Ashkhabad to Moscow. I was in better shape then, of course. And now what do you want to do?"

"In general or today?"

"Today," Guvanch said. "We can talk more later. You will come later to the mountains. We can swim there, and grill lamb. We will have time to talk. But right now, what do you wish to do?"

"To see horses."

"Of course," smiled Guvanch. His mouth was full of gold teeth that sparkled when he smiled.

"He has good Japanese camera," said the Bulgarian in Russian. "He can make most good photos of horse."

"Of course," said Guvanch again.

And it was done.

"Of course" in Russian is *konyechno*. I would find out in the course of the next year that it was one of Guvanch Djumaev's favorite words. *Konyeeechno*, he would drawl out, his lips curled in a smile. Then everyone at the BEVIKO cooperative picked it up from the boss. They became the Konyechno Kids. Guvanch Djumaev's enterprise forged a kind of can-do, go-for-it, break-down-the-barriers spirit. "Of course" was their corporate slogan, their marching tune, their anthem. It was infectious: I would soon start saying it, too.

That afternoon I went with Alex, Sasha Reebok, and Sasha Skorokhodov, one of Guvanch's Russian partners, to the stables at the Ashkhabad municipal hippodrome. The Bulgarian wanted to show me the "most good" Akhal-Tekes, and I was ready. The racetrack was on the outskirts of town. On the drive over, it developed that Alex was eager to purchase one of the stallions stabled there. He wanted to take it back with him to Bulgaria on this trip. Most of all, he wanted to know if I wanted to go in on the deal with him.

"This is most good horse in world," he declared bluntly. "You can sell the babies this horse for one hundred thousand dollars in your country."

He was mistaken on two counts. One, there was no way anyone could sell an unknown breed in the United States for that kind of money; secondly, I couldn't sell them for anything. "I'm a writer, not a horse trader," I reminded him.

"You will see this horse. Very, very good. Very strong. Then you will change your mind," he said.

The unfinished hippodrome was anything but prepossessing. From a distance, stretched against the flat buff horizon, it looked like nothing more than a cinder-block foundation. In fact, it was an unfinished concrete grandstand with no roof to protect race fans against the searing sun, no clubhouse to get a bite to eat or drink between races, and no parimutuel windows. Construction had begun five years ago, but as everywhere else in Ashkhabad, little progress had been made. Piles of precast concrete blocks were strewn around, and the obligatory construction cranes were there, stationary and well rusted. There were neither construction workers nor fans in sight: By tradition, the Turkmen race only on Sunday afternoons. When or if they will actually complete the hippodrome remains a mystery.

The track itself was a simple sand-dirt affair, with a low rail only on the grandstand side. It was unusually long for a racetrack, and the following Sunday, when I attended the races with Guvanch, I was surprised to learn that the shortest races of the fourteen-race card were still one mile or more, while the main event was a whopping six kilometers, more than twice the length of our typical races. The stables were on the far side. They were ugly, utilitarian concrete sheds with iron-fenced paddocks, and stableboys sprawled asleep on bare metal bedsprings outside the doors. Six or eight stables were lined up in a row. Between them were brown felt yurts, the ancient tent dwellings of the nomads, standard across five thousand miles of Eurasia. The jockeys and trainers lived there. With the first smell of horses, horse manure, leather, and hay, I felt exhilarated.

The horses were stabled inside during the heat of the day, but Sasha Skorokhodov convinced the stableboys to bring out half a dozen. In Turkmenistan, you never go into a stable to see horses. They bring them out to show you, rather like a fashion show put on for the foreign guest's aesthetic and sensual pleasure.

The models—in this case, some of the finest racing Akhal-Tekes in the Turkmen republic—were brought out one at a time. The first was a palomino, the second jet black, the third dappled, the fourth a bay, the fifth a golden color certainly unique in the equestrian world—shining gold like a pure bar of the stuff from Fort Knox, held up to the sunlight. The black stallion and the bay also shone brilliantly. Their iridescence could only be compared to a beautiful tiny hummingbird. Their coats radiated a light that made their colors glow. Each was brought out in turn and stepped high and lively several times around a circle in the sand, then posed while I took its portrait in color, and was held on a lead line while I inspected each horse at leisure with the Bulgarian.

"You see why I love these horse?" he asked.

I did. They were unlike any other horses I had ever seen. Alex had removed his shirt and was wearing only sweat pants and sneakers in the glaring sun. He put his arms out along the neck of the bay he wanted, to show me how long it was. From the withers to the top of the ear was almost the length of his two arms outstretched. "Look at this long neck. Why this horse carry the head so high, you see? Is the most good for the dressage. Look at the skin of this horse. It is fine like the doe skin. They no use the clip. That is natural length of hair. You see this horse?"

The radiant bay, his dark coat blending into burnished gold, was indeed a stunning animal.

"I say this stallion worth the one million dollars," Alex whispered. "Maybe I buy now for the fifty thousand dollars. We make the business together. I sell the babies in the Europe. You sell the babies in United States."

76

It was a familiar kind of greed. All horse lovers suffer to one degree or another the desire to possess the most beautiful, the most graceful, the most winsome—the most good horse. Horses have been bought and sold for too many centuries to pretend they still have a pure attraction, disinterested and separate from all financial considerations. Maybe it is the same confusion between beauty and value that has led so many racehorse owners to the poorhouse. Nevertheless, if I'd had twenty-five thousand dollars in my pocket at that moment, I would probably have gone into partnership with the overexcited Bulgarian.

But other, very different ideas gripped me. In two days in Ashkhabad, I had seen only squalor, disorder, dryness, dust brigades, drunks standing in line, and statues of Lenin. There was more than enough food to eat in Ashkhabad, but there are other forms of starvation. In the desert one can starve for visual affection. When the powerful, sleek stallions stepped high and proud into the wincing afternoon light, it was like a visitation of demigods to the dusty hell of the Kara Kum. Their exploding colors blinded me to reality, and I could see why the Turkmen valued these horses above all earthly things. The Akhal-Teke is not only the Turkmen's national pride, but also their cultural treasury and patron saint.

I took out my cameras and went to work, and by the end of two hours had made more than one hundred exposures. The Akhal-Tekes were quite different from the picture I had in my mind—the same picture, by the way, that everyone unfamiliar with the breed has. That is, the picture of a stout, shaggy, small horse, almost like a pony, which Westerners probably associate with the pictures of Asian nomads we've seen in *National Geographic*. In fact, nothing could be further from this image than the long-legged, lean, lustrous Akhal-Teke, with its trim musculature, sparse mane, and veins rippling out of its thin, fine, shimmering coat. Although actually compact, short-barreled, and narrow in the chest, the impossibly long neck and high, strong legs give the altogether opposite impression of a large, streamlined animal—taller, for instance, than an Arabian. They also carried themselves, like larger horses, as if possessed of a high, courageous spirit fully aware of their unique place in this sector of creation. I realized in those moments that if Akhal-Tekes were so valuable and bred for racing, it was unlikely that I could afford, much less obtain, a mount to take off into the desert. Still, how could I be disappointed in the presence of such horses? Their sparkle and energy were unexpected in a land where dry heat turned everything to slow motion. In the brilliant afterimages of that parade of Akhal-Tekes, I knew I had found my way to one of those sacred places on Earth, where humans have, in one small instance, in the case of one species, combined their talents for breeding with natural evolution to achieve something truly miraculous: a work of art that can trot and canter.

The Turkmen were no fools, I thought as we drove away, though I was not so sure about the Bulgarian. He still took me for a rich American— or rather, an American and, therefore, rich. He sat bare-chested and sunburnt in the backseat, talking incessantly about our future together as business partners. It was interesting to be trusted solely on the basis of national origin. The bay stallion was the deal of a lifetime, he maintained, but that wasn't the end of it. Now he had decided that maybe he would bring the horses back to Bulgaria overland by tractor trailer. "The big *mashina*," he called it. Guvanch could get him the big truck. As long as he was driving, he would bring other Turkmen animals— some less good horses for pulling phaetons, some Bactrian camels, and some onagers. The guy was becoming the Noah of nascent Eastern European capitalism.

"What are you going to do with all these animals, Alex?" I asked.

"Okay. I explain you," he said. "September I hold the Akhal-Teke auction in my home. You come to auction as my guest. There we ride, swim. My home, Kavarna, on Black Sea. Is many pretty girl in the resort, every week another. Is the resort place. Before, under Communists, could not buy the land. When go away the Communists, the land cost the five dollars one hectare. Now go up. The hectare now maybe the fifty dollars. I know this business very good. We can buy the small resort, make the park for riding the animals. The people can come to ride the horse, the camel. Many people come from the Europa, from America, to make the holiday. You need only maybe the ten thousand dollars."

"Haven't got it, Alex."

"Maybe then you bring the American investors with you. You know some the rich Americans?"

"Regrettably, no."

I could tell he didn't believe me. I could also see from his darting eyes and desperation that he didn't understand why I was refusing to go in on a deal with him. "I tell you," he tried again, "no one here know what will happen in the six month from now. Will be the communism, the capitalism? Maybe the Iran will take over. I must make the business with horse now. Next year no good. Maybe they sell the horse to the Italia. I don't know."

He was so worried that I began to wonder if there wasn't something fishy going on. From what Guvanch had told me earlier, his was the first Turkmen enterprise trying to deal Akhal-Tekes on its own account, free of Moscow's deadening hand. There was no reining in the Bulgarian, though, so I just let him romp briskly at the mouth. I surmised that the original plan to lease a cargo plane to carry the horses to Bulgaria had run into an insurmountable obstacle: There were no direct flights from Turkmenistan to anywhere but Moscow. Therefore, the new talk of the *mashina*. Yet the overland route, across the desert and over several thousand kilometers of Russian territory to the port of Odessa on the Black Sea, also entailed huge risks. Politically, legally, and economically, the old Soviet empire was in chaos. There must be thousands of corrupt officials and hundreds of mafia gangs between Ashkhabad and Odessa. Was exporting horses even legal? Or had I innocently walked into a horse-smuggling plot?

We dropped off Sasha Reebok, who had an English class to teach downtown, then drove out north of Ashkhabad parallel with the mountains. I didn't know exactly where Sasha and Alex were taking me, but I didn't care. I wanted out of the city, which I was already coming to think of as a place where ex-nomads drove around endlessly in cars looking for their lost way of life. For the rest of the day, I wanted to see no more rubble, no dry fountains, no statues of Lenin, and especially no Turkmen Friendship Society building. The two-lane road was a mayhem of noxious vehicles, military vans, Jeeps, and eighteen-wheelers all trying to overtake the slower ranch vehicles, with the noses and butts of animals sticking out over tailgates. What was worse, the uninspiring face of the Number One Comrade followed you out of town: Every few kilometers there was a placard of Vladimir Ilyich, pointing his determined hand toward the equivocal future (sand dunes), or urging people to remember the GLORY OF THE CENTRAL COMMITTEE OF THE COMMUNIST PARTY (sand dunes). It seemed ludicrous to have Comrade Lenin gazing out like a patriarch and prophet over these wastes, his squat billboard and pole legs stuck deep into the shifting desert. Did the Communists want credit for making the desert or for fighting it? one wondered.

Fifteen minutes from the noisome scratch of Ashkhabad we were in the Turkmen countryside. It was a poor, worn-out, aching landscape, and the people moved slowly through it as if in biblical grief. The land close to the road looked as if it were made of pure salt. Another billboard screamed THE DESERT HAS A FUTURE! But old bearded men in dark fur hats led columns of filthy camels by the side of the road, as they must have done for a thousand years. Little boys on asses herded sheep in the spring desert, suddenly bursting forth not with grasses, but with low, tough, broad-leafed vegetation, wild mustard and rhubarb. Women squatted on their haunches, or picked radishes and potatoes in long truck garden patches. Then neat, pruned orchards of apples, apricots, and pomegranates spread away from the roadsides for we were paralleling the Kara Kum Canal now, a blue pencil line in the hazy distance. The irrigation canals delivering water to each row of trees formed geometric patterns like the complex designs of Bukhara rugs. Here one could see how these ancient carpets kept the memory of settled agriculture alive, which must have been useful when centuries of warfare between nomads and settled agriculturalists, between one nomadic tribe and another, made the transfer of written knowledge from generation to generation an impossibility. It is nonsense to think of nomads only as people constantly on the move. They moved to find pasture, and, most of all, water. Where there was water, they stopped, not giving up their herds, but adding the grain and the vine to their stores until the next drought-stricken tribe attacked. By providing irrigation water from the canal, the

Soviets had created anew the conditions of settled life, but it wasn't the Soviets who had first planted fruit orchards here. If they had engineered a future for the desert, they constructed it on top of the ruins of a past remembered in rugs.

A horse probably spied a human being for the first time during the great intercontinental exchange that took place between Asia and North America in the Ice Age. Such enormous quantities of water were required to form the vast ice glaciers that sea levels were lowered worldwide and, as a result, a land bridge emerged across the Bering Strait, connecting Alaska with Siberia. An animal with the mobile skills and roaming habits of the horse, which the fossil record shows evolved first in the New World, would have found it simple to cross this new neck of earth and radiate into the broad grasslands waiting on the other side. At the same time, the first of the Mohicans was heading in the other direction.

No individual animal or single herd would have made the entire trip across the large landmass of Eurasia that was soon to become the heartland of the horse. Like humans, horses migrated in a variety of directions, at many different times, over various distances, for diverse reasons, over tens of thousands of years. As few as four, or as many as one hundred, distinct species and subspecies of horses—including ponies, tarpans, and onagers—participated in this wholesale migration, the majority of which species eventually died out, hybridized, or were later subsumed into the bloodstocks of domesticated breeds.

The disappearance of wild horses from the American hemisphere and their entry into Asia during the great exchange set the stage for equus's transformation from wild animal to domesticated species. From this time on, the major events in the history of the horse took place in the world's largest area of grassy plains, fertile valleys, semiarid steppe, and true desert. The range of wild horses stretched for five thousand miles, from the northern shores of the Black Sea and black-soiled Ukraine in the north, the Iranian plateau in the south, east across southern Russia, Central Asia, and Mongolia to northern China. This extensive belt subsequently also became the zone within which domestication took place. It was here that humans turned from being hunters of horses to their keepers, assumed nature's job of selection and distribution, and finally lifted themselves onto the backs of horses to become the first riders.

Many scenarios for the domestication of the horse have been suggested. Some think that hunters may have begun capturing young wild horses to raise, and later to breed, for meat. Others, while agreeing that horses were certainly first hunted for food, think that the process of domestication could only have been accomplished in sedentary farming communities possessing the means to pen horses for the long periods of time it would take to accustom them to captivity and milking. Still others point out the important role of reindeer herding in primitive stock raising.

Reindeer were more widely distributed across the northern temperate zone during the Ice Age than they are now, as is shown by the many cave paintings portraying this stolid, hardy, easily tamable creature. Ancient written sources mention certain Mongolian and Scythian tribes who went mounted on "stags." In his account of his travels through the empire of Cathay, Marco Polo also wrote about tribes north of the Great Wall who rode stags. Even at the beginning of the twentieth century, Russian ethnographers still found small pockets of reindeer-herding cultures surviving in Siberia and the Sayan Mountains of Mongolia. The equipment they used for reindeer riding was similar to equestrian tack only more primitive—for example, their bits were fashioned out of bone.

Toward the end of the Ice Age, as the glaciers retreated, changes in climate shifted the moss-eating reindeer's range, and they migrated northward, following the tundra that grows at the edge of the northern forests. According to this theory, the herding knowledge acquired from the domestication of the reindeer was then adapted to horses when the climate became more favorable to equids.

During the late Ice Age, the pressure of cold air over Europe had forced the Atlantic rainstorms to travel east along a southerly track, turning much of western and Central Asia into a continuous belt of lush grasslands that was inviting to wild horses. With the ending of the Ice

Age about 7000 B.C., however, global climate patterns gradually began to change again. For the next eight millennia the Atlantic rains moved along an increasingly northern route, subjecting the entire Mediterranean basin and Eurasia to a long period of gradual desiccation.

What had been swamps surrounding the rivers feeding the Mediterranean, Black, Aral, and Caspian seas now became meadows and fertile valleys, hospitable for the first time to human habitation. With the help of this change of climate, humans came out of their Paleolithic isolation, traveled the rivers, and communicated with their kind. The Near East gave birth to agriculture, in Mesopotamia and along the Nile, in the fifth and fourth millennia B.C. On the Iranian plateau and in Central Asia, which had not yet become salt desert, great rivers descended from the surrounding mountains to provide water for the irrigation of crops. The development of Neolithic agricultural irrigation is still little known, but already by 4000 B.C., for example, there were small communities practicing irrigation farming and husbandry of sheep and goats in the foothills of the Kopet-Dag.

These Neolithic settlements had a complex mixed economy that included agriculture, stock breeding, hunting, and fishing. The Neolithic farmer knew how to harvest the nutritious emmer wheat and six-rowed barley, how to sow the alfalfa and sorghum his animals required for grazing or winter fodder. It was probably during this time, perhaps around 3000 B.C., that humans made the transition from simply keeping horses primarily for milk and meat to mounting them for transport or harnessing them for draught.

As long as there were adequate resources to keep the Neolithic revolution watered, the effects of the drying climate were positive. But between 2000 B.C. and A.D. 700 conditions worsened; the climate got drier faster. Severe droughts came with more regularity and lasted longer. The grasslands turned into dry steppe, and then ultimately into desert. Herds of sheep, cattle, and especially goats became too large for the carrying capacity of the land around settlements. Goats may be tougher than other domestic animals when it comes to surviving on little water, but they are also more destructive since their sharp hooves break up turf, exposing loose soil to wind erosion. The desertification of most of North Africa and the Mediterranean basin seems to have been mainly the work of goats.

Because of the failure to obtain adequate water, protourban communities founded on irrigation began to disintegrate. Those who had mastered horse riding and could drive their domestic herds of sheep and goats in search of pasture adapted to the drying climate by becoming nomadic. In this sense, nomadism was a successful adaptation to an ecological crisis. The nomadic pastoralists were far better able to exploit the desiccated lands of Eurasia than agriculturalists. With the help of their horses to move sheep herds along, guard them from predators, and scout the route ahead, the nomads followed a well-devised system of seasonal migrations, always moving toward a perpetual spring, which assured the most expedient exploitation of sparse, intermittent Central Asian pastures.

By the first millennium B.C., however, the nomads had become so adept at horse riding that land conflicts and warfare became practically inevitable. When the rains were sufficient, the horse-mounted nomads spent their time hunting, drinking fermented mare's milk, and smoking hemp (apparently both women and men continuously smoked pipes). But when droughts came, the nomads prepared for war.

For the next two thousand years, the pattern repeated itself again and again. Some tribe at the center of a nomadic geographic area suffering drought pressed its neighbors for grazing lands or water. The neighbors, dislodged, in turn conflicted with their neighbors, and so on, until at the fringes of the steppes the nomads conflicted with the settled peoples who had managed to hold on to their way of life. Should the tribe moving out from the center have some new technological advance in weaponry or military science, it would sweep across the steppes destroying everything in its path, and continue into Europe in the west, or China in the east. The Indo-Europeans, the first mounted warriors, erupted from the drought-stricken Iranian plateau. Then the Scythians, from what is now southern Russia, dominated the steppes by deploying the first mounted archers. Next, the Sarmatians displaced the Scythians with their use of armored cavalry. Then the Huns displaced the Sarmatians by their invention of the compound bow, which could penetrate armor. It was to protect against the depredations of the nomads that the Chinese built their Great Wall.

This historical calamity only really ended when the lands bordering the steppe zone came under the control of formerly nomadic peoples— the Huns in Hungary, the Bulgars in Bulgaria, the Turks in Turkey— who could defend themselves against the next wave of nomads because they already used nomadic military tactics.

Until the turn of the twentieth century, it was universally supposed that nomadism developed and existed *before* settled agriculture as the primitive prelude to the beginning of "civilization" in the valleys of the Tigris and Euphrates. From the time of Herodotus to the time of Marx and Engels, nomadism was viewed as an intermediate "stage" of human society between the hunting clans of the Paleolithic and the sedentary farming of the Neolithic. Hard and fast distinctions between the "steppe" (nomads) and the "sown" (farmers) are no longer so easily drawn in the light of more complete knowledge of climatic change and its effects on the environment. Human populations in Eurasia were already settled and irrigating crops for thousands of years *before* some of them developed into pastoral herders and horse-mounted warriors. Domestication of the horse made warfare on a grand geographical scale possible. But it was the drying out of the climate that set in motion two millennia of nomadic warfare, leaving Central Asia a retarded, enfeebled region, centuries behind Europe when the Russians invaded there in the late nineteenth century.

About fifty kilometers out of Ashkhabad a pink-washed restaurant with an Islamic crescent sign stood at the side of the road like a Mexican cantina but surrounded by perfumed rose gardens and delicious running fountains. Sasha Skorokhodov suggested we stop; he wanted to take me to lunch in this typical Central Asian establishment. He had never met a foreigner before, much less an American, and he couldn't pass up the chance for offering hospitality.

We went in through beaded curtains. Miracle of miracles! There was a bar, tables and chairs, eastern dervish music from a cassette deck, even indirect lighting. It was a real old-fashioned Silk Road joint where the weary traveler could refresh himself. We sat down, but the Bulgarian went over to another table, where he had recognized acquaintances from his hotel. Probably potential business partners. There was a guy wearing dark glasses at the table with a girl on each arm. He was smoking Marlboros and flashing gold jewelry. A Turkmen playboy?

My attention turned to Sasha, who had in the meantime ordered vodka and *zakuski* [hors d'oeuvres]. He was a descendant of Don Cossacks; his grandfather had been sent to Turkmenistan as a cavalry officer after the Russian victory at Geok Tepe to patrol the border with Persia. Sasha had grown up in a town called Firyuza in the nearby mountains. It had been an Iranian area, populated mostly by Kurds, but the shah had given it to Stalin. Sasha was a man of about fifty, entering middle age trim and fit, graying at the temples, and displaying the forcefulness and correct manners traditionally ascribed to Cossacks. Like Guvanch, he had also been a Komsomol official before leaving political service to join the BEVIKO enterprise.

The waiter came with vodka and *zakuski,* which were oblong chopped-meat patties garnished with parsley, onions, and radishes. Sasha poured a shot for me and one for himself, then asked with a courtly smile if he could offer a toast. He held up his glass and considered for a moment, smacking his lips, then fixed his eyes on me and said, "I never thought I would ever be sitting in a restaurant in Turkmenistan toasting an American across the table. What's more, an American who knows about Akhal-Teke horses. For years we were told Americans are devils. Today I saw with my own eyes that this is not true. I want to welcome you here to us with a little history. You should know that the Turkmen aren't the first breeders and guardians of these horses. The Turkmen have only been here for several hundred years. Long before them, the Parthians fought the forces of Alexander of Macedon from horseback. Alexander's phalanxes marched through this region after his conquest of Persia. The phalanx, which his father Philip had perfected, consisted of a strong line of infantry with horse-drawn chariots on the flanks. But the Parthians had light cavalry on swift horses; they were archers fighting from horseback. They attacked the Greek phalanxes from all sides, day and night. They rode up, shot their arrows at close range, then rode away, sending a second volley as they retreated, shooting over the rumps of their horses. This was known as the 'Parthian shot.' They refused to meet Alexander on his terms; they would not fight a large-scale infantry battle. Instead, they attacked at a gallop, then vanished into the desert. They fought the first guerrilla war. The Greeks had only seen cavalry for the first time in Persia. The Parthians paid tribute to the Persian empire in horses and cavalrymen. Alexander had no means to counter such light cavalry tactics. They couldn't chase the Parthian cavalry, which would return to its encampments for fresh mounts and then attack again. Day and night they fought. These tactics inflicted heavy losses on Alexander's forces, but he retaliated, they say, in two ways. First, he burned the Parthian city of Nisa, which is very nearby; I will take you there another day, if you would like. Second, he incorporated the Parthians into his empire by marrying Roxanna, the daughter of the Parthian satrap. He had conquered the Persian empire in one year, but his troops spent two years trying to subdue the native tribesmen from these hills. By the end of that time, Alexander of Macedon was won over, and from that time the West began to learn to employ cavalry."

Sasha looked down at the table and paused before finishing. "I hope this history tells something more about these horses. In my early life I worked for many years as a sailor on fishing vessels. I was in the national police for more then ten years. I always liked my work. But I *love* working with Akhal-Tekes horses, so I want to share what I know about them with you in the hope that our acquaintance broadens into friendship."

We clinked glasses and drank, "to the bottom," as the Russians say.

About ninety kilometers out of Ashkhabad, the road took a bend through the rocky foothills of the Kopet-Dag. We left the car in a parking area at the foot of a five-thousand-foot escarpment, which veered dizzily up at a 55 degree or 60 degree angle from the flat edge of the desert. The towering hills were mantled in bright spring green, not to be confused with watered lawns or rain-soaked greenswards. Boulders protruded boldly in the afternoon sun. If ever there was a more natural boundary between two cultures than this one between Turkmenistan and Iran, it must be the infinite spaces between other inhabited planets. Yet what appeared topographically as a dramatic divorce on the surface turned out to be a mysterious geologic liaison under the earth.

"You would like to swim?" asked Sasha.

"Very much so. Where?"

"You will see."

The Bulgarian nodded knowingly. We entered the large mouth of a cave. Just outside someone was selling entry tickets, but we went right in. Inside we descended flight after flight of steep concrete steps, down and down into the dank, warm bowels of the Earth. Immense, garish lights glared down from high wooden stanchions. The stairs went on for what seemed like miles. Day and night vaporized. At the bottom, however, several thousand feet below the surface of the Earth, was not hell, as one might have expected, but a scene out of Hieronymus Bosch: fifty Soviets in bathing suits desporting themselves in a huge underground pool of slightly steamy water. This ballroom was lit up like a prison yard by a single stationary searchlight.

I took off my clothes, put a safety pin over the fly of my boxer shorts for decorum's sake, and dove in. The water was too warm to be really refreshing, but it felt cleansing, and thankfully tasted more like minerals than bat guano. It was hard to distinguish the color, but it wasn't clear. I swam to the far end of the pool, where the underground lake ebbed into a narrower but level passage of the cave, and turned around to admire the vastness of the place. The bulbous white figures of the bathers, backlit by the scary yellow light, showed that most of them were probably Russians. They seemed pale and flabby to American eyes.

As my eyes grew accustomed to the lighting, I started looking for bats on the ceiling or gallery, which actually started at water level on all sides of the oblong pool and ran up to about fifty feet at the highest point. All schist. Just then I recognized Guvanch Djumaev's round brown torso and thin, sharp nose. He was bathing near some rocks at the edge with Alexei and some others. Alexei looked uncomfortable as a swimming spelunker, but Guvanch resembled a happy porpoise. I swam over, and we paddled together toward the dark outer edge of the pool. What a strange and unexpected pleasure, I told him, to swim in an underground lake, buried inside a mountain.

"The cave is called in Turkmen '*Kou-Ata*,'" Guvanch said. "It means 'the father of caves.' The sulphur-lime water is thought to have healing powers. If you follow the lake all the way down the passageway, it will come out in Iran, three kilometers away."

Having grown up near the ocean, I am a good swimmer, so I decided to swim to Iran. I wanted to see if there was a barbed-wire fence across the border line. But as I swam out of the searchlight, I discovered I couldn't follow the twists and turns in the dark. What if the border wasn't marked at all? Why would it be, a thousand feet underground? What if I got lost? What would I do if I came out in Iran in my boxer shorts? Having swum out to the point where resolution gave way to prudence, I turned back. Still, returning toward the light I could see the roof of the gallery better. There were bats aplenty on the ledges, all hanging upside down and twittering softly among themselves. Also, I now saw, swallows building nests. Later I learned the cave had once supported the largest bat colony in the USSR, but that must have been before they built the concrete steps and turned the father of caves into the natatorium from hell.

After thirty or forty minutes, everyone got out at the same time. It was only then that I realized they were a group; in fact, Guvanch was their host. I found out from Alex that they were the representatives of trade unions of workers in the new cooperative enterprises all over the Soviet Union, holding their first national organizing session in Ashkhabad. This explained why Guvanch was the only Turkmen among them, though an important one, it would seem, as he had organized the conference.

I waited until all the Soviets had pulled on their clothes and huffed and puffed their way up toward the surface, then I did the same. The trip up the stairs was far worse than the one coming down. I thought my radiator would boil over; they would have to call a tow truck to get me out of there. When I finally emerged from the cave, I found Guvanch's group just across the road. They were beginning to feast around a thirty-foot-long table on a broad concrete patio with a sweeping view of the Kopet-Dag range behind it.

The table was set simply. Bottles of vodka and mineral water were set out, and small plates of raw spring vegetables—green onions, flat-leafed parsley, and the obligatory red radishes. From a booth in the closed restaurant, several men were issuing bottles of beer and glasses of lemonade. Over at the side of the patio, Sasha and several Turkmen were grilling lamb for *shashlik* on two-foot spits over a concrete pit. I had eaten enough meat to put a lion out of business in the past twenty-four hours, but the aroma of the grill revived my appetite. Lamb and mutton, it had become abundantly clear, are the mainstay of Turkmenian cuisine. With Guvanch in charge and Sasha doing the grilling, I had no doubt the results would be delectable.

Sasha smiled, gestured me to have a drink—this is done in Russia by plunking the neck twice with the index finger—and waved me over to the drink booth. I took a bottle of beer and sat down off to the side with Alex, who was drinking lemonade. It wasn't our party, and no one was offended that we didn't join them. For several moments we gazed up at the mountains almost directly overhead. Even Alex was too awed to mention business. The summits of the Kopet-Dag were already turning iron blue with the sun behind them. I was not in the mood for a party. My faltering attempt to speak Russian all day, photographing the Akhal-Tekes in the midday sun, drinking vodka, and the descent to and return from the underground lake had worn me out. I wanted only to be a fly on the wall. There was one especially fat man in a frowsy tie and rumpled jacket, very jovial and toasting his colleagues repeatedly with vodka. The people sitting near him laughed at his jokes and quips. Almost half the group were women. A young man from Kiev, in a white short-sleeved shirt and dark slacks, was giving his business card to a woman colleague sitting next to him. The table would unite for several minutes while someone offered a toast, then break into dozens of smaller groups and conversations. They were having a good time. Guvanch was down at the far end, talking with a woman with badly peroxided hair. When he drank, he rifled the vodka down in one gulp, screwed up his face as if it were turpentine, and immediately grabbed some vegetables and stuffed them into his mouth as a chaser.

But unlike an American cookout, the volume diminished the more people drank. The men from the closed restaurant brought out hot round loaves of unleavened bread; the guests pulled them apart and started to chew. Conversations dwindled. The amiable mood grew melancholy. It was as if they had forgotten themselves for a few moments in the alcohol, companionship, and wondrous natural beauty of that spot. But then the same things that had made them forget suddenly made them all remember and struck them dumb. It was as if everyone there had again remembered that they were part of something senseless, tragic, and absurd: Soviet history. The stolen moment of happiness together was the bittersweet herb that made them remember. It was not a bond that could keep an empire together voluntarily, but it was a bond nonetheless.

Sasha started serving the *shashlik*. The big skewers held huge hunks of grilled mutton that were piled on common plates. There was no silverware; we ate with our hands, pulling apart the grilled meat with our teeth, until the warm fat drizzled down our mouths. The delegates had probably never seen so much meat. Neither had I. The fat man laughed, handed me a piece of bread to use as a napkin, and said, "Do you know the anecdote about the man who had the dream that the whole world became Communist? No? Well, a man had this dream, and in the morning he wakes up with his face ashen and says to his wife, 'I have had the most terrible nightmare.'

"And his wife says, 'What was it about?' "

The whole table was listening. The ones who smiled must have known the anecdote.

"So the man says, 'I dreamed Comrade Brezhnev made a speech to the central committee, and they carried it on television, and he announced to the Soviet people that the revolution had been victorious in every country in the world.'

"His wife asks him, 'So what is so terrible about that? Hasn't the party always told us that the whole world would one day achieve communism?' "

And the man says, "Yes, that's all very well, but where will we buy our bread now?"

I reached Dr. Shikhmurad's *microrayon* not long after dark. It hadn't cooled off much, but at least the ebb of traffic reduced the noise and dust. Inside, I found my host family faint with worry over my absence. True to form, Dr. Shikhmurad had panicked and run off to borrow a car and organize a search party for me. The bewitching Yedesh had gone to work at the birthing hospital, but Mrs. Dr. Shikhmurad and the two boys crowded around me in the entrance hall as if the prodigal son had made an appearance.

"We thought something had happened to you," Mrs. Dr. Shikhmurad said, with her palms to her face. "Something terrible. You poor man! Where were you so long?"

"I was photographing Akhal-Teke horses at the hippodrome."

"You don't say! You must be hungry. Did you eat?"

"Yes," I told her. "All afternoon."

This did nothing to deter Mrs. Dr. Shikhmurad. She was convinced I had narrowly escaped death by starvation, and was not yet out of the woods. She ran to the kitchen to start emergency procedures. Meanwhile, I sat down at the dining-room table. Iceland was playing Finland in ice hockey. The younger son came back quickly with a plate piled high with meat raviolis, then a bowl of *plov* with pieces of chicken. Whatever else you may say about the Turkmen, they're not worried about diets and thin thighs. Mrs. Dr. Shikhmurad herself carried in a pot of green tea and a pitcher of grape compote. When she saw I was only drinking, she stood over me and cooed softly but firmly, "Eat. Eat."

I could no longer remember how many times I'd eaten, but there was no way to ignore such affecting maternal concern. At least, I told myself, it would be the last meal of the day. I moved some rice and chicken around slowly in my mouth, smiling agreeably. Finally, assured my vital signs were okay, Mrs. Dr. Shikhmurad sat down at the head of the table and fanned herself slowly with a dish towel. When Finland scored a go-ahead goal, the family cheered since Finland was an ally of the USSR.

Soon, Dr. Shikhmurad came in. When he saw me, he was visibly shaken.

He grabbed me by the shoulders. "What happened to you? Did you become lost?"

"No," I assured him. "I was looking at some Akhal-Teke horses. Then some friends took me swimming in the underground lake."

"We didn't know where you were."

It was true. I told him not to worry if it happened again.

"We are your hosts," he remonstrated. "It is a shame upon us if we do not know where you are."

"Let him eat," said Mrs. Dr. Shikhmurad. Then to me, "Go ahead, please. Eat, eat."

I assured the family I would try to keep them informed, but it wasn't always possible, and I couldn't very well telephone.

"Our telephone works," insisted Dr. Shikhmurad.

"But none of the others do."

"I will blame myself if something happens to you."

"Look, nothing happened. I'm perfectly fine. What's more, I ate."

"Please," he pleaded, "let us arrange things for you."

"I will try. But remember, please, I am an American. To Americans it is pleasing to go away by themselves. Not unfriendly. Trust me."

He didn't understand. "Now we are very late," he said.

"Late for what?"

"We are supposed to go to a party tonight."

"No!" I stamped my foot. "I am not going to any party tonight. You go without me. I've had a long day. I'm tired. I wish to take a bath and go straight to bed."

I looked at Mrs. Dr. Shikhmurad. It was all right with her; she wasn't invited in any case.

"But the party is in your honor," her husband said meekly.

"That may be, but no one told me about it, and I am very tired. I am going to sleep now. *Do svidaniya,* Dr. Shikhmurad."

On the cab ride over to the party, it turned out that Djura had been on the telephone to Dr. Shikhmurad all afternoon, checking on my whereabouts. Sasha Reebok had been called to the Turkmen Friendship Society for an impromptu meeting. This accounted in part for Dr. Shikhmurad's desperation to get me to the party. The other part, he confided in the cab, was that he wanted to visit the United States. He could possibly go with his wife in a delegation of Ashkhabad doctors that Sally Alice Thompson was trying to invite to Albuquerque. The formal invitations and the makeup of the delegation would be issued and decided by the Turkmen Friendship Society.

In short, he needed brownie points with Djura. It was just the poor guy's luck to get me as his foreign guest. I wasn't likely to win him any points; I was more likely to get him busted.

Dr. Shikhmurad promised that we would stay at the party for only thirty minutes, just long enough to prove I was back on the program for the delegation.

The party was across town at the apartment of the news photographer Gennadi, an Armenian with thick curly black hair and mustache, who reeked of tobacco and sweat. It was just him, his rail-thin Russian wife,

Greg, Sally Alice, Djura, and Djura's son, the big oaf. They had been drinking vodka; the table was littered with colorful exotic dishes and several empty half-liter vodka bottles, the standard Soviet size.

"Maslov!" Djura greeted me squinty eyed and with a grim smirk. "So here you are. We thought you escape on Akhal-Teke horse. We had to send intelligent agents look for you."

"Where did you find any around here?"

He laughed, but he wasn't joking. I said, "Djura, your agents can't move fast enough to keep up with me."

"Oooooommmm." His eyes were hooded in drunkenness. His head swayed slowly from side to side, like an old cobra, menacing but without fangs. "You real Turkmen cowboy, Maslov."

They seated me directly across the table from him. He was drunk, and growing nastier by the minute. He dominated the conversation like a monomaniac. After a few preliminary jibes at my absence without leave, he started issuing terse commands: You will be at the Friendship Society, nine o'clock tomorrow morning. You will give me your passport. You will go on Sunday to a party in the mountains. You will go Saturday here or there.

One hell of a party, I thought.

"Now you drink vodka, Maslov!"

I was in no mood to answer. I put my elbows on the table, centered my iciest stare back on him, and watched him guzzle booze and wolf down food.

"Time to drink vodka, Maslov!" he repeated. "You need drink vodka now!"

Next he called for his son to take a Polaroid picture, made everyone stand in the living room, and tried to place his arm around my shoulder. I rebuffed him and went out to the porch behind the kitchen to smoke one of Gennadi's Marlboros, which Gleason had evidently provided him. Soon Gennadi trotted out after me. He had noticed my camera bag at the musical reception the day before and wanted to talk about photography.

"I use the two-and-a-quarter square format at the newspaper," he said. "But here is very difficult, almost impossible, really, to find the color film."

"Now he wants my passport," I snorted, jabbing the reeking Armenian in the solar plexus with my forefinger. "Not now, Gennadi. Not

94

tomorrow. Not ever! If that jerk wants my passport, he'll have to take it over my dead body."

"Please?"

"How can you even have that snake over to your house? You think he can hear me yet? I can talk louder!"

"You would like to see my camera?"

"Your what?"

Gennadi went back inside and returned a moment later with his big black clunker of a Soviet camera, a Zvezda—Star—which looked like an armored beetle.

"Which is your opinion of this one camera?"

"Crap!" I said in English. I handed it back to him. "Piece of junk. The Japanese were making better stuff than this six minutes after the end of World War Two."

He understood me, and nodded sadly in agreement. "I would like some day to own Hasselblad. You can help me get color film for my camera?"

"No problem. In the States you can buy color film on every street corner. Write down what you want and give it to Gleason with your address. We'll send it to you from the States."

"Please," he stammered, "I would be so grateful."

"Don't mention it."

"You would like to see my pictures?"

Back he whisked into the apartment again, to return with a folded newspaper. "This is my newspaper, *Turkmen Red Star*. Two years ago we celebrated our fiftieth anniversary issue. I did these photographs on front page. I would like to show them you."

He unfolded the paper. It was as large as *The Wall Street Journal*, with a red-ink banner slashing diagonally across the whole front page announcing the *Red Star*'s anniversary. The center photo, bathed in red, was of one of Ashkhabad's statues of Lenin. There was also a picture of a fountain, and one of a big gray monumental concrete building. But no people.

"This one I am most proud of." He pointed to an ordinary cityscape of a high-rise building with the Kopet-Dag behind it.

"Very nice," I told him. "Why are you most proud of this photo?"

Gennadi looked at me. "The mountains, of course. Because of the mountains."

"The mountains? I don't get it, Gennadi."

"Yes, sure. You don't see the mountains? This was the first photograph of this part of Kopet-Dag published in Turkmenistan. My picture."

"Why? What's so unusual about the mountains?"

"It is state security zone. The mountains are border with Iran."

Oh, yes, I thought. It made perfect sense. The mountains form the border, so you can't portray them in a photograph. Although every single citizen of Ashkhabad must see the Kopet-Dag several times each day—in fact, every time they leave the house—the newspapers were required to act as if they didn't exist. It was a simple case of Stalinist denial: natural geography sacrificed to state security. I recalled the story Dr. Shikhmurad had told me about the catastrophic earthquake. Six thousand dead, as Stalin claimed, or a hundred fifty thousand? We shall never know. Volunteer workers from other republics buried the bodies in huge mass graves, landfills dug with earthmovers. But what did Stalin fear about having the world know that Turkmenistan had been struck by a natural disaster? What would be the consequences of admitting that the Kopet-Dag Mountains were more or less where they had been for millions of years? Would the West immediately launch an attack on Turkmenistan? Would the Turkmen revolt? To the Westerner there can be no immediate comprehension of such lunacy, only pity for the victims, alive and dead.

But there was no time to pursue such thoughts: The dreaded Djura had come out to the porch, too.

"Where you were today, Maslov?" he badgered.

"None of your business."

"We look all over Turkmen republic for you."

"Well, you've got your job and I've got mine."

He held out his hand. "Now give passport!"

I blew smoke in his face and glided back inside. The party was breaking up. I nudged Greg Gleason off to his room next to the dining room and blew my cork.

"I don't want to wreck things for the delegation, but I can't take much more of this guy. It seems his whole job is to prevent us from seeing or learning anything here."

"Are you surprised?" Professor Gleason asked. "I've been in this game a long time. They've been at it for thousands of years."

"Do you think he really sent agents out after me?"

"Sure."

"Now he wants my passport."

"He claims he needs it to buy our tickets to Bukhara. We're supposed to fly there on Sunday and come back to Ashkhabad Tuesday."

"Are you giving him yours?"

"No. I'm going to go with him to buy the tickets; otherwise, he'll screw it up. I think Sally Alice gave him her passport. She's having a tough time with Djura, too."

"What do you advise me?"

"Put your cards on the table. Tell Djura that if he doesn't want to help you, you'll leave for Bukhara and *adiós!* Be pleasant but firm. Offer him ten bucks. He'll change his tune."

I did not really want to leave for Bukhara. I had only just met Guvanch Djumaev, whom I was to visit again the next day. Furthermore, I had high hopes of traveling east to Repetek, the desert research station, or south to Badkhyz on the Afghan border, through Professor Sopiev's assistance. As I had hoped, accompanying the Albuquerque delegation was presenting opportunities. Therefore, following Professor Gleason's counsel, I decided to bribe Djura. I required his bureaucratic cooperation if I was to get out to the *zapovedniki* through Sopiev. At the party I had noticed he was extremely fond of his Polaroid camera. However, I reasoned, if Gennadi the sad-eyed photographer couldn't get standard color film in Ashkhabad, where could Djura the Horrible obtain Polaroid film? I happened to have a supply in my camera bag. In a trice, my plan was hatched: I would pay him off with one of the film packs.

So much of a surprising, exalting, fascinating, and galling nature had happened that day that I was positive nothing more could occur. As usual, I was wrong.

Back at Dr. Shikhmurad's place, I said good night, went into my room, threw open the windows to see if some small breeze might enter to cool off the concrete walls, which had been accumulating the heat of the sun all day, and sat down at the table in boxer shorts to write in my journal:

Sometimes a traveler absorbs a country through his senses, sometimes through a revealing moment. There are layers of reality here, which cannot be made intelligible by impressions and intuitions. As water flows deep under the mountains, so the oriental game of intrigue and deceit weaves its patterns beneath local apparent noon. They've been at it here for a thousand years, as Professor Gleason put it. How ironic to be in the open desert, native land of the legendary fleet horses of antiquity, and feel so stalled and cornered—like a chess pawn, surrounded by pieces of superior mobility. The vestiges of Stalinism are everywhere here. I can't say they are only vestiges. Like the beauty of the Akhal Teke rising from the deadness of the desert, Stalinism makes every human gesture seem all the more remarkable and inspiring: The open curiosity of Guvanch Djumaev; the quiet dignity of Professor Sopiev; the heartfelt toast of Sasha Skorokhodov in the roadside restaurant. How did the Akhal Teke survive the great desertification of Central Asia? How did humanity survive the great wasteland of Stalinism?

At this point I stopped writing for a moment and chewed the tip of my black Bic pen. Thinking of Sasha's toast had reminded me of Alexander the Great, and that, in turn, of the well-known story of how young Alexander won his black stallion Bucephalus. But just then I happened to glance out the window as a car rolled up in front of Dr. Shikhmurad's apartment house. It was a heavy black sedan, which stopped directly in front of my windows, only about fifteen feet across the dirt frontyard. The motor died. The headlights blinked out; the red running lights remained on. The windows were rolled up. The tiny yellow glimmer of a cigarette lighter flickered momentarily: I could make out two men inside. I peered out at them, and they returned the courtesy. Although I could see their forms, I could not make out their faces. I could, however, confidently conclude I was now under surveillance. It had not been difficult to achieve spyhood. In retrospect, it occurred to me that every single thing I had done since arriving in Ashkhabad was suspicious. My cameras, the telephone calls, the unexplained absences from the delegation's program, especially my request for a street map! The truth is that every traveler is a spy of sorts.

Damn them, I thought. I was not going to fall for this clumsy and toothless cloak-and-dagger intimidation, glasnost or no glasnost. I would press on regardless. And so determined, I tossed my Bic down, drew the curtains across the window, and fell asleep thinking of Alexander and his horse.

Alexander won Bucephalus when he was only twelve years old, but an extraordinarily precocious lad, not only because his tutor was Aristotle, but also because his mother, Olympias, and father, King Philip, hated each other's guts, which makes any intelligent child an early actor in his own life's drama, and a sharp observer of behavior and character. Philonicus the Thessalian breeder brought Bucephalus to Philip, offering to sell him for thirteen talents, a high price, about three times the normal price of a hunter in those times, or the equivalent of approximately ten thousand dollars today. The king of Macedonia was himself a great horseman, having been the first to introduce into the conduct of Greek warfare a significant role for his cavalry of aristocrats known as the Companions. Under Philip, the Macedonians used the infantry phalanx not as the attacking line, like the Athenians and Spartans, but to pin down the enemy so that the cavalry could swing in from the flanks like pinball flippers, cutting down the enemy. Aside from waging war, the favorite occupation of Macedonian aristocrats was hunting birds, foxes, bears, lions, and hares from horseback. Alexander hunted from horseback every day, not only for pleasure but also because, as Xenophon wrote, every hunter was by definition a "good man." The Greeks lacked saddles and stirrups, calling for superior strength in the legs and extraordinary upper-body suppleness to wield their spears. Riding was still a relatively new art among the Greeks. The very fact that Xenophon had thought to write down, two generations before Alexander, his knowledge of horsemanship points to the novelty of equestrian training.

Since no one would pay so much for an old horse, it has always been inferred that Bucephalus was young, though whether he was the exact same age as Alexander, as some sources claim, is not known. The Greeks knew nothing about aging horses by their teeth. When the king and his men took the black stallion onto the Macedonian plains to try him out, they found Bucephalus so violent and untractable that he reared up every time someone tried to mount him, and went wild at the sound of the voices of Philip's attendants. (According to another tradition, Bucephalus was worse than merely unmanageable and was a man-eater; when

Alexander first comes upon him, there are human arms and legs lying around him in his cage!)

How a stallion attained the age of twelve without being broken by a rider, or why a wild twelve-year-old was worth so much money, are questions Xenophon would have addressed had he been there. Since the historians who came after—Plutarch, Arrian, Quintus Curtius Rufus, et cetera—seem to have known little or nothing about horses, these questions will never be answered. In any case, King Philip ordered Bucephalus to be taken away as useless. As the horse was being led from the field, young Alexander, who had been watching nearby, complained what a shame it was to lose so excellent a horse because no one was skilled and brave enough to manage him. Perhaps he was even then thinking of Xenophon's advice to lead a frightened colt by the hand through crowds or unfamiliar noises, teaching him "not by irritating but by soothing him, that there is nothing to fear." Xenophon said that this alone was enough to tell the amateur about horse breaking.

At first, Philip ignored the boy as any adult would ignore a twelve-year-old kibbitzing from the bleachers. When Alexander continued to voice his objections, which were a form of taunting, the king turned coldly to his son and said, "Do you reproach those who are older than yourself, as if you knew more, and were better able to manage him than they?"

What a question! Of course Alexander thought he could do better. Did a young man ever think he could do worse than old men? The question was itself a generational challenge that Alexander could not let go unanswered. "I could manage this horse," he replied coolly, "better than others do."

If not, what then? His father bid him wager the price of his rashness.

Alexander bet the horse's entire price, much to the amusement of the Macedonian elders. This must have reinforced Alexander's determination, especially since all accounts of his boyhood hint strongly that he was regularly a victim of homophobic gossip—now said to be dominated by his mother, now derided as overly sensitive, with a fey, high-pitched voice, always in the company of his "best friend," Hephæstion, and contemptuously flirted with by the "normally" bisexual adults.

With the wager set, Alexander immediately ran to Bucephalus, took hold of his bridle, and turned him directly toward the sun. The others had simply tried to force the black stallion into submission. Alexander had observed carefully and noticed something no one else had: The others had been trying to move the horse away from the sun, making Bucephalus shy from his own shadow. Now Alexander firmly led Bucephalus forward by the bridle, with gentle caresses in the places horses like to be touched and soothing sounds. He settled down the skittish stallion, proving Xenophon's central point: "The one great precept and practice in using a horse is this—never deal with him when you are in a fit of passion. . . . Compulsion and blows inspire only the more fear."

Then when the moment was right, Alexander let his garment fall and mounted the horse in one leap—though it shouldn't be forgotten that all unarmored Greeks mounted the same way, grasping the halter with the left hand and the reins and mane with the right, so as not to wrench the horse's mouth, then using either a spear as a pole vault or raising the body on the stiffened right arm, springing into place by swinging the right calf cleanly over to the off-side. It's not known how big a horse Bucephalus was, but if he was from Thessaly, the former division of ancient Greece where the best Greek horses came from, he was probably of medium height, at most fifteen hands. It is well known that Alexander was a martinet when it came to physical training, competing in the Olympics and rigorously developing the strength and agility he would later demonstrate a hundred times in battle.

The laughter stopped as men held their breaths, fearful that the prince would be thrown and killed. Alexander brilliantly kept the reins loose at first and did not try to ride Bucephalus on the bit—or, as they say, "get in his mouth." Nor did he strike him or spur him on. He merely sat still and maintained a firm seat, letting the horse become accustomed to the strange feel of human weight on his back. Little by little he curbed the horse with his hands, until he had him gathered and ready, as Plutarch says, "free from all rebelliousness, and only impatient for the course." Only then did Alexander, with a commanding voice and laying his leg on him, ask Bucephalus to canter. The wild black stallion obliged like a twenty-year-old gelding at a dude ranch. Straight off they loped, Alexander turning Bucephalus at the end of the course and returning in open triumph for what he had accomplished, to the astonished applause and acclamation of everyone gathered there.

King Philip was so moved by his son's performance that he wept tears of joy and kissed Alexander as he came down from his horse, telling him to look beyond their homeland for a kingdom worthy of himself, "for Macedonia is too little for thee." The conventional moral, of course, has to do with how a boy becomes a man with heroic courage and blazing intelligence, but from the equestrian point of view, one may also conclude that each horse is a mystery unlocked by its own special key. The excellent rider grasps both the bridle and the key, too, never forcing an animal with such a highly developed nervous system to work against its own nature. The trick was to reduce Bucephalus's fear by winning his confidence. By turning him into the sun, Alexander showed that he understood Bucephalus perfectly. Loose reins and soft hands let him succeed where hardness, punishment, and trying to dominate the wild-spirited stallion had failed. If riding is a metaphor for the way humans relate to the world, it was King Philip who learned a lesson, for he now considered his son, as Plutarch relates, "to be of a temper easy to be led to his duty by reason, but by no means to be compelled." From then on, the father "endeavoured to persuade rather than to command or force [Alexander] to any thing." He treated his son as Alexander had treated the horse. It was just after this incident that Philip sent for Aristotle, the most learned and celebrated philosopher of his time, to be Alexander's tutor.

In the morning, woozy from lack of sleep, I drank green tea alone in the darkened dining room of the apartment while Mrs. Dr. Shikhmurad fixed my breakfast in the kitchen. Dr. Shikhmurad was already out trying to scrounge a car so he could be my chauffeur again. I now assumed that the reason for his keeping close tabs was pressure from the Turkmen Friendship Society. The boys were off at school. Gulya had come home after a thirty-six-hour shift at the birthing hospital, and was asleep in the back bedroom.

As I sipped my tea, I considered my situation. I did not want to further involve the Shikhmurads, who were, after all, only implicated by happenstance in my little crimes and misdemeanors. I decided not to mention the black sedan that had sat parked outside their house all night. Why upset them? In the morning light it seemed more amusing than frightening. I couldn't completely discount the possibility that I might be taken into custody and packed off to Bukhara with the delegation, or even booted from the country. Since the black sedan was now gone, the more likely probability was that it had been a bluff. Just in case my time in Turkmenistan was to be cut short, I decided to ignore my appointment with Djura and pay another call on Guvanch Djumaev instead.

Mrs. Dr. Shikhmurad spread before me a breakfast fit for a khan. There were chicken legs with *plov*, hardboiled eggs, radishes, and green herbs as well as a glass of hot milk—camel's milk, judging from its sour taste. When I complimented her on the excellent chicken, she went back to the kitchen and proudly returned with the plastic packaging. There, written in Russian, were the words "Chicken . . . product of Jackson, Mississippi, U.S.A."

"Where do you receive this food?" I asked her, using the correct Russian verb *poluchit'*, which can mean either to receive or to obtain.

"From the party," said Mrs. Dr. Shikhmurad, without shilly-shallying around the issue. "We're good party members. We joined when we were students. We always believed in The Party. Now," she shrugged, "you can buy everything at the bazaar, but it's too expensive. This isn't *perestroika;* it is speculation and profiteering. For us it was better in the time of Brezhnev."

She said this in the same way Americans might say, "I like Ike," or "I'm a Kennedy Democrat."

"Eat, eat," she added. "Dr. Shikhmurad will be here soon."

She padded back into her kitchen and began scraping plates and washing dishes as I ate. I was getting to like Mrs. Dr. Shikhmurad. It wasn't only the home cooking, though being a breakfast person myself, this helped. More than that, it was her candor and lack of pretension. Admitting that she got special groceries because of her Communist affiliations came perfectly naturally to her. It wasn't something to hide out of shame. A full-time doctor and homemaker, she never seemed hurried, and radiated a kind of fat person's stability, which has become all too rare in my country, with its absorption in weight and dieting.

Dr. Shikhmurad came in smiling. He winked at me and gave me the thumbs-up sign: He had bagged another clunker. He was surprised to find me leisurely enjoying my breakfast when I was supposed to be meeting Djura at the Turkmen Friendship Society at 9 A.M., but he sat down himself and drank a cup of green tea.

Then he asked, "Shall I call the Friendship Society and tell them you'll be late?"

"Thanks, but not necessary," I told him. "I've changed my appointment with him till tomorrow."

"You did this? How?"

"That's my business."

"As your host, I should be informed."

"I'm sorry, but you weren't here."

"I went to find a car."

"Yes, I know. I'm sorry you went to the trouble. If you prefer, you can go to work instead. They must need you at the medical institute more than I need you to drive me around."

"It is an honor. Would it be different in your country?"

"Yes, very different. In America, foreign guests can obtain maps and use telephone books. You wouldn't need the head of a medical institute to take whole days off from work to drive you around."

"But I am your host!" He grew excited.

"Americans are an independent people. We like to go our own way and make our own friends." I didn't expect him to understand.

"Where are you going today?"

"To meet the same friends as yesterday, the people who helped me to photograph the Akhal-Tekes. The office is on University Street, one hundred meters from the tourist hotel. I can get there by taxi."

"No, no!" he cried frantically, as though someone had just told him one of his children had been run over in the road.

"Listen to me, Dr. Shikhmurad," I said, raising my voice. "Maybe I should leave your house and take a room at a hotel. Maybe it would be better for both of us." I tried to think of the Russian word for "guilt," but couldn't remember it. Nor could I command enough Russian to tell him that I understood, and would even sympathize with him, if he wanted to see the last of me. How could I explain that American journalists don't make very good "foreign guests"?

Dr. Shikhmurad pushed his glasses slowly up his nose like a day laborer pushing a barrow of bricks up an inclined plane, and said, "You will allow me, please, to drive you to University Street."

"With pleasure," I said in perfect Russian. It was the least I could do to placate him.

We braced the crosstown traffic in a well-dented blue Moskvich, and reached the BEVIKO offices a little before a big meeting between the principals in Alex's horse deal. Alex and Sasha Skorokhodov were already there awaiting the arrival of the Akhal-Teke breeder, Geldi Kiarizov. In the meantime, Guvanch was clearing the *divan* of other matters, taking time to chat briefly with Dr. Shikhmurad, who drank a cup of green tea and obtained Guvanch's assurance that I would be safely returned to his apartment by evening.

After Shikhmurad left, Guvanch asked me, in between phone calls, correspondence, and signing contracts, about my first impressions of the Turkmen horses. I used a lot of superlatives, and he smiled and nodded to show me he was listening. Alex sat looking dour. After a while, he sidled up to me and whispered, "I must make fast the business. There are not so many *loshadi* [horses] here. Now everyone come to buy."

"Like who?"

"Italians. British. I learn that British princess was here the one month ago to buy the Akhal-Teke horse. Guvanch talk with Italians here. I must buy now fast."

At length, Geldi Kiarizov strode in with a fat briefcase under his arm. He was a tall, sunburned Turkmen with proud black eyes and an angular desert face. Although he was dressed in a dark-blue pinstriped suit without tie, his rangy movements and enormous rough hands marked him as a man who worked out of doors. To look at Geldi, you would never think he was of the same tribe as the slighter Mongolian-visaged Guvanch. A few hundred years ago his ancestors probably weren't.

In matters of horse business, however, Guvanch and Geldi were blood brothers; he had ridden with Guvanch on the famous 1988 marathon. Once more Guvanch took down from his office cabinet the scrap book of the *probeg*. There they were, entering Moscow side by side in the saddle, each dressed in traditional scarlet silk robes and huge white sheepskin hats. A year later, Geldi led another *probeg* six hundred kilometers across the Kara Kum Desert to demonstrate the surpassing endurance of the Akhal-Teke. For the past ten years, Geldi—the name means "welcome" in Turkmen—had been establishing the first, and so far only, private Akhal-Teke stud farm in Turkmenistan. Now Geldi and Guvanch were working together on the Bulgarian deal, the first in which Turkmen would deal directly with foreign buyers without Moscow middlemen. I would come to know Geldi Kiarizov as the single most knowledgeable person where Akhal-Tekes were concerned. When he spoke, he made a speech, and when he made a speech, it was about only one subject. The Akhal-Teke was his religion.

Geldi had brought with him a Russian equestrian magazine, and now he showed me the back cover illustration. It was a poor-quality reproduction of a sensual eighteenth-century portrait by Franz Kruger of an Englishwoman in black skirt and habit riding sidesaddle. Geldi said, "I can positively say that horse is Akhal-Teke. Positively."

"How?" I asked.

"Number one," he said, "is the color, golden yellow. It is the unique color of the Akhal-Teke horse. No other breed possesses that bright golden coat. Number two, look at the pasterns. The pasterns on this horse are very thin between the heavy foreleg and hoof. Fine, delicate pasterns are another Akhal-Teke characteristic. It has been so with Turkmen horses since the earliest times. In the Pazyryk Hills in southern Siberia, archaeologists have discovered skeletons of domesticated horses twenty-five hundred years old. They were preserved in burial mounds in ice, like the Siberian mammoths. I have studied these skeletons at the Institute for the Study of the Horse in Moscow. These skeletons have the same anatomy as the Akhal-Teke. Third, you see the head? Look at the way the horse holds its head up high."

Geldi stretched his own neck up and ran his hand along it to demonstrate the upright posture. "This is the desert horse, the ancient Turkmen horse. In the desert the horse needs to hold its head up high to see far and smell danger a long way off. Turkmen have always admired the long neck more than any other characteristic. In the desert our grandfathers would dig a hole in the sand, and put the colt's food down in it to make the colt stretch its neck to eat. You can always recognize the Akhal-Teke by its long neck and high head. The Arabian horse holds its head down."

I asked how it could come to pass that Turkmen horses from Central Asia would be ridden by eighteenth-century British ladies.

"We know the answer to this question." Geldi held up one finger as he spoke. "The British! The British army was here, in Afghanistan, in

Persia, in Turkey, in India. The British took our horses back to England. There is no doubt of it. I have researched this. Between two hundred and three hundred Akhal-Teke mares and fifty stallions disappeared from Turkmenistan when the British military was fighting in Asia Minor and Central Asia. They took Turkmen horses to make the English Thoroughbred."

I expected him to add, "And we want them back!" But baring his teeth slightly, Geldi said instead, "You are occupied today?"

"Not at all."

"You will be my guest, then. You would like to see my herd?"

"Yes, very much."

"*Ochen khorosho.* Very good. We will go to my farm to see my horses, and then you will come home to dine with me."

The business meeting about Alex's deal began, dominated by Geldi. He said, "I estimate that there are fifteen hundred pureblood Akhal-Tekes in total. Between six hundred and seven hundred are at the Ashkhabad Komsomol Konnozavod. Altogether there are maybe five hundred pureblood Akhal-Teke horses in the entire rest of the Soviet Union. According to the stud book, there are a hundred thirty-four registered stallions; seven hundred forty-two mares. Last year they gave birth to two hundred sixteen foals."

The Bulgarian sprang to his feet. "I buy all of them!"

Geldi paused, gave Alex a slightly contemptuous look, and replied, "Only yearlings are for sale. We must build up our breeding stock here or the Akhal-Teke breed will cease to exist. We should not let certain horses go out of Turkmenistan. The Soviets have all but destroyed this breed. Only fifteen hundred purebloods survive. And from how many, in the herds of ancient times? Think of this: In the days of the Parthians, the Medeans, and the Bactrians, the tribes contributed twenty thousand sabers to the Persian Empire. Each saber had a stallion, so there were twenty thousand stallions. In order to keep a force of twenty thousand horse supplied with remounts, you must have eighty thousand to one hundred thousand mares. That is how many horses were kept here in the days of the Persian Empire. The Parthians first planted the *luzerna* [alfalfa] grass in the grazing areas, in the river valleys, and along the edge of the mountains."

"The only place to buy *luzerna* now is from Russia," Guvanch added.

"Until the time of Gorbachev," Geldi continued, as much to me as to Alex, "there was no supervision of breeding Akhal-Tekes. No thought went into it. The apparatchiki in Moscow set production quotas in the five-year plan. They took the best colts to Moscow, like Mele Kush, which Khrushchev gave to the queen of England. Some of our best horses ended up in the private stables of generals and party leaders. The ones left here they sent to the meat-processing plant!"

After the meeting broke up without anyone agreeing to sell Alex anything, Geldi whisked me off to his stud a few miles out of town. There was plenty of land to be had there, but none good enough to pasture horses year-round. Despite the fact that it was only April, all that sprouted in the sandy soil was a poor sedge, already turning brittle. In another few weeks, the shoots would break off and blow away, driven on the desert wind, and there would be nothing to graze on at all. Outside Geldi's makeshift stallion pens, a large pile of fresh green lucerne grass had been delivered.

Probably no Turkmen can pass up the chance to show off his horses. Geldi led his stud's foundation stallion, Kaplan (meaning Tiger), out for me to admire. He was a tall, high-spirited nineteen-year-old with an exquisite black coat, a champion racer in his day. It was almost as painful to look at the light reflected off his glossy coat as it would have been to look directly into the sun. I had already found out the day before at the hippodrome stables that there was a special word for this electric black coat, *voronoy,* denoting the Akhal-Teke's lustre and distinct from *chyorny,* the common Russian word for black. The Russian Cossacks who occupied then-Turkestan in the late nineteenth century and started breeding Akhal-Tekes are said to have been responsible for introducing other colors by interbreeding with their Orlovs and Dons—in Geldi's view diluting the Akhal-Teke's blood. But it seems doubtful that the Turkmen could have gone hundreds or even thousands of years in as crisscrossed a place as Central Asia without interbreeding. The great Tamerlane, for example, was supposed to have sent five thousand Arab mares to Merv to reward the Turkmen for their service in his campaigns of conquest. As it happened, Geldi's horse was the sire of a slightly smaller *voronoy* stallion I had fallen in love at first sight with at the hippodrome. They were both from the most outstanding Akhal-Teke blood line, tracing back more than one hundred years to a famous black stud called Boynou (Long Neck), already alive at the time the Russians first came into the area. The stallion took a few mouthfuls of the lucerne grass, then rolled in the sand, enjoying his bath, while his owner and I looked on.

Geldi's herd of mares and foals was turned out a mile away in an unfenced area of scrub trees near a man-made watering hole that caught the overflow of the Kara Kum Canal. There, twenty-five or thirty mares with half a dozen foals were tended by two barefoot boys with sticks. Most of the herd was parked in groves of saxaul, a tiny-leafed desert tree that provided hardly any shade. The midday sun made the horses drowsy and slow. It was too hot to spend more than forty-five minutes taking photographs; then we drove back to Geldi's home in town.

His family lived in a quiet, leafy neighborhood of whitewashed dwellings on Karl Marx Street, across from which a new mosque was being built. The Muslim religion had not been suppressed in Turkmenistan under the Soviets, only put to sleep. The Gorbachev era was reawakening the Muslim genie. They were building an unpretentious octagonal concrete house of worship, with a shiny tin dome and a tin crescent rising above it like a weathervane.

It was a neighborhood of walls. Through an iron gate we entered a sunny courtyard with a gushing water pipe serving as fountain, a grape arbor, a dog on a chain. Even the light was different from that in the Soviet-style apartment houses. There you went from the wincing brightness of the street to the uniform darkness of the Shikhmurads' apartment. Here it was the opposite: From the shady street, you came into the light and airy courtyard with its gurgling oasis, its vineyard, its pet—the desert domesticated. There was room for silence here, perhaps even space for a life of the mind. Under the vines Geldi's brother, Kakysh, sat wearing cotton pajama bottoms and strumming a guitar. He was a younger, heavier-set, coarser, sluggish version of Geldi, who had apparently inherited most of the family's brains, looks, and fire in the belly. The brother rose and stretched, slapping his meaty sides before crushing my hand. If Geldi needed an enforcer, however, Kakysh fit the bill.

Together they showed me into the coolness of the dilapidated old house, which rose several stories. I removed my shoes and entered a narrow kitchen. The room had the profound quality of darkness of Rembrandt's backgrounds: the old mother and aunt sitting at a table in sackcloth and black veils, the steam of the dinner pot vanishing into the ceiling, the beaded curtain in the doorway, through which could be seen only another doorway. When I was introduced to the mother, I went up to shake hands, but she did nothing and only fixed her gaze on me. She was a striking, powerful woman with a look of medieval intelligence in a face that receded deep into the inner recesses of her black shawl. If eyes are a window on the soul, this woman was in big trouble. She was in no hurry to finish her assessment and continued to look at me from the cruel black orbs of her eleventh-century eyes. She had centuries to spare. I stood there feeling as though she were about to ask her son to slice off my ear to see if I was edible, but Geldi interrupted her with a light kiss on the forehead and told her to serve dinner. From this I gathered who was nominally in charge here.

The house was strictly divided into separate quarters for men and women. In the men's dining room, Geldi offered me pillows and showed me how to dine Turkmen-style, reclining on the carpet with the pillows propped under my arm. The brother sat on a sofa on the side of the room, continuing to alternately slap his fat deposits and strum his instrument. The walls were decorated with posters and photographs of Akhal-Tekes; one showed a unit of Turkmen cavalry armed with swords before the Bolshevik Revolution. Their horses wore jeweled necklaces. Another was a portrait of the famous Boynou circa 1900. He was a handsome, muscular stallion, though rather stocky and short at the withers.

Geldi took out his fine collection of old black-and-white photographs of Akhal-Teke stallions. I went through them one by one, reveling in the exotic sounds of the names rolling off Geldi's tongue: Fakir Pevan, Saparhan, Jeren, Alcona, Galishiklee, Absent, Mele Kush, Mele Chep, Teleke, Kirsakar, Ckak, Yel, Caparjen, Paracat, Kara Kir, Kara Kush, Hadji Bai, Dovlet Ashan, Dor Bairam, Perzent, Kizyl, Polotli.

Geldi could speak with authority and had an opinion about every horse—its blood lines, its characteristics, its racing record, and its place in the history of the breed. It was the beginning of one of Geldi's long stump speeches lasting two hours through dinner, while the mother and aunt served green tea along with candied figs and meat soup with thick unleavened bread. But at the end of that time in Geldi's company, I had learned a good deal about the background in front of which these Turkmen beauties paraded before my eyes.

Until the time of the Russian victory at Geok Tepe, the Turkmen raised their horses according to tribal traditions. The Tekes, who populated several oases and irrigated zones bordering pure sand desert, were never able to graze herds on their skimpy pasturage. From a very early time, natural conditions determined a unique form of horse breeding. Each Turkmen kept one horse—or at most, if he was rich, an additional mare and foal. By profession the Turkmen was a mercenary for the local despots. Agriculture was secondary. In times of peace between the khans, the Turkmen continued as warriors on their own account, organizing raids against other settlements. Their one recreation was, of course, horseracing. In this Spartan military existence, they were indissolubly bound to their horses, which were always hand fed, watered daily, covered in felt blankets against the summer sun and winter cold, and kept tethered winter and summer on a long rope outside the Turkmen's *kibitka*. Whether fighting or racing, the Turkmen showered all his affection and attention on his horse, trained it himself according to precise customs, and prepared his sons to continue the equestrian tradition. From the time they were two years old, the children were made to grip boulders between their legs to develop their riding muscles. The great expanse of Kara Kum Desert lying to the north and east ensured that no infiltration of northern horse types could occur from Mongolia and Kazakhstan. No Turkmen would adulterate the tribal stock with genes of the smaller, shaggier, phlegmatic Mongolian horses, which were considered inferior in every way. Hadn't the great Genghis Khan himself conquered the khanates of Khiva, Bukhara, and Merv to obtain tribute in what the Chinese called the horses of heaven?

With the Russian takeover of Turkestan in the 1880s, however, the mercenary armies were disbanded and the first attempts were made to settle the nomads. The economic and social base for horse breeding began to disappear. Rather than lose their most cherished traditions, many Turkmen moved their tents and horses farther into the desert, or to eastern Iran, Turkey, and Afghanistan, where more than one million Turkmen reside to this day.

Thereafter, the Akhal-Teke in Turkmenistan was bred mainly for racing, but not the piddling seven-furlong jobs we know in the States. Local races, usually held at weddings, were commonly twenty-five, fifty, or one hundred kilometers. In the meanwhile, the Russians sent Cossacks to occupy Turkmenistan, and they, with their own cavalry and equestrian traditions, began to Russify horse breeding. In 1897, the Russian governor, Alexei Kuropatkin, founded the Zakapiisky breeding stables near Ashkhabad in the village of Keshi. A Kuban Cossack named Mazan was put in charge, and his selections became the foundation of the modern Akhal-Teke breed. Mazan's most outstanding stud was the same Boynou on Geldi's wall. The Zakapiisky stud acquired him as a fifteen-year-old, after a mediocre racing career, but he proved so prepotent that 80 percent of today's pureblood Akhal-Tekes descend from him. The Zakapiisky stables were therefore critical in saving the breed during the transition to Russian suzerainty, though tribal breeding and training continued at some level in the desert oases.

With the Bolshevik Revolution, horse breeding went through another convulsion in Central Asia. In 1918, even before the Reds had defeated the last khan of Khiva and consolidated their hold on Turkmenistan, Lenin promulgated a decree, "On Pedigree Livestock Raising." During the 1920s, all Akhal-Tekes were registered with the state, private ownership of horses was banned, and scientific breeding was introduced among the herd of seventy pureblood horses at the Zakapiisky stables taken over by the Komsomol and renamed, unimaginatively, Konnozavod #59 (stud farm #59).

It was now that things began to go radically wrong for the golden horses of Turkmenistan. The new Soviet managers, perhaps better versed in genetics than the average Turkmen nomad, had very different ideas about what was desirable in a pureblood Akhal-Teke. Where the tall sons of Turkmen warriors wanted a tall, lean horse with a fighting spirit, the Red Army wanted a four-legged tank. The most famous Soviet cavalry officer, Marshal Semyon Budyonny, who became minister of war under Stalin, hated the Akhal-Teke and installed a breeding program to produce Red Army cavalry remounts by introducing Donski (Russian Thoroughbred) blood into Akhal-Teke lines. By the mid-1930s, the pureblood Akhal-Teke was in danger of extinction, and it was this that motivated the Turkmen to conduct the famous 1935 *probeg* to Moscow in an effort to bring the stamina and courage of their breed to the attention of the Soviet authorities, and to stop the adulteration of the Akhal-Teke bloodstock. What a bold and noble impression these Turkmen riders must have made parading through the gray streets of Stalin's Moscow on their luminous fiery horses, riders regaled in their silk robes and karakul hats—the only ethnic group in the Soviet Union, Turkmen say, to keep its national costume intact through the years of Soviet efforts to break down nationalities and mold the bland "Soviet Man." And what a daring adventure for the Turkmen, crossing the bandit-ridden desert, the vast wastes of the steppes, in eighty-eight days to a Moscow reception they could hardly have imagined beforehand. It must have been even money they would either be welcomed by their smiling "Little Father" or simply arrested, taken to the edge of town, and liquidated.

In the event, neither occurred. When they reached Moscow in the late summer of 1935, it was in the midst of the brief thaw that came between the forced collectivizations of the early thirties and the purge trials and mass executions, which began in 1936. The totalitarian campaign to "proletarianize" every aspect of life in the USSR was taking a respite. The arts and sciences bloomed in the fashion of sick apartment plants put out in healthy sunlight. Music, movies, and sports flourished. The Turkmen participated in a challenge race circling the entire capital, and won the first sixteen places with their Akhal-Tekes. The favorable impression they made in 1935 can be gauged by the fact that ten years later Marshal Georgi Zhukov, the hero of Stalingrad, led the victory parade ending World War II on a pureblood white Akhal-Teke.

But the Turkmen horses were now firmly tied to the gyrations of the Soviet state. When the screws came down in the postwar period—the grimmest period of Stalin's rule in many respects, for it is always more difficult to reestablish total control of a country than to maintain it from the start—Akhal-Teke horses were among the many victims. These were the years, continuing after Stalin's death through the Khrushchev period, when the state was hell-bent on fostering mechanized agriculture. The tractor driver was elevated to the status of national hero, and all vestiges of national "backwardness" were to be eliminated. Khrushchev returned from his trip to the United States so impressed by the cornfields of the Midwest that he ordered a crash program to make the Soviet Union the world's biggest corn producer. New laws were issued ordering the liquidation of all draft horses. As the antihorse campaign gathered momentum, the economic five-year plans decreed by the Communist party began to treat horses as nothing more than a food product. The state farms in Turkmenistan were issued quotas for horseflesh, and Stud Farm #59 was slated for closure.

The Turkmen could not stand idly by, watching the animals that defined them as a people butchered and ground up for sausage, mainly to feed the influx of Russians and other nationalities who repopulated Ashkhabad after the 1948 earthquake. Escape over the borders of Iran and Afghanistan was too dangerous then; getting caught in the frontier zone smuggling "state property" was a capital crime. So the old nomads turned inward, to the harsh, pitiless land of their ancestors, the Kara Kum Desert. They released their horses to run free and survive on their own in the desert, back to the place where the wild Central Asian bloodstock had flourished long before the Turkmen existed. The breed had evolved under harsh desert conditions and was biologically equipped to survive the hot, dry climate, especially in the absence of many extinct animal predators. To Russians and Westerners the desert is a place of evil and death. The Turkmen bears no such fear, Geldi told me. He quoted the Turkmen poet Atakopek Mergen, who said, "I would never change the beauty of the desert for the beauty of a woman."

No one will ever know how many Turkmen sneaked away into the desert night to leave their horses a bale of pilfered fodder, knowing they would be cruelly dealt with if caught. In their souls burned the pride of their ancestors. Like the biblical prophets keeping the holy laws of the Hebrews alive in desert exile, the Akhal-Teke kept what was sacred to the Turkmen alive during those dark days.

Then in the early 1950s an event of the first importance took place. One of the USSR's most famous horse breeders, Vladimir Petrovich Shambarant, came to Turkmenistan from the Tersk region of Daghestan in the Caucasus, where he had been working. Shambarant knew the story of the desert horses, and came for the sole purpose of mounting an expedition into the Kara Kum Desert to save the Akhal-Teke as a breed under domestication. He captured several feral horses and took them back to the horse-breeding zone of Daghestan in Russia, carefully establishing a breeding program which produced Galishiklee, the prepotent Akhal-Teke stallion of that time. Geldi's black foundation stallion was a grandson of Galishiklee. Shambarant's salvage operation once more snatched the Akhal-Teke from the jaws of extinction. It was only through Shambarant's timely intervention that the possible progenitor of the modern racehorse was saved.

We reclined on the rugs till late in the afternoon, talking about horses and drinking green tea. Then Geldi drove me back to Dr. Shikhmurad's *microrayon,* and left me with an invitation to attend his brother's wedding the following Saturday. Perhaps some Turkmen prenuptial ritual was the reason the brother had been walking around in pajama bottoms in the middle of the day.

I reached home at nearly five, but Dr. Shikhmurad didn't arrive till past seven. We were running late for the Friendship concert to be held downtown at the Ashkhabad municipal auditorium. The Turkmen Symphony Orchestra was going to play a program of music composed by an Albuquerque composer in honor of the respected American delegation from Ashkhabad's sister city in the United States of America, and I had promised Sally Alice to photograph the event for the Albuquerque newspapers. Still, it was hard to drag myself away. There was an ice hockey game on the tube. The Soviet Union and Canada! Mrs. Dr. Shikhmurad and Gulya had joined the boys in the dining room, broaching Muslim custom in the interests of rooting for the Soviet Union. Whenever Gulya spoke, I wondered how she achieved that voice without smoking a pack and a half of Lucky Strikes and drinking a fifth of Jack Daniel's every day.

Dr. Shikhmurad had commandeered the car of his cousin Mahmut, the traffic cop, for the drive downtown, minus Mahmut, who was on duty. We arrived when the introductions were just about over. Greg and Sally Alice were onstage, winning a round of applause, and she had another bouquet of long-stemmed flowers in her arms. They invited me onstage, but I ducked down in front and started clicking pictures, looking around the half-filled hall. Gennadi, the news photographer, came down from his seat and knelt beside me, stinking of tobacco and sadness. Sasha Reebok was sitting with his wife in the front row.

"What was this place?" I whispered to Gennadi.

"The old caravansary for the Silk Road," he said.

Before I could take in the architecture, the Russian maestro in black tie and tails took the podium and the concert began. The music was unbearably tedious, atonal and without melody, so I could see why the

Turkmen might have liked it. The general theme seemed to me to convey the modern inability to finish a thought, though it could equally have represented a night washing pots and pans in the kitchen of a truck stop. It went on for so long that I was glad to have a professional pretext for keeping my hands occupied.

When the concert was over, the applause was less thunderous than that which had greeted Sally Alice and Greg, and the audience fled like kids let out on the last day of school. Before I had packed away my camera gear, the building was deserted, the front doors locked. Only now, in the darkness and silence, could I hear the ghost voices of caravan travelers, and see the yellow flames of their campfires lick the walls. I found my way in the dark to a side door and slipped out into a courtyard with a fountain. People were standing around in the dark smoking cigarettes. It had just occurred to me that our little delegation's arrival had probably flooded the Ashkhabad market with Marlboros when suddenly the bottom seemed to drop out of the gravity holding the Earth together, and from the desert a demonic wind attacked without mercy. One could feel the gaping jaws, the hot breath, the sharpened teeth. Some kind of white tree tassels swept across the courtyard like a blinding snowstorm. The water from the fountain, only a few seconds ago splashing tamely, stood up like wraiths in twisting, misshapen sheets. In another few seconds, a sandstorm was pelting the old caravansary, the tiny grains stinging our faces and hands. People lowered their heads, covered their faces with handkerchiefs, and fought to remain standing. In an instant the tranquil courtyard was blotted out in a terrifying whiteout. The wind whipped, whistled, and howled. A billion billion grains of sand rattled against the old protector of the caravans. You couldn't see where you were, you couldn't see where to go, and even if you could have, you couldn't get there. It was like a dry hurricane; if the wind and sand kept up like that for even half an hour, anyone caught out in the storm would perish. But in what must have been less than a minute, it was gone, like an ominous warning from the desert to caravan travelers dead hundreds of years.

When I found Dr. Shikhmurad, parked waiting for me on the street side of the municipal theater, I found out that Turkmen call such a wind "Urugan"—an amazing cognate of the Amerindian name for the evil spirit of such storms, Hurakan, which Spanish expeditions from Columbus on learned in the Caribbean; it was later incorporated into English as "hurricane."

I suppose there are different kinds of night dreamers. Some are prolific dreamers, but others may have Gothic productions in wide-screen Technicolor. There are nightmare sufferers, of course, and those who spring from bed in the morning convinced that they never dream at all. My own dreams tend to be in the form of a pithy paradigm (I am brought in to pitch in the ninth inning with runners on base), an aphorism ("All my best thoughts come when I am on horseback"—Montaigne), or an outright message (buy two hundred shares of Kaiser Steel).

I slept badly that night, perhaps because the surveillance car was parked outside the apartment house again, but awoke with the lucid memory of just such a slumberous one-liner: "You can never cross the same river twice."

This was no cryptic psychic puzzle. I could remember exactly where I'd heard the saying before. It was Ilona Ujheli, my riding guru, explaining, as I walked a horse named Copper Flash around the ring, why riding is an art, not a science. Just as the water in a river is constantly changing and never the same, the equestrian has to sense and react to a particular horse in a particular place on a particular day to get anything accomplished.

"Ride the horse you're on today," Ilona often tells her students, who are almost all girls and young women. It is not enough to simply know how to make the horse trot, stop, back up, or canter. Hand and leg aids have been instituted over a long period of history, not to mechanically command, but to communicate with the animal. Ilona likes to compare the process to driving a car. Of course a car is a machine. Turn on the key, and 999 times out of 1,000 the engine will start. (Ilona has never been to Ashkhabad.) Turn the steering wheel, and normally the car will turn in that direction; apply the brakes, and the car will come to a stop. But horses are not machines, and sometimes they are not even as reasonable as humans. Nature has made them into changeable creatures with highly evolved central nervous systems. You can train to ride physically as much as you like, but until this training is put into the service of an understanding of the moods and emotions of the animal, you will end up fighting the horse to get where you want to go.

I filed my dream away for the moment and, hoping this might be the day I actually rode an Akhal-Teke instead of just dreaming about it, rose to prepare for my showdown with Comrade Djura.

I got no farther than the bathroom, however, when I suddenly became aware of a serious solid-waste crisis in the Shikhmurad household. Ever since my arrival they had been depositing the organic garbage in a wastebasket in the bathroom; with putrefying four-day-old meat bones giving birth to a swarm of flies, you came out of the bathroom dirtier than you went in. What made it worse was that since wastewater simply plunged to the floor whenever the bathroom sink was used, the floor had developed a coating of slippery wet stinking slop. At first I found it appalling that a houseful of medical professionals knew so little about basic sanitation, but actually the problem had probably originated with me. Before the advent of the "foreign guest," they wouldn't have created so much solid waste in a solid month. Still, as so often in Soviet life, I felt I had just penetrated a front curtain and was staring suddenly at the real thing in all its horrors.

It was clearly time for some Boy Scout ingenuity, so I taped the sink pipes back together with the duct tape I always carry, and mopped up the floor with hot soapy water and an old towel. When Mrs. Dr. Shikhmurad saw it, you would have thought an angel had descended, or possibly a licensed engineer; a miracle had taken place!

I had washed and shaved and put on a clean shirt and necktie when Sasha Reebok telephoned around 9:30 A.M.

"What is the problem, Jon?" he barked down the line. He had been leaned on, there was no further doubt of it. For all I knew, he was one of the cats smoking in the black sedan. I said to him, "Is this line safe to speak on?"

"Yes."

"Good," I said. "The problem is that your friend Djura was drunk when I made an appointment to see him. He forgot the appointment. He's drunk every time I try to talk with him. He's so drunk he forgets what I tell him, if he listens in the first place. He has broken his promises to me. That is the only problem. But don't worry, Sasha. I'm on my way to see him now."

That should get Djura where it hurts, I thought, in case anyone was listening in.

"How will you arrive there?" Sasha asked. It disheartened me that he was so subjugated by the tin-pot pasha, but there was no harm in answering his question. After all, unlike Richard Nixon, I had nothing to hide.

"Dr. Shikhmurad went to borrow a car. If he doesn't come back in fifteen minutes, I'll take a taxi. If Djura doesn't show, I'll leave. I have other things to do today. Everything will be fine."

"Shall I meet you at the Turkmen Friendship Society?"

"Thanks, but it's not necessary. I want to speak to Djura alone."

"What will you tell Djura?"

"I will introduce the concept of incentives and bonuses to him. If you want, you can meet me at the agricultural institute at noon. Maybe we'll go see Professor Sopiev together," I said, and rang off.

Dr. Shikhmurad arrived a few minutes later with a teacher from the medical institute and the teacher's car, yet another output of the Mosk-vich line. Of course it wouldn't start.

"Sit down, please," my host said to me, opening the back door like a lackey.

Having won over Mrs. Dr. Shikhmurad with my plumbing skills, I was determined to conquer Dr. Shikhmurad with my auto mechanics. "Dr. Shikhmurad," I said, "open the hood, please. In America we know all about cars. I will get it started without fail."

Sure enough, when I lifted the hood I saw loose and detached spark-plug wires. Inside of a schoolboy's minute we got the car running and headed at a Soviet streak for the Turkmen Friendship Society. It felt great to be an American in the morning.

Upstairs, Djura was alone in his office, looking over papers.

"I need to speak with you, Djura," I said.

"I am very busy man," he replied. "Must go to airport."

"If you don't have time to see me, I'll go. You won't see me again, though, I promise. *Do svidaniya.*"

"Sit down, please," he said, relenting.

"I need to speak with you alone."

"Yes." He ordered Dr. Shikhmurad to leave with an uncouth wave. When the doctor had closed the door behind him, I waited until Djura got the idea that he had to pay attention. When he finally looked at me, I began, "Do you ride horses, Djura?"

"No, I don't ride. But I know Turkmen horses very, very well."

"Do you? Look, Djura, what I have to say to you is simple. If you get on a horse and pull the reins tight, that horse is going to buck and throw you. But if you keep a light rein, that horse is going to work with you and you'll get along fine. Now think of me as a horse. An American horse that you've never ridden before. Do you understand?"

The official face remained impassive. Without a pause, he said, "Yes. Understand."

"I need loose reins, Djura. I want you to back off. Get it?"

"Yes." He looked out the window. "Understand."

"And I have brought something for you that I think may help you to remember." With that, I brought out a twin pack of Polaroid film from my camera bag.

Djura continued to show no expression or emotion whatsoever. He simply picked up the film pack and set it closer to him on his desk. Then he took out a piece of fresh paper. His tone of voice unchanged, he said, "What you want, Maslov?"

"Number one, I want to obtain a permit to go to the nature reserves in the deserts and mountains—meaning the ones in the border zones. I need a letter from the Turkmen Friendship Society to the head of the

120

agricultural institute saying I have permission to go there. Number two, I want to extend my visa . . . am I going too fast for you?"

Djura was writing it all down, but had stopped to finger his film pack with evident pleasure. "Polaroid very good camera," he said. "I have one."

"I know."

"Can only buy film U.S. and Germany. Very hard for me."

"Is that so?"

He got up from his desk, went over to the metal office cabinet, and took out an old pack of Polaroid film to compare with his new one. Suddenly it occurred to me that he might have an old model Polaroid that used a different film pack; if so, the deal would go down the tubes. To keep his mind occupied and away from such a discovery, I blurted, "It's a twin pack. Hey, twice as many pictures, Djura. Very, very good. Twin pack—very expensive in the West."

"Yes," he agreed. "Cost twenty dollar. Maybe nineteen."

"It cost $21.99, to be exact, as you can see from the pricetag still on the box. And, Djura, one more thing: There's more where that came from. But I'll only give you more film if you do exactly as I tell you. I want to be left alone. I want to go where I want to go and do what I need to do. I want to meet the folks I need to meet and make my own friends. All I'm doing here in Turkmenistan is studying Akhal-Teke horses. I don't want you interfering, and I don't want to be followed. I want you to back off. I want loose reins. Is that clear?"

Djura picked up the film from his desk and admired the blue package. I had never seen greed gleam so brightly in a man's eyes. I don't think he was paying attention to anything I'd said. But he got on the telephone, and inside of ten minutes everything was arranged for my trip to the nature reserves. "Dr. Balakaev, head of agriculture institute, will await you at ten A.M. tomorrow."

"Good. Do I need a special visa to go to the border zones?"

"Not necessary."

"What about extending my official visa?"

"How long you wish to stay?"

"I want to stay six weeks at a minimum. The agriculture institute will be my host, not the Turkmen Friendship Society. I repeat, *not* the Turkmen Friendship Society."

"Take more time," he said smoothly. "How long you go to desert, Maslov?"

"I don't know—four or five days, maybe more."

"I will work on it while you away in desert. Give passport, please. Need passport to extend visa."

I provided him with photocopies of my passport's identification pages, which he accepted without complaint. Then I rose to leave and shook his hands.

"Nice riding with you today, Djura," I said.

"Mmmmmm," he hissed like a sleepy cobra. "You, too, Turkmen cowboy."

I trotted out to the front gates with my head so high—like an Akhal-Teke—that Dr. Shikhmurad, who must have realized by his dismissal that I was bribing Djura, smiled.

"All satisfactory?" he asked.

"All satisfactory!"

"And where to now?"

"The agricultural institute, please."

It was only two minutes away on the other side of the city park and botanical garden. I would have enjoyed the walk, but instead I sat in the backseat and in victory smoked one of the Marlboros I had brought to give away as trade gifts. Dr. Shikhmurad, too, was in a lighter mood, pointing out to me what are called in Russian "*dostoprimechatelnosti*"—tourist sights, to be exact.

"And that," he said proudly, "is our Lenin!"

It was one of those full-stature Lenins, pointing toward the road to the future (out of town). There were some wedding couples and other appreciative native tribesmen dressed in silk robes and fur hats standing in rapt awe below him. "Who did you say it was?"

"Lenin," said Dr. Shikhmurad.

"Who is he?"

"Vladimir Ilyich Lenin, the father of our revolution."

"Revolution? What revolution? Did you all have a revolution here?"

"Lenin! The Bolshevik Revolution of 1917!" He pounded the back of the seat. "You don't know about it in the West?"

"I'm afraid not."

Sasha Reebok was waiting for me at the entrance of the Kalinin Agricultural Institute. While Dr. Shikhmurad dropped me off and went to check in at the medical institute, I suggested that we take a stroll in the botanical gardens and perhaps find something cold to drink.

"Cold?" Reebok said. "But there is nowhere to buy a cold drink in Ashkhabad, Jon."

"Let's go for a stroll in the gardens, then," I suggested. "I've been in Ashkhabad for days, and I haven't stretched my legs yet. You know us cowboys feel out of place in the big city."

Sasha gave me a look that said all right, but it won't work.

He was right. It didn't work. We hadn't got past the gates of the botanical gardens when we were stopped by the guards. They were four old coots in blue uniforms and hats, sitting around a table in the dirty little courtyard outside their guard booth, drinking vodka and smoking those Russian cigarettes that are like a Texas carburetor—an air tube made out of cardboard with a hit of strong black tobacco at the front end. They were all potted. None of them wore any medals, but you could bet your life they were veterans. One of them got up, staggered over to us, and told Sasha we needed permission from the director of the botanical gardens to enter.

"I will get in touch with the director immediately, yes, Jon?" Sasha volunteered. "Right now. I will call him on the telephone, okay?"

"Let's go away on foot," I said in plain Russian.

As we were leaving, I handed out Marlboros to the old men. As soon as they saw the colors of the package, they groveled. Oh, come in, come in, they said, walk anywhere you like, stay as long as you want, pull up any plants you don't care for. I took a photograph of them lined up behind their little party table, some straightening their hats, others raising their vodka glasses, while one, too drunk to realize he was having his picture taken, struck a match on the table to light his smoke.

As we were leaving by the gates we had just entered, what should appear out of nowhere, waiting at the curb to pick us up, but a big black sedan, just like the one that had sat outside Dr. Shikhmurad's place at night.

"Is this the part where I get arrested?" I tried not to sneer.

But it wasn't—yet. Sasha Reebok, of course, was utterly at a loss to explain the car. The humiliation of exposure was only rivaled by the humiliation of the stumblebum tactics and cartoon amateurism. To see the old war veterans grovel for Marlboros was sickening enough, but now I had to watch Sasha, the unhappy KGB man, self-destruct.

"But . . . but . . . but . . ." he stammered. His face grew intensely tense, almost orange, like an October moon. His tongue protruded a little, and you could see the pressure behind the eyeballs. I realized suddenly I had never seen anyone actually die of apoplexy, and wouldn't know the symptoms. Would it be like a horse with colic? Or like a raccoon with rabies? Most important, should I try to dispel the attack with the Heimlich maneuver?

But then Sasha disgorged. "It is a car from the Turkmen Friendship Society. It will take us anywhere you wish to go, Jon!"

"*Prikrasno!*" I said in plain Russian. "Wonderful! Let's go drink a beer!"

We got in. The driver was not a Turkmen, but an Uzbek with a drooping mustache and eyes like a killer with nothing on his mind. Sasha said, "You mean you want to stand in line in the hot sun with a big jar, as people do here? It would be very uninteresting, I think. These people have nothing to say."

"Nothing to say? Why, because they're drunks? Look, if I had to live under this system, I'd try to stay as drunk as I could, too. Well, how about a Coke, then?"

At this, Sasha brightened somewhat. He was finally inspired with an idea he was sure would please me. We happened to be just down the block from Ashkhabad's diplomatic hotel. It was bound to have some sort of indoor facility with cold drinks.

"Let's go on foot," I said, but no, that made too much sense. It was far more unreasonable to drive half a block, so that's what we did. We hadn't gone half of the two hundred yards between the botanical gardens and the diplomatic hotel, however, when a turtle appeared in the street directly in front of us.

"Stop!" I ordered the Uzbek. As we had hardly got going, the car was still going slow enough to stop before crunching the poor turtle under the tires. Coming from New Jersey, where thousands of terrapins are killed by vacationing drivers every year while crossing roads to get to their nesting grounds at the Jersey shore, I am acutely sentimental about turtles. I got out, picked him up, and came back to the car to take a look at him. He was dark yellow and light black, just a little bigger than a box turtle, but with bigger, stronger claws. The Uzbek was terrified.

"Turtles are inoffensive creatures," I told him. "See?" And I shoved it up to his face. For a moment, I thought he would run away and leave me to drive the car. Obligingly, the quick movement made the reptile hiss.

I pulled the turtle back. "Oh, see that? You scared him! You tried to kill him by mindlessly running him over, and now he's scared. Shame on you for scaring a poor dumb creature. What did a turtle ever do to you, Mr. State Security Uzbeki chauffeur?"

I released the turtle on the other side of the road, in the botanical gardens, the direction in which it was moving at the moment of capture. More concerned with having its feeding cycle interrupted than with my having saved its life, the turtle thrust out its head and legs with a good-bye hiss, and crawled off into the foliage.

I walked across the street, heading for the hotel. Idiotically, the black sedan swung around to drop off my personal agent, and we went in. To the guards at the lobby door I tipped my cowboy hat and said, "Howdy."

They were dazed, and let us pass.

There was a public room off the lobby that seemed to combine the functions of a hotel bar and restaurant with an employee cafeteria as well as a souvenir and news shop. Several well-dressed men were sitting at tables eating *pirozhki*—greasy cupcake-size pies filled with meat, potatoes, or cabbage, usually cabbage. It's Soviet street food, but can do double duty as a paperweight.

There was no Coke, but there was Pepsi. It was written out in Russian on the bottles, all lined up along the back counter as if they could dance like Michael Jackson after everyone went to bed at night. At first they didn't want to sell us any, but they changed their tune when a dollar bill was flashed.

As soon as we sat down at one of the tables, I could see that Sasha Reebok was drowning in luxury.

"*Shishkas,*" he said.

"*Shishkas?*"

"Yes. It means pinecones. We use this word for what you call the big shot. This is the hotel for the diplomats, the *shishkas*."

The waitress came with our drinks. There was no ice, of course; nor did they have the sense to keep the sodas in the fridge. What came out of the warm bottles, however, wasn't warm Pepsi in any case. It was a flat, syrupy, dark brown substance like the ones our grandparents were forced to swallow. Sasha took the opportunity to load up on boxed candy, which he happened to notice was for sale. It was for his wife, he said. When he had paid the waitress for the candy, he began, "Jon, I would like to ask you a question."

"Proceed."

He couldn't spit it out. His face contorted in difficulty. He was sweating. Finally he said, "Jon, I would like to emigrate."

"Oh?"

"I would like to go to America. Life has become too very hard for us here. I have my wife and three-year-old son. Tell me, if a person like me went to the United States, could I expect to receive employment and earn money?"

I told him that if he had papers, he would probably be allowed to work—a very different thing from "receiving" a job.

"And how much money would I earn?"

"That depends on the job."

"I have been thinking," he said. "Perhaps I could go to Los Angeles and be a businessman."

"What kind of business did you have in mind?"

"Do you think I could start a business making drawings and blueprints when a building was going to be built?"

"We have a lot of people who do that. They're called architects and engineers."

"You do? But let's just say I started such a business. How much would I earn?"

"I wouldn't know," I told him. There must be millions like this man, thinking about jumping the Soviet ship on its way down. I wondered how many of them would do a little KGB work on the side to curry favor with the authorities or receive a few extra groceries. I saw now the double game Sasha Reebok was playing. He was working for Djura on the one hand, reporting my activities, and perhaps even the conversations he was privy to. Mightn't this lead to foreign travel to America on the delegation from the Turkmen Friendship Society? If he could only reach America, he was already dreaming he could become rich as a construction draftsman. No wonder he was trying to learn colloquial English. On the other hand, he was trying to keep my friendship, if not my trust, perhaps thinking I could arrange his exit or be of some use in his emigration scheme.

"Stay here," I told him. "The last thing we need in the United States is another Russian building contractor who doesn't know his ass from the wallboard. New York City is full of them."

"But Jon," Sasha persisted, "here we operate only from fear. I do not want to live only acting from fear."

"Who would?"

"Would I, for example, from some business venture earn enough to buy meat? Not every day, you understand, but maybe four or five times a week?"

"Sure. In America you can eat meat four or five times a *day* if you like. But forget it; in order to immigrate to the United States now you need to have immediate family members already living there. I checked the rules before I came here."

"But I have!" he objected. "I have aunt in Los Angeles."

"Aunt's no good. They mean parents or children or brothers or sisters," I told him harshly, wary of continuing a conversation that might be construed as urging a Soviet citizen to defect, and determined not to get any more tangled up in the nets of Djura, the greedy fisherman of Turkmenistan.

Upstairs at the agriculture institute, Professor Sopiev was locked in a meeting; again I had come without an appointment. We were invited to wait in the office of his junior colleague, Andrei Kozlov. Kozlov was a young Russian ornithologist who spoke no English, tall and straight like a white birch tree, with a trim black mustache, dark hair that stood up in formation, and slightly dreamy blue eyes. One might expect to see him in a peasant's tunic and baggy trousers, chasing butterflies uselessly up and down a meadow on a summer afternoon in a novel by Turgenev.

"I have never met an American before," Kozlov said apologetically, "so, of course, I have many questions. Is it pleasing to you to answer a few questions?"

"Of nothing!" I told him in plain Russian, folding my arms across my chest the way I'd seen Tolstoy do in a photograph.

Kozlov had heard that in the United States ordinary people—not just scientists, academicians, and professionals—go out in the fields and forests to watch birds in their natural surroundings. Was it true? he wanted to know.

I told him there were thousands of such local bird-watching clubs in the National Audubon Society, and that millions of Americans take an interest in bird life, both at home and on vacation. I told him that millions of Americans go camping every summer in national and state parks and nature reserves for no other reason than to see some birds, catch some fish, and dangle their feet in cold running water. He was amazed to hear that each year thousands of amateur American birders take part in the Audubon Society's nationwide Christmas census, counting birds in their own local districts and pooling the results to get an overall idea of bird populations, species distribution, and so forth.

"I would so much like to see this," Kozlov said, not gloomily, but as an agnostic might say, "Someday I would truly like to see an angel." He thought there were probably fewer than a thousand bird watchers in the entire Soviet Union. The majority of them were, of course, professional ornithologists. Hunters? Oh, lots of them, he said, but though you could ride around with any kind of hunting firearm you wanted, the Soviet system didn't encourage people to go wandering around the countryside, with or without binoculars. Even when he, a university-trained scientist with a Ph.D., wanted to go into the field for professional research purposes, he had to obtain permits. "But sometimes I ignore the state and just drive off into the mountains for a few days to observe birds. I have a car now," he confided. "It's easier."

The problem of the borders with Iran and Afghanistan, however, made it nearly impossible to study birds, Kozlov went on. "We have no information whatsoever about the birds on the other side of the borders, and we can't go there ourselves to see if our birds are also over there. We cannot study birds' range or migration. It's most frustrating, like living in a flat world; at the edge, all knowledge disappears."

Kozlov spoke so ingenuously that I was delighted to listen. There was one bird, for instance, the scaled woodpecker, he said, which inhabited the forest that once fringed the desert rivers of Turkmenistan—the Amu Darya, the Tedzhen, the Murgab. Since World War II, the Amu Darya had been severely depleted to provide water for the Kara Kum Canal while the remaining woods around the Tedzhen had been cut down for agriculture. As a result, no one had seen a scaled woodpecker since 1960.

Kozlov had undertaken a special search as a doctoral candidate at the agriculture institute, making field trips along the rivers to look for the bird, but hadn't discovered a single one. "In the spring, at this very time of year," he said, "the male woodpeckers would hammer on the poplar trees to call to the mate. But time after time I heard nothing; the poplars have all been logged out. Is the scaled woodpecker extinct? Here in Turkmenistan, yes, but does it perhaps survive in Afghanistan or even India? We have no idea. If we had international scientific communications, we could perhaps arrange to repopulate our riparian habitats with woodpeckers from Afghanistan."

I told Kozlov that this didn't seem at all realistic to me. After all, woodpeckers that couldn't withstand ordinary agrarian development would not be likely to have survived the war going on in Afghanistan for seven years between the Soviets and mujahideen. And what good would it do to raise captive woodpeckers if there were no poplar trees for them to peck when they were released? "Anyway, what you need aren't only international scientific contacts, but also some kind of voluntary citizens' group that will support saving local species from extinction."

"But we do have such an organization here," said Kozlov. "It's the Turkmen Society for the Conservation of Nature."

"No relation to the Turkmen Friendship Society, I hope?"

"No. This is our national conservation organization. It was founded in the 1950s."

On closer questioning, it turned out that only scientists and academics belonged to the organization. Students at institutes of higher learning could probably have learned about it and joined, but common citizens wouldn't have even known the Turkmen Society for the Conservation of Nature existed, much less its purposes. Most of the comrades didn't know what conservation was. At the ag institute, Sopiev and Kozlov were the only two members.

We were talking in a sunny little office, no more than a cloak closet, which Kozlov shared with another junior academician, just off the second-floor corridor. Just as Kozlov was pouring green tea, Professor Sopiev came in with a bouncing step and shook hands as warmly as before.

"I am delighted to meet you again, my friend. You know that you have a meeting tomorrow morning with our institute chairman?"

"Yes."

"This will be an important meeting in relation to your hopes to travel in Turkmenistan."

"Yes?"

"Another American will also be there."

"Another American?" I was caught by surprise. "Who could that be?"

"I don't know." He shrugged. "Another American is here in Ashkhabad."

"Professor Gleason, I bet," I said. "We're part of the same American delegation. Good man, Professor Gleason. Will you be at the meeting, Professor?"

"Yes, of course. I will tell our chairman that we would like to invite you to visit Repetek *zapovednik* and tour the desert institute. It so happens that a colleague of mine from the Academy of Sciences will be going there by train on Saturday morning to meet a delegation of American zoologists. He is a herpetologist, Professor Shammakov. You may travel with him."

"*Otlichno!*" I told him. "Excellent!"

"Unfortunately," he said, "at the moment Professor Shammakov is in the hospital."

"The hospital? Is it serious?"

"I think so. He has high blood pressure. But he is in the special hospital for party big shots," his eyes twinkled, "so maybe he will live."

Professor Sopiev sat down with us in Kozlov's office for a cup of tea. We all popped hard candies into our mouths, then sucked the hot tea through the sweets, Turkmen fashion. I thought, now if only the candy was a piece of ice. But most Turkmen have never enjoyed a cold soda or beer. They are a civilization that has survived without convenience stores. They continue to drink their tea the old-fashioned way, hot from the teakettle. It was getting hot in the room, too; the window glass was burning orange. Well, I thought, at least they will never be short of solar energy. What with Kozlov and his officemate, me, Sasha Reebok, and now Professor Sopiev, the little office was packed so full of brains that it was beginning to steam. The light green paint made it seem more like a home for the mentally insane.

Professor Sopiev said, "So what have you learned here in Turkmenistan since our first conversation?"

I had Sasha translate. "Professor Sopiev," I said, "I want to thank you for the trouble you have already gone to in order to assist me. But mostly I am grateful for your advice. You were absolutely right about how slowly things move around here. I am learning to go slower each day in Turkmenistan, just as you advised me. I have also learned here that one can get into trouble with the KGB by trying to go too fast."

"The KGB?" Sopiev lifted his widow's peak, and something went through his mind, perhaps the way an old dance tune from the war would go through the head of a veteran. He said, "Please believe me, whatever you encounter here now is nothing compared to what it was before perestroika. I remember well how it was for foreign visitors under Stalinism, and that was only three or four years ago here. Whenever we hosted a foreign scientist then, the KGB would always assign a man to follow him around. We never knew if it was because they were afraid of what we might say to the foreign scientist or what he might say to us. Perhaps both. But everywhere we took the foreign guest, the KGB man was sure to be with us. Usually he would be introduced as a colleague or a driver. At that time all the KGB men were heavyset thugs in black leather coats and dark glasses. We couldn't possibly introduce some of them as our scientific colleagues to the foreign scientist; they would have laughed too hard.

"Let me tell you an anecdote. I was going to take an Austrian biologist into the field for a week, camping out in the mountains, and the intelligence officer came to meet with me beforehand—you know, to get our story straight. I asked him if he knew anything about science. He said no. 'How shall we explain your presence, then?' I asked him. He said he didn't know, but he was coming anyway. So I looked him over. He was a short guy with a giant belly sticking over his pants, like a big fat bear.

" 'Can you cook?' I asked him.

" 'Oh, yes, Professor,' he says to me.

" 'Fine.' So we brought him along as the cook and camp manager when we took the foreign scientist into the field. For five days the KGB man set up the tent, prepared the meals, washed the dishes, and so forth.

And all the time in his black leather coat and dark glasses. I can tell you, it was delicious!"

Professor Sopiev finished with a not-so-subtle arched eyebrow directed toward Sasha Reebok, sitting in his black leather jacket and dark glasses, who looked away stonily and lit a Marlboro.

The next morning, for the usual reasons, I was an hour late for the meeting with the director of the agricultural institute. When I got there, the meeting was already under way in the first-floor conference room. Professor Sopiev met me outside and rushed me in. As we went through the outer offices, he said to me, "Our director is Comrade Professor Balakaev."

"A musical instrument, is he?"

"No, that is *balalaikev*. Comrade Balakaev is not only director of the agricultural institute, but also a deputy in the Turkmenian parliament and a member of the politburo of the Turkmenian Communist party."

"Oh, I see. I'll be very nice to him."

As I had suspected, Professor Gleason was already there, sitting alone at a conference table for thirty. He gave me a friendly handshake, and then I was presented to Comrade Director Balakaev at the head of the table. He hugged me, but I suppose it was all right because he didn't know me. As soon as I sat down Balakaev rose and started to talk. He was a short, fat-faced, white-haired man in a gray suit, somewhere between fifty and eighty—the quintessential party boss, so bland and one-dimensional that I wondered as I looked at him if he was a cartoon. There was something about him that reminded you of the melting clocks in certain paintings by Salvador Dalí.

Comrade Director Balakaev grabbed the lapels of his suit jacket and thrust his arms open wide. It was a gesture I had never seen before— maybe some stunt Al Jolson would have done in vaudeville, down on his bended knee. Where did these guys go for acting lessons? "Welcome, foreign guests to the Socialist Republic of Turkmenia!" said Comrade Director Balakaev. "Let us speak one with the other! Let us speak frankly and openly! Let us become friends! We will work to develop our cordial relations between our peoples. Why not? Why should we not be friends? I say to you, come, my American friends: Let us drink green tea together!"

That was the end of Comrade Director Balakaev's remarks. They had lasted about a minute, and he had said nothing in as many words as possible. He ended up leaning over the conference table, with his hands still holding open his suit coat as if offering his breast to any assassin with a dagger handy. He had a smile on his mouth as fake as that on the mouth of a goatsucker bird, which opens its mouth up like a trap door, but only to let more insects in. Sweet biscuits and chocolate candies with gooey centers were brought in to go with the green tea. I couldn't think of anything phony enough to say to the Comrade Director, so I ate some of the chocolates and let Gleason handle the formalities. I didn't follow what he said to Balakaev, but only sat there in astonishment at his fluency in Russian. I think he was peddling a computer as part of a cooperation deal of some kind. After the two of them had vented a lot of friendly hot air at each other, Balakaev presented us with "little gifts," as they are called in Russian. They were blue plastic briefcases with snap tops. The initials of the Agricultural Institute in the Name of Kalinin was embossed on them in fake gold paint. Balakaev handed them to us one at a time and shook hands warmly.

"Thank you," I told him. "I will cherish this plastic briefcase always."

Satisfied, the Comrade Director went back to the head of the table and sat down.

I said, "I also would like to present my friends at the Kalinin Agricultural Institute with little gifts."

I rummaged in my camera bag and brought out the three mini hand calculators that I had bought for a few dollars in the drugstore back home. Since my little gifts trumped the institute's little gifts, Balakaev was displeased. He handed one calculator to Professor Sopiev, who in turn handed it on to Andrei Kozlov, who had happened to enter the meeting room just then. Leaving the others on the table, the Comrade Director buttoned the coat of his gray suit and quickly left the conference room. The meeting was over.

Afterward, Professor Sopiev wanted to show us the agricultural institute's natural history collection upstairs on the second floor, but as soon as our meeting with the Comrade Director broke up, I darted over for a short consultation with Greg Gleason.

"Sorry if I wrecked your meeting," I told him. "I'm afraid I'm hopeless as an Albuquerque citizen diplomat. If the delegation wants to purge me, I'd understand completely and make a full self-criticism."

"Not to worry, Comrade," Gleason said, as unflappable as ever. "I've pretty much accomplished what I wanted to do here in Ashkhabad anyway."

"Which was?"

"Well, one of the things was to set up a conference on water policy involving their scientists and academics and ours. It would be held next year in the States, so I have invitations to the United States to give out. As you can imagine, that's made me very popular. Everyone has been extremely helpful to me here."

"I suppose you'll invite your friend the lady economist?"

"Stranger things have happened," he said.

"I'm glad I could catch you for a minute. I didn't know whether I'd have the chance. The last few days have been pretty helter-skelter. They've been watching me night and day. They think I'm a spy."

"They think all foreigners are spies because when they go abroad *they* are all spies. It's amazing how superficial de-Stalinization is here. Did you come to some mutual understanding with Djura?"

"Oh, yes. At least I think so. I bribed him with a pack of Polaroid film."

I waited to see by his expression if he thought I had paid too high a price. Obviously, I had, but Professor Gleason was cool enough not to say it. Would five dollars have been enough? Or two? Maybe just a pack of Marlboros. I didn't bother to tell him it was a twin pack; I felt foolish enough at having introduced bribery inflation in Turkmenistan.

"What about Bukhara?" I asked.

"Sally Alice and I will fly there Monday morning—if Djura comes through with the tickets. I'm just sort of floating till then."

"Look, I'm not going to Bukhara with the delegation. Professor Sopiev has arranged for me to go out to Repetek, where the Turkmen Academy's Institute of the Desert has a field station out in the Kara Kum. He's a terribly nice guy, Sopiev. What do you think?"

"I'd go for it, absolutely. We don't have anything set up in Bukhara, really. We'll probably just meet the folks and be entertained."

"How long will you and Sally Alice be there?"

"Two or three days tops. What about you?"

"I dunno. It depends on what I find out there in the desert. Maybe I'll run into the Akhal-Teke of my dreams, but I suspect I'll be coming back to Ashkhabad within a week to see about my visa extension."

"Let's talk on the phone when we both get back to Ashkhabad, then."

—

The small museum upstairs was a dry, brittle room full of pinned insects, stuffed birds and mammals. Inasmuch as I was going off to Repetek, Andrei Kozlov wanted to brief me on some of the critters I might meet up with while Gleason and Sopiev had a chat in the corner.

When I was young, I was afraid of snakes, mainly because where I grew up in New Jersey was the northernmost range of water moccasins. My run-ins with them were never less than petrifying, and I emerged from boyhood hating snakes as much as Indiana Jones. I remember one time as kids we were playing ice hockey on a frozen pond. It must have been January or February, and the wind was blowing hard, giving the illusion it was cold enough to keep the ice hard. But the puck slid across to the far edge where the ice wasn't thick enough and plopped into the cold water, sinking to the bottom. When I skated over to fetch it, I recklessly tossed off my mittens and plunged my hand into the freezing water to retrieve the puck. Instead, I came up with a big water moccasin that had been lying in the mud at the bottom of the pond. Luckily for me the serpent was too torpid to do anything, but it scared the hell out of me. Whenever I encountered a snake around the yard, my first impulse was to get a long-handled shovel and beat it on the head until dead. I remember one memorable battle with a cottonmouth down at the little stream that ran at the end of our property. It was autumn, and I was down there raking the leaves that had mucked up the stream. Moccasins are perfectly camouflaged for lying on dull-colored autumn leaves, and the first thing I knew I had lackadaisically raked a three- or four-foot moccasin toward me. Moccasins don't like getting raked. It twisted its head up and opened its mouth, and that was the very moment I learned why they are called cottonmouth snakes in the south. The inside of its mouth was as white as an undershirt. Fortunately, I had my weapon already in hand. I gave it a good swack with the iron end of the rake, pinning its head in the sandy mud, then reached for the shovel on the bank nearby and struck off its head with a couple of blows.

But as a naturalist and outdoorsman traveling in snaky places for years, I decided about ten years ago that this wouldn't do. I determined to overcome my fear in the prescribed manner: by catching and handling serpents I could identify as nonpoisonous, which is most of them. I started off with little rat and garter snakes, and worked my way up to black, grass, and hognose snakes. It took some practice, but in this way I got to the point where, when I first see a snake, I no longer jump back in panic or run for my machete to kill it. Instead I identify it, pick it up, and hold it for a few minutes before letting it go. Now if I see snakes in the yard at home I avoid them with the lawn mower, sparing their lives, or simply step over them when I am in the fields or forest. Nonetheless, I've noticed that even after overcoming my fear of the legless ones, I still can't bring myself to actually like or even admire them, and I probably never will. Whenever I see them it seems to me they're always up to no good. Either they're crawling up to destroy a bird's nest and eat the babies, or they're invading a bat nursery to eat the babies, or they're attacking a mouse nest to eat the babies—always out for number one. Even a snake that is harmless to humans is destructive to practically everything else that lives, especially birds and small mammals. You never see a snake building a nest or licking its young. You never see them having sex (or even French kissing; what a waste of those long tongues!). You never even see snakes minding their own business, unless it's sunning themselves to get enough energy into their cold-blooded frames to go out and kill again. Whenever you meet a snake it's on the way to or from some nefarious act of life destruction. Snakes don't have good moral qualities. They're not the kind of animals one wants to be associated with. They don't have family values. In short, I look at snakes as the serial killers of the natural world.

Snakes, however, are the big show in the Central Asian desert. The institute's reptile collection in a glass case covered almost an entire wall. It contained skins of the three most dangerous Central Asian serpents, and Andrei Kozlov was happy to tell me about them. "The three most dangerous snakes are cobra, first, of course, then gyurza, and the one called efe. They are very distinct forms. The gyurza has a fat head and long fangs. It bites quickly, then retires to let the prey die before returning to consume its food. The cobra, on the contrary, waves its neck and puffs up its hood when it's threatened, but actually, as you see, it has quite a small head and tiny fangs. Therefore, in order to inject more venom, the cobra strikes and holds on to its victim, shaking its prey to death."

"Thank you for that most illuminating lesson. Can we get out of here?"

Much more to my liking was a wall display in the corridor on the work of the Stalin-era Russian geneticist Nikolai Vavilov. My friend Victor Fet had told me the story of how Vavilov, Russia's most brilliant geneticist, ran afoul of Trofim Lysenko, Stalin's geneticist from hell, whose mad theory that hereditary characteristics could be acquired through training threw Soviet biology into a generation of darkness. Vavilov was liquidated in the 1930s, but left behind a botanical garden at Kara Kala. He had collected native plants of the Turkmen region for decades in the early part of the twentieth century.

Sopiev and Gleason joined us, and Professor Sopiev began to explain the wall map. "Some of the plants Vavilov collected are illustrated here, at the places where Vavilov collected them. As you see, it is a map of the Iranian plateau, the Kopet-Dag Mountains, and the steppes and deserts of what used to be called Russian Turkestan to the Syr Darya River. Vavilov's work proved that many most valuable agricultural products originated in this region, especially wheat, which was a grass of the Iranian plateau and mountain steppes."

In addition to the favorite food plant of humans, the map of Vavilov's discoveries also included grapes, pomegranates, apricots, peaches, marijuana, pistachios, and licorice.

But perhaps his most intriguing find in Turkmenistan was the legume alfalfa, or lucerne. Never the favorite food of people (even alfalfa sprouts on salads are nasty tasting, some would say), but the decided favorite of horses—and especially valuable in growing big strong horses that the Turkmen favor. Alfalfa is probably the oldest plant cultivated by humans. Its seeds have been dug up at Persian archaeological sites six thousand years old. Alfalfa was prized especially in ancient times for its high protein content and its almost unbelievable durability. It is a perennial legume that can yield as much as ten tons per acre. It has such a remarkable proclivity for regeneration after cutting that up to thirteen crops of alfalfa hay may be grown in one growing season. There is no food crop on Earth more drought and heat tolerant. This is because the plant sends down vast tap roots. Two-month-old alfalfa seedlings are known to penetrate three feet down into porous soil. It is also amazingly long-lived. At the age of twenty years, an alfalfa plant may possess tap roots more than fifty feet deep. Yet although highly tolerant of drought conditions, it uses large quantities of water in producing its nutritious leaves, whether forage or dry hay.

"There's something that puzzles me, Professor Sopiev," I said. "This exhibit proposes that Turkmenistan was an area of settled agriculture at one time, where *luzerna* was domesticated for forage in the same place where the big Turkmen horses were bred. But this is now a desert region, and the Turkmen are a nomadic people by custom. How do you account for this apparent contradiction?"

Both Sopiev and Kozlov smiled when they heard my question. Kozlov said, "There is an old Turkmen legend that once upon a time the Amu Darya River flowed into the Caspian Sea, not the Aral Sea as it does today. At that time the Great Silk Road to China followed the Amu Darya through this land, and a great wealth of trade passed through this region. Then an evil khan of Khiva, wanting to capture the caravan trade for himself, diverted the Amu Darya River to the east. The Turkmen tribes were left without trade and water. Since then this became the Kara Kum Desert, and the Turkmen became nomadic."

It sounded apocryphal, but perhaps only because it was told by a Russian to a foreign visitor aware of the drying out of the Aral Sea as a result of the Soviet diversion of the same Amu Darya River back across the desert. I turned to the real Turkmen among us. "And what do you say, Professor Sopiev?"

"It is a correct question you ask," said Sopiev thoughtfully, "but again you are moving too fast. I could give you an official answer, which is that humans made this desert in the era of feudalism and that the Soviet state, by building the Kara Kum Canal, is reclaiming the desert for humanity. I could also give you my own opinions, and the body of scientific evidence. We certainly know that the winter snow-fields of the Kopet-Dag play the role of a giant reservoir in the ecology of this region. Many rivers run down onto the plains of Turkmenia. The two major ones, the Syr Darya and the Amu Darya, both now flow into the Aral Sea, but in ancient times the Amu Darya drained into the Caspian Sea. The old bed of the river can still be studied. You will be going quite soon to Repetek and the Institute of the Desert. You will be in the company of my colleague and friend Professor Shammakov, the great herpetologist of Turkmenia. Wouldn't it be better to go and see for yourself? Perhaps you will find an answer to your questions in the Kara Kum. When you return to Ashkhabad, we can discuss what you have learned."

Would there be a final exam? I wondered. But what Sopiev had said seemed so sensible to me that I simply nodded.

Dignified, professorial, slightly inscrutable, Professor Sopiev was a falconer. He knew just when to release his bird into the air, when to retrieve him, and how to motivate him for the hunt. I was getting antsy to put Ashkhabad behind me for a while, especially to get out from under the awful aegis of Djura the Horrible. I found myself wishing I could cross the Kara Kum tied by a leather thong to the wrist of Sopiev the Falconer.

In the *Histories,* Herodotus says: "It does seem to be true that the remotest regions, which surround the inhabited countries and lie to the outside of them, produce the things which we believe to be most rare and beautiful." In Herodotus' time, for example—a century before Alexander—amber was thought to come from near a river then called Eridanus, which flowed into a remote northern sea beyond Europe, but no Greek had viewed either river or sea firsthand. Tin supposedly came from the "Tin Islands." No Greek had ever visited those islands, either. It was thought that gold was procured by a race of one-eyed men, the Arimaspians, who stole it from griffons, the flying dragons that nested in golden lairs in their caves. Herodotus says he doesn't believe it, but offers no alternative theory.

What about horses? The most rare and beautiful horses also came "from what one might call the ends of the earth." These were the horses

Herodotus called "Nisaean" horses, sacred to the Persian kings. "Now these horses," Herodotus wrote, "are so called because they come from the great Nisaean plain in Media."

Herodotus described with black relish how ten such magnificent horses—"decked in the most splendid trappings"—were prominent in the perverse parade ordered by the Persian King Xerxes. Xerxes was angry because old, ailing Pythias, whose five sons were serving in the Persian campaign against Greece, asked that just one of them be released from duty to take care of him. Whereupon Xerxes cried, "You dare ask me to concern myself about your son?" and immediately ordered Pythias' most beloved son sliced into halves and set up on the road like goalposts for the Persian army to march through.

In this grand procession, Herodotus continues, King Xerxes himself came between front and back infantry columns of men of all nations, tributaries, and mercenaries. The king was preceded by a thousand horsemen chosen from all the various realms and tribes over which he lorded. Then came a thousand spearmen "with their spears reversed." Next came the ten Nisaean horses, followed by the holy chariot of the sun god Ormuzd. (The Greeks often brought images of their gods onto the battlefield; the Persians brought the god's car.) Unfortunately, Herodotus does not describe these horses in detail. He does not even say whether they were ridden or pulling chariots; archaeological artifacts, such as the reliefs at Babylon, indicate chariots.

Media was a longtime Asian satrapy of the Persian empire, but somewhat short of the end of the known world even in Herodotus' time. Herodotus, who in his lifetime apparently traveled to Egypt, Babylon, and the Black Sea but never to the Iranian plateau or Central Asia, was often confused about geography at the "ends of the earth," and admitted basing his own accounts on unsubstantiated hearsay. Possibly he was confused about the location of the Nisaean plains where the sacred horses were bred because there seem to have been several Nisas in the ancient world. Perhaps the sacred horses actually came from the area around Nisa, the capital of the Parthians. Parthia was somewhat closer than Media to the end of the known world, which from time immemorial was the Jaxartes River, now the Syr Darya, on the Uzbekistan–Kazakhstan border. In fact, Stary Nisa (ancient Nisa) was built on a site only about twelve kilometers from the present site of Ashkhabad.

Later in the *Histories,* Herodotus speaks of the lands of some of the famous horsemen who surrounded the Persian kings on the battlefield, whose tribes contributed the mounted bowmen who made the Persian light cavalry a new and particularly devastating weapon against the Greek phalanxes, which at first lacked cavalry altogether. He tells of a great grassy plain in Asia that "formerly belonged to the Chorasmians, and their lands still adjoin it and so do those of the Hyrcanians, the Parthians, Sarangeans & Thamanaeans."

This plain, according to Herodotus, was surrounded by a ring of mountains with five clefts, or passes. Through these five passes flowed five channels of the river Aces, irrigating the lands of the five tribes whose territories bounded the plain. The Aces is the ancient name for the Tedzhen River, one of the numerous rivers that still cascade down from the Kopet-Dag, Gissar, and Pamir ranges to the Turkmen and neighboring Uzbek flatlands below.

But since the Persian conquest, Herodotus says, this plain and its river had become "the property of the king." The five tribes found themselves in a tragic pickle for the Persian king blocked up the five gorges and built sluice gates to control the flow of water. The river Aces flowed in as before, but no longer had any means of egress. As a result, this lush plain, abundant with water for the tribes of Asian horse herders, was turned into a private lake of the king's.

This was a disaster for the five tribes, because they depended entirely on this water. In winter "the god rains upon them as upon other men," says Herodotus, but in summer they had no water to irrigate their millet and sesame crops. (Herodotus does not mention alfalfa, which was not known in Europe until early Christian times.) The tale goes on that when the Chorasmians, Parthians, and others found themselves at planting time without water, they were reduced to begging. "They go to Persia with their womenfolk," he writes, "and stand before the doors of the king's palace, crying and howling" until at length the Persian king would give the word to open the sluice gates to the lands that thirsted most.

But just as water no longer flowed freely, it was no longer free of charge, either. Subjugation to Persia also meant economic exploitation by the Persian state. "I am told," Herodotus concludes, that the Persian king "only opens the sluices upon receipt of a heavy payment over and above the regular tax."

We have no idea whether one word of Herodotus' story is true, and if it is, when it actually took place. What is interesting about his tale is the portrayal in folk legend of life-giving water disappearing by human action, in this case the arbitrary rule of a Persian king. Herodotus was retailing the story of the five tribes in order to blacken the repute of the Persians, and not without reason.

It was just the kind of irrational cruelty Xerxes dealt Pythias, and just the kind of arbitrary oppression the Persians forced on the five tribes when they shut off their water that made the Greeks hate the Persians as Oriental barbarians, and made them dread such absolute monarchs. By the seventh century B.C. the Greeks had already begun to develop the forms of politics and warfare that, by checking regal absolutism, became the foundation of Western democracy. The Greek assembly of aristocrats placed certain restraints on the king or ruler precisely in order to avoid the mad exercise of power by unfettered monarchs like Xerxes.

Even, or especially, the characteristic way the Greek city-state went to war exhibited a community solidarity to thwart such tyrants. This was the classical Greek phalanx, made up of hoplites (heavily armed infantrymen). In *The Greek and Macedonian Art of War*, F. E. Adcock defined the phalanx as "a body of infantry drawn up in close order in several ranks which are also close together." The hoplites took their names from their shields, the use of which was essential in their fighting tactics. These round shields about three feet across were held by the left arm's passing through a ring to a grip for the left hand. The shield covered most of a man's body, leaving the right hand free to wield a long spear or short sword. At first the ranks of hoplites were filled exclusively with nobles, but soon they accepted anyone from the upper or middle classes who could provide his own shield and weaponry. They were not professional soldiers, but citizen-soldiers, who answered the call of their city-states in wartime but spent the vast majority of their time involved in nonpolitical civilian pursuits. In battle, phalanx confronted phalanx. One infantry line tried to break or split the other. When one phalanx succeeded, the other would take to flight; the battle was over, and battles were usually of short duration.

As Adcock explained, the hoplite's shield most effectively covered his left side. His right side gained lateral protection from the shield of his neighbor on the right as they advanced shoulder to shoulder in close ranks. The effectiveness of the phalanx as a whole, therefore, depended not only on the skill of the front rank in wielding its weapons or the physical and moral support provided by the ranks behind, but also on the all-important factor of the continuity of the line, and the mutual dependence on comrades. As Adcock said, "Every man in line knows that his life depends on his neighbour's fighting as steadily, as skilfully, and as bravely as himself. No form of combat could so plainly exhibit the community solidarity that was of the essence of the Greek City-State."

The Greeks tempered the power of kings with the custom of assembly, and might have expressed the heart and soul of their growing democracy on the battlefield with their hoplite phalanxes. But on the margins of the Eurasian steppes, where the cautionary tale of Herodotus supposedly took place, there was no democracy. It was not just human tyranny that Central Asians were confronted with. All five tribes downstream from the legendary reservoir of King Xerxes were practicing settled agriculture and raising big warm-blooded horses on alfalfa at the time they were subjugated by the Persian empire. This accords with modern anthropological findings that the horse was almost certainly first domesticated by sedentary agriculturalists, who required an infrastructure of pens for captured animals, a secure supply of fodder from permanent fields, and lengthy periods of time to accustom wild animals to captivity. Archaeological evidence shows that by the fourth millennium B.C. villages of about thirty-five acres were engaged in irrigation farming and the husbandry of sheep and goats in the foothills of the Kopet-Dag.

Yet within human memory, if not written history, these settled horse herders, shepherds, goatherds, and camel keepers abandoned their homelands and slipped away into the churning wastelands of warfare and migration that was Eurasian nomadism from the Kopet-Dag mountains to the Great Wall of China. Against human tyranny there are answers, but against the tyranny of nature herself, humans are helpless as newborn babies. The global climate was changing. The world was getting drier. The rains vanished. The rivers stopped. The goats cut up the turf with their hoofs, and the soil turned to dust and blew away. From the Gobi to Saharan Africa, from 3000 B.C. to about A.D. 700, the gods of the winds, sun, rain, rivers, and soil angrily took back what they had generously given their inhabitants. "All life is grass," said the prophet Isaiah, who lived at this time in the Holy Land. He might have added, "And all grass is water." Without water, the grass was burning and dying:

> Your country is desolate; your cities are burned with fire:
> your land, strangers devour it in your presence.
>
> —ISAIAH, I:7

Forced by these circumstances, the peoples of Central Asia turned increasingly from sedentary agriculture to seasonal migrations in search of grazing pasture. Not only the Chorasmians, but also the Scythians, Huns, Kazakhs, Kirghiz, Mongols, and many hundreds of other tribes, large and small, were forced into movement to find pasture for their livestock. In winter they tried to keep to the warmer valleys; in summer they made for the richer vegetation of the cooler mountains and foothills.

But always there were disputes, conflicts, and continual warfare, and in time the demands of the terrible struggle for survival on the steppes—where one raid could wipe out an entire tribe—made the unlettered nomads forget where they had come from. Those who roamed the steppe with a horse between their knees learned to despise those who sowed the earth. Nomadism was hemmed in on either end of the Eurasian landmass by the two great empires of settled agriculturists, Persia (later the Arabs) in the west and China in the east—both of whose civilizations were based on slave labor. The nomads neither possessed slaves nor would they ever submit to slavery. They disdained the very idea of private property in the sense of owning land. Religion and law seemed to them mere tricks—devices that despots employed to oppress their subjects. They were anathema to the creation of unified states.

On the vast desiccated wastelands of the Eurasian steppes the whirlwinds swept history to hell and back. Those who lived in cities and towns or farmed the edges of the steppe looked across the river toward the empty plains in fear of the dust cloud that foretold an imminent attack by the barbarians. Those who adapted and survived the ecological tyranny became implacable foes of those they saw literally looking down on them from their fortress towers. It was two thousand years of savage havoc from the beginnings of nomadism until Genghis Khan and the Mongol Horde returned to the original lands of the Chorasmians, now known under Islamic rule as Khwarizm, trampling and burning crops, demolishing mosques and libraries, looting and torching cities, leaving nothing but scars on the face of the Earth, massacring populations and turning survivors out to die in the desert. Genghis Khan forbade his Orkhons to show mercy to any enemy. No prisoners, no slaves, no survivors. Liquidation, not subjugation, was the ultimate law of the steppes. "For an enemy conquered," Genghis Khan said, "is never subdued, and will always hate his new master."

144

It was Saturday morning and everyone in Ashkhabad was supposed to do what is called *sybotni,* or voluntary labor. Not foreign delegates, you understand, but true Red citizens of the classless society. Such he-man/ she-man Reds were supposed to get out in the streets one Saturday a month to perform public service of the physical kind. Not the worst idea in the world, and in bygone days, when the party was king, maybe no-shows had to pay a price. This kind of public-spirited Soviet machismo, however, didn't play well in Muslim Central Asia anymore. The few who still obeyed society's call, probably loyal party members like the Shikhmurads, were out in the streets with brooms and bandannas over their faces, sweeping Ashkhabad.

I was driving with Professor Sopiev, Andrei Kozlov, and my personal KGB agent, Sasha Reebok, to the so-called Hospital for Pinecones. There we were to meet the man I would be traveling into the desert with the next day, Professor Shammakov, the renowned Turkmen herpetologist, currently a patient there.

"This is where the bosses get sick, Jon," Reebok repeated with a slight sneer as we walked in. "The hospital for everyone else is simply terrible. Probably in America you wouldn't let your little doggy get an operation there."

It was a thickset, whitewashed stone building from the Stalin era with a lot of windows and other touches of Soviet modernism. It was probably built in the early 1950s as part of the city's reconstruction after Ashkhabad's earthquake. It had only three stories—a sensible height, it seemed to me, in an unstable geological area. Inside, there was no sign that you were in a hospital. The first floor could have been the lobby of an old Miami Beach apartment building, except that it lacked the smell of chicken soup. There were no hospital personnel in evidence, only a toothless old babushka in a blue work dress minding the door.

Up the stairs (there was no elevator, which seemed odd for a hospital) we came onto a wide landing used as a common room. Four or five middle-aged patients sat around a jumbo black-and-white television. The men were unshaven, the women frowsy-haired; all were in bathrobes and slippers and were watching Saturday-morning cartoons with dull faces.

Here, at least, an attendant was mopping the floor. The thought crossed my mind that he was performing his voluntary labor, mopping the floors of the hospital for *shishkas* once a month. But this was proved wrong when he went off down the hall to tell Professor Shammakov we were there to see him.

In an Ashkhabad minute Professor Shammakov appeared. He was an inoffensive toad of a man, small, dark, round, kind of wet. You could imagine him sleeping under your porch at night, or hopping around your feet in an outdoor shower. If you shone a light on him at night or nudged him with your boot you could imagine that he wouldn't hiss or strike at you, but simply jump out of the way and go back to minding his own business.

Professor Shammakov did not appear at all well. His voice was low and pale; his movements slow and lethargic. The whites of his eyes bulged. Sopiev kept the discussion brief. Professor Shammakov was leaving in the morning to travel by train to Repetek to meet up with a group of American zoologists arriving from Moscow by train to go naturalizing. He would be happy to have me accompany him. He made a small bow from the waist and padded away back down the corridor.

Out in the hospital courtyard, Professor Sopiev wasted no time. First, he wrote me a note of introduction to the director of the Repetek *zapovednik* on the back of an envelope, then instructed me to meet Professor Shammakov at the Ashkhabad train station at 7:00 A.M. the following morning. We would take the eastbound Turkmenistan express for twelve hours across the Kara Kum Desert to Repetek.

"Will the professor really be ready in the morning?" I asked.

Sopiev fixed his dancing eyes on me and hoisted his bushy eyebrows. "Ready for what, a funeral or a field trip to Repetek?"

There was one more obligation to fulfill before leaving Ashkhabad, and this was to attend the wedding of Geldi Kiarizov's younger brother, Kakysh. Weddings are the main event on the Turkmen social calendar and customarily take place on Saturday, the Muslim sabbath. It was no different on this bright Saturday, rife with the air of the desert spring's fecundity. Sometimes it was a procession of desert-beaten little cars racing behind each other bumper to bumper at breakneck speed, all honking their horns full blast. In other places, women were setting long tables for wedding guests in the open-air courtyards of the high-rise apartment buildings. In their festive tribal dresses and ornately jeweled head pieces, heavily laden with silver necklaces for the occasion, the women offered a bright splash of finery to the stark monotony of the housing complexes. Five hundred to one thousand guests at a Turkmen wedding is normal, but, as in so many instances, the traditional tribal weddings of Central Asia have had to be modified to fit into the pattern of Soviet life.

Yet as long as the Turkmen tribes survive, their traditions are always ripe for renewal, so now and then I would see a young groom on horseback, trotting proudly down the center of the street in the Turk-men warrior's costume the men still wear for ceremonial occasions: a tall, fluffy, white lamb's wool hat, resplendent red-and-yellow silk robe, gray pantaloons, and high black boots. They say that in Uzbekistan, the neighboring republic (or one *Istan* to the east, if you like, an *Istan* being defined as the distance from one republic with the name ending in *-istan* to the next), weddings are still celebrated in rural areas with the traditional bride chase in which the prospective bride gallops off and the groom must capture her on horseback. Now that Turkmen are permitted to keep private horses once again, the horse is returning as a member of the wedding, though at present still in vestigial form. These wedding-day rides must be hell on the horses' hooves, because they jog their mounts over the hard pavement of Ashkhabad's streets; desert horsemen have never shod their horses, which have never been bred for hard hooves, either.

Late that afternoon Sasha Skorokhodov and Alex picked me up, and we drove to meet Guvanch at his apartment before going over together to the Kiarizov family house on Karl Marx Street, where I had lunched the week before with Geldi. With two foreigners in our party, we were taken up an outside staircase to wait for the wedding to begin with the elders and dignitaries in the airy office of Geldi's father, a Marxist scholar and professor of philosophy at the Turkmen university. He was a courtly gray-haired gentleman in his early sixties, reclining with the older men on a Teke carpet, drinking green tea and eating sweets. We removed our shoes and were invited to stretch out on pillows. The walls were lined with books and journals, and after introductions the father wanted to know where Alex and I were from, and what had brought us to Turkmenistan. He was especially pleased to welcome an American guest to his home.

"It is a great honor to have you as guests in our home on the occasion of this *svadba* [wedding]," he said. "I want to say that this would have been impossible even to imagine before the time of glasnost. We were always told that Americans are our enemies. Now we have the opportunity to meet Americans in our own homes, sit down together, talk, and become friends. It is only thanks to Mikhail Gorbachev that such things can now take place."

There was no doubt where his sympathies resided, but Alex said to me in English, "I don't think this man know what he talks. He is the Communist party man."

But Professor Kiarizov was also a Turkmen elder, a university scholar, a political philosopher, and I wanted to hear him out. After all, before the Soviets took control of Turkmenistan, no Turkmen had *ever* attended a university. I asked Alex, whose Russian was much more fluent than mine, to ask him about other changes taking place in Turkmenistan under Gorbachev. It was a faux pas; the professor spoke for five minutes, but the Bulgarian wouldn't interpret, insisting that the father was lying and that he really knew better.

Alex said, "When I was here first time, I would ask the people the name of this street or this village. They run away. They are afraid. The people always afraid with Communist system. The people here live like the animal."

Alex had finally stopped entreating me to join his grandiose business schemes, but even at the wedding he could not lay aside his immediate concern. Just then a call came through to Geldi's house from Alex's boss in Sofia. He was trying to get his front office's okay for the Akhal-Teke deal he had arranged with Geldi through Guvanch. He had decided to buy forty Akhal-Tekes, but to take only two to Bulgaria with him now, in a truck loaded with twenty-four tons of Guvanch's honey, a sure seller in hapless Bulgaria. It would be a test run. If all went well on the long journey across the Caspian, through southern Russia, and around the Black Sea to the port of Odessa, where he would take a ferry for Sofia, he would turn around, return the empty truck, and pick up a large horse trailer that Guvanch had somehow located. When he returned from his call, however, Alex was beside himself; the connection was so bad that he hadn't been able to discuss the deal. He no longer wanted to remain at the wedding, but to return to his hotel immediately and use the telephone there. He didn't have the sense to realize that his hosts would take offense if he left the wedding; nothing mattered to him but closing the deal. Guvanch, of course, could not walk out like that, even if Alex was the representative of his Bulgarian partners. Alex was trying Guvanch's patience, but he remained calm and authoritative, sending Sasha Skorokhodov to drive the Bulgarian. As they left, I could tell by Guvanch's silence that the social breach had offended his Turkmen's commercial spirit by setting business against national custom.

Down below in the courtyard, the wedding party was revving up. There must have been two hundred or three hundred guests sitting at tables under the leafy grape arbor. Before them were bottles of vodka, beer, and soft drinks. There were tables for men, tables for women, and one long table for children. The half of the courtyard near the head table was for the family, who sat with the men and women together. A popular Turkmen band called Akysh was playing Central Asian rock with an electric keyboard, electric bass guitar, and drums. Their shouting songs sounded like Muslim prayers set to a fluid Oriental rhythm.

Then the bride emerged from the house, her head and shoulders covered in a bloodred carpet, and led by the mothers, aunts, and grandmothers. She would remain covered, according to Turkmen custom, through the whole affair, like a veiled statue, not eating, not drinking, not dancing. I wondered what it would be like, in years to come, when a Turkmen wife remembered her wedding day. Would she experience her own marriage like a wood floor under a Teke carpet? Kakysh came out with her in a starched white dress shirt, smiling and looking very much like the cat that swallowed the canary. They sat at the head table, and the eating and drinking commenced in earnest.

We had lamb soup and vodka. Geldi's father made an elaborate speech in Turkmen on the singer's microphone. We had lamb *plov* and vodka. The father of the bride made a speech. We had roast chicken and vodka; then Geldi himself delivered a speech. It was a long, mellifluous speech, but the only thing I understood was that it was the main event, and that Geldi, the horse breeder and owner of the only private herd of Akhal-Tekes in Turkmenistan, was obviously considered the head of the family.

They had roasted several sheep for *shashlik*, the main course at every true Turkmen gathering. Guvanch was really packing it in. We would drink a glass of vodka, then he would chase it with a piece of grilled meat and raw green onions. He urged me to do the same, claiming that as long as you kept eating you wouldn't get drunk. The problem with Russians, he said, was that they drink vodka on an empty stomach. This sounded sensible, and since I hadn't gotten drunk once yet in Turkmenistan, I followed my friend's example. As a result, my memories of the rest of the wedding became increasingly clouded. I remember taking out my Polaroid and all guests wanting their pictures taken as a souvenir. I snapped the happy couple, the parents, aunts, uncles, cousins, children, even the old women guarding the outhouse out back. I must have given away twenty snapshots. It was my first experience of being mobbed in adoration by total strangers. They marveled at the instant photographs, as exotic to them as the Turkmen wedding was to me. I also remember wild dancing, the children in a swarm around Geldi, who was laughing, spinning around and around, with ruble bills held high in each hand.

What I remember next is sitting in the front seat of Guvanch's car, driven by Sasha Skorokhodov, with the front doors flung open. We were parked somewhere in Ashkhabad, it was dark, and in the backseat Guvanch Djumaev, ex–first secretary of the Ashkhabad Komsomol, was wailing out the Beatles song "Yesterday" at the top of his lungs, and I was wailing with him. Oddly, he knew all the lyrics in English, a language he didn't speak at all.

"How did you learn these songs, Guvanch?" I asked.

"When I was at university I played guitar in a rock band. We only played Beatles songs. John Lennon was my hero."

"*Konyechno!*" I was thinking in our drunken revelry what an amazing fellow this man Guvanch was. It's one thing to share a meal or a conversation, but quite another to share a mutual memory of youth. Was it possible that we two men on opposite sides of the world, from cultures that couldn't have been more different, had both felt the same spark of Beatlemania and rock music so long ago? We shared something generational and global that struck a deep fraternal chord. Perhaps it was only the vodka making me maudlin and misty, but it was one of those rare moments in the life of a traveler, when you stop feeling like a stranger in a strange land, if only for an hour, and somehow the notion arises within you that you have crept inside another culture.

As if reading my mind, Guvanch said, "We Turkmen have a saying: 'The first time you meet someone, you become friends. The second time you drink with your friend you become allies. And the third time, brothers!' When you return from the desert, you will be my guest at my house. Then you will be one of my family. What do you say?"

I looked at him and sang out the first verse of "Rocky Raccoon." Guvanch joined in, and together we bleated Beatles to the Ashkhabad night.

When I returned to Dr. Shikhmurad's place, Saturday night was in full swing there, too. Everyone was watching television in the living room except Yedesh, who was still at work. They were watching a news report; Gorbachev was in Japan on a big trade mission. Then the ice hockey game came on, what they were all waiting for. It finally dawned on me that for desert nomads ice hockey must be sensationally exotic, like a sport from the moon. I went into my room and packed the things I'd be taking next morning to Repetek while Mrs. Dr. Shikhmurad went into the kitchen to rustle up a small supper of leftover chicken and four gigantic meat raviolis. I had been eating and drinking nonstop for five hours, but to avoid a fuss I nibbled a chicken leg, ate half a ravioli, and drank a pitcher of Mrs. Dr. Shikhmurad's delicious yellow grape compote.

Luckily for me, Sasha Reebok arrived with my train ticket and sat down at the dining table.

"Look, Sasha," I said in English, "I've been to a wedding and have been eating since three o'clock in the afternoon. I can't touch another bite. You must help. Eat the rest of this food Yenye has prepared for me. I don't want to insult her on my last night here, but I'm stuffed."

"Well, Jon, if you insist."

"I insist. Also, tell Dr. Shikhmurad for me that I would like to propose a toast and present them with some little gifts."

I went back into my room and found the stethoscope, blood pressure monitor, and bottle of one thousand aspirins I had brought along from home, apparently for this very occasion. Actually, I had brought them in case the delegation toured a hospital, the way Sally Alice had brought five hundred disposable syringes for the same purpose. She had told me over the phone that after asking day after day to visit the Ashkhabad Hospital without result from Djura and the Turkmen Friendship Society, she had finally insisted one morning that her hosts take her there. She said she had been so adamant that they probably began to think she was ill.

When I gave Dr. and Mrs. Dr. Shikhmurad my little gifts they were amazed. Dr. Shikh's glasses got steamy. Mrs. Dr. Shikhmurad said she had always wanted her own stethoscope. Blood pressure units existed at Turkmenian hospitals, but not privately owned ones. Mrs. Dr. Shikhmurad said they also had aspirin at the hospital where she worked, but not all the time; she would give them to sick children and keep some at home for relatives and neighbors. I had paid less than twenty bucks for the blood pressure unit at a mall drugstore, and the aspirin was cheaper. The incalculable difference between our standards of living made me feel more embarrassed than proud. It is wonderful that America has such products readily available for everyone, but it is uncomfortable to feel the shame of the recipients of gifts who believe you must have paid your family fortune to obtain them, when they actually cost less than a good restaurant meal.

Dr. Shikhmurad knew just how to smooth jagged edges and uncorked a bottle of bubbly to celebrate the occasion. I was sure the Turkmen Friendship Society had provided it, but what did I care? I took my glass and rose to my feet, asking Sasha Reebok to translate.

"I would like to offer a toast to my hosts. In the short time I have been with you, I feel that I have become one of your family. We have eaten together. We have talked together around your dining-room table. We have slept under the same roof, and waited for the bathroom together in the morning. We have even had our quarrels. This especially has made me feel a member of your family. I want to say how very grateful I am for your generous hospitality."

Even Mrs. Dr. Shikhmurad drank a glass of Champagne, which I later found out is considered a lady's beverage in the hard-drinking old Russian empire.

That night I dreamed I saw Genghis Khan in a roadhouse bar in west Texas. He wasn't anything like I had always imagined. He looked like Kenny Rogers in a chain-mail hood, and he was drinking Jim Beam. He turned around at the bar and asked me for a Marlboro, then lit it with a torch of flaming naphtha. When I recognized him, I was so terrified I woke up instantly. It was pitch black. For a moment I couldn't figure out where I was—at home? In my childhood bed? In a Motel 6? Then I found I didn't know which end of the bed I was lying in, or, for that matter, whether I was in a bed. It was the strangest sensation—like levitation, I suppose. The dream had been so lucid and frightening that at least I was sure I was alive. Then the physical disorientation became fun; I was floating in the blackness and didn't really want to find my bearings. When, in the space of a few seconds, I came back down to consciousness, then got up and looked out the bedroom window, the surveillance car parked outside in its usual space struck me as idiotically comic. Only fools could imagine I was a spy. What a foolish spy I made; my mission was to find out if Akhal-Teke horses were the root stock of the modern Thoroughbred. Obviously, it was top secret information; if the news got out at Churchill Downs, it could mean war.

In the morning, Dr. Shikhmurad volunteered one more time to drive me, this time to the train station to meet Professor Shammakov. Perhaps it was a sign of how relieved he was to have survived my visit that the new borrowed car arrived fifteen minutes early, its engine actually running. Or maybe it was a going-away present from the Turkmen Friendship Society, which also had every reason to be glad to see the back of me for a while. I had left most of my gear and trade gifts with my hosts since I expected to reconnoiter the Kara Kum for horses and routes, then return to Ashkhabad to see about my visa extension. I was also glad to give the Khogyshevs (the family's actual surname) a little holiday from their rebellious American guest.

In Central Asia, you always take off your shoes and exchange them for slippers before you enter any home, and Dr. Shikhmurad's apartment was no different. I was lacing up my Reeboks on the way out of the apartment, nursing a small Champagne hangover, when Mrs. Dr. Shikhmurad trundled out of the kitchen to say good-bye and give me a plastic bag of provisions for my trip: *cherek*, salt, radishes, green onions, and hard-boiled eggs. I had bought a kilo each of raisins and pistachio nuts at an Ashkhabad market the previous day, and was carrying a two-liter plastic Coke bottle of tap water, cleansed for drinking with an eyedropper full of laundry bleach. Now I was thoroughly provisioned. I was so touched by Mrs. Dr. Shikhmurad's thoughtfulness that I threw my arms around her as if I were her own son, and gave her a big hug good-bye.

"But you haven't eaten breakfast!" she cried.

"To me sorrow," I told her in plain Russian. "Time not exists." But she put up such a fuss that I was obliged to eat, standing in the foyer with my traveling shoes on, a hard-boiled egg and drink a glass of boiled milk. I have no idea what kind of animal the milk was from, but it was fresh, invigorating, and welcome.

"To me it is necessary to leave," I told her again.

"Eat, eat." She was standing over me to make sure I finished. It reminded me how when I was a boy, I would wait for my mother to leave the kitchen, then dash to the sink and wash down the breakfast oatmeal I hated so much that my throat would actually constrict and refuse it entrance.

I said, "Say good-bye to Yedesh for me, please."

"She's asleep in the back room," Mrs. Dr. Shikhmurad said. "She was on forty-eight-hour shift at the birth hospital."

And may she be as attentive a nurse in her forty-seventh hour on call as in her first, I thought. It was too complicated to try to put into Russian, so I just said, "Until the next viewing!" and went out.

—

The Ashkhabad train station was a small neoclassical gem, probably constructed after the 1948 earthquake toward the end of the Stalin era, when there were still slave labor and newly emigrated craftsmen. The walls were pastel pink plaster with sturdy white columns holding up a rotunda ceiling. The high molding was brilliantly ornate, everything in gold leaf, and the floors were off-white marble. The only thing wrong with the train station was you couldn't buy a ticket. At each end was a bank of ten ticketing windows, all shut, even though a line of people that stretched halfway across the station stood in front of one. Maybe the locals knew something I didn't, or perhaps they were simply waiting on line as Soviet citizens were supposed to do. Maybe when they opened the window they would be selling car parts or toilet paper. Luckily Sasha Reebok had obtained my ticket the previous day through connections.

We went out to the platform, where the old iron horse known as the Turkmenistan Express already stood steaming and hissing and pawing the ground. Desultory Turkmen with tattered plastic bags of food and clothing waited out of the sun on benches under the eave of the roof. It was my first experience of railroad travel in Asia, and I didn't know the rules. I took a photograph of the windows of the train, smartly decorated with light blue camels on the train's white cotton window curtains. Immediately a militiaman in uniform came over to stop me, admonishing the foreigner in the cowboy hat that photography was not permitted at any Soviet transport installation, including airports, train stations, highways, and bridges.

"To me sorrow," I said, instead of "I'm sorry." I pointed at the train windows and spoke to him in English. "You see? I was just taking a picture of the camels. The camels, you see?"

When I put the camera back into my day pack, the militiaman went away. We waited on the platform thirty minutes for Professor Shammakov, until just before the train was set to depart, and then found him already in the compartment we were to share.

"Happy path," said Dr. Shikhmurad, and we shook hands only two minutes before the Turkmenistan Express pulled out punctually at 8 A.M.

We had the roomy compartment to ourselves. I sat back on the seat across from Professor Shammakov and heaved a sigh, delighted to be under way at last out of the Turkmen capital, even if it was not on a real horse. The professor, too, seemed perkier than he had been in the hospital, sitting on the edge of the seat in his old black snake-hunting boots, with his curved snake stick jutting out of his gym bag beside him.

"How do you feel, Professor?" I asked.

"Ahh, now better and better." He smiled a broad bullfrog smile. "I did not like hospital. Better to go to desert. I love life of desert." He was from Mary, he said, formerly the ancient city of Merv founded after Alexander's death. Our route would take us six hundred kilometers, at first parallel to the Kopet-Dag until we reached his native city, then swinging east northeast toward the Amu Darya River.

"Will we see the Amu Darya?" I asked.

"Won't see," he said. "Repetek is located seventy-five kilometers from city of Chardzhou, located on banks of River Amu Darya. But we will see other Turkmen Rivers: River Tedzhen, River Little Tedzhen, and River Murgab."

I wanted to tell him how exciting this was because these were three of the rivers Herodotus probably wrote about in his story of the Chorasmians, but it was too complicated, so I just stuck up my thumbs and said, "Excellent! And when will we actually enter the Kara Kum Desert, Professor?"

The train had already attained a slow, rocking rhythm. We were only five minutes out of the capital, but already there was not a single tree in sight. Professor Shammakov gestured with a sweep of his arm across the window; "Please," he said.

The train ran parallel to the Kara Kum Canal, through an irrigated agricultural district where women and children were harvesting white potatoes in the fields. It seemed to me an unforgivable folly to use the water that had apparently come at such a steep environmental price to produce nothing more than white potatoes.

What amazed me was how the desert ran smack into the two tiers of mountains on our right. There was no transition zone at all between desert and mountains. It was the earthbound view of what I had seen from the window of the jet as we landed: an immense flatland with a wall of gray-brown snowcapped peaks at its edge rising up as sheer as a stone curtain. The single tier of foothills was knobby and green in the exuberance of spring. The professor said this would last no more than fifty or sixty days; afterward, the desert heat and the wild Kara Kum winds would make vegetative growth impossible. The perennial plants would more profitably spend their time sinking their root systems deep into the sandy soil, and the land would return to its usual sunny tans and golden browns—the standard colors, by the way, of the Akhal-Teke horse.

We had been under way only for twenty minutes when Professor Shammakov looked up at me with a slightly anxious expression, as if he had forgotten until now to say something important, delicate, almost of a personal nature. He said it in English: "I vant drrrink grrreen tea. You like drrink grreen tea? Zis no is vodka."

"*Konyechno,*" I found myself saying, the way Guvanch Djumaev said it: with a positive-sounding thump.

The professor beamed, and whatever ice there was between us was broken. The way to a Turkmen's esteem is through his teapot. Professor Shammakov had brought his own, plus a glass jar of loose tea leaves. He went out into the corridor and boiled water on a Rube Goldberg contraption of pipes, tanks, spouts, and levers next to the car porter's compartment, which served as a public samovar for the entire car. In a few minutes he poured the hot water into elegant old glasses held in the traditional pewter or silver plate holders apparently provided by the railroad. We drank our tea with some of my raisins substituting for the traditional Turkmen sweet.

The professor smacked his lips and drained his glass. He said it was the best medicine for his high blood pressure, and anything else that ails you. I said I was drinking it to cure a hangover from the wedding I had been to, and Professor Shammakov assured me that it was also the best thing for any stomach problems. It was getting stifling on board the Turkmenistan Express, but the hot tea made us sweat and kept us alive.

While we drank the tea and gazed at the desert, I told the professor the story of picking up the turtle in the street outside the agricultural institute. I described the animal's coloration, and Shammakov immediately identified it as the common Central Asian turtle, *Testudo horsfieldi.* He described its strange life to me. For ten months of the year, the turtle remains in a state of torpidity under the sands. Then in spring it becomes active, digs its way up to the surface, feeds like mad, digs its nest, and lays three to five eggs, which produce young turtles in sixty to seventy days. Then the baby turtles lie torpid for ten months before surfacing to see the world for the first time. Professor Shammakov said the turtles live for many years—perhaps as many as one hundred if they don't get run over trying to cross the road in downtown Ashkhabad—though as for living, it seemed to me an animal that only crawls above ground for two months of the year hardly has a life at all, at least by luxurious mammalian standards. I couldn't imagine having to spend all that precious time lying dormant underground just because of the climate. I learned that they don't even have a friend to get torpid with.

"This is life of desert," said Professor Shammakov proudly, and no one knew better than he. He had been studying the biology of the Turkmenian desert for more than thirty years, working on his magnum opus, *The Reptiles of Turkmenistan*. He had personally collected seventy-nine species of indigenous reptiles—three turtles, twenty-nine snakes, and forty-seven lizards—plotted their distribution, and kept records on their populations.

"In the course of thirty years, I worked too hard. Now high blood pressure." He shrugged, then added in English, "Professor vant drrink grreen tea. Professor vant study of foreign language. Study of foreign language is greatly developed in our country. Vat does zis mean?"

He had memorized the sentence in an English course he had taken at the Turkmen Academy of Sciences where he worked, but hadn't the foggiest idea what it meant. We agreed I would be his professor of English, and he my professor of the desert.

"During course of thirty year, I worrk-ed my book."

"I have worked on my book for thirty years," I corrected.

"Turkmenistan have forty-eight thousand square kilometer."

"Turkmenistan has four hundred eighty thousand square kilometers."

"What karakul sheep eat, pleash?"

"Sheep eat grass."

"Vite down dis vord, pleash."

"With pleasure," and I did so.

We drank another pot of tea. The truck farms became cotton fields. Masses of red poppies, tiny yellow chamomile, and a small purple wildflower I didn't know lined the tracks, spreading in paisley splashes to the plains beyond. In the distance, oil and gas derricks pricked up between blotches of white sand.

We drank another pot, and Professor Shammakov's mood improved. "Dis wery gut fixation, study oder languages," he said. "After many days I know you many vort."

"After a few days, I will know many words. I will increase my vocabulary. You see?"

"Vat does zis mean, pleash—incrrease?"

"To become larger. To get bigger."

"Yes! Understand! Incrrease range efe snake, from Kopet-Dag Mountains to Kara Kum Desert."

"Exactly. Excellent, Professor! I think that after a few days you will speak English better than I speak Russian."

"I sink after many day, we will drrrink many grrreen tea!"

Every hour or so we passed a small *aul,* or village, walled with unpainted bricks, etched crisply in the searing sun. None had a single shade tree, grape vine, or palm. These walls, never more than five or six feet high, were not built to keep out human enemies. Perhaps a hundred years ago they could have deterred a raiding foe mounted on horses. Now they stood solely to keep out the winds. The corrugated or brick roofs of the crude huts within were to keep off the sun. There were no people in the streets, if indeed these *auls* had streets. The population was hiding inside their mud huts, seeking relief from the terrible sun and stinging sands. In the West we have long been used to the notion that humankind's war against nature is essentially over, and that except for hurricanes, floods, earthquakes, and the like, we humans have won. But here the people were pinned inside their dark bunkers by the elements without mercy. On the attack for three millennia, nature had fought humankind to a standoff, sweeping all but the most hardened herders off the surface of the Earth. Every human resource and action—from the architecture and making of bricks to the domestication and breeding of desert-fortified animals to the daily hours of work and rest—was marshaled for survival against the relentless onslaught of nature. It was impossible to see these settlements without thinking back to the times of the Great Silk Road, for the Turkmen were still fighting for survival with the weapons of those centuries. Modern technology had made no inroads other than the railroad itself. Under siege by the desert, they were waiting for the eighteenth century—the Age of Enlightenment and industrial progress—to arrive and save them.

Sometimes the train stopped at the larger *auls*, and poor folk descended, dragging their luggage and parcels of radishes and green onions along the concrete platforms while fresh replacements with equally bedraggled effects boarded. After reaching the Amu Darya, the Turkmenistan Express would swing north and head all the way to Moscow.

We drank another pot of green tea as the train rocked on across the Kara Kum. It was really a good old train, and riding it was like making love to an older woman. Some of the sparks and heat might have cooled, but the motion comforted the soul and the accommodations were quite ample. Then the cotton fields became less continuous, the canal disappeared, the mountains moved farther away, and the train started to bear east. Grasses and small herbaceous shrubs took over in spring profusion, and with them the herders. Flocks of karakul sheep appeared every few miles as black specks in a sea of chalky green springing up from the desert floor. Professor Shammakov explained that this variety of sheep, little changed by humans from the original wild breed native to Central Asia, carried a special bag of fat under its tail in order to survive the lean months when little fresh fodder was available.

"Good day. Good noon. Good evening. Good luck. I speak English nice."

"No, Professor, you speak English well."

It was early afternoon when Professor Shammakov told me that we were pulling into the town of Tedzhen. I wished to see the river, so we stepped out of our compartment and leaned against the windows in the corridor. There was a pretty young Turkmen woman, maybe twenty years old, in a blue cotton dress at the next window. For all the world, she looked black Irish with light blue eyes, jet black hair, pale white skin, and full lips. I thought there was no way she could come from the same ethnic stock as the swarthy professor. Our eyes met, and I was surprised to find hers holding our mutual gaze, Western girlish modesty being unknown in Central Asia. She asked the professor in Turkmen where I was from. When he informed her I was an American, she was suddenly awestruck and speechless. She had never seen an American before and was obviously taken by surprise and momentarily scared out of her wits. But she held her ground and didn't run away, her eyes coursing hungrily over me, as if her passionate curiosity would consume me head to toe. I asked in Russian where she was from, but Professor Shammakov interpreted because evidently she didn't speak Russian.

"She is girl from Tedzhen," said Shammakov.

"Please tell her she looks Irish, Professor."

Shammakov interpreted, and the girl smiled. Although she probably had no idea what Ireland was, she must have realized I was paying her a compliment.

When the train came to a halt at the Tedzhen station the girl gathered her belongings and got off. As she walked away across the platform, she put down the bags she was carrying in each hand and turned back to wave shyly. I waved, too. She turned away again, and passed through a jagged hole in the concrete retaining wall of the platform, then across a vacant, dusty field. Every twenty or twenty-five yards she would stop, put her bags down, look back to see if I was still there, and wave. She was walking away into the perspective. Her waves got broader as she got smaller until finally she appeared only as a tiny waving blue reed at the horizon. Then she disappeared into a town I had never heard of before and would never know, but would remember forever for this unexpected human gesture between strangers from opposite sides of the world.

The Turkmenistan Express pulled out.

"So pretty girl from Tedzhen?" The professor smiled like a froggie that had just eaten an exceptionally delicious fly on a warm summer evening. We were out in the corridor, leaning against the windows to let the other passengers get by.

"The pretty girl is from Tedzhen," I corrected him.

Momentarily I regretted not following her into the perspective, not jumping off the train and dashing after her. We were passing a three-story wooden lookout tower next to the tracks. It must have been a hundred years old, built around the same time the Russians had built this railway through Central Asia, and taken over all trade in the region, which was their prime purpose in conquering the Turkmen tribes. The windowless tower had a military cast to it.

If only I could have found out her name. What then? Nothing.

"But, Professor, where's the Tedzhen River?"

Shammakov gestured with his hand again. "Pleash."

The Tedzhen River was here, on the other side of town. We crossed it on an old steel bridge like those you sometimes see when coming into old industrial towns in America on passenger trains. The river was only thirty feet across, a sluggish, shrunken, sickly khaki green.

"Kara Kum Desert eat rivers," said Professor Shammakov. He explained in Russian that all the rivers flowing out of the Kopet-Dag Mountains die out in the desert sands. Surely he thought it must be due to removing water for irrigation.

I went back into the compartment and brought my map out to the corridor to study the course of the Tedzhen River and find out when we would cross the next river. Just as I unfolded the map and located the tiny Tedzhen, a Red Army officer in uniform lumbered down the corridor. He was middle-aged, tall, and blond, carrying a black briefcase under his arm. When he got close enough to see the map, he stopped dead in his tracks. His eyes bulged, first with disbelief, then with rage, and the hateful look he gave me stopped conversation in the car. People came out into the corridor to see what all the silence was about.

"Who is this person?" the officer asked Professor Shammakov in the voice of authority. Shammakov's head receded quickly into his neck. I would have preferred that he look like a snake, snap his head back, and hiss.

Then began a half hour of wrangling during which the officer called out the train conductor and demanded to know how a foreign passenger had been permitted to board the Turkmenistan Express with a map of the frontier region. The officer obviously hadn't been glasnostized. The conductor, an obsequious little man in a uniform and hat two sizes too large, who collected tickets and handed out glasses for tea, had nothing to say. This meant the officer could upbraid him, me, and Professor Shammakov. I tried to stay out of it, but I got the gist. The officer repeated endlessly how he was walking down the corridor when he suddenly apprehended this foreigner breaking Soviet law. Didn't the conductor and Shammakov realize it was strictly forbidden to possess such a map (which I had purchased in a bookstore in Munich six months ago)? He demanded that the conductor ask for my papers. He demanded a full investigation of this serious breach of Soviet law. He demanded an explanation from Professor Shammakov. He demanded that the conductor take the map away from me. I was half afraid he would demand that I be put off the train.

To make matters worse, at precisely this moment the train actually passed a detachment of Red Army troops sidetracked with their armored personnel carriers and tanks equipped with howitzers. They must have been en route back from Afghanistan. It seemed I couldn't avoid spying no matter what I did. If they were going to throw me off the train, I wished it had happened in Tedzhen. At least I sort of knew somebody there.

The conductor was too perplexed to do anything. Shammakov took a low-key approach; his health wasn't up to contradicting the officer. On and on it went until finally I simply folded up my map, and without a word reentered the compartment, shut the door behind me, and sat down by the window. It worked. A few moments later, Professor Shammakov entered and nodded twice with his eyes lifted toward heaven, as if to say, "Thanks be to Allah, the incident is settled." Then we both nodded out. An hour or so later, the train's halt in Mary shook me awake.

"This professor home," said Shammakov. "When was child, professor play in sands of Mary." He pointed out the window to the sands, for we had not yet reached the station. Then his amphibious eyes kindled with mammalian warmth for the first time. A man in a brown sheepskin hat was leading a string of camels alongside the tracks.

"Distribooshun of dromedary is in Turkmenistan, Uzbekistan, middle Asia, Iran, Afghan, Saudi Arabia, Algeria."

"*Otlichno,* Professor!"

"Distribooshun of two-hump camel in Kazakhstan, Mongolia, western China."

When the train stopped, we climbed down and strolled the bustling platform, looking for the professor's nephew, who was supposed to meet him. It had been so hot inside the train that I was sure we would get a breath of fresh air outside. On the contrary, it was even worse. I couldn't believe the heat. I had never experienced anything remotely like it. You could feel your uncovered skin burning like a slice of white bread in a toaster. Even though there was no humidity, I was pouring sweat. People scurried from the shade of the steel cantilevered station to get to the boarding steps of the train. The movement on the platform resembled what you see when you uncover an ant's nest with your foot.

Professor Shammakov finally found his nephew, and a good thing, too, because he had brought the professor a plastic bag of provisions for our expedition to Repetek. He had three flashing gold teeth. I didn't catch his name. We went under the cantilever to check out the provisions. He had brought Shammakov red radishes, green onions, two round loaves of *cherek,* and a clear plastic bag of *kissloe,* a dairy concoction made from curdled sheep's milk. Shammakov offered me some. It tasted like unflavored yogurt with the texture of cottage cheese. It was probably just the right thing to eat for stomach disorders; however, for someone with high blood pressure it was probably like taking slow poison. But this was the professor's comfort food, and he seemed comforted by it.

The train pulled out of Mary alongside a huge old cotton mill, like the dilapidated gins still to be found in Mississippi and Alabama. The Murgab River was the same color as the Tedzhen, but almost completely stagnant—dammed either fore or aft of the railway to make a reservoir. Mary has some of the best archaeological artifacts in Central Asia, but they are spread over several sites as the city was built, added onto, and rebuilt repeatedly during centuries of various dynasties and continual warfare. By studying the dreadfully translated booklet on the Silk Road that Sasha Skorokhodov had given me as a going-away present, I was able to figure out a thumbnail chronology.

At the time of Alexander's march, the lands along the Murgh Ab, or River of Birds, were known generally as Margiana—i.e., the margin of the known world. The Seleucid dynasty built the city of Antioch under Hellenic influence in the century after Alexander. King Antiochus Soter, "being striked by the land fertility of Margian" (*sic*) ordered a 250-kilometer contoured wall constructed with four gates. Highways cut the city from north to south and east to west.

Merv was founded next, its vast suburbs spilling out from the defensive wall left by the Seleucids. The Sasanid period was marked by religious tolerance because, in addition to the official state Zoroastrian necropolis, the Sasanids left behind in Merv Christian temples with wide staircases and Buddhist temples with large clay statues of the Buddha. By the sixth and seventh centuries, numerous fortified country seats like the castles of feudal Europe were built, with walls up to forty-five feet in height. Then came the conquest of Merv by Islam, and rule by the Arabian caliphate. Merv reached its height in the eleventh and twelfth centuries under the Muslim Seljuq dynasty, when the city occupied the crossroads of the northern and southern caravan routes and considerably exceeded in size not only the Near East cities of Damascus and Jerusalem, but such European cities as Paris and Milan. As the booklet put it, "Splendid erections—mosques, *madrasahs* [universities], libraries, mausoleums, palaces, and rich townhouses—adorned Merv at this period." The Madjan Canal crossed Merv from south to north, supplying the entire city with plenty of water from brick overflows.

From the windows of the Turkmenistan Express, I managed only a fleeting glimpse of the mausoleum of the Seljuq Sultan Sandjar (1118–1157). It is the most remarkable architectural work of Central Asia's medieval period, when Merv was called "the jewel of the sands, the pleasure city of the Shahs" by Arabic travelers. The mausoleum of Sultan Sandjar stood off by itself a mile or so from the railroad tracks, a sandstone tower at least one hundred feet high, with a dome shorn of its original tiles. Nothing could be more impressive and spooky than this priapic monument standing naked against the cloudless desert sky, and no work of human hands could better symbolize the terrible calamity that followed soon after its construction.

It was less than a hundred years after Sultan Sandjar's death when Genghis Khan's youngest son Tului entered Persia in pursuit of the Khwarizm shah's son, Jalal-ad-Din. After a furious twenty-two-day seige outside the walls of Merv, during which the Mongols employed their Chinese engineers to build an earth embankment against the city's ramparts, Tului sent word to Merv's governor Merik that surrender would save his life. He invited Merik and his intimates to dine in the Mongol tents, then asked for a list of the six hundred richest men in the city. The governor and his friends obediently wrote down the list. Then, in front of the horrified Merik's eyes, the Mongols strangled his companions. The six hundred rich men were taken from the city and put under guard, and the Mongols entered the streets of Merv. The inhabitants were ordered out onto the plains. The evacuation took four days while Tului sat on a gilded dais, singling out military leaders, who were immediately decapitated. The men, women, and children were separated and handed over to Mongol soldiers, who raped, strangled, and slashed to death all but the four hundred craftsmen Tului wanted for rebuilding the city as a Mongol fortress. The six hundred rich men were tortured till they gave up their treasures, then done away with. The vacated dwellings were put to the torch, the irrigation system completely destroyed, and the walls of Merv razed. The only survivors were some five thousand devout Muslims who had hidden in cellars: The Mongols returned and hunted them down, and Merv was left empty of human life.

Only the mausoleum of Sultan Sandjar remains, in a sea of sand no longer watered by the great irrigation works along the Murgab. The jewel of Islam had been turned into the lifeless waste one can still view from the windows of the Turkmenistan Express eight hundred years later.

We reached Repetek at 6:00 P.M., unloaded our packs and provisions, and started to walk along the sand lane beside the railroad tracks to the biological research station. It was only a ten-minute walk past the end of the *aul,* but it felt as if we had entered an experiment in solar power. The station was rudimentary—a few bungalows to house visiting researchers, a shower room with huge, strange red lights, and a stinking outhouse. Sand dunes spread in every direction.

Except for the toilet and the red-light shower room, you could probably accomplish the same research half a mile out of Ashkhabad. The famous Repetek—a world biosphere site anointed by the United Nations—was like practically everything else I had officially seen in the USSR, a place to show foreigners. In czarist times, de Custine had called this Russian effort to display a pleasing façade to foreigners the "conspiracy of smiles." Nevertheless, there was nothing phony about this ecological specimen of pure sand desert, the result of the colossal drying out of the inland sea that once covered the Eurasian steppes.

The American zoologists hadn't arrived yet; they were supposedly coming by rail from Bukhara in the other direction. Only four Soviet doctors from Novosibirsk and an eccentric Indian moth hunter in a turban were working at the site. The moth man had set up a sheet with a flashlight behind it to attract moths for collection right outside his bungalow. The four doctors in shorts and sandals were drinking vodka and smoking cigarettes, watching the Indian. Their work seemed indefinably different from a camping vacation.

The professor and I put our gear in the third bungalow and followed the path to the house of the director of the *zapovednik,* who wasn't in. Outside his house, on a wooden platform with a carpet made for dining, lay a great fat court eunuch of a man, flat on his back with his legs splayed, sound asleep with a piece of newspaper over his head to keep the flies and sun off. Professor Shammakov knelt and woke him up, whereupon he lurched into an upright position, screwed up his eyes, and looked about him in a most unfriendly manner. He was completely hairless on top, with a fat, round, stupid, angry face, which reinforced my impression of a court eunuch from the Arabian Nights who waits with his scimitar to lop off the heads of anyone who gets out of line with the pasha. For a moment I was worried lest he grab poor little amphibious Professor Shammakov by the gills and chop off his legs for dinner. However, he took my letter of introduction from Professor Sopiev and said he would give it to the director. The professor seemed to think all would be well arranged for me when the director came back. He gave a satisfied nod, and said, "Now make grreen tea?"

"*Konyechno!*"

The bungalow had an electric kettle and porcelain cups, which delighted the professor.

The sun was sinking low. After tea, we walked behind the station for a quarter of a mile or so into the beautiful rippled dunes. The sands were crisscrossed by ribbons and tracks in minimalist patterns, memories of the insects, lizards, and snakes that had crawled by that day. They would be gone overnight.

With the sunset it had begun to cool down. We followed a snake track into a small arroyo until it disappeared under some scrub bushes, then came to a rise, and sat on the sand ridge, listening and watching the night come on. In the twilight, small bats and nighthawks were out flying low over the sands to catch insects. Their agile turns and dips among the contours of the dunes were a pleasure to see.

Professor Shammakov sighed. "Professor love life of desert."

The stars emerged swiftly. A few electric lights from Repetek winked on. An owl hooted, throwing its voice to appear as if it came from several locations. A herd of sheep bleated from the *aul*. Dogs barked. A speeding train pounded through, shaking the earth with Soviet power.

Shammakov gazed at the dusk with regret, and said, "Ah, Professor love life of desert. Not life of city."

Next morning we rose two hours before dawn and went into the field before it became too hot. The American zoologists had arrived during the night—Julian, Ray, and Steve, along with their keepers, two English-speaking Moscow zoologists who managed to look like fit, bearded outdoorsmen and emaciated Moscow intellectuals at the same time. My fellow countrymen had come stupendously overequipped for the expedition, with lightweight field glasses and Japanese cameras, featherweight jogging shoes, breathing cotton clothing, a charcoal-filtered water purifier, and pith helmets with solar-powered fans. It was a moving demonstration of superior American technology.

We hiked a couple of kilometers past the *aul,* keeping parallel to the railway, though there was little need to worry about getting lost. As soon as it became light, you could see 360 degrees from the top of any sand dune. In a landscape marked only by limitless undulations of sand, I found myself missing the sight of the mountains. Mountains, like streams and greenery, soften and beautify nature, making them places of life. In the middle of a sand desert, as in the middle of the ocean, nature is harsh, silent, desolate, as uncontrollable as death itself.

The Americans turned out to be excellent field naturalists and good companions. They stopped to examine every wildflower and herb, as eager as Boy Scouts to explore the Kara Kum. One of them, Steve, was an obsessional herp man. He and Professor Shammakov had a wonderful time together, chasing down snakes and sneaking up on lizards to seize them bare-handed. They even caught a tortoise, the same species as I had saved in Ashkhabad, but Steve refused to pick it up, because, he said, the tortoise's short season above ground is so attenuated that even a five-minute examination by a human could mean the difference between survival and death.

What a fierceness was revealed as the sun climbed the cloudless sky. What an absence of succor, comity, nurturing tolerance. Here were nature's true savages, the ones with teeth, talons, venom, armor. The predominant tree, the saxaul, looked like a dead stump in full leaf, its leaves so narrow and mean that they cast no shadow on the ground. By an hour after dawn, the spiders, scorpions, beetles, and worms were busily digging foxholes to escape the coming heat of the day. The temperature went up thirty degrees Fahrenheit in two hours, and the air became so dry that it seemed to lack any smell.

Although it was spring, the festive season of bird courtship and mammalian birth, we saw none of Turkmenistan's indigenous warm bloods: no wild asses, no goitered gazelles, no larks. There was no time for such frivolous beings. The desert is not merely for killers, but for well-disciplined, hard-working, never-take-a-minute-off killers. What use is home and family in the shifting sands? After a hard day's night, none of it is there anymore for the desert winds have blown your sand castle miles away. Your children have been eaten by a swaggering monitor. Your wife has run off with another scorpion. All you've had to eat is a noxious millipede, and you're too tired to start life over again. Better to be on one's own. Who needs others, anyway? What good is affection or friendship? Where do they get you?

By ten o'clock, it felt like walking through the Book of Job. Is it any coincidence that desert prophets fill the world's angry religions? Can any care but redemption fill the soul of the desert dweller?

"I've always wanted to catch one of these," said Steve, holding up a thin green-brown snake about two feet long. I noticed he didn't worry about upsetting the snake's schedule. "Would you mind taking a picture?"

"Konyechno!" I found myself saying in Guvanch-tinged Russian.

Ray explained the narrow leaves of the saxaul trees: They lose less water that way. Desert plants have various strategies for overcoming drought. Some have thick leaves with thick cell walls, which prevent penetration of the aridity. One plant has small air sacs or bubbles on the underside of its leaves. It fills them with water at night and sips them by day. But none of this solves the problem of shifting sands. For this, the shrubs and trees have elaborated a catalog of different root systems. Some plunge straight down for a hundred feet, others stretch out for a hundred meters, or they grow in communities of root networks, new members growing from accessory shoots.

By late morning there wasn't a scrap of shadow anywhere. The sunlight was perfectly relentless; and our thermometers recorded 125 degrees Fahrenheit. We headed back to the station. It was then that I saw a pair of sparrows flitting about in the scrub. I stayed to watch them while the others went on.

They were the first birds I had seen all morning, and the sight of them returned to me a modicum of energy and enthusiasm. I followed them through the scrub, watching them with my field glasses. They were only a pair of common sparrows—the kind that raise the kids, pay the taxes, and play by the rules. They were a kind of dusky brown and black with a touch of chalky bluish-white—nothing special in the bird world of outrageous cross dressers and feathered mandarins. Yet as I watched, these two ordinary birds chased through the trees in a mating game lovely to see in the Kara Kum. The male swooped up into the air to catch an insect, and then looked for his girlfriend to pass her the morsel. While she ate, he perched next to her on the branch, shaking his feathers with seductive pleasure, then flew off again to find her another present.

I flopped down in the bunkhouse, roasted by six hours of direct exposure to the desert sun. At the shimmering edge of consciousness, armored lizards were crunching down armored beetles. I had only just dropped off to sleep when Professor Shammakov came to say the director wanted a word with me.

By now the director would have read my letter of introduction from Professor Sopiev, and I expected he or she simply wished to welcome me formally to the desert research institute. I threw on a T-shirt, and we walked the short path from the bunkhouse to the administration building. It was an elegant old building, probably dating from the 1950s, built in the comfortable Russian colloquial style that went back a hundred years before that. It had a wide front porch with ample half columns. I was shown into a high-ceilinged office like an old rural school principal's office, paneled with painted boards. In the corner stood an old-fashioned cylindrical coal-burning stove made of green metal that went from floor to ceiling.

At a desk along the side of the room, a heavyset woman in a lavender dress offered me a seat beside her. Her hair was so orange that it was almost purple, and was stuck to the sides of her head with some kind of perfumed lard. When she opened her mouth, I saw two terrifying rows of gold teeth.

"Who are you?" was her first question. Her mouth appeared to vibrate when she spoke.

"Why are you here?" was her second question. She did not leave any room to answer in between.

Over the desk was a wall map of Turkmenistan. Above the map—what else—a portrait of Lenin. I was glad to see the Number One Comrade portrayed in a nice camel's hair coat for a change, looking more like a smoothy from old Harlem than a dangerous radical. Above him was written the slogan MAN BELONGS TO EARTH.

How fatuous, I thought. What was it supposed to mean? It could be a truism, a cliché, a nationalist slogan, or even the kernel of a wise insight into humanity's relation to nature. Or it could be the fortune in a Soviet fortune cookie. Like water, it could fill any shaped vessel of linguistic usage. Behind such banalities lay the heart of human corruption and the root of evil. But was it any worse, really, than the West's slogan, EARTH BELONGS TO YOU AND ME?

"Your documents?" was her third question.

This startled me. No one expects an interrogation at a nature refuge. But if I had done something wrong, I couldn't take it very seriously. Now Madame Commissar sat kind of sidesaddle next to me, facing the wall. With her flaming orange hair and sharp gold teeth, she looked like a villain from a James Bond movie. Having studied my passport and visa for several minutes, she swiveled her chair toward me and explained in a bureaucratic monotone that she would now proceed to write out criminal charges against me, as I had broken the laws of immigration and registration of the Union of Soviet Socialist Republics.

"The what? Look, I'm sure you're making a big mistake," I said. "I'm an American. Here's my passport. Here's my visa. I'm a member of an American delegation visiting Ashkhabad."

"But you are not in Ashkhabad Oblast; you are in Chardzhou Oblast. That is precisely the law you have broken. Why?"

"Haven't you received the letter of introduction I delivered yesterday from Professor Sopiev of the Agricultural Institute in the Name of M. I. Kalinin to the directorate of the Repetek *Zapovednik*?"

"We have received no such letter."

That Commie eunuch lying on the slab yesterday had neglected to deliver my letter of introduction. Little wonder the authorities wanted to know who I was. I blamed myself first; I should have bribed the eunuch, or held on to the letter from Sopiev in order to present it at the appropriate time—which seemed to be now, unfortunately.

"I will ask questions now," said Madame Commissar—and she wasn't kidding. She picked up her pen and began to fill out the forms of the legal complaint in longhand. This took about two hours. There must have been forty or fifty questions, including a full family history on both sides going back for two generations.

At this point I immediately claimed I didn't know any Russian, and I answered only in English, trying to be as unhelpful as possible in the hope Madame Commissar would see how silly this arrest was. "Now if I remember right, my granddaddy on my mother's side was born in, let me see, was it 1870 or 1780?"

But you couldn't pull the wool over the eyes of Madame Commissar. She saw on my passport that my surname was Russian; Maslow, or *maslo,* actually means "butter"—probably the name of some cow keepers originally. She cleverly started to repeat questions at intervals, as if to trip me up.

"Where born?"

"I already told you. Long Branch, New Jersey, though I grew up in Belmar."

"In Soviet Union?"

"No, ma'am. Belmar is in New Jersey. And New Jersey is not in the Soviet Union. It's in the U.S.A."

After more than an hour of struggling to understand my answers and write them down, Madame Commissar's eyes hurt so much that she had to stop interrogating me and rest for a few minutes. It was during this time that I found out her name was Serebryakova, Serafima Vacilyevna, and that she was indeed a commissar for OVIR, the state agency responsible for tracking every foreigner's whereabouts and enforcing the visa laws. Such laws seemed particularly ludicrous in the middle of the desert, border or no border. Wasn't it just these sorts of restrictive laws against free movement that made the Mongol nomads of Genghis Khan's day implacable enemies of the Chinese and all other settled peoples? Didn't the Mongols despise all settled peoples and hate the rulers of unified states from China clear across the steppes to Persia? They saw with their own eyes how settlement led inexorably to the privatization of lands, to the end of freedom of movement, thus to enslavement of the multitudes by an elite.

Maybe the barbarians had a point.

When Madame Commissar finally completed the criminal charges against me, I refused to sign them.

"No understanding. No lawyer. No signature," I told her in Russian. "Where is Professor Sopiev's letter to the director? I tell you again, that letter will answer your questions concerning me."

Madame Commissar conferred with another official, a timid, knife-faced man in a militia uniform. These were not exactly the tough, ruthless agents of totalitarianism you come to expect from Cold War movies. But after another half hour of rigmarole, it seemed Professor Sopiev's letter had disappeared.

"I will go get Professor Shammakov, whom I came with by train from Ashkhabad," I said. "He will tell you how I came to be here. He's right outside, I think."

"For the moment you are under my custody," said Madame Commissar. "You may not leave the building."

"Well, then, we'll sit here all day." I was determined to hang tough. "I'm not going to sign a document I can't read, and that's that."

The legal charges against me, as much as I could understand, were not serious. I'd entered the Chardzhou Oblast without something called a *razreshenie,* and I had not registered at the OVIR office in Ashkhabad, as all new foreign arrivals were required to do. I sniffed the dead hand of Djura Semedov behind this whole contretemps; surely he knew the registration requirements for foreign visitors.

"You are Russian by birth, correct?" Madame Commissar returned to her favorite theme.

"Nyet! Amerikanski!" I ratcheted up my voice. "Born in the U.S.A."

"And what are you by profession?"

"I'm a writer, a journalist. I have already told you this."

"A writer"—she screwed up her eyes as if she'd finally trapped me—"or a journalist? Before, you said you were writer. Now you say journalist."

"What is the difference? In case I choose to write about my arrest and interrogation here this afternoon, who would believe me? In this world, you do not need to invent anything to become a writer. A writer is just a journalist without a job."

Madame Commissar banged her whole forearm on the table in front of me and bared her gold teeth. "A writer and a journalist are not the same profession," she insisted.

"You win," I told her. In an interrogation, thoughtfulness must always appear as a sign of guilt to the interrogator, the point at which your story has broken down and you are left without words.

She continued, "And where were you born—really born?"

"What means this 'really'?" I asked her.

My trials were not half over. Once the indictment had been drawn up, we moved down the hall to the director's office for my speedy trial and swift injustice. It took another hour and a half. They had to go over most of the same information yet again. Since I could not imagine that my crimes would be viewed seriously (except perhaps in wartime in the country of the enemy, which was not the case here) I was not so much scared as exasperated. There was a familiar inevitability about the whole process: It was like getting caught red-handed by the local sheriff in a small-town speed trap on a Sunday night; you knew you should have never got off the interstate; you knew you were going to have to pay a big fine; you just wanted to get it over with and get back on the road.

I now had three inquisitors—Madame Commissar, the timid militiaman, and the director of the *zapovednik,* a dark-skinned Turkmen official face who seemed neither friendly nor hostile, neither interested nor uninterested. The two men were happy to let Madame Commissar run the show.

"What is purpose of your visit to Repetek?" she asked again.

"I have told you repeatedly, to observe the wildlife of the desert." I tried again to speak Russian, though I was so fatigued I must have made a hundred mistakes per sentence and sounded like a moron.

"Why you failed to register at OVIR in Ashkhabad?"

"No one informed me I must register. I am a member of an American delegation. The delegation members were never told to register."

"Who is your host in Ashkhabad?"

"Turkmen Friendship Society. Director's name, Djura Semedov." I insisted they note his name down on the bill of indictment. I spelled it out for them. I had gone into the desert essentially on Djura's say-so. Perhaps I had been too eager to get out of Ashkhabad, and Djura, hunting from a stand, had less trouble than he thought he would picking me off. He had gotten the carrot in the form of the Polaroid film, and I had gotten the shaft. There was something especially soporific about this second interrogation. It seemed to be happening in a slow-motion dream. It was like having your teeth drilled by a dentist in the old days, with a whining old drill, the slow speed adding to the pain. The botflies in the stagnant air seemed to float, and to remain for a long time when they landed.

I no longer tried to persuade my interrogators that my crimes against the state were simply the innocent mistakes of a foreigner. I didn't try to say that I had been misinformed by my host. I did not apologize, or say I did not mean to break any Soviet laws, only to see the Kara Kum Desert. I did not even try to convince them that EARTH BELONGS TO MAN. I simply could no longer find the words in Russian, and to babble in English was a waste of time. I lapsed into lethargic silence.

At length they prepared a protocol; I also refused to sign this document. "I do not know what it says. Perhaps I am giving approval for you to send me to concentration camp?"

All three were truly horrified at this suggestion. They could see no connection between this procedure and Stalin's gulag. They conferred, and decided to call in Sergei, the English-speaking Moscow zookeeper accompanying the American zoologists at Repetek. When he arrived, they asked him to translate the protocol to me in English.

If nothing else, I thought, I'll learn some new Russian vocabulary.

"Sorry, Jon," he apologized to me before he began.

"It's all right, Sergei, I understand your position. It's not your fault."

The document repeated that I had broken two Soviet regulations— they weren't called laws—crossing into the Chardzhou Oblast without the *razreshenie,* and not registering with OVIR. By breaking these two regulations, however, I had explicitly violated the terms of my visa to the Soviet Union.

"How could I have known that?" I interrupted Sergei.

He asked them. Madame Commissar said the rules were printed on the back of my visa. I took it out of my passport, unfolded it, and turned it over. Sure enough, there were about a hundred lines of fine print in Russian. Madame Commissar went on to explain, through Sergei, that I wasn't supposed to leave the cities the visa was issued to: Ashkhabad and Bukhara. In consequence, under the terms of the protocol, I would agree to return immediately to Ashkhabad and to register with OVIR.

I asked Sergei to interpret. "Look," I said, "this is not a matter of my refusing to follow Soviet laws. There has been a mistake, not a crime. I do not even know what a *razreshenie* is. It means 'destruction'? Like physical destruction? Demolition of a building, for example?"

"No," said Sergei, without waiting for the commissars to reply. "That is *razrushenie*. It is a different word. This is *razreshenie*. It means a special permit required for internal travel."

"No wonder!" I exclaimed. "No wonder I could not figure out what Madame Commissar was talking about!" I turned and flashed her a smile and said, "Forgive mistakes of me in tongue. I already study Russian language one and one half year only."

When Madame Commissar heard this subtle plea for leniency, her big mouth flapped open like a hippopotamus yawning, and I had an excellent opportunity to study all those gold teeth again. The two bottom front teeth were the only white ones in her mouth. I think she was laughing. She pounded on the table, but only with her fist this time, and said cheerfully, "Ten years back, we would seize you and immediately put on plane out of country for what you did."

A hundred years ago they threw foreigners caught traveling in the old khanate of Bukhara without permission off the tower of death into a pit full of Asian cobras. Fitzroy Maclean, a British diplomat who wrote a memoir, actually saw this tower when he visited Bukhara in the 1930s. This was why the Hungarian adventurer Ármin Vámbéry, from whom we have one of the few reports on Central Asia in the nineteenth century, traveled disguised as a Muslim dervish. I suppose there was some good news to report. Times have changed even in the Kara Kum Desert. Humanity has progressed! Not civilization yet, of course, but clearly in the upper ranges of barbarism.

At length I decided it was better to sign the protocol and return to Ashkhabad than continue the standoff. I had no leverage, no power, and nothing to bribe them with because my good trade items had all been left back in the city. I also did not want to kill sickly Professor Shammakov, or get him into trouble on my account. Besides, there were no horses out here whatsoever, and no point in my staying. This was strictly camel country; I'd had enough of it.

As soon as I signed, everyone relaxed. I thought for a minute they would serve me green tea or butcher the fatted calf in my honor. Madame Commissar sat back in her chair as if she had just achieved orgasm and said, "So how do you like the nature of Repetek desert refuge?"

"I saw half a day," I told her. "Insufficient time to construct opinion."

"Oh, then you ought to return to us as guest," said Madame Commissar.

"Another time, maybe. I can go now?"

I trudged back the short path to the bunkhouse in a black funk. It was the middle of the afternoon, and withering hot. All activity had ceased; everything that could go underground was down there already. Professor Shammakov shared my low mood. He had sat in on the second part of my criminal proceedings, subdued, sickly, and silent. They had not asked him any questions, and he had not volunteered. I had sensed only the spiritual fatigue of an elderly toad from the corner in which the professor sat, but only now it struck me with particular force what he had been croaking about on the evening before as we sat on the neatly windblown sand ridges above Repetek watching the bats dart near the ground while the red fireball of sun set over the desert.

Professor Shammakov had said, "I have studied snakes all my life because I want to be left alone."

In the office during my trial he had seemed a shriveled, weary old toad, as if the snakes had been hunting him. I, on the other hand, felt as if I had been cantering along nicely when my horse had suddenly halted, tumbling me over his head so that I landed with the wind knocked out of me. I had cased the settlement when we arrived the day before, and the chances of escape were low to nil. The whole place consisted of a hundred or so dirty hovels and the desert institute headquarters, surrounded by who knew how many miles of sand dunes with saxaul trees. To go out there on foot without supplies or water was certain death. There were no ridable mammals of any sort around, let alone a road. Although plenty of other trains had gone slamming through during the twenty hours or so since our arrival, no others had stopped. I suspected that a passenger train stopped at Repetek only once a day in each direction. Since my sentence was to immediately return to Ashkhabad, and there was no other way out of town, there was nothing more to struggle against. *Que sera sera*, I told myself. I was considering how to put this phrase into Russian when I suddenly became so weak and insubstantial that I could hardly move my legs forward.

When we reached the bunkhouse, I slumped down on the stoop. The professor looked at me, and recommended, "Drrrrink grrrreen tea?"

"*Pazhaluista*, Professor," I said (please).

"I now make."

While Shammakov prepared the tea inside, I sat on the single concrete step in a profound bad mood. I had traveled tens of thousands of miles to Central Asia, and for what? To be sent back like a misbehaving schoolboy by a madame commissar with a mouth like Fort Knox? To prove that totalitarianism is just as banal at the anus of the Earth as elsewhere? Moreover, I understood all too clearly that my arrest and interrogation meant I would probably not get to ride across the Eurasian steppes; indeed, I was not likely to get any farther again than Ashkhabad. No one would help a convicted cowboy to go snooping around on the Afghan border. I would certainly not get a visa extension. In short, not only had I been thrown, but there was no immediate way to get back in the saddle. The only mitigating circumstance was that, what with the wholesale changes going on in the Soviet Union, I suspected that this whole contretemps would never get recorded properly, and so would not impede future travels in Central Asia. This speculation turned out to be correct.

I drifted over to take a drink at the water spigot outside the bunk-house facing ours. An apparition was drinking there, a bearded, strapping Russian in nothing but a skimpy pair of athletic shorts and sandals. He was drinking and smoking one of those high tar and nicotine jobs the Russians suck away at. Only a fool would expose his white skin directly to the desert sun, I thought. He was turning electric pink and lobster red at the same time.

I offered this apparition a Marlboro, and he told me in good English that he was an entomologist, now in charge of his own Moscow research laboratory for the Soviet space program. This explained his lack of common sense. He must have mistaken me for one of the American zoologists.

"What is a space researcher doing out in the middle of the Kara Kum Desert?" I asked.

"I am directing study of beetles."

He told me the scientific name of the beetles, *Tenebrionidae,* but I shrugged; it meant nothing to me, so he darted inside the doorway of the bunkhouse and brought out a live specimen in a matchbox. It was a large black hunk of beetle, well armored, with a shiny black rounded carapace like a soldier's helmet. It also had two bristly antennae thrust forward, which made it look like an earthmover with its scoop replaced by twin keyhole saws.

"And what in particular are you studying about these beetles?"

"These beetles," he said, "have very unusual biorhythm adapted to desert climate. During day they dig into sand and remain in torpid state. Then come out at night when it is cool. We are studying beetles' biorhythms in order to help learn about best times to work in space. First we reproduce desert habitat in laboratory; later we will send beetles into space. We will see if they maintain biorhythm, or perhaps they can be retrained."

"You will train beetles to work in the Soviet space program?"

"No, I don't think," he shook his beard solemnly. "Absolutely not. On contrary, we learn if we can retrain cosmonauts in space program to adopt biorhythm of beetles."

"What a great idea," I said. "But why stop at cosmonauts? You could make the Earth itself into a desert and turn the whole human race into armored beetles that only come out at night. Think what a breakthrough that would be for Soviet science."

He looked at me suspiciously for the first time. "And what do you doing here?" he asked.

"I'm an American spy," I said. "I came out here to hunt mammals with gold teeth, but I've been arrested for not having a hunting license."

At this the man stuffed his beetle back into the box and marched off without another word.

The authorities had told me to return to Ashkhabad on the first train, but how was I to travel? I had no ticket, no reservation, and no train schedule. This mystery was solved after tea, when the state eunuch, the fat man who had lost my letter to the director, arrived at the bunkhouse to lead me away. Professor Shammakov came with us to interpret, since the court eunuch did not speak Russian, let alone English. With his swaggering belly and angry Mongoloid face, and his little birthday party porkpie hat, he was taking us to arrange for my railroad ticket at the request of the director of Repetek, who would help arrange the booking.

"What about my letter?" I said, but Professor Shammakov, already resigned to fate, would not interpret this into the local argot.

We walked on burning sands the one kilometer to the settlement. Repetek the settlement, as opposed to Repetek the field station, consisted of one sand street lined with low-roofed huts made of scrap metal and scrap boards, which began at the edge of the railroad tracks and ran in one direction a couple hundred feet, where a second street of hovels exactly like the first went off to the right. The only difference between the two was that the trains going by night and day were probably louder on First Street. On both there were filthy, mostly naked children running around squalid penned yards; they had domestic turkeys in Repetek, and the children's playpens were carpeted with turkey dung. If you stood at the top of town near the tracks and looked down First Street, the most prominent feature of the settlement was the rusty heavy construction equipment. There was even a small crane. Big pipes for sewage were deposited up and down the street. Unfortunately, whatever ditches had been dug to accommodate the pipes had long since been filled in with drifting sands, and most of the heavy pipes had been broken before they had ever been laid. There would be no sewage system in Repetek anytime soon.

We halted outside the second hovel on First Street. In the yard a woman and her daughter were baking bread in a hot clay oven. I took their picture, and the woman sent the little girl trotting over with a loaf of fresh *cherek* for me. I thanked her with a smile and a wave, and decided this would be my rations on the train ride back to Ashkhabad.

180

There wasn't a scintilla of shade in Repetek. The state eunuch went into this house near the tracks to rouse the railroad ticketing agent. He was gone about fifteen minutes, during which the professor and I were left to roast in the sun. It was a fine form of torture to stand there, and after the morning in the desert and the afternoon in custody, I was sinking low. I was starting to hallucinate that the state eunuch would come leaping out with his scimitar flying, and my head would ascend to heaven on a Bukhara rug while my body remained on Earth for beetle cutlets. Instead, the door finally opened slowly, and what emerged was the railroad agent, who was so drunk that no sooner had he stepped out of the house than he fell down, rolled over on his back, and began to moan like a whipped dog. His eyes rolled up into his head. Eventually he managed to right himself and crawl across the street on his belly. It was amazing how everyone there was turning into some kind of insect or reptile. For several minutes he leaned against the hut across the way, moaning and crying, then managed to slither inside and shut the door.

My God, I thought: Maybe the world isn't round after all. Maybe it's flat, and Alexander's geographers were right: This area right here is the end of the Earth.

Again we waited in the sun. I memorized the view up First Street, shimmering in the insane heat. But this time the ticket agent's wife, who turned out to be the woman who had given me the bread, came over and told us that her husband's name was Escavat, and that he was drunk because he had a terrible toothache, and there was no medicine or doctor. The scene began to make sense. She said he was now telephoning down the line to Chardzhou to find me a place on the train. The director of Repetek had telephoned personally to order this; otherwise Escavat never would have roused himself. Still, it took another half hour, so our solar torture continued.

Finally Escavat swam out again, now holding his head together with his hands. By the time he reached us he was able to raise himself to his knees, in which position he looked like a drunken Humpty Dumpty with a black mustache. He told the professor to tell me that he had reserved a berth for me, and to buy my ticket at the railroad station at 9:00 P.M. The westbound train for Ashkhabad was due at 9:35 P.M.

The professor and I shambled back to the bunkhouse without the state eunuch. There were still several hours before my train, and I wanted to spend them resting out of the sun. I put my head down on the cot, but every time I shut my eyes I remembered Joseph Brodsky's infamous advice to travelers in a poem called "Advice to Travellers in Central Asia": sleep with your head in a corner, so that when they come to chop it off with an ax, they won't have room to swing properly.

Back at the bunkhouse, the American zoologists were hurrying to get out into the field again before dusk, and invited me to join them. But the professor, casting his eyes down in shame, said I could not go. In effect, I was now under house arrest—only it wasn't my house. Furthermore, the professor said I would have to pay for my stay at Repetek. Poor Professor Shammakov. When he had to tell me that they were going to charge me for my visit, it was his blood pressure I thought of, not mine. In the end, he, too, had conformed, like Sasha Reebok, like almost everyone obliged to trade in their freedom for survival. There is a much-used Russian verb: *molchat'*. Literally it means only "to remain silent," but around this definition floats a world of circumstances under which it would be better for one's health to remain silent. This, of course, was one such circumstance, and Professor Shammakov one such patient. How sorry I feel for such men, who will never know what it is like to express themselves freely, who will never know the supreme satisfaction that is to be found in spitting in the eye of authority, who will never experience mentally what galloping is to the horseman or horsewoman—the feeling of flying free from the Earth and from gravity. I would rather have Alex, the crass, ambitious, grubbing Bulgarian capitalist as my friend a thousand times over, I thought, than to have these poor frogs with whom the authorities bait hooks.

By this time, though, I had reconciled myself to the outcome and consequences of my misadventure. I was even looking forward to my journey alone on the night train back to Ashkhabad, to chewing my *cherek* slowly and drinking water from my plastic jug.

Shammakov said yet again, "Green tea? You vud like grreen tea?"

It was his answer for everything, his nutrition, his tranquilizer, his stimulant, his palliative, his aphrodisiac, expectorant, and the best friend he had. We had our tea and bread in silence. I was not angry with the professor, not at all. He was no informer, nor a true collaborator. What could he have done for me? Nothing. For that matter, what could he have known about forming alliances and friendships with other men? He had been out with his snakes in the desert too long. Has anyone ever seen two snakes team up?

He said sheepishly, "You know what is *fonar*?"

"It means 'flashlight,' yes?"

Yes, and he wanted a good American flashlight for snaking at night. Could I send him one from the States?

I said yes, but only to keep up appearances: I knew a good flashlight would never survive a mailing from the United States to Turkmenistan. There was no point in even trying. But when he asked if I could put his book *The Reptiles of Turkmenistan* in a good American library, I could be more honest, as well as helpful. Why shouldn't I? None of what had occurred was Shammakov's fault, and I certainly didn't want it adversely affecting his health. I told him I would have his book put into the Library of Congress or the library of the Academy of Natural Sciences in Philadelphia. Later, when I returned to the States, I was surprised and delighted to learn through correspondence that the Library of Congress already had a copy of his book, so I placed the one he gave me in the Academy of Natural Sciences library.

After dark a knock came at the door. It was Escavat, the railroad agent, and he had Nabi, the state eunuch, in tow. One had brought my bill, the other my train ticket. The railroad agent looked a little more alive than the last time I'd seen him, howling in pain and writhing on the ground. He wanted nineteen rubles for the ticket, about eighty cents.

I returned to the bunkroom to get it from my money belt, and handed Escavat the exact change. He looked at it contemptuously and said something gruff in Turkmen to the professor. I didn't need a translation: The guy wanted a tip!

The professor began to wave him away, but I told him to stop, and went and got from my rucksack a plastic disposable razor and a pair of panty hose. I have no idea why I should have felt generous toward anyone in Repetek. There was no justification for it; I might more logically have punched him in the mouth.

Escavat was so satisfied that he beamed as if I had handed him a precious gem. He only wanted to know from Shammakov what the items were. When Shammakov explained to him that he could shave with the razor, he went home very happy. I gave the state eunuch a condom and a packet of Chiclets, but didn't tell him what they were for. I hope he didn't get them mixed up.

There was still more than an hour to go. I stepped outside, where the stifling air was beginning to cool after the long day. Birds were coming in to roost in the trees planted around the bunkhouses, and I felt like staying close to them after twenty-four hours with reptiles and insects. A lovely pair of grosbeaks with pink wing spots. A whole family of small falcons perched in a leafless tree. The flying mice were out: *lyetushaya mysh*, which the professor had taught me is Russian for bat, like the German *Fledermaus*.

I sat for a while with the professor on the bench outside the bunk-house, assuring him I didn't blame him for what had happened. We talked a little about how the system of nature was different from the systems of men, and agreed that nature's system was better.

"I love life of desert." The professor repeated his maxim.

Then it was time to go. I had my rucksack with my water jug, and the loaf Escavat's wife had given me. We walked together up the dark path and onto the sand road. There was a ring of haze around the moon. The air smelled of piss and burned rubber. I felt as if I were on the way to my own execution.

"Look at the ring around the moon, Professor," I said. "At home in America it means it will rain."

"Yes," the professor agreed softly.

In a few minutes we reached the station. The platform was deserted and dark, the station lit and open, but also empty. We sat down on a bench outside to wait, passing the time with the professor's last English lesson.

"Beautiful girl lives in Tedzhen."

"I have made error."

"An error," I corrected him.

"I have made an error."

"Right. Very good. What else?"

"I did not achieve plan here Repetek."

"Here *in* Repetek. You sure as hell didn't."

We could hear dogs barking from one end of Repetek to the other. Across the tracks, away in the middle distance, was a whitewashed concrete house. Kids were running and playing in its yard under a harsh yellow light. A car of some sort pulled up near the house; I couldn't see if there was some sort of road there or not. I had seen no other vehicles in Repetek. At the sight of the car, the mother ran outside, herded her children to the far edge of their perimeter, and stopped. For a moment I thought they would start to bark; you could sense the fear in their flocking movements as they waited to see if danger was imminent. But the vehicle made a U turn and went away.

After a while, Nabi the state eunuch arrived with Escavat the ticket agent. Approaching us in the dark, one fat and short, the other thin and long, they looked like Laurel and Hardy. They had come to make sure I got on board. They chatted with the professor in Turkmen; every half minute, one or the other of them spat on the platform. The state eunuch sent Escavat to turn on the platform lights. Perhaps it was the signal for the passenger train to stop. The overhead lights flickered on weakly, illuminating nothing. A freight train pulled in opposite us. An engine went by. They moved me down to where they thought wagon seventeen would stop, where I was supposed to board. We moved under the overhead light, but immediately beetles the size of golf balls started raining down. Disgusting giant winged insects pelted us and landed at our feet. The Turkmen didn't seem to notice; they certainly didn't seem to mind. Escavat gave me my ticket.

The professor said, "You will have a place, an upper berth near the toilet."

Perfect, I thought; that will smell just great. I offered my guards Marlboros. They had the odd habit of taking a drag, then spitting on their cigarettes, after which they had to light them again. Maybe it was to make their smokes last longer. Maybe they enjoyed the sulphur fumes when they struck a match. The beetles were still dropping like rocket-propelled grenades. The state eunuch was wearing a blue workman's uniform, and stood, beefy, bareheaded, and bald in the beetle shower, not a guy to mess with.

"Beautiful girl lives in Tedzhen," pronounced Professor Shammakov. "I did not complete plan here."

I shook hands with the professor, and told him once more he was not to blame. Nabi and Escavat wanted to shake hands, too. They thought they had turned into my protectors and helpers. What the hell, I thought; what does it cost me to be polite? They would probably be talking about the Turkmen cowboy in Repetek for years.

At last the train's big front light appeared. They told me to step back. Of course wagon seventeen stopped exactly where we had been waiting before we moved, in front of the station at the other end of the platform. All four of us ran toward the front end of the train, and everyone but Professor Shammakov came on board to find the commissar in charge of my car. He was in his little room with a friend, playing dominoes amid cabbage leaves and other garbage. They got him to give me a sleeping car. He said I would be by myself; this proved incorrect. Nonetheless, he issued me sheets, and a few minutes later I began my return to Ashkhabad.

If the train forged through the desert night back toward Ashkhabad, I was oblivious to it. No sooner had we cleared the Repetek station and I opened my journal to fill in the tale of my misadventures in the Kara Kum than I conked out. It was more like a coma than sleep, but during the night I was aware at some fuzzy level of human activity in my compartment, of doors opening and closing, of commotion, and of laughter. None of it was strong enough to wake me from my numb slumber. What I wasn't aware of was that I slept through an all-night drinking party.

Unlike Willie Nelson, who went to bed at two with a Ten, and woke up at ten with a Two, I went to sleep alone on a train and woke up with an Eight and a Half. She was young, black-haired, and *zaftig*, and was sprawled diagonally across the two lower berths beside me with several curves hanging out of her slip. Somehow our bodies had meshed front to back in the night, following each other's contours like two stacked spoons. I was attempting, on first waking, to understand the significance of the empty vodka bottles and cigarette ashes around us, as well as the hairy male leg dangling down from the upper berth, when she turned over, draped her arms around my neck, moved her thighs up between my legs, and without opening her eyes, planted her mouth firmly on mine. She must have mistaken me for the hairy ape in the upper berth.

Never has a traveler stared naked temptation so squarely in the eyes. Never has a man faced a more open invitation to anonymous sex. The Eight and a Half was a handsome young woman, nationality unknown, with a round white face and pointed chin, bulging breasts, and a frame like a '57 Chevy. That I was able to overcome moral turpitude was involuntary, for as soon as our tongues mingled, I tasted such a hellish mix of booze and tobacco halitosis, her unwashed body emitting such strong perfume of sweat and stale female secretions, that I was thrown back against the wall of the compartment in revulsion, where I found my writing journal.

This inspired a sudden idea. I took my Bic pen from my jeans pocket, sat upright against the compartment wall, and began to scribble:

4.15. Notes for an essay on why men don't ride horses anymore. Dr. Freud wondered what women want, but everyone knows what men want: to get laid. As much as possible, at every opportunity, no matter their culture or even their gender preference, whether it's a wife of 30 years or the checkout girl at the Piggly Wiggly. As natural selection produced a female human always capable of a roll in the hay, nature supplied a male sex drive that just won't quit, and an ever-ready external organ that keeps going like a Duracell battery. Therefore, every civilization has had to deal with the question of how to keep men's pants zipped. Freud called it sublimation—the transformation of the sexual drive into productive or creative activity.

Europe's special contribution to the problem of sublimation was chivalry—from the French *chevalier,* the horseman. These horsemen weren't like the rapacious Greeks or the raping Mongols. Chivalry matched the feudal rider against a set of virtues, which emanated formally from Christianity, but in practice came from men's association with horses: courtesy, honor, generosity, valor, and physical dexterity. The knight on his charger carried these standards in his head, no matter with whom he trysted. In this sense, chivalry was like golf, where you score points against yourself and thus can never win.

Inherent in the ideology of chivalry was a new ideal of manhood. The chivalrous knight had to be prepared to lay down his life for a maiden in distress before he'd even fucked her. Even when shooting his lance through the Infidels during the Crusades, the knight was obliged to spare Mohammedan women dishonor. It was something of a revolution in the relations between men and women.

From the time of the Italian Renaissance, chivalry was itself transformed from its martial aspect of individual combat to rationalism and athletic performance. In riding, reason bloomed. Horses got light, finer, one dares say more intelligent. Horse breeding became more scientific. Training became more precise and sophisticated. Hundreds of complex dressage maneuvers were devised to perfect the physical, mental, and aesthetic collaboration of horse and rider. The canter came into its own—a finely controlled gallop, throwing the horse into a smooth, rocking, three-beat rhythm (the exact rhythm of human sexual intercourse). The cavalier or dashing hussar of the Enlightenment committed himself to an art of horsemanship as exacting and splendid as romantic love, and these twin disciplines called upon men to address both horses and women as reasonable beings and consenting adults. Chivalry, which challenged men to curb their primal lust by treating women as well as they did their horses, evolved into a manly aesthetic-athletic endeavor, a high-water mark for sublimation, a major step forward in male self-control.

Now that women outnumber male equestrians by a hundred to one, they call the vestiges of chivalry in everyday life patronizing. Now that it's mostly girls and young women who develop a deep and passionate affection for horses, men scoff at horseback riding as the nonpareil prepubescent substitute for sex, not as the sublimation which has probably led to whatever civilized behavior Christian manhood has been able to muster. Now men drive fast cars and watch power sports on television; everything is a paradigm for economic competition. Even the kids hug fur dinosaurs—a contradiction in terms if there ever was one. What are dinosaurs except the big corporations of the animal world, greedy, plundering, combative, and out for numero uno. Male self-control is supposed to come about nowadays solely from the substitution of ambition, greed, and the desire to win, and riding horses has been definitively dropped from our modern definition of manhood.

Before I could finish jotting down this rubbish, my Eight and a Half woke up, and shortly thereafter so did her friend in the upper berth. He climbed down without shirt or shoes, and they smoked a cigarette, hacking at each other. The two of them were as hung as a painting by Picasso. I figured it was even money they weren't husband and wife. They brushed their teeth with some remaining vodka, which they spat on the floor. They were real party animals. She had evil gray eyes; he looked like a public enemy.

I tried not to attract their attention, which was about as possible as shoeing a horse while riding it. Surely they already knew I was a foreigner: Who else would be sitting in the corner in a cowboy hat writing? They gaped at me as if I were an alien from Venus trying to sell them life insurance.

Finally I broke off my portentous scribbling and offered them Marlboros. It was just to be friendly, but the gesture was misinterpreted. The guy thought I wanted to buy sex from Eight and a Half with my smokes. No questions asked, he got up to leave. Then I knew, of course, that they weren't married, but would she really have sold herself for a pack of American cigarettes? More interesting, would she have split the take with the boyfriend?

"*Nyet, nyet,* sit down." I motioned him back. "Friends. You see? Only *druzya,* okay?"

"Okay," he said, "*druzya.*"

But now that I had offered my Marlboros and my friendship, I was obliged to converse with them. He owned a bar in Mary; she was the barmaid (and the bar harlot, by the looks of it). They went up to Ashkhabad every week to buy liquor for the bar, apparently exploiting the train trip for a little dalliance.

"I am Muslim." He pointed to his chest. "Son attends new mosque in Mary."

"There's a new mosque in Mary?"

"Not finished. They build now. But already open."

"I understand."

"Muslim must treat everyone as brother."

"Yes?" What about drinking alcohol, I wondered.

"If everyone followed Koran, there would be no war," he declared.

If everyone followed the Koran, there'd be nothing *but* wars! Somehow he turned the conversation to the subject of women, but left Eight and a Half out of it for the moment; in any case she was too hung over to talk.

"A Turkmen should have twelve wives," he declared.

"Twelve? You don't say?"

"Timur had three hundred sixty."

"That must be some kind of record." Timur is Tamerlane, the bloodthirsty Asiatic conqueror who was Genghis Khan's great-grandson.

"First wife runs Turkmen home," the Muslim bar owner went on. "When Turkmen comes home, wife should have everything ready for him. Second wife should cook for him. Third wife to serve him. Fourth is young wife, wife to sleep with. When fourth is pregnant, Turkmen sleeps with fifth wife. You see?"

"You mean a harem?"

"Da, khareem!" He was delighted I had heard of it. It was the Turkmen custom, he said, before the revolution.

"What about all the children?" I asked.

"What about?"

"How do you feed them?"

"Turkmen not worry about feeding children," he answered. "Children are gift of Allah. Turkmen never thinks of how to feed. Allah will provide. Turkmen only wants to have more. His children are his riches, too."

The bar owner invited me to come to his café in Mary. He would make cucumber soup with yogurt. Eight and a Half would make *plov.* I could drink as much as I liked: vodka, cognac, Georgian champagne. He would hire a camel to be there when I came, so I could go for a ride. Allah would strike his children dead if he ever charged me a single ruble.

The train reached Ashkhabad around eight A.M. I was in no hurry. I watched Eight and a Half and the Muslim barkeeper climb the stairs of the track overpass. They slogged across the platform and off to the booze depot. I suppose I should have felt depressed, returning to the capital on the heels of my aborted trip to the Kara Kum. Yet I slung my small rucksack over one shoulder, tipped my cowboy hat back, thrust my hands into my jeans pockets, and went off whistling a tune.

It was a sunny morning with the Kopet-Dag veiled by gossamer haze, and no one was expecting me in Ashkhabad. No one even knew I was here. Suddenly it occurred to me that by getting myself arrested and sent back, I had finally evaded all my keepers. I was that rarest of all beings, a free man in Turkmenistan. At last there would be no one to tell me what I could or couldn't see, no one to stand between me and my curiosity, no one to make me go by car. At last I could do what travelers the world over have been doing from time immemorial: walk the streets of a foreign city and observe the ways of a strange people.

The long train trip had left me hot, thirsty, tired, and unwashed, but my newfound freedom of movement exhilarated me. I still had no street map but with no time constraints, there was no need to know where I was going. All I wanted was to use the two legs God gave me to see something of the city. Besides, I could always take a cab, if only to get my bearings from the driver.

I strolled up Shevchenko in my cowboy hat as if it were the most normal thing in the world, looking in the windows of the small tailoring workshops, stopping at two bookshops, taking time to browse the works of Gorbachev, Brezhnev, and Lenin that they had for sale. At a little streetside produce market, I watched women line up for the radishes and green onions piled in the stalls. Mothers were buying ice cream for their children at nine o'clock in the morning. I stopped at a café and drank two glasses of lemonade, though they had nothing to eat for sale. I stopped pedestrians to ask directions just for the pleasure of looking into their eyes and working out which Russian verb of motion to employ.

From the street, I spotted the fountain built as a memorial to the victims of the 1948 earthquake, and made a beeline for it. It was an abstract red metallic erection, giving every evidence of having been designed by a plumber. It stood amid minimalist landscaping on a wide concrete apron in the middle of a stark sandlot that ran between two major avenues. I had become so used to seeing things unfinished in the Turkmen capital that by now it seemed natural that the park surrounding the memorial fountain had never been completed.

I didn't care. Seven powerful jets of water shot twenty feet in the air, and came down in a gurgling, bubbly, cast concrete basin. I stared at the water as if it were the visage of the Lord. I bathed my eyes and my soul in it, then leaned over and dunked my head. The spray made by the water splashing in the basin felt gorgeous on my face; the cool water felt delicious flowing over my toes. Only now could I imagine what life without water would be like—like a life without a mother's love.

The day was already hot, and bound to get hotter, as well as more polluted, judging by the thickening pall in the sky. What about a nice, cold, refreshing bath? I looked around. There was no one at all within view, only an old man with a broom sweeping the concrete platform like a Turkmen Sisyphus. He didn't care. In a flash, I tossed off my jeans and sank into the fountain up to my neck, saved and gloriously happy.

Restored by my bath, I decided to visit the Ve-De-En-Kha, the Exhibition Hall of the Accomplishments of the Turkmen People. Every Soviet republic had one, with the biggest, of course, in Moscow; every student of the Russian language gets to visit the Moscow Ve-De-En-Kha in his language textbook:

DIALOGUE A

TOURIST: Excuse me, please. How to reach the Ve-De-En-Kha?

MUSCOVITE: You are on the wrong bus. Get off at the next stop and transfer for the number eighteen. Then take the metro at Mayakovsky.

TOURIST: Thank you.

MUSCOVITE: You are foreigner?

TOURIST: Yes, I am an American spy.

MUSCOVITE: In that case, you must hurry or you will miss the bus.

TOURIST: Thank you for the information.

MUSCOVITE: I gave no information.

Just for spite, I flagged down a cab to take me. It was straight down Leninski Prospect, said the driver, now called Makhtymkuli Avenue. The exhibition hall was an imposing modern steel-and-glass shed with two pompous flights of concrete steps out front to make visitors feel like beetles. Inside, the artifacts were in glass cases arranged on three levels skirting the walls, with connecting flights of stairs—a rectangular imitation of Frank Lloyd Wright's Guggenheim Museum. The center well was occupied by a boring collection of photographs featuring the central committees of the Communist party of Turkmenia, going all the way back to the 1921–23 civil war won by the Bolsheviks. The Russians and later the Bolsheviks had liberated the Turkmen from the absolute rule of the khans, but the central committee had gotten shorter, older, fatter, and balder with each generation, until they were now official Soviet faces, indistinguishable from Russians, no-frills model leaders turned out at the same factory with no thought to design or packaging. There, staring out from the 24th Congress of the Turkmen Communist Party, was the old goat and famous writer Mr. Ataev, probably reading from his novel about oil and gas production.

The exhibits went from the top-floor display of the great agricultural and industrial accomplishments to the traditional folk crafts on the basement level. So many smiling women harvesting apricots, melons, pomegranates, pistachios, and licorice wood; so many wise, bearded elders pointing out oil rigs to enthusiastic young pioneers; so many sober, hard-working people sitting at the rug machines in the world's biggest rug factory, where they turned out Bukhara rugs with cameos of Lenin. They didn't know this was the one ingredient that would make the rugs impossible to sell outside the U.S.S.R. The biggest Oriental rug in the world, or so they claimed, was hung on the second level. It was a Bukhara-patterned rug on a traditional wine-red background, maybe seventy-five feet by fifty feet, but since it was divorced from any possible use except as an exhibit, it lacked the mystery and history that add so much to the beauty of Oriental rugs.

I peered at the models of happy gas refineries and cheerful cotton gins. Unfortunately, the electrically powered model of the hydroelectric plant and dam was out of order: a bad plug. Babushkas in blue smocks minded the exhibits, four to each floor, one for every side of every floor, ready to inform you immediately of the whereabouts of the bathroom or the location of the stairs. One was doing her ironing on the job; another was cooking a midday meal on a hot plate; still another was working at a small sewing machine. I liked this informal exhibition of the real life of the Turkmen Soviet people.

On the top level were displayed all the glorious consumer goods produced by the glorious Turkmen Socialist economy under the leadership of the glorious Turkmen Communist party. There was a radio console so big that it looked like Glenn Miller was hiding inside, black-and-white televisions, and bread-mixing machines (though I hadn't seen a single mass-produced loaf of bread, and doubted anyone ate anything but the traditional *cherek* made in clay ovens). There were gas cooking stoves, electric radiators, and—wonder of wonders—car tires!

From all this I concluded that the Turkmen people were making a slow onslaught toward a consumer society. Laden down with the gifts of modern life, it was unimaginable they would ever return to living in felt yurts, moving their herds with the seasons. The Soviets had freed them from the poor nomad's life, as well as the life of mercenary warriors, which was the paid occupation most Turkmen pursued under the khans. Now even people born in desert tents like Dr. Shikhmurad could become doctors and ice hockey fans. The only horses to be seen were the ones ridden in the old black-and-white photographs by the Bolshevik cavalry. The authorities weren't encouraging the tradition of Central Asian horsemanship, nor its modern continuation in horse breeding: There was not a single reference to Akhal-Tekes in the entire exhibition hall.

Later that afternoon, I decided to drop in on Guvanch Djumaev at the BEVIKO office on Universitetskaya Street, so named because the university had stood there before the big earthquake. When I arrived, Guvanch's *divan* was in full swing. I did not get the seat of honor this time because an Armenian businessman was working out with Guvanch and Sasha Skorokhodov the contract for a deal by which BEVIKO would swap sheep hides for a used Mercedes automobile. Guvanch's secretary was taking down the exact wording of the contract in longhand. I sat down at the lower end of the table with BEVIKO's junior colleagues.

"You are back soon," said Erik, a young Armenian employee. "We expected you would be gone at least five days."

"They arrested me and sent me back."

Guvanch looked up. "What?"

"Tell Guvanch what happened to you," said Erik.

"You were arrested?" asked Sasha.

"They took me into custody at Repetek and sent me back by train because I did not have the proper permits to remain in Chardzhou Oblast."

Sasha's smile turned to a warning. "Don't believe that anything has changed here from five or ten years ago. It is all still the same as before. Don't believe what anybody tells you, whether it's about horses or documents."

It was then that Guvanch asked, "Did you know that all the men who met you at the airport were KGB?"

"No. Then I didn't, but I do now."

They hurried to wrap up the contract with the Armenian, after which Guvanch motioned me forward.

"In future, when you wish to go somewhere or do something in Turkmenistan, you only need to ask either me or Sash. What can I do for you now?" Guvanch folded his hands on his desk to listen.

"Guvanch," I began, "I had hoped to stay longer than two weeks in Turkmenistan, but now, after my arrest, I'm sure I won't get a visa extension. I want to come back to your country. I have only just begun to know the Turkmen, and I want to ride your horses. Where is Alex, by the way?"

"He left for Bulgaria."

"With or without horses?"

"We obtained horses for him to take to Bulgaria for auction, but the *mashina* wasn't ready, so he left without. He will come back next month for the horses, we think. But please continue."

"I want to come back to Turkmenistan. I think we can do a deal together. You provide me with an invitation and a place to stay here, and I'll come back for a month or more—as long as you will have me. I will make color photographs of all Akhal-Teke stallions. You can use these photographs for publicity purposes, for marketing your horses abroad, or for the historical record—whatever you like."

Guvanch took a phone call, signed the contract with the Armenian, settled three or four other issues, then came back to me with his decision. "Of course we want you to come back to Ashkhabad. It will give me pleasure to be your host. I would invite you even if it had nothing to do with trade because I see you love horses, and pursue this interest in a serious way. We used to say that the Turkmen loves his horse more than his wife. Of course you may photograph any Akhal-Teke horses you wish. Your idea is a good one, but I have an idea, too. The Akhal-Teke is well known in the Soviet Union because of the *probeg* we made to Moscow as well as the breed's success in sporting competitions. You are aware that the Akhal-Teke Absent won the dressage competition at the Rome Olympics, with Sergei Filatov riding?"

"Yes."

"But Akhal-Teke horses are not so well known, I think, in Europe, and especially in the United States," he continued. "The American oilman Armand Hammer obtained one hundred Akhal-Tekes through Moscow. He intended to take them to the United States and hold a show, but he died. No one seems to know what happened to these horses. We hope to sell our horses in the West. Not our breeding stock, you understand, but a certain number of horses each year once we get our breeding stock up to sufficient numbers that the breed's survival is secure. Now the number of pureblood stallions is less than one hundred. Only in the past two years have we been able to take control of our horse-breeding industry from Moscow. Now our associate Geldi Kiarizov, whom you met, has the first private breeding herd. In August we will hold the first auction of Akhal-Tekes, in Bulgaria, to see what interest there is in our horses in Europe. We need to begin marketing Akhal-Tekes. I would like to have a promotional video made to introduce our Akhal-Teke horses to the West. Could you make it?"

I thought for about two seconds. If I worked on a video for Guvanch Djumaev, I could probably get access to any aspect of the horse culture I wanted. I might even get to ride one. How hard could it be to make a video about horses? *"Konyechno!"* I agreed. In my mind, I was already packing my riding boots and breeches.

Guvanch took a piece of paper to make notes. He was in a hurry; the telephone hadn't rung for almost three minutes. "When will you come back?"

"It will take several months to organize. I must get the video equipment together, and so forth. Let's say three months. I will come back in August. You will provide me with a formal invitation?"

"Konyechno, but this, too, will take several months to prepare. It must go through the proper ministries."

"I will be prepared to come, let's say, around the twentieth of August. I will come as soon as I receive the invitation."

"Should we obtain a tourist or a business visa?"

"Guvanch, I don't want anything to do with the Turkmen Friendship Society. As long as they are not involved in any way, I don't care what kind of visa."

"A business visa, then. You will send me a written proposal. As soon as I receive it, I will start the paperwork."

"How will I send the proposal? The post isn't secure. A letter can arrive in two weeks or two years."

"Post not necessary. We will have a fax machine here at BEVIKO starting next week. It was given to us by a Canadian company we sold cotton to."

"A fax? Guvanch, you are a man full of surprises."

"*Konyechno,*" he readily agreed, flashing his handsome gold teeth.

For the days remaining until I was to leave Turkmenistan, Guvanch remanded me to the custody and care of Sasha Skorokhodov. Although I went back to stay with Dr. Shikhmurad and his family in the *microrayon* on the outskirts of town, I lived like a delegation dropout. Sasha picked me up every morning in his classic 1960s-model Moskvich sedan, lemon yellow and shaped like a lemon drop, and dropped me off each evening to spend an hour before bed with my host family, watching ice hockey or translating rock lyrics from their cassettes for the kids.

These were my favorite days, for Sasha Skorokhodov was a born guide and courtly companion. He had been born and raised in Firyuza, a little mountain resort an hour out of Ashkhabad, so his knowledge of Turkmenistan was copious. He had a thorough command of the roads and routes and a collection of Russian popular music tapes, which he played on a small cassette deck he kept under his feet when he drove.

Like Guvanch, Sasha had also been a Komsomol apparatchik, and had served as an officer in the Soviet navy, then in the federal police. He had risen high enough in the Komsomol to become a Turkmen deputy to the National Komsomol Chamber of Deputies, and one afternoon, when I went to his apartment to meet his wife and stay for supper, he brought out photographs of himself as a young Komsomol deputy from Turkmenistan, taken in Moscow where the chamber met. He was young, clipped, tough, clear-eyed, and extremely good-looking—obviously a guy who was going places. In the end, however, where Sasha Skorokhodov was going was away from the Communist system; his stint in Moscow as a deputy was the first step.

"They gave us hotel rooms in Moscow," he reminisced. "They gave us whatever we wanted to eat and drink, but that was all. We didn't debate issues or learn to govern; we didn't even hold meetings. The deputies lived in the hotel, drank vodka, and ate caviar. We stayed in Moscow for four months like this, then went home."

This disillusioned and disgusted Sasha. He had always liked to work. It was the one thing potentially interesting about life in the USSR. It was the one area where you could use your intelligence and energy. By the time he was twenty-five he was aware that the Soviet economic system was bankrupt and could not deliver the goods. Without simple things like housing and food, private life was a constant round of frustration and privation. No mastery of one's personal or economic life was possible, but at least a man's work provided the opportunity to put his soul on the line for something. Now he had learned that life as a Komsomol big shot deprived a man of work as well, deprived one of that sense that can only come from work, the sense of mastering a small sphere of human action. He quit Komsomol and joined the merchant marine, working on Soviet fishing vessels for twelve years. He had sailed the Seven Seas, yet never set foot on foreign soil, since fishing vessels never stopped at foreign ports. Once, he told me, "we sailed right along the French Riviera. We were so close to shore that with field glasses we could see the girls in bikinis. I can say in truth that I have seen the French Riviera."

But he was not bitter about never visiting foreign lands, and had no great desire to visit them today. "I have a wife and daughter now. Anyway, we should try to make some sort of new life here. To make a free life is the only way to prevent a return to Stalinism."

Each morning Sash would say, "So what would you like to do today? Where would you like to go?"

One day I said, "I would very much like to visit the Komsomol stud farm."

In thirty minutes Sasha delivered me there, introduced me to the stud's commercial director, whom he knew, and accompanied me on a tour. The commercial director, Yusup Anaklichev, was also president of the Akhal-Teke Association of Turkmenistan, and a friend of Guvanch's since childhood; both were passionately interested in horses as well as American rock music. Yusup had not ridden on the 1988 marathon, but had been in Moscow to greet the riders and arrange what to do with the Akhal-Tekes. Distinct from Guvanch's assertive, decisive personality, Yusup had softer Persian looks and manners; his own views on horse politics in Turkmenistan were equally distinct from Geldi Kiarizov's. It was true, he said, that Lenin's 1920 decree depriving individuals of domestic animals was hugely unpopular and caused a massive hemorrhage of horseflesh because half a million Turkmen fled to settle in Iran and Afghanistan, taking their horses, sheep, and camels with them. But by creating the Konnozavod (literally, "the horse factory," but actually meaning "the stud farm"; there are certain concepts that simply baffle the Russian vocabulary), the Soviets had introduced scientific breeding for Akhal-Tekes, put the breed on a sound genetic footing, and stopped the flow of horses out of Turkmenistan.

Yusup treated me like a foreign potentate rather than a humble American delegate. We stood outside the stables together on a tiny patch of real grass, which must have gotten there by mistake, and the stable hands began to bring out the Akhal-Teke stallions one by one on lead lines for me to see. It was a show of horseflesh as impressive and seductive as what I had seen before at the hippodrome. Akhal-Tekes' coats are iridescent in a unique way that has spawned a special vocabulary to describe their colors. There was a *voronoy* (black) stallion with a coat like silver river water under a full moon. There was a *bulanyi* (golden) stallion whose coat could only be described as what a bar of gold out of Fort Knox would resemble if held in the sunlight at high noon. Finally Yusup had them bring out the most famous living Akhal-Teke stud, Polotli, twenty-six years old, three times champion of breed in the USSR, son of the champion Peren and sire of numerous champions whose twenty-five-foot-high statue stood at the mouth of the entrance road to the Komsomol stud. He had lost his muscle tone from years at stud in the Komsomol stables, and was looking decidedly pinkish in his dotage, but it was interesting to meet a legitimate celebrity horse.

After the show, Yusup took me gently by the elbow and led me to the pen for colts and the pen for mares with foals, always speaking to me in soft, earnest tones. He murmured, "Turkmen horses spread all over the world from ancient times to modern times, Jon. Trade caravans took Akhal-Teke horses as far as China and India, in the other direction through Iran to Arabia, and from there to Europe and England. Alexander's horse Bucephalus was Akhal-Teke. The British took Akhal-Teke mares when their cavalry was positioned in Turkestan against the Russians after the Russian withdrawal from World War One."

"How's the horse business now, under perestroika?" I asked.

He said one of their horses had fetched twenty-eight thousand dollars at the annual Essen equitation show two years ago—a record price for an Akhal-Teke, even though it was not one of their best. Up till now, he went on, there had been only one horse auction in the entire Soviet Union, the Moscow auction. Now they were planning to open an auction in Ashkhabad and invite foreign buyers. "Our main idea is to keep the money here in Turkmenistan instead of having the apparatchiki in Moscow steal it. But money is the problem; Moscow has cut Komsomol stud off entirely from state funds. Now we must find interested outside parties—investors. We have to invest money in the horse-breeding industry. The other problem is lack of training. No one knows the skills of the horse trade after so many years of isolation from the rest of the world. For example, we don't have one veterinarian in the whole Republic of Turkmenistan. We have no one to do blood work on our horses. We have no farriers. All we have are jockeys who can ride fast and stable hands who drink vodka."

Before leaving, Yusup asked a personal favor. "You know the American Akhal-Teke breeders Phil and Margot Case?"

"No."

"I thought perhaps they had sent you here."

"No."

"I have never met them," Yusup said, "but we have corresponded for several years." He took their last letter from his pocket, dated more than a year previously. Their address was Staunton, Virginia. "I have not written back to them. I am ashamed. Perhaps you could meet them in America and tell them how much I appreciate their letters?"

"Obyazatelno," I said. "Without fail." I told him I would return to Turkmenistan in August; perhaps I could carry a letter from the Cases to him.

"It would mean so much to me. I know from their letters that Phil and Margot love Akhal-Teke horses. Do you ride, Jon?"

"Da."

"When you come back, I will give you my own horse, Tarlan, to ride in the Kara Kum."

"To me, honor." I slapped my heart.

—

Another day, I said to my genie, "Take me to a Russian steam bath. A real, old-fashioned *Ruskaya banya* where I can soak the dirt and sand out of me."

Sasha grinned. "You mean today is cultural program? Okay, let's go!"

In minutes we were headed straight for the mountains and the border with Iran. There was an almost unused road there which ran through stony foothills exactly parallel to the frontier. It had almost certainly been built by the military to patrol the border. The road twisted up through a pass of no great elevation. On the other side was a classic Soviet border zone with patrol towers and a four-foot-wide gravel trench with concrete posts every ten feet to which were attached two strands of wire radar devices at about ankle level and two strands of barbed wire at about neck level. No one was living on either side. The foothills were inhabited only by giant wild rhubarbs, huge dill flowers, and yellow mustard. Was all this security to keep Soviet citizens in, I wondered, or Iranians out?

For half an hour we drove along the border, spooky and deserted, surrounded by eight-thousand-foot snowcapped mountain peaks. Then we turned a curve, and an even higher summit came into view on the Soviet side, a huge chunk of black rock slanting out of the earth at about a 60 degree angle. "That's where we go hunting for mountain goat," Sasha said enthusiastically. "The last one I shot, I tracked for four days in January on that mountain."

I was paranoid about getting caught again in a border zone without a permit, but the mountain views were so powerful that I made Sasha stop so I could take photographs. At length we swung around to the west, and headed uphill into a small valley lined with leafy green mulberry trees, the ones that silkworms love to munch. The air grew radically fresher as we ascended to the mountain resort town of Firyuza, which Sasha said had formerly been Iranian, given by the old Pahlavi Shah to Stalin. The population was mostly Kurdish with a Farsi minority, and the usual smattering of Turkmen and Russians. Past the Pioneer and Komsomol camps we came to the State House of Rest, where Sasha easily convinced the Kurdish manager—like him, a Firyuzan by birth— to let us into the bathhouse, which wouldn't officially open for the season until the following week.

"An American guest is something special," the manager agreed behind his bushy mustaches. "Anyway, the attendant is already there. Forgive us if we lack bath sheets."

But they didn't. In a few minutes we were sitting in the bathhouse anteroom, which was hung with drapes of chintz in a big red rose pattern. The table was covered in white linen, spread with lovely blue lilacs and a tea service. Everything seemed old and worn, but somehow comfortable. Posters on the wall showed how to take a sauna and how to perform massage.

We stripped and went into the sauna; the steam room really wouldn't be turned on until May first, when the season started. At last all the bangs and twists and jolts of the last weeks floated away as we alternated for an hour between sweating and plunging into a bracing cold pool.

"If only we had some beer to pour on the hot rocks of the sauna," said Skorokhodov. "Breathing in the steam from the beer is very good for your health."

"Maybe for a Cossack's health, not mine," I said.

Afterward we returned to the antechamber, our skins red and pulsing, to wrap ourselves in old white cotton bath sheets and to take tea. A woman attendant came in with a hot teapot, set it down before us, and left. There is nothing under heaven like hot tea after a hot bath; it does for your insides what the hot bath has just finished doing for your outside. I was feeling good in my brain for a change, and was soon riding a wave of senseless speculation that the Soviet Union could only be understood by someone when he was drunk, and that what had gone wrong in the USSR was not, after all, Stalinism or communism, but merely the triumph of nostalgia and tastelessness over the original impulse to create something new.

Sasha rejected my claim out of hand. The problem was leadership, he said. "Look, Jon, I was apparatchik; Guvanch also apparatchik. First you become a Pioneer when you are a child. You learn slogans, discipline, and memorize ideology. Then you graduate to Komsomol, where you study and practice ideology and party politics. Then you leave Komsomol to become a full member of the Soviet Communist party. You are assigned various political jobs. If you rise within the party, you will receive greater and greater responsibilities. You will manage factories, work in ministries, run large bureaus. But what does the apparatchik really know? All their lives all they've done is politics. They know the party line. When it changes, they change with it. They know how to maneuver themselves upward in the system. They know how to win rewards for themselves. They know how to go to meetings, party congresses, to make speeches. But they know nothing about economics, technology, or management. Maybe this would not be so bad; what is bad is that they know so little about the way ordinary people actually live. Is it any wonder Soviet society is collapsing?"

It sounded grim: a bunch of know-nothing, self-satisfied, good-for-nothing politicians completely divorced from everyday life, running the country on hot air and personal greed. I was sure glad that nothing like this could happen in the U.S.A.

We drank our tea in moody silence. The steam from his cup made a melancholy curl under Sasha's nose. "Now maybe you begin to see why perestroika is a sham," he said. "These new slogans—perestroika, *demokratizatsia,* glasnost—are as meaningless and senseless as the last generation of slogans. If tomorrow the party said something completely different, the apparatchiki would simply salute that, too. But come on, let's get dressed."

We left the cool green of Firyuza to return to the brittle ugliness of Ashkhabad. On the way across town we passed a big placard that read: WHAT HAVE YOU DONE FOR *PERESTROIKA* TODAY?"

I was packing at the Shikhmurads' on Saturday night for my Monday departure when Djura arrived to say good-bye. Those two words were actually all I had to say to him, but I knew him well enough by now to realize that he wasn't showing up just to be polite. He wanted something, and he had brought his wife along to help him get it. We sat in the dining room. She looked like Madame Nhu, the Vietnamese Dragon Lady, wearing a silk dress and gaudy costume jewelry, and bossing around the poor Shikhmurads as if they were servants. In particular I didn't like the way she spoke to Yedesh.

When she told the girl to take away the dishes and bring her something, I told Yedesh, "Not necessary," in Russian and watched for the wife's reaction. She said something in Turkmen, then brought out a crystal and tried to place it on my forehead.

Of all things, a New Age queen! I ripped the cord from her hand and flung it brusquely into the hallway. She hustled after it, seemingly without the least embarrassment. Then she called Dr. Shikhmurad and his family into the kitchen on some pretext in order to get Djura and me alone.

"No like crystal, eh, Turkmen cowboy?" Djura smirked. He'd been drinking, as usual. He was wearing a zippy white nylon windbreaker he claimed he had bought in Toledo, Ohio. "I spent three thousand dollars shopping in Toledo, America," he boasted. "Jacket cost forty-eight dollar. What you think?"

"It's a piece of shit, not worth twenty. You got ripped off."

"I buy sixteen tennis rackets in America. All for me! Ohh, so good to shop in Toledo! Now I will go America again, to Albuquerque with Turkmen doctors delegation."

"Congratulations."

"Alice-a Thompson-a make me invitation."

"I heard you the first time."

"I go to America. You see? Here I got color television, VCR. Got car. Got dacha in mountains. Very good life. I only get for me." He guzzled down a double shot of vodka. "I will go Albuquerque in August. Alice-a Thompson—"

"Djura, what's your pitch? What do you want? Because I know you want something."

"I could speak with you man to man, Turkmen cowboy?"

"Don't make me laugh."

"Polaroid film difficult to receive here. Very hard! I take pictures only my grandson with Polaroid film."

"You have the audacity to come here and ask for more film? You know what you are, Djura? In plain English, you are a scumbag."

"Don't know this word."

"What about my visa extension?"

"Was impossible." He shrugged. "I try."

"What about your agents following me around night and day like I was a spy?"

He changed tactics. "I pay you for Polaroid film."

"Okay, Djura, I'll tell you what I'm going to do. I'll sell you a twin pack of Polaroid film for exactly what I paid for it in America. No charge for transporting it here. That will be twenty-two dollars, plus two dollars sales tax for Governor Florio."

"Don't know him," said Djura.

"It doesn't matter. Twenty-four dollars, please."

Djura slumped. I knew he didn't have the scratch. "Very big money for Turkmen. Equals my six weeks salary."

"It's a tough world, Djura. Well, I guess this is good-bye." I got up to leave.

"Please, Turkmen cowboy, sit down!" Djura cried in desperation. He was a living example of dialectical materialism gone haywire. As for me, this revenge was too delicious served up hot to wait for it to get cold, as Balzac advised that revenge be enjoyed. I had a barbed hook through his lip, and all I wanted was to play with him some more and make it hurt before using the gaff. It wasn't a very nice thing to do; I wasn't cruelly toying with him out of ideological antipathy, even though he was KGB, but was simply enjoying this little cruelty. I should have been ashamed, and I was—but only to a limited extent.

I sat down and folded my arms across my chest. "Okay, Djura. What's your offer? It had better be damn good."

"Have idea!" he brightened. "You bachelor, Turkmen cowboy. Maybe you need Turkmen wife. You like Shikhmurad daughter? She old enough to marriage. Very good family, Dr. Shikhmurad. I can arrange."

"I don't need you for that."

His eyes narrowed so much they disappeared from his head. "What you want?"

"I want a Teke rug."

"I am Teke tribe!"

"What a shame for the Tekes. You'll get me a rug? If you bring that rug to the airport on Monday morning, I'll give you the Polaroid film."

"How big rug you want? How much meters?"

"Oh, I want a very big rug, Djura—say, three meters by two meters."

"Not permitted bring more worth than fifty rubles out of Turkmenistan."

"That's for you to organize. I want the rug and a document permitting me to take it out of the country. Otherwise, no film."

"Big rug not exist in Turkmenistan, Turkmen cowboy."

"Bullshit. I saw one a hundred times bigger at the exhibition hall. And by the way, I don't want a rug from the factory. I want a handmade one."

For once Djura said nothing. Even a big man like him couldn't obtain a good rug on such short notice. The game was over; I'd won the final round. He knew it, I knew it, and he knew I knew it. I swore to myself then and there that if I did manage to return to Turkmenistan, the so-called Turkmen Friendship Society would never find out I was here. For a moment I stared into his drunken eyes, still full of arrogance, and savored the modest pleasure of knowing I would never meet Djura Semedov again this side of hell.

Can the joy of homecoming ever be sweet if you have never tasted the sourness of a journey? I had never intended to end my trip to Central Asia in Ashkhabad, stuck in the same area of the Kara Kum Desert where I had started. I hadn't raised my aging carcass into the saddle so many times at home to not have ridden a single minute in this wild country of untrustworthy sand dunes. Yet when, on my last day in Turkmenistan, Guvanch and Sasha took me to the races, I found myself trading my dream of riding across the Eurasian steppes for the friendship of my new Turkmen comrades, and without regrets.

When we reached the hippodrome, it was already the third race of a twelve-race card on a searing Sunday afternoon. It couldn't have been less than 110. There was a paltry bit of white cirrus stretched thin in a cobalt sky. Turkmen wore their brown sheepskin hats, which they believe keeps their heads cool.

The Ashkhabad hippodrome had opened seven or eight years back, and although still not completed, like every other public work in Ashkhabad, it opened anyway, and now races every Sunday throughout the year. The dirt track itself is long—twenty-two hundred meters around—and dusty. Between races a World War II–vintage humpbacked tank truck crept around the track like a mechanical beetle, drizzling a weak stream of water from a nozzle on the front bumper, which accomplished nothing but holding up the start of the next race. I noticed there was no lovely pond for race fans to soothe their eyes on, as at lovely Belmont Park. There were no indoor television screens for the gamblers, either, or parimutuel windows, bookies, beer and hot dog stands, advertisements, or urinals in the men's room. In fact, no men's room at all: If you needed to pee, you walked down to the end of the track, and watered the desert. It was also the first track I have ever been to where no money was involved.

In the uncovered concrete grandstand sat three thousand or four thousand boys, men, and bearded elders, almost all of them keeping cool in their big fur hats as they followed the races. When the horses closed in on the finish line, the boys jumped to their feet, yelled, pounded the air with their fists, and slapped their programs against their sides. The elders stroked their wispy white beards and waved their cigarettes, which they smoke in holders. No one paid the slightest attention to the heat; they were exposing themselves to the cruelest of suns for no other reason than their love of fast horses. The trainers brought Akhal-Tekes from the state and collective farms all over the Turkmen republic, not to run for the gold—there were no stakes, no purses, no claiming races, no trophies—but for the pure pleasure of the competition, the chance to go home knowing that your horse was the swiftest. Only the jockeys stood to gain materially, the winners receiving a new carpet, television set, or, once, two hundred rubles cash, about an average month's wages.

We bypassed the grandstand and went down to mingle with a knot of the hippodrome cognoscenti congregated on a raised dirt mound near the finish line, just in front of the booth on wheels where the starter rang the bell. You could tell from the way the men stood with programs and pencils in hand that these were the trainers, the breeders, and probably, the apparatchiki of the horse business in Ashkhabad. They kibbitzed with each other, and called the jockeys over for last-minute instructions before the race.

They race long in Ashkhabad. We saw several two- and three-kilometer races for two-year-olds and fillies, but four- and five-year-old stallions are expected to win over distance, and the featured race on the card was a six-kilometer affair, almost four miles.

"It is because the Akhal-Teke horse is so strong," declared Geldi Kiarizov, who was standing with Yusup Anaklichev.

Yusup took me softly by the elbow again. "Jon, the Akhal-Teke has great endurance. Tremendous! Before the revolution, the Turkmen would gallop his horse all night. They would ride from here to Persia to raid for slaves. If they captured someone, they put them behind their saddle and galloped their horses fifteen, sixteen hours back home, with the horse carrying two. This is the Akhal-Teke horse!"

I noticed they were about to start the eighth race. "Can you pick a winner?" I asked Yusup.

"You would like to bet, Jon?"

"How much?"

"Oh, just for sporting interest." Yusup smiled nervously, perhaps remembering he was still an apparatchik who shouldn't be caught wagering on the Komsomol's own horses—or against them, as the case might be. He quickly looked down at his program, read the line of entries, and without hesitation chose the number seven entry, Bagitli, a Komsomol horse.

"You will see," he said.

Yusup put the program in my hands to choose. I saw that four of the seven horses entered were from Komsomol stud, two from the Leningrad state farm, and the last from the Sverdlov state farm. I knew nothing about any of them, and there was certainly no racing form to record their latest workouts. But I noticed the name of the number one horse from Komsomol; it was "Guvanch."

"It seems that's mine."

It was one of the shorter races—fifteen hundred meters, or only about one mile—a tune-up race, Yusup explained, for a big race that would take place on the following Sunday. The old-fashioned blue starting gate had been brought into position at the farthest turn across from us, and we could see the stable hands struggling to get the fiery horses locked in. The crowd hushed. With a crisp snap, the starter rang the bell, and the horses broke in a swirl of desert dust. They went flat out from the gate. There was no reason to hold them back in such a short sprint. There was no strategy; the race was a pure test of speed over two turns. All seven horses stayed together in the back stretch, but

Yusup's horse pulled ahead at the first curve, and increased his lead without the whip in the final curve. He was a dapple gray with a boy, maybe all of twelve years old, aboard. Three lengths ahead with the last quarter to go, the jockey pulled back on the reins, still no whip, and the Akhal-Teke took off as if shot out of a cannon. I scrambled down the knoll to get a photograph at the finish line. By the time the horse galloped by, he had increased his lead to win by a full seven or eight lengths.

Turning back, I gave the thumbs-up sign, and Yusup acknowledged it. He then proceeded without fail to pick the winners of the next four races, yet I am sure they were not fixed. He merely knew every horse on the track. He should; he had been a director at Komsomol when most of them were born, raised, and trained.

While Yusup demonstrated how to pick winners, I was noticing how the cognoscenti came to pay their respects to Guvanch. One by one they came over to shake hands, exchange embraces, and to chat for a minute before the next race started. As the former head of Komsomol and the man who had personally led the Akhal-Teke marathon to Moscow, then appeared on national television riding his horse up to the Moscow city soviet where he delivered a speech, Guvanch must have seemed to them like a combination of Michael Corleone and Joe Montana, with Bruce Springsteen thrown in for good measure. His post in the Communist apparatus, Sasha had told me, had made Guvanch one of the two or three most powerful young men in the Turkmen capital. No one had to groom Guvanch Djumaev for anything; whenever he saw a bootstrap, he just naturally lifted himself up by it. He had maintained his party position until after the marathon, then boldly broke with the Communist party and organized a private enterprise, where he seemed by all odds not only incredibly successful, and making lots of money in trade, a time-honored profession in Central Asia going back to the days of the Silk Road, but also a key man in privatizing the horse industry and saving the Turkmen's main cultural symbol. He was young, handsome with a round face and crooked Mongolian nose, clean-cut, and had an air of authority about him. In addition to a relentless gift of gab, Djumaev had the politician's ability to give each man he talked to his undivided attention for three or four minutes—during which, however, he did most of the talking. Could anyone be so good? In my mind as I watched him, I thought, what a contrast to Djura Semedov: Could anyone be so bad? It was almost too symmetrical to believe. They were exact opposites in any category you chose. It was hard to believe they were both Turkmen—indeed, even members of the same human race.

Yet how much of their opposite characters, I wondered, emanated from the same sources: the Soviet system, which had first liberated Turkmen from the old culture of tribal warfare and slave raiding, then Russified the place; and the treacherous desert itself, where change usually means death. Also where every man wages war between the nomad and the settled man inside himself—between the elemental forces of nature that make him look upon other men as mortal threats to his survival and the human impulses that drive the city man to look on others as allies necessary for his survival. Why does one man succumb to greed in a stifling, corrupt system while another plays his hand wisely and rises above conditions to become a hero of his time? Perhaps it is nothing more than intelligence. The only thing I knew was that one was Turkmenistan's leading horseman while the other weaved webs of intrigue and deceit from an office at the Turkmen Friendship Society. Were it not for Guvanch, Semedov would have driven me irrevocably from any thoughts of ever returning to Central Asia. Because of my chance introduction to Guvanch, however, I now felt sad about my imminent departure. A part of me did not want to leave.

But it was not only Guvanch. Through the dumb luck of meeting him, I had also found a band of brothers with whom I shared the passion for horses: Geldi, Yusup, and Sasha Skorokhodov. The Akhal-Tekes were their love, their trade, and their culture. I have no real brothers, yet somehow I remembered this feeling of brotherhood, as if I had experienced it in a former life thousands of years ago; now it was returning, on the other side of the world, to make me whole.

As the afternoon wore on, the restless boys in the grandstand tore from their seats at the end of each race and ran onto the track. Policemen gave chase, but half a dozen cops can't stop a hippodrome full of wild boys.

"That was me as a boy." Geldi smiled as he watched them. "When I was their age, seven or eight, I was working at the stables of the old hippodrome. I never went home. I slept with the horses in the stables. That was how I began."

After the last race, Guvanch decided we should have a going-away party for me, so the four of us packed into his plush tan sedan—Geldi had to go home to make sure his horses were fed—and bumped along in the Sunday afternoon traffic to a café he knew about somewhere in downtown Ashkhabad. The decor was late Mongol Horde: dark, smoky, with glimmering blue-black beaded curtains and strange Turkmen music squealing from a cassette player. The owner was a portly young man who insisted on standing us to drinks and a meal, and started delivering bottles of vodka and delicious hors d'oeuvres to our table. He toasted us by saying it was a great honor to have Guvanch Djumaev and an American guest in his café on the same evening.

Guvanch belted his vodka back, closed his eyes, inflated his cheeks, and immediately stuffed something in his mouth to take away the burning taste of the raw liquor. He didn't like the taste of vodka, only its effect. As we drank, he grew more expansive than ever, talking, inevitably, about horses. "We are only the temporary keepers of the world," he said. "The Turkmen have a duty to future generations to preserve the Akhal-Teke breed because it was here before the Turkmen ever came to this land."

"Truth?" I asked in Russian. "What proof?"

"There is archaeological proof that the Akhal-Teke breed long preceded the Turkmen nomads here." Sasha picked up the point in his more precise, analytical style. "There would be historical evidence, too, but the Mongols destroyed all the written records of the Islamic scholars at Merv and Khwarizm."

The archaeological evidence had been found at Pazyryk in southern Siberia, in the Altai Mountains. It is a Scythian burial site dating back to about 500 B.C. The Scythians buried their kings and aristocrats along with their horses. The site was permanently frozen underground so everything found there was in perfect condition. At Pazyryk they dug up sixteen complete horses of different kinds. Some were the slaves' ponies, some pack animals. The king had to take with him all he needed for his journey into the next world. They also dug up the first horses known to be used primarily or only for riding. They knew this because of the saddles and tack found with them, and also because they were gelded. A carpet found at the site—the oldest carpet in the world, Sasha added—showed Scythian aristocrats riding these horses. They were large, averaging some fifteen hands, and those who studied the carcasses found that they had the same anatomical characteristics as the Akhal-Teke. In addition, the skins were so well preserved that the very same golden shine, unique identifying mark of the Akhal-Teke, could be observed. "It is not actually known when the Turkmen tribes came here, but the first mention of them in Western literature is in Marco Polo, who came at the end of the Mongol invasions. Marco Polo stayed a year in this region, we know, because of the danger of travel on the Silk Road during the Mongol wars. The Turkmen may have first come to this region as mercenary cavalry to fight for the khans of Khwarizm or Bukhara or Merv against the Mongols. If so, they didn't arrive here until after A.D. 1200, so it is certain the Akhal-Teke type of horse existed long before the Turkmen tribes came here."

At this point, Guvanch staggered to his feet. "Talking, please," he said in broken English, with a big, wide golden-toothed grin at me, as if to say, I'll bet you didn't think I could do that. The others raised their glasses. Guvanch spoke seriously of our new friendship—how it must continue and how I must return to Turkmenistan as his guest. For the Turkmen Muslim, he said, nothing was as important as foreign guests. He quoted a Turkmen proverb, "The guest is higher than the father." When I came again, he said, everything would be prepared for me to make a film about the Akhal-Tekes. Everything would be taken care of. If I wanted to ride, Guvanch would provide a horse. If I wanted to see the rest of Turkmenistan, he would go with me himself. And no one would try to arrest me!

"Are you sure?" I interjected.

"*Konyechno*," he laughed. He returned to being serious. "Now we are in a difficult situation in Turkmenistan. After the marathon to Moscow we made in 1988, the Turkmen were able to win back control of Akhal-Teke horse breeding from Moscow. This is good. To control our own economic and cultural resources is a first step toward joining the modern world. But now the economy and political situation of the Soviet Union is so unstable that no one knows what will happen. We can be sure Turkmenistan will remain part of the Union. In a referendum 95 percent here voted in favor of remaining inside the Soviet Union, whereas the other Soviet republics voted for independence. The Russians protect the Turkmen from Iran. The Turkmen don't want to trade Gorbachev for the Ayatollah Khomeini. But with the Soviet Union sinking, the situation for the Akhal-Teke is dangerous. Most of the horses are on the big state farms and collectives. What will happen a year from now when the people are starving and have no meat? The party has taken our horses to the sausage factory before. That is why we have decided to ship some Akhal-Teke horses to Bulgaria now through our colleague Alex. We will try to have horses and capital outside the Soviet Union if things come to the worst here."

A few minutes later claps of thunder like bombs shook the café. We must have have looked disastrously drunk. Yusup was wearing my cowboy hat; I was smoking Russian cigarettes with Sasha Skorokhodov, holding them between my thumb and index fingers, Cossack style. We all staggered outside to see what the noise was about, but got no farther than the concrete awning over the entrance when the sky burst. The rain came down in solid sheets. It was more like a waterfall than a rainstorm. No ground could accommodate so much water so rapidly. We stood under the awning staring at the puddles and rivulets.

"It will be the last rain until next spring." Guvanch folded his arms across his chest with satisfaction.

No one disputed him. We went back inside to finish our party.

The next morning I flew to Moscow to meet Sally Alice Thompson and Greg Gleason, who had gone on to Moscow from Bukhara. We stood in a tiny park in an old commercial district of the city and ate fresh cabbage *pirozhki* with mugs of tea in a cold May drizzle. Sally Alice was tired but unbowed from all the partying. Her main worry was the invitation to Albuquerque that Djura had extorted from her as part of the delegation of Turkmen medical doctors she was trying to bring to the States. I advised her to tell the State Department that he was KGB; maybe it would cancel his visa. Greg Gleason was to stay in Moscow for another week on academic business.

Our plan was to call it an early evening since Sally Alice's and my flight to Frankfurt departed at six A.M., and we had to leave for the airport at three. We were staying at the apartment of another of Sally Alice's international hosting friends, a bright, affable young scientist named Leonid Kordonski who had quit the Soviet Academy of Sciences to join a private joint enterprise selling imported Western computer equipment. When we met him at his office in downtown Moscow, he showed me his company's computer and telecommunications system, complete with answering machine and fax.

"Leonid," I asked, "is there any chance that you could communicate with Ashkhabad, Turkmenistan, by fax?"

"Konyechno," he said with more of a drawl than Guvanch's delivery. He was a skinny kid with a wiry, light-colored beard and melancholy eyes. "All that is necessary is the fax number there."

"Leonid, I need to send a fax to Ashkhabad in May, and to receive a fax from Ashkhabad in June. If I paid you the charges plus your time—"

"But you don't have to pay me, Jon," he cut me off. "Our company has a telephone line reserved one hour a day for a friend in Boston, Massachusetts, to do business. I would be happy to transmit your fax documents."

Could it ever be that easy? But nothing involving remote Margiana, the edge of the old Russian empire in Central Asia, could be so simple. The Soviet Union was disintegrating; no one had any idea what to do next. Nonetheless, in the months to come this chance encounter with Leonid Kordonski turned out to be a crucial connection for me. With this new link to Moscow, my travels to Ashkhabad and the Kara Kum as an Albuquerque delegate became the prelude for a return to the land of the sacred horses.

PART III

In the Shadow of Bucephalus

It had taken so much time and effort to arrange my first trip to Turkmenistan that I did not look forward to going through it all again when I returned to the United States at the beginning of May 1991. While my new friendships with Guvanch Djumaev, Geldi Kiarizov, and the others would make the next journey immeasurably more productive and pleasurable, especially from an equestrian point of view, I was aware that I had essentially been thwarted and obliged to come all the way home in order to arrange for new documents to go back—all because of Djura the Horrible at the so-called Turkmen Friendship Society. It was a bit like climbing to the top of a high mountain with great effort, then, without having a chance to savor the view, being forced to return to base camp and made to climb it all over again.

Even so, I felt bound and determined to return to Turkmenistan. The most exciting things going on in the States that summer were the double-dip recession and the guy in Milwaukee who liked to eat boys after raping and murdering them. I still had not ridden an Akhal-Teke in the Kara Kum Desert, let alone across it, but now I had a unique opportunity to document one of the world's most exotic and beautiful breeds of horses, perhaps a missing link in the evolution of horses and horsemanship. Most of all, I wanted to find out what would happen next in the country of the sacred horses.

Having once gone through the enormous rigmarole of obtaining the right documents and getting myself halfway around the world to a remote Central Asian republic populated by ex-nomadic Muslims, I was

cognizant now of all the difficulties in getting such an expedition together, especially in terms of communications, and slightly anxious that
the record of my arrest and interrogation in the desert might somehow
prevent my obtaining a new visa, though this seemed a remote possibility
in the chaos reigning in the then Soviet Union. It seemed more likely
that political upheaval itself might prevent me from returning to Central
Asia. Gorbachev had recently abandoned the reformers and was moving
into an alliance with the hard-liners on the right, which had Americans
and Soviets alike wondering how much longer the policies of glasnost
and perestroika would last. A return to Stalinism, even sugar-coated
Stalinism, would almost certainly be accompanied by the reinstallation of
restrictions on travel to places like Turkmenistan, and probably by
reinforced restrictions on citizens' contacts with foreigners as well. The
boys at the Turkmen Friendship Society would welcome it as open
season.

Such considerations were out of my hands, but they created a certain
urgency. If I was ever to go back to Turkmenistan, it was necessary to
try sooner rather than later, so I decided to proceed as if my plan to
return in August would, in fact, come to fruition. If it didn't turn out,
I would never regret the riding or the time spent memorizing ten
thousand Russian verbs. Perhaps the short course I put myself through
in video production might serve a purpose in some other endeavor. On
the other hand, if my second journey actually did come off, I would be
ready.

This meant hurling myself into a kind of single-minded training
mission for the next three months—riding, studying Russian, learning
video technique, writing up the journal of my first trip while it was still
fresh in my mind, and trying to answer some of the questions about
horses and Turkmenistan. In May, as agreed, I wrote out a proposal
for Guvanch, including some of the things I wanted to document
about Akhal-Tekes—breeding, feeding, training, racing, et cetera—as
well as a list of the locations in Turkmenistan where I wanted to film,
and some of the people I wanted to interview. When it was done, I
had my literary agent fax the document to Leonid Kordonski in Moscow with a request to transmit it to Ashkhabad. Unbelievably, my frail
little communications network actually worked: A few weeks later, my
agent's office called to say it had received a document in Russian for
me by fax from Moscow. Sure enough, when it arrived in the mail, it
contained a formal invitation from BEVIKO to Turkmenistan for me and

Moira Ratchford, a young Washington sovietologist whom I had enticed to come along to Turkmenistan to assist in documenting the Akhal-Tekes on videotape. Moira had made numerous trips to the Soviet Union, several as a guide for American tourist groups, and from the beginning she proved an invaluable colleague. The next thing was to arrange for air tickets, and Moira knew a discount service with an 800 number for cheap seats on Aeroflot. I reserved two seats to Moscow for August 20, and saved eight hundred dollars over what TWA-Lufthansa would have charged. Of course, we would have to fly an airline with one of the worst air-safety records in the world, but at least I knew enough to bring sandwiches. With the invitations in hand and the tickets purchased, Turkmenistan II was looking increasingly like a go. At the end of June, I made arrangements to travel to Staunton, Virginia, to visit the Cases—the American couple breeding Akhal-Tekes whom Yusup Anaklichev had told me about—to photograph their horses for Yusup and to show them the slides of the Akhal-Tekes I had taken in Turkmenistan.

Staunton is about an hour out of Charlottesville, in the rolling horse country toward the West Virginia border. The Cases' Akhal-Teke stud farm occupies the top of a long sloping ridge, which starts downhill at the barn and rises through lush green pastures to a comfortable cedar dacha built in the round. As I drove my pickup truck in, I experienced the strange sensation of seeing a herd of Akhal-Tekes at pasture in Virginia. I would have recognized their dished faces and fine, glowing coats anywhere. But standing on green grass? Where was the desert beneath their feet? Was it just my imagination, or did these American-raised horses look plumper, perhaps from richer fodder? Did they lack that lean, hungry, wild, and almost primitive look of their cousins back home in Turkmenistan?

It was a close early-summer afternoon, about 110 percent humidity, very much *not* Turkmenistan weather. Margot Case met me outside the house, and walked me down to the barn; Phil, a paper-company executive, would be home from work later and would join us in time for dinner. Margot is a soft-spoken, introspective woman, more comfortable around her Akhal-Tekes than around strangers, especially ones with cameras. But our mutual enthusiasm for the breed quickly overcame her shyness.

For more than ten years, the Cases have been breeding Akhal-Tekes in the United States, trying to introduce them into different kinds of equestrian competitions, including show jumping, cross country, three-day eventing, dressage, even steeplechase. Akhal-Tekes are just as good for one event as another, and look great when performing in shows at their smooth, high, trot—a unique rhythm, which Margot attributes to an exceptionally loose shoulder joint. Anyone who feels that rhythm becomes intrigued and impressed, but the name of the game in the horse business, she told me, is getting a winner before the riding public to familiarize Americans with the Akhal-Teke breed, and to show them that a horse they may initially consider too exotic can compete successfully against big warm bloods and high-priced Arabians. Introducing a new and foreign breed in the conservative world of equestrian sports is a daunting task requiring time, patience, smarts, capital, marketing, luck, and a healthy sense of irony. So far, said Margot, their successes had been limited to producing some regional winners, but not the major national splash they would like. "To create a winner like that," she said, "everything has to click just right: the rider, the horse, the training regimen. It's a union of many factors. The program has to be designed around the horses. Akhal-Tekes can't be forced. They have to trust their rider. Once they do, they perform like no other, but if you try to push them, they'll balk. If you break trust with them, they won't work with you. We have had trainers who didn't really understand this. One thought she should be able to bring the horse along fast, before she had really established that trust relationship. When the horse wouldn't perform up to her high standards, she tried to discipline it as you might a Thoroughbred. It didn't work. You have to work *with* the Akhal-Tekes, not *on* them. That's what people mean when they say that Akhal-Tekes are temperamental. It's not that they are high strung, only that they are so loyal they seem to have an emotional key different from other breeds. Once that loyalty is established, however, the Akhal-Teke will do anything for its rider."

At the barn, I was introduced to Sue, who manages the Cases' stables. She wondered if she could send along some written questions to ask Yusup at the stud in Ashkhabad. Since the Cases are the only Akhal-Teke breeders in the United States, specific information about the breed has been hard to come by. What do the Turkmen feed their horses? How do they train them? How does their breeding program operate? Sue said they'd had several foals born with contracted leg tendons. Were the Akhal-Tekes in Turkmenistan also prone to this condition? If so, what caused it, and what could be done about it? She also spoke a little about the differences she had noticed between working with the Akhal-Teke mares and the stallions. "We use a heart monitor to gauge variation with exercise," she said, "but I've noticed how a mare's heartbeat also varies with emotional situations. For example, when we take a mare away from the herd and isolate her, her heartbeat definitely increases. When she's returned to the herd, it goes back down to normal. Generally speaking, the mares are harder to handle; they don't want to leave the group."

The stud's handsome foundation stallion, Senetir, a classic golden chestnut Akhal-Teke with long legs and a haughty eye, was brought out, and I shot him with my old 35 mm. Nikkormat on a tripod. The Cases have chosen Turkmen or Turkmen-sounding names for their horses, in keeping with the breed's roots, and meticulously enter their Akhal-Teke pure bloods in the Akhal-Teke stud book published in Russia. Soon the barn hands led out the stallions, mares, and offspring—too many of which, unfortunately, still reside in the Cases' barn—to have their pictures taken: Senova, Sentor, Sengar, Danska, Dari, Kashman, Oliva, Dekka, and Melekush U.S.A., the last from the same blood line as the famous Akhal-Teke Melekush, which Nikita Khrushchev presented to the Queen of England. We spent the better part of the afternoon leading them out onto the greensward. As I looked through the lens, I thought how tickled Yusup and my other Turkmen friends would be to have pictures of their beloved Akhal-Tekes from the United States—but also how strange they would probably find the color of the land, for the Turkmen have not known a time when their lands were not desert.

Before we had finished, Phil Case arrived home from work and came down to the barn in shorts and high rubber boots, his Labrador retrievers nipping and jumping at his ankles. Case is a tall, rugged man with a hard handshake and a forceful personality to match. He has taken on the Akhal-Teke as a cause as much as a business venture, and launched the Akhal-Teke Association of America to work on conserving, researching, and stabilizing the breed. "The more you work with them and learn about them, the more you realize that the Akhal-Teke is a genetic heirloom," he said. "I've read just about every work there is on the breed, and it's clear to me that this was the horse from which the Thoroughbred derives."

"The Turkmen say the same thing," I told him.

Over dinner that evening, the Cases were eager to hear about my experiences in Turkmenistan. Phil spoke about his dream that someday he and Margot could themselves travel there, but he spoke with the sigh of a horse owner who must be there always to care for the horses.

"Why don't we go together?" I suggested, not wanting to let anyone as nutty about the breed as me get away. "Your friend Yusup Anaklichev is dying to meet you. I'm sure he would issue an invitation. Here's what we'll do. When I go to Turkmenistan in August, I will suggest a cultural exchange between the Akhal-Teke Association of America and the Akhal-Teke Association of Turkmenistan. First, I'll invite a delegation of Turkmen horsemen to the States. We could ride a marathon together, the way the Turkmen did in 1935 and 1988."

"There's the International Horse Show in Washington every autumn," said Margot.

"Could we ride there on some of your horses? It would be great publicity for the breed."

Phil Case regarded me thoughtfully, but said only, "It's possible."

"Then they would invite a return visit by an American delegation," I said. "We'll go—when? Maybe next winter? I'd love to see Turkmenistan in the winter."

"Christmas in Ashkhabad." Phil Case laughed. "That would really be something."

"Can I propose it on behalf of your association when I go over there in August—if I go, that is?"

"Why not? It sounds so silly that it just might work out."

A few days later, I stopped in at the library to look up the 1948 earthquake in Turkmenistan. In Ashkhabad they had told me that 150,000 had been killed in twenty minutes, and the entire city reduced to rubble, after which the Stalin regime had the bodies bulldozed into a common grave, and repopulated the city with other nationalities. I didn't expect to discover the truth; I merely wanted to see what the world had known about the Ashkhabad earthquake and when it had known it.

The first item I found appeared in the back pages of *The New York Times* on Saturday, October 9, 1948. It was a classic Associated Press "shirttail" of about three column inches, datelined Moscow. The headline read INJURED EXCEED 6000 IN MID-ASIA QUAKE. The AP quoted Moscow radio as saying that "Six thousand persons injured in an earthquake October 6 in the city of Ashkhabad, Central Asia" had been evacuated by air and special trains to hospitals in the region. The AP described Ashkhabad as the "capital and largest city of Soviet Turkmenia," in the foothills of the "Kopet-Daga Mountains" (sic), about 150 miles north of the Iranian city of Mashhad, which had also been devastated by an earthquake about midnight, Tuesday, October 5. So Ashkhabad was not alone: There had been more than one temblor. The report noted that the Moscow broadcast "did not say how many were injured in the quake."

The following day the *Times* carried a slightly longer account headed QUAKE DEATH TOLL HIGH. This time it was the United Press International quoting Tass to the effect that "a large but unstated death toll" had been reported from the "severe earthquake in the southern Soviet Republic of Turkmen (sic)." Tass was still using the figure of six thousand injured, but added the puzzling information that six hundred children had been orphaned. In addition the agency was quoted as saying that the epicenter of the quake had been just fifty miles from Ashkhabad, and that "industrial enterprises, administrative buildings, railway stations, communications, and cultural institutions were destroyed." A thousand doctors had arrived in the area from Moscow, accompanied by the chief Soviet health officer and the chief surgeon of the Soviet army. The high number of medical personnel cast doubt on the casualty figures.

That was all. There was no follow-up, no relief forces sent, no attempt by Western reporters to reach the quake site. The Ashkhabad earthquake was never mentioned again in the American press. Perhaps no one knows how many people died, only that there were so many that the Turkmen subsequently became a minority in their own homeland. Nature has never been kind to the Turkmen, and Stalin got away with whatever he wanted.

Spurred by my conversation with the Cases, I decided to try to learn more about the background of the English (and American) Thoroughbred breed, but was surprised to find out there is apparently no standard contemporary reference work on this subject. I slogged through Professor William Ridgeway's massive 1905 tome, *The Origin and Influence of the Thoroughbred Horse,* only to find that he devoted nearly five hundred pages to his idea that the Thoroughbred descended from the Libyan horse from North Africa, not the Turkoman (sic) horse from Central Asia, and spent less than ten pages discussing the actual founding of the breed. Ridgeway, a Cambridge don and professor of archaeology, was convinced that North Africans gave their light, swift Barb horses to the Arabs as the bloodstock for Arabian horses, which later became the foundation of the Thoroughbred. He based his case mainly on color: the bays and browns and chestnuts of the Arabian being originally Barb colors while western Asian horses are typically yellow, dun, gray, or white. Ridgeway thought that Turkoman horses derived from "Turcoman ponies" crossed with Arabians which had been introduced into Central Asia by Tamerlane in the thirteenth century. He seemed unaware that Chinese and Persian emperors and Mongol khans alike had been lusting after the big warmblood horses of Central Asia for millennia. Ridgeway must never have seen a Turkoman horse, because he repeatedly referred to them as small and shaggy, like the Mongolian pony—about as far as you can get from the tall, fine-coated horses represented today by the Akhal-Teke. This makes everything else Ridgeway said in his book suspect.

The origins of the Thoroughbred are not so much shrouded in mystery as hampered by simple lack of information. This is probably in character with the men who breed horses for the turf, a secretive lot who fervently believe in the pecuniary value of inside information. But it was also in keeping with late seventeenth- and early eighteenth-century England, when foreign horses were imported as an adjunct to the rising tide of British imperialism—which is to say captured in war, taken as booty, accepted as tribute from subject potentates, dubiously acquired by merchant-adventurers, or just plain stolen. Under the circumstances no one asked for written pedigrees, and no one wrote anything down—a wise policy when dealing with hot goods.

The problem of the Thoroughbred's origins is further complicated by the fact that at the beginning, breeding racehorses was intuitive and random. There was no plan, no concept, no proposal, no contract. No one ever consciously thought, "Now we will begin a breeding program by which, at the end of one hundred years, there will emerge a noble horse with the splendid speed of the Oriental warm blood and the indomitable strength of the British hunter, the fastest horse the world has ever seen, full of energy and spirit, with an outstanding competitive urge, and a heart full of courage." On the contrary, it was a hit-or-miss business; the three so-called pillars of the Thoroughbred stud book weren't even recognized until several generations later, when their grandsons and great-grandsons proved themselves on the turf—and when, of course, it was too late to go back and breed them to more carefully selected mares.

In addition, the English traced a horse's descent through the sire, whereas Arabs traced lineage exclusively through the mare. Radically different systems of pedigree reflected different beliefs about inheritance and breeding practices—none of it, however, based on a scientific understanding of genetics: Mendel and his magic beans were still a long way off. Set in their beliefs, the British were on the prowl for stallions—usually undocumented, because the Arabs did not care about them—while the Arabs were reluctant to let go of any except their most inferior mares. This is surely the reason why Thoroughbred breeding began almost exclusively with imported stallions of vague origins being put to domestic mares. This fundamental difference between two equestrian cultures resulted in the absence of records of the importation of a single mare of any Eastern breed into England during the period of the Thoroughbred's founding. The first edition of the General Stud Book in 1793 mentions only 174 "foreign Sires"—89 classed as Arabs, 47 Barbs, 32 Turks, 4 Persians, and 2 stallions not identified by country of origin.

This does not mean, however, there were no foreign mares involved in the founding of the Thoroughbred. On the contrary, the author of the stud book, James Weatherby, Jr., recounted in his introduction that after the Restoration of 1660, Charles II sent his Master of the Horse, Sir John Fenwick, to the Levant with orders to purchase Oriental mares for the king's racing stables. Fenwick went as far as Smyrna on the coast of Turkey, where the bazaars presumably provided him with Turk horses to become the royal broodmares.

Within a few years Charles had the best running horses in England. This king didn't sit up in the clubhouse tipping his hat and drinking Pimm's Cup. Charles II was himself a furious competitor, and won several big races. He was the leader of a generation of English aristocrats who found racing and hunting so much more to their liking than warfare that they fostered a breed of horse exclusively for their pleasures. At Newmarket Heath in Suffolk, where Charles sponsored development of the racecourse and stables, competitors typically ran three- to four-mile heats, the winner taking the best of three with a half hour or so between runnings. These distances and repetitions were far too strenuous for the heavy domestic chargers favored by the mounted knights of medieval times, and helped stimulate interest in Eastern breeds known for their stamina as well as their speed. This push from the top is why the real beginning of the Thoroughbred breed is usually dated from the reign of Charles II.

Unfortunately, no one thought it important enough at the time to record the royal broodmares' names, descriptions, types, or geographic origin, much less to paint their portraits, so we might have some idea how they appeared. After the death of Charles II, the king's horses were sold, and the royal broodmares were eagerly purchased by the leading breeders of the day. Again, however, no records were kept. Afterward, they were sometimes referred to by the names of their new owners, such as the D'Arcy Royal Mare or the Sedbury Royal Mare. This is about all we know of them except that the pedigree of the first truly dominant racehorse and prepotent stallion, Eclipse, was laced with no fewer than six royal broodmares.

The use of the terms "Arabian," "Turk," and "Barb" also does not diminish the uncertainty surrounding the Thoroughbred's origins. As early as 1580, Thomas Blundeville was writing about horses "from Turkey" coming into Italy and thence to England: "not verie great nor strong made, yet verie light and swift in their running and of great courage." Among the breeds of horses Blundeville thought "most worthie" of mention to his English readers were not only "the Turk," but also "the Barbarian." The latter emanated "out of King of Tunnis land, out of Massilie Numidia," by which Blundeville meant North Africa. These Barbarians, he says, "for the most part be but little horses, but therewith verie swift, and able to make a verie long cariere, which is the cause why we esteeme them so much."

In the same year that Blundeville's book was published, a commercial treaty opened Constantinople and other ports of the Ottoman Turkish Empire to direct trade with Britain, making possible for the first time the legal importation of Eastern breeds. A few years later, Shakespeare was shortening "Barbarian" to "Barbary horse" (in reference to Othello, the Moor, himself out of North African stock). The bard mounted Bolingbroke on a "roan Barbary horse," and Barbary horses are also mentioned in *Hamlet*. One can, therefore, conclude with confidence that Barbs from North Africa and Turks from the empire of the Turkish sultan were well known in Elizabethan England and already valued for what their speed and stamina could contribute to the native breeds. This was almost one hundred years before the Byerley Turk arrived.

Blundeville made no mention of "Arabian" horses, but this term also was shortly to enter the lexicon. The duke of Newcastle, famed horseman and Charles II's boyhood riding instructor, recounts in his classic *New Method of Dressing Horses* that in 1616 he saw "one of these horses, which Mr. John Markham, a Merchant, brought over and said he was a right Arabian; He was a Bay, but a little horse, and no Rarity for Shape; for I have seen many English Horses farr Finer." Newcastle relates with unconcealed hostility how Markham sold this "right Arabian" to King James I for the outrageous price of five hundred pounds at a time when forty pounds could buy a fine English courser. When the Arabian was trained and raced, Newcastle reported with a smug sniff, "Every horse beat him."

The Weatherbys, who published the General Stud Book, passed along unchallenged this story of the overpriced foreign import in the fourth edition (1868). But Professor Ridgeway went to the considerable trouble of actually looking up the terms of the deal in the Exchequer of Receipt Order Books, and found the entry dated December 20, 1616, which says that Markham was paid 154 pounds, not 500, as Newcastle said. This evidence, Ridgeway proclaimed triumphantly, "puts it beyond doubt that no Arab horse had been imported into England prior to 1616." At any rate, no earlier record exists.

Whether the terms "Turk," "Barb," and "Arabian" were employed with more accuracy than poetic license is doubtful. I have been unable to find out, for example, why the Godolphin Arabian is sometimes called the Godolphin Barb, although the Darley Arabian is always called the Darley Arabian, and nothing else. Perhaps "Turk" and "Barb," coming into use earlier, generally referred to geographical origin while the later term "Arabian" was a more generic name for any horse of Oriental origin. In sum, the founding stallions' last names probably had little bearing on their true lineage.

Of the three commonly recognized pillars of the stud book, to which 80 percent of the half million or so Thoroughbreds in the world today can be traced back in about thirty-five generations, the first to arrive in Britain was the Byerley Turk. Like most Oriental horses, he took his name from his British owner. Captain or Colonel Robert Byerley was a mercenary cavalryman in the service of Prince Eugene at the siege of Vienna by the Turks in 1683—the very last wave of attack from the east on Western Europe, by the way. Byerley literally snatched this handsome dark bay stallion from the Turks in battle and brought him home to Ireland to serve as his charger. After fighting for William III at the Battle of the Boyne, where the famous stallion was said to have saved his master's life when he was surrounded by King James's cavalry, Byerley retired in 1690. The Byerley Turk stood at stud until his death, the year of which is not known. Like the other founding fathers, the Byerley Turk never won a stakes race himself; he did not even cover many mares. His hallowed place in the stud book was only realized later, when his great-great grandson Herod was hugely successful on the racecourse; Herod sired the winners of more than a thousand stakes races. The Byerley Turk's story serves to highlight the blind nature of early Thoroughbred breeding: No one knew where the Byerley Turk really came from and they had no idea now where his genes were going. In retrospect everything worked out for the best. John Wootton's romantic engraving of the Byerley Turk shows a tall, dark, and handsome stallion held by a turbaned sheik amid some classical stone ruins. The stallion has the splendid long neck, big legs, and comparatively slender body associated with Turkmen horses, but since the engraving was made in 1718, after the Byerley Turk had passed on to the Big Pasture in the Sky, we cannot credit it with anatomical accuracy. The Hungarian equestrian scholar Jankovich thought the Byerley Turk was "most likely" an Akhal-Teke. Even Professor Ridgeway would not dispute that he was at least a Turkmen horse of some sort.

The Godolphin Arabian probably had the most obscure beginnings of any of the three pillars of the stud book. He was born about 1725, maybe of Yemeni stock, which would make him a Barb, though he never had a pedigree and was always said to have been stolen. He was a brown-bay horse about fifteen hands high with some white on his off-hind heel and was apparently presented to Louis XV of France by the Bey of Tunis as either a five- or seven-year-old. How such a valuable stallion ended up pulling a coal cart in the streets of Paris, as legend has it, no one knows. An Englishman named Edward Coke discovered the stallion in his reduced Parisian circumstances, purchased him, and carried him off to England, where he was 1) sold by Coke to Sidney, Earl of Godolphin, or 2) left to the earl by Coke at his death, or 3) given by Coke to a coffeehouse proprietor named Roger Williams, who later presented him to the earl. Whatever, the horse ended up in Lord Godolphin's stables at Gog-Magog near Cambridge, where he remained at stud until his death in 1753 at the age of twenty-nine. There is no record that the Godolphin Arabian ever raced. His contribution to the Thoroughbred breed was not recognized until his "get" began winning big races. In the stud book Weatherby says that "almost every superior horse of the present day partakes of his valuable blood." Little more is known about the Godolphin Arabian except that he was painted in his lifetime by both George Stubbs and John Wootton, the two principal equestrian painters during the period of the founding of the Thoroughbred breed. Stubbs painted the Godolphin Arabian outside, standing alone against a stone wall. He rendered a strong, powerful horse of quite dark color, with a long, thick, arched neck and a shapely, narrow head. Wootton also portrayed him as a stunning animal, powerfully built, with fine legs and a full, arched neck. But Wootton pictured him inside a stone barn, standing on his straw bed discussing life and art with a tabby stretched out on the stallion's blanket as if he owned the place. The cat was Grimalkin, for whom the Godolphin Arabian developed an "extraordinary affection" at Gog-Magog, said Weatherby, and they became inseparable companions. Perhaps on long winter evenings the Godolphin Barb liked to tell Grimalkin the story of his early life in lands beyond the dawn while they sipped mulled wine and listened to the wind howl. If so, Grimalkin never told, and took the stallion's secret to his grave. (The stallion went wild when the cat died, became unmanageable and did not long outlive his bosom pal.)

More is probably known about the Darley Arabian than the other founding fathers; he was the only one, for example, whose original name has survived: Ras-el-Fedowi ("the Headstrong"). He was also the only one of the big three acquired above board, when Thomas Darley, a British consul, purchased him in 1710 for his brother at Aleppo in northern Syria, the principal market of the Middle East. He was described by Darley in a letter as an "exquisitely beautiful" dark bay stallion. Wootton's 1720 engraving shows him with three white boots and a prominent white blaze. In other respects, the Darley Arabian seems to have resembled his cohorts, with an elegant leanness and compact barrel, a dished or concave face, and small ears. In the 1930s, the Russian authority Dr. W. O. Witt claimed the Darley Arabian "could not possibly be taken for a thoroughbred Arab" because of his height (15.2 hands high) and his exterior, which closely approximate the better specimens of the Akhal-Teke.

Witt argued in his book *Breeds of Horses in Middle Asia* the exact opposite of Ridgeway, claiming that the Akhal-Teke, the best representative of the Turkmen horse, is the true forerunner of the Thoroughbred. He traced back through classical sources to prove that the Arabian was bred from horses of "Persian breed," not vice versa. Up until the time of Mohammed, the Arabs had a small number of horses; only after their conquest of Iran and Middle Asia did they obtain bloodstock for their special breeds subsequently developed in Arabia. During the epoch of the British Thoroughbred's development, Witt says, Europeans generally considered Arab horses "inferior to the Turk" in performance, and held them "in very low esteem." The duke of Newcastle's remarks certainly seem to support Witt's claim that Arabians won their reputation in the latter half of the eighteenth century, when large numbers of Arabians were imported to Europe to meet the huge demand for cavalry remounts after Turkey's defeat in numerous wars made trade safe.

This would explain why the Arabian was so often mentioned in connection with the Thoroughbred, when, in the event, the three foundation studs were probably a Barb and two Turks. Witt then goes on to demonstrate that the Darley Arabian was a Turk stallion to begin with, a conclusion not disputed by Professor Ridgeway. Even he recognizes that the horse Thomas Darley bought at Aleppo was bred in the desert of Palmyra in northern Syria by the Anazah, a tribe of Bedouin nomads. In the 1860s, when Wilfred and Anne Blunt made a famous expedition into central Arabia to discover the true roots of the Arab horse, they reported that the Darley Arabian was "perhaps the only thoroughbred Anazah horse in our stud book." Ridgeway quotes the Blunts approvingly, and later comments that the horses of the Levant, Iraq, and western Asia "are generally inferior to the pure-bred horses of the Anazah tribes." Dr. Witt says these Anazah Bedouins migrated into northern Mesopotamia in the seventeenth century, where they came into contact with Turkmen nomads and put some of their mares to the Turkmen stallions. This mixture of Anazah with Turkmen found its highest expression—and closest approximation of the Akhal-Teke—in the Maneqi (or Muniqi) el Sladji blood line, which reached its present form just a few years before Consul Darley went shopping in Aleppo. Witt says the Darley Arabian was "without doubt Maneqi."

Witt associates the Turkmen horse of the Thoroughbred's foundation era with the prized Oriental warhorse raised by numerous equestrian cultures of western Asia, including the Parthians, Chorasmians, Medes, and Bactrians, as well as the Turkmen nomads. But Witt was not unbiased. He was trying to bolster the reputation of Turkmen horses to the Soviet government in order to generate interest in saving the Akhal-Teke breed, which was in imminent danger of vanishing entirely because of the Red Army's preference under Marshal Budyonny for heavy cavalry mounts. Under the circumstances, it is hard to fault Dr. Witt if he was stretching the truth when he wrote that "fundamentally it was not the Arab horse which founded the British thoroughbred." Perhaps between the lines he meant the Soviets when he wrote that the czarists had "criminally underestimated the historic importance of Turkmenian breeds."

I don't pretend to be an expert on this subject, nor to have made an exhaustive study of the matter. Besides, I'm not objective; for me, the Turkmen horse, immediate forebear of the Akhal-Teke, is the obvious sentimental favorite.

It was late on Sunday night before our scheduled Tuesday departure for the USSR when I heard about the coup attempt against Gorbachev taking place in Moscow. All that summer I had been sleeping on the living-room couch, not because it was cooler than upstairs in the bedroom, though it was, but because for some reason I had convinced myself that sleeping in my own bed at home would somehow jinx my trip to Turkmenistan. I had almost finished packing; I had been packing for a good two weeks, owing to the peculiar nature of the journey.

In order to fulfill my promise to Guvanch, I was bringing along a video kit of camera equipment, designed to survive the kind of harsh desert conditions we'd be shooting under. Sand, wind, and high temperatures play havoc with such gear, so I had tried to bring two of everything, but had to fit it into one large, heavy-duty camera bag. I was almost finished packing now, and the floor was strewn with battery chargers, boxes of 8 mm. cassettes, canvas camera covers, and spare plastic bags. My riding boots were standing on a plastic bag of toilet articles and a first aid kit. The four straw cowboy hats I was going to bring as gifts for my Turkmen friends were stacked in the corner. I had managed to borrow a sturdy tripod from a public-television channel.

I flopped down in the midst of this disorder about 12:45 A.M. A storm with the absurd name of Hurricane Bob was curling up the North Carolina coast, heading toward my home in Cape May, New Jersey, and I clicked on my small transistor radio, another piece of equipment I was packing, for a weather report. Instead, I heard the news flash that Mikhail Gorbachev had been ousted by a group of hard-liners.

When I opened my eyes early the next morning, the rain had stopped, the sun was coming out, and the day was cool, bright, crisp, and golden. Hurricane Bob was a major flop, and the television and radio were full of the news from Moscow: Gorbachev removed, tanks rolling in the streets, Boris Yeltsin calling for resistance and a general strike. Like everyone else, I was stunned, confused, and hungry for information. The twenty-four hours before departure now seemed to stretch infinitely into an unknown future.

I clicked on CNN shortly before it started broadcasting the press conference of Gennadi Yanayev and the junta that claimed to be the government of the Soviet Union. It was a joke in the worst of taste. Yanayev was explaining that Gorbachev was "very tired" after all the stress he'd been under for so many years. He needed to "rest." Perhaps he could return to office later. Even George Orwell couldn't have written a better parody.

The press was outraged, and their questions were pregnant with contempt. The correspondent from the Italian newspaper *Corriere della Sera* asked, "Before undertaking your actions, did you consult with General Pinochet?"

Yanayev was visibly trembling. It occurred to me that he might be drunk, but it is hard for a naïve American to believe that one of the leaders of a coup d'etat in the Soviet Union would appear before the world in that condition. Would a president of the United States come out drunk to announce he had toppled the Senate? I preferred to think of Yanayev as the fall guy. Clearly he had been set up by the others: If it later came to trials, it would be Yanayev mouthing excruciating falsehoods in the videotape submitted as evidence. He was the small, not terribly bright boy egged on by his older brothers. Yanayev was shaking like a leaf on a tree. Perhaps when the history of the failed Soviet coup of August 1991 is written, it will be concluded that the vodka the coup plotters drank to toughen their spines was the very thing that ultimately accounted for their loose resolve and the coup's collapse.

But Yanayev was nothing compared to the man next to him, Interior Minister Boris Pugo, whose face looked exactly like his name; he had the blank expression and empty eyes of a psychopath. Then there was Vasily Starodubtsev, who had the best name of any of them. Starodubtsev, the celebrated star of Soviet agriculture, head man at the Lenin Collective Farm, looked like a Soviet version of Donald Trump. That these apparatchiki believed they could come out in front of the world press in 1991 and get away with the black-and-white lies of the 1950s showed how out of touch they were with the reality of a world irrevocably miniaturized by television. I had seen American presidents from Lyndon "I won't send your boy to die in Vietnam" Johnson to Richard "I am not a crook" Nixon, and I am happy to report that our production values are a lot higher.

Later that day, American television carried reports of Yeltsin's stirring appearance outside the Russian White House, calling for resistance and the reinstatement of Gorbachev. It was at this moment that Boris Yeltsin became a historical leader of his people. Meanwhile, the U.S. State Department had issued a traveler's advisory warning Americans not to travel to the Soviet Union. In any case, all flights from the United States to the Soviet Union were canceled. Moira had learned through her contacts that the Moscow airports had been closed down by troops. In addition, the private visa service one had to hire in Washington to deal with the Soviet embassy called to say the embassy had stopped issuing visas, which they usually grant only twenty-four to forty-eight hours before your flight. When they reopened the visa office—who knew when?—we would have to reapply, at an additional cost of $150, if we still wished to make our trip.

What to do? Nothing at this point but wait. I had spent most of my savings on the video equipment and air tickets. To carry videotaping equipment into the Soviet Union without press credentials in the midst of a coup was not smart. The authorities would confiscate it at the airport, and I would immediately be arrested or deported—or maybe both.

On Tuesday morning, I called Victor Fet in New Orleans, my Russian friend and adviser on all matters fat and lean. He was in a rare black mood—pessimistic, I thought, even for a Russian. "The fascists are in power," he said bluntly. "It may be that they will put Gorbachev on trial. In any case, they will look for scapegoats. For the Jews it will not be emigration; it will be evacuation. I think the Russian people will accept this junta. Their history is that when they wake up one morning and it's Ivanov in the Kremlin instead of Petrov, they shrug and go to job. These events will support the view of the older generation—that it's better not to know and to keep silent. You know the joke about Russian factory?"

"No," I perked up.

"One day a decree comes to factory, so the boss calls the workers together and announces, 'Tomorrow, every third worker will be hung. Any questions?'

"Everyone sits there silent. Then one worker gets up and asks, 'Should we bring our own ropes?' "

My own veil of depression lifted a little when I heard this. I knew that if Victor could find a laugh in the situation, it wasn't a lost cause. Russia, or the Russians, or maybe just Russian humor would probably survive.

"Soviet Union was on the edge of abyss," Victor concluded, "and Gorbachev took a bold step forward."

It was also on Tuesday that President Bush came out of his summer house in Kennebunkport, Maine, and denounced the Soviet coup. This was when he coined the term "coup people." He said, "We hope those, er, coup people over there . . ." Immediately thereafter, the coup mysteriously started to collapse. Yeltsin stayed inside the Russian parliament building; he was not arrested, taken to a KGB base, and executed. The tanks and troops, which had killed several people in the streets the night before, began to withdraw without shooting. Nobody could explain these occurrences other than as a crack in the attempt to overthrow the government. By Wednesday morning, National Public Radio was reporting that the coup people had fled from Moscow.

Then suddenly we were seeing Gorbachev arrive at the Moscow airport in a skimpy wind breaker, looking like somebody's lost uncle from Minsk, making his egregious mistake of still supporting the Communist party, which had just tried to topple him, and failing to thank the people in the streets who had shown themselves ready to shed their blood for democracy.

In any case, the Soviet Union was back in business, at least in the short term, and we were on our way.

Numb and disoriented from the flight across seven time zones, we arrived in Moscow five days after the aborted attempt to reinstate some version of the totalitarian past. In the taxi on the way to Leonid Kordonski's apartment, the cab driver chattered nonstop to Moira about the events of the past hundred hours. He insisted on driving us through the center of the city so we could see the Russian flag, hanging limply from the tower of the Kremlin in a shivering late summer rain; perhaps, in the end, climate does rule history.

I was more interested in seeing the remnants of the barricades in front of the Russian White House. The downtown area near Red Square looked like Washington as I remembered it in the wake of one of the big Vietnam-era antiwar marches. Two caved-in red buses—run over by a tank?—had already somehow been dragged into the yard of the Moscow City Museum; whether as an instant exhibit or a mop-up operation to unblock traffic none could say. I was content to let Moira do the listening, and sat back to look at Moscow in its postoperative recovery, but all I saw was the usual bland façade of Russian life: shabby apartment houses, fuming traffic, the billowing steam plant, unsmiling women standing in lines in their mouse-dun coats and head kerchiefs. Why wasn't everything magically transformed by the sudden advent of democracy? Why weren't the streets full of deliriously happy people celebrating their great victory over the villains? Why hadn't new shops with bright neon signs sprung up on every street, billboards advertising Sony and Hitachi, bistros on every corner? Where were the guillotines? Under the dirty face of the city, the dark, misunderstood soul of Russia was still lurking in its lair; it wasn't about to be seduced by the firebird of freedom anytime soon. It was hard not to simply feel glad that the cold war was over and pity the losers for the way history has abused them century after century. The Russians love history more than life itself.

Leonid had stayed home from work to meet us. I didn't feel the emotional impact of the Moscow events until I saw one Russian standing at the top of the stairs looking so tentative, subdued, and relieved, his face oddly shadowed, sculpted in the dark hall like a figure from the blackest strokes of Rembrandt's brush. Suddenly, I became teary-eyed, pulled his beard, and hugged him.

"You made it," I told him.

He looked at me quizzically; then his eyes flamed with irony. "No," he said, "you made it."

Inside, Leonid introduced Moira and me to his girlfriend, Tanya, a Ukrainian with a Ph.D. in nuclear physics, sweet cream in her cheeks, and hot ice in her blue eyes. She had come up from Kiev on the train, as she does every other week, to bring Leonid a dozen eggs and some fresh vegetables from her parents' dacha. On arriving, she had cleaned the whole apartment, washed the dishes, scrubbed the floors, cooked some fish and potatoes, and was looking ravishing, as well as virtuous, in a checked wool suit and tight white sweater.

We sat down to have tea with them. Not knowing whether Moscow would be worse off materially or spiritually, I had brought Leonid New York bagels, Genoa salami, a Spanish onion, a Jersey tomato, a Sunkist lemon, and a two-volume illustrated Bible. I think he liked the Bible best. During our meal we learned that he had been in touch with Ashkhabad by telephone. When Guvanch had confirmation of our arrival through Leonid, he had dispatched his junior colleague Erik to meet us in Moscow and arrange our flight to Turkmenistan. He would need our passports to arrange the tickets; the plan was to be in communication with us by telephone during the course of the day.

Leonid had to go to a business meeting and Tanya to the station to catch her train home. We promptly fell asleep waiting for Erik to contact us through someone named Victor Mikhailovich, who called about midafternoon. Moira answered, and gabbed for a good half hour. She could hardly get rid of him, and rolled her eyes when she finally put down the receiver.

We met Erik at the *aerovokzal*, a terminal downtown where they sell airline tickets and run ground transport out to the airports. In his round metal glasses, white shirt, and black tie, he looked like a Ross Perot employee. It was his first trip to Moscow, Erik said, using one of my favorite Russian words—*komandirovka*—a business trip. His instructions from Guvanch were to locate a BEVIKO contact at the *aerovokzal*, but we were told at the ticket window that she wouldn't be working until tomorrow morning. The complication was that BEVIKO wanted to pay for our tickets in rubles. In rubles a ticket from Moscow to Ashkhabad cost about three dollars. If you paid foreign currency, it would be sixty dollars or more.

We spent from 8 A.M. till dark the next day with Erik trying to obtain our airline tickets to Ashkhabad. The BEVIKO contact at the *aerovokzal* sent us to the Ministry of Civil Aviation to show our passports to the proper authorities. When we reached the correct office on the fourth floor, it was 8:45 A.M., so we were told to wait in the hall. At 9:05, a man with a briefcase swept by us into the office, slamming the door shut behind him. At 9:30, I persuaded the obsequious Erik to knock and open the door. The official, who was sitting at his desk reading the newspaper, jumped up and told us excitedly that he was not receiving anyone for an hour.

Ten minutes later a woman from the next office came out into the corridor. We collared her, and Erik showed her the official letter of invitation Guvanch had arranged for the Turkmen Cinematographers' Union to send to the Ministry of Civil Aviation on our behalf. The woman said the letter was no good because the Ministry of Civil Aviation's international department had recently changed its name, so the letter was addressed to an incorrect agency. I protested that we could hardly be refused because of a bureaucratic name change, and after a little discussion the woman agreed to sign off, and sent us upstairs to room 725 for a final okay.

Upstairs in room 725, however, a twitching bureaucrat in a white shirt and tie decided the letter had the wrong date on it because we were four days late arriving in Moscow. He wanted a new letter Telexed from Ashkhabad with the proper date of our arrival. I pointed out to him that the reason the date was incorrect was because events in his country had prevented us from traveling, and that we could hardly be blamed for this. He twitched in a negative way and turned back to his typewriter. At this point I lost it, leaped out of my chair, and started ranting in English about "fucking bureaucratic assholes."

"I good understand English," said the twitching bureaucrat without smiling.

"Well, then, understand this," I told him. "We're not getting a new letter Telexed. Our documents are in good order. Now do us the courtesy of signing off and we'll go away and leave you alone."

This incentive must have sounded good enough because at this point he relented and said he would send the required Telex to Aeroflot permitting the purchase of our tickets in rubles. We had only to go to the office on Petrovka, where they actually sold tickets to foreigners.

On the way out to the elevator, a table was set up offering Aeroflot timetables. I picked one up. An Aeroflot advertisement on the back of it said, "Where would you be without accurate flight information?" Right here, I thought.

—

When we reached the ticketing office on Petrovka, there were twelve ticket windows, all but one closed. There were no signs or information of any kind, no one to speak to, and a ragtag line of third-world students who had obviously been waiting for days to get out of the USSR in its time of instability. Naturally, no one there knew anything about a Telex from the ministry; we had been tricked by the twitching bureaucrat. I felt like leaping through the glass window, flopping prostrate on the ground in tears, and begging whoever came by first for a small personal favor. I had read about this method in Gogol stories. Moira said they wanted to be paid off. Poor Erik was flummoxed and didn't know what to do. He said he would consult with Victor Mikhailovich, whoever he was, and telephone Guvanch in Ashkhabad for instructions.

"No," I shot back vehemently. "We're not getting anywhere like this. We will go back to Leonid's, get our gear together, go out to the airport, and offer someone waiting for the Ashkhabad flight to buy their tickets for dollars."

Outside, a bone-chilling drizzle had started. By the time we got back to Leonid's and scraped together a meal of buckwheat kasha with onion, we realized that buying tickets at the airport was impossible because passengers are identified on their tickets by passport number. I was stuck in Moscow with the Ashkhabad blues again, hearing saxophones in my head by this time.

I relented. Otherwise, we might still be in Moscow trying to buy an airline ticket. Next morning Moira and I went back to meet Erik at the circus on Petrovka, and after several hours in various lines finally managed to purchase tickets for a night flight to Ashkhabad. What was amazing was how, after you gave in psychologically, the bureaucratic logjam suddenly seemed to break up for no better reason than it had formed in the first place. However, the whole imbroglio left me with a sore throat and a bad taste in my mouth.

Erik picked us up to go out to Domodedovo at 9 P.M. for a 1 A.M. departure. There was no point in leaving too little time for something to go wrong. He showed up at Leonid's apartment house in a big, boxy, black chauffeur-driven Volga.

"What's this?" I asked.

"The state limousine of Turkmenistan. The president uses it when he comes to Moscow."

"I see." Somebody had been pulling strings like mad. It seemed odd that we rated the president of Turkmenistan's limo, but couldn't manage to buy a simple airline ticket. Still, I was glad that Erik had the chance to regain his self-image after all the bureaucratic humiliation he had suffered during his first *komandirovka* to the big city. I tried to act duly impressed.

We drove out to Domodedovo in plush, funereal silence. I mulled over important questions of state policy, like whether they would feed us on the flight. At the precise moment I stepped out of the limo and saw all eyes turn my way, I suddenly knew what it must feel like to be a celebrity: like your head is too big for your neck.

Arrival by limousine, however, couldn't protect us from the nightmare of Domodedovo. The so-called transit lounge was packed with comrades trying to go somewhere, but their passage was blocked by families of every different Soviet nationality huddled in the middle of the floor as if shipwrecked, waiting for flights. There were no benches or seats of any sort. Mothers with babies in their arms were curled asleep around their hampers and cardboard boxes. Men were sprawled asleep over big, cheap, broken-zippered plastic suitcases. Brothers and sisters slept in tangles of arms and legs.

As a result, slurries of humanity oozed slowly around the sloppy floor, sometimes colliding with oncoming slurries. Individuals abandoned their slurries to wriggle into others. They pushed each other, slipped, fell, got stepped on, stepped on others. Tempers flared; shoving matches broke out. A tall comrade with a shaved head suddenly started shaking his fists, shouting at the top of his lungs, "This is life in the Soviet Union, Comrades!"

There was no place to move, but hardly any place to stop. You couldn't see too well, either. The lights were low and yellow, as if it were 1934 and Stalin was watching from behind a one-way mirror, snickering at the havoc he had created. Over the noise of the crowd, a mechanical female voice droned out flight departures, but there were no gates.

I was mostly worried about Moira, who was carrying her own heavy rucksack and the heavy-duty tripod. Despite being fluent in Russian and brilliant and beautiful, she was not used to such rough riding. I kept her in front of me where I could see her. We pushed toward a corner, drew the wagons into a circle, and stayed there guarding the gear and fending off the fringes of the mob while Erik forayed to discover when and where we could board. At length the uniformed security guards gave the gear a dose of X rays that was sufficient to shrink tumors and let us out a side door to walk to the jet across the tarmac in the dead of night, dodging the jets taxiing in and out.

When we boarded, the cabin wasn't half full, so I put my heavy bag with the video gear down in the rear, but a stewardess immediately stomped toward us, barking "Not permitted! Not permitted!" By Aeroflot regulations, the seats had to be filled front to rear. I showed her that we were carrying seven bulky pieces of baggage, and that it would be far easier for everyone concerned if we sat in the rear. *Nyet,* she insisted; no exceptions allowed. So we carried all seven pieces to the very front of the cabin, poking and stabbing poor Turkmen comrades every step of the way up the narrow aisle. By the time we had arranged the gear and squeezed into our seats, we were marked as the troublesome "foreigners" on board. Up in the crowded front, the air reeked of jet fuel, unwashed bodies, sheep dip, camel breath, rotting onions, and fermenting pumpernickel bread. The air vents above the seats sprouted some kind of unreassuring, steamy vapor. Fifty pairs of eyes were preparing fifty painful deaths for us.

Oh, well, I thought, if you pay in rubles, you live in rubles.

But eventually the jet took off without incident, and three and a half hours later, still unfed, we came in for a landing. Out one side of the plane it was black night; on the other was a single pink stripe of dawn. Another adventure in Turkmenistan had begun.

At the airport, Guvanch threw his arms around me in a big hug. Our own odyssey flying through the aftermath of the coup couldn't be compared with the incredible journey Guvanch had undergone on our behalf. He had taken his wife and children to Bulgaria for the Akhal-Teke auction and a summer holiday, intending to return via Moscow in order to meet us in person when we arrived. They flew from Bulgaria to Moscow on the twentieth, the very day the trouble started. The roads into Moscow were already full of tanks and troops. They managed to get downtown, only to find the hotels closed. He managed to stash his family in a hotel outside of town, where at least they found out what was going on by watching television. At this point they realized that we would not be arriving, due to the closure of civilian airports, and that they themselves would not be leaving anytime soon. The next evening Guvanch left his wife and children at the hotel and went downtown to join the demonstration outside the Russian White House. He ended up spending the night there, witnessing the initial attack of the army troops on the barricades set up by the demonstrators, and taking part in the defense of democracy and the Yeltsin government. He had been there when Yeltsin came out and made his famous rallying speech. By pure coincidence, Guvanch had participated in history, and returned to Turkmenistan two days later with a tale to tell his grandchildren.

In Ashkhabad, Guvanch had arranged everything splendidly for Moira and me. We would be lodging with Donatar, his wild young Turkmen driver, who just happened to have a spare house in which we could stay. Donatar was getting married in October and, according to Turkmen custom, had been building his bride a new home in the Sverdlov neighborhood, a few kilometers from downtown. Until the wedding, he was living there by himself, and was not averse to a little stimulating foreign company in the dwindling days of his bachelorhood.

Donatar was a rangy six-foot-plus twenty-five-year-old with thick black hair and black eyes that could equally well kill you or die for you. It was a surprise when his house turned out to be something of a private palace. The rooms were forty feet long, the walls hand-painted in fantastic Arabian Nights patterns and mad arabesques, with stars and crescent moons on the chocolate-brown ceilings. The bathroom was lavishly tiled with colorful murals of fish and a large new imported porcelain bathtub. The exterior was painted gray trompe l'oeil, making the building look as if it had been built of stone blocks. A broad cement courtyard with a fig tree and high iron gates completed the feeling of Asian splendor, though the furnishings would arrive only after the wedding. I had been to Guvanch's apartment on my first trip to Turkmenistan: The chauffeur's dwelling place was more impressive than the boss's.

"To you it is pleasing?" Donatar asked.

"It's fantastic," I said. "I've never seen anything like it."

"For my Gulichka." He winked. "My bride. Gulya is her name."

"Has she seen it yet?"

"What are you saying? The bride see the house before the wedding? Absolutely not! Never. It's not allowed under Turkmen custom."

"She must be very special to you."

"Yes," he said proudly. "I'm paying fifty thousand rubles to her family for her!"

From the window of the central room a scene of biblical simplicity caught my attention in the adjacent courtyard of a poor Turkmen family, where the clothes were washed and hung out to dry, children played, wood was chopped for the clay bread oven, and the fodder chopped for the sheep kept alongside the house in a makeshift, lean-to manger. A tattered piece of patterned cloth hung in the doorway in place of a door. Sunlight struck the yellow wash of the mud-brick walls with a lambent warmth. The comrades next door moved slowly through this light as if reenacting scenes from Deuteronomy and Leviticus. Guvanch turned on the air conditioning and left us with orders to rest after our long trip. But as soon as he went home, Donatar returned with *cherek* still deliciously hot from the clay oven in which it had been baked. He made a pot of green tea in an electric kettle, and sat down to schmooze. He, too, it turned out, was a veteran of the 1988 Ashkhabad–Moscow marathon Guvanch had led, and he showed me the tiny plaque on the small Teke carpet presented to him as a souvenir. He kept the carpet draped over one of the dining-room chairs.

"That's not all I got," he said. "They gave me a television, and later a cassette player. I sold it for two thousand rubles."

"It must have been an incredible adventure, to ride an Akhal-Teke from Ashkhabad all the way to Moscow."

Donatar whooped, whistled, and whipped his imaginary mount to show me his keen horsemanship. Then he made a grunting sound through his nasal passages and flexed his biceps to show how young and virile he was. He nodded with satisfaction. "That's when I started to work for Guvanch."

"Tell me, did you ride your own horse?"

"*Nyet!*" Donatar waved his arms furiously above his head. "I rode horse of Guvanch! Guvanch was the leader. You think he had time to ride every day? *Nyet!* The boss was busy finding provisions, meeting officials, getting the truck running. He had a lot of things to do, so Donatar rode Guvanch's horse for him. Now I drive his car for him, and now I drive his car for you. Wherever you wish to go, you ask Donatar. Whatever you want, ask Donatar."

"But, Donatar," I said, "how did you manage to build this beautiful house on a driver's salary? It really is magnificent. It must have cost a fortune."

"Marriage in Turkmenistan costs and costs," he replied. "The house cost a hundred thousand rubles. In a few months I must buy a car; it will cost seventy thousand rubles. I must pay my bride's father the bride price, fifty thousand rubles. The wedding itself will probably cost another fifty thousand. It's too much!" Without saying where he would obtain so much money, he pointed with his index finger to his temple. I wasn't sure whether he was signaling that he was clever enough to find the dough or crazy to get married, or perhaps both.

In the afternoon Guvanch returned with his Russian wife, Alla, for lunch, which they brought with them. They carried in platters of grilled lamb, smoked chicken, marinated eggplant, eggplant caviar, buckets of fresh tomatoes, peppers, salamis, sausages, watermelons, local Persian melons, three kinds of grapes, bags of pistachios and walnuts, candied figs, pears in sugar, pickled squash, soda, Champagne, vodka, and even ice water. There was enough food to open a catering business. At a time when there were widespread food shortages in Russia, it seemed that Turkmenistan had a surfeit. In fact, Turkmenistan is the only Soviet republic where there was no rationing. In addition, Guvanch and his brother, Bigench, had been investing in agribusiness and could obtain all the food they wanted from their own farms.

It was my first opportunity to get to know Alla, who certainly felt more comfortable with Moira there than if she had been a lone woman among men. In fact, if Moira hadn't been there, Alla probably wouldn't have come at all. Though I had no way of knowing, I wondered how a Russian woman married to a Turkmen navigated the heavy seas of male dominance in the patriarchal Turkmen culture. In this respect, Guvanch's choice of a non-Turkmen wife was yet another indication of his own cosmopolitanism.

Alla Borisovna was short, plump, round-faced, black-haired, white-complexioned, and very Russian-looking. She had been raised in Ashkhabad, and said she fell in love with Guvanch when she was sixteen. It had taken him a year to notice her. While she was out in the kitchen with Moira, Guvanch took me aside and pressed a thick roll of crisp new twenty-five-ruble notes into my hands for walking-around money. I couldn't refuse without offending him.

There could be no doubt about it: As Guvanch Djumaev's guests, we would be treated as visiting royalty. For a Westerner raised on tales of desert khans throwing foreigners off towers of death into pits full of vipers, it is hard to credit the level of hospitality one can meet in Central Asia. It reminded me of the anecdote of Hungarian traveler Ármin Vámbéry about his caravan's arrival in Turkmenistan in 1862. Thousands of men, women, and children rushed out with extended arms to greet the pilgrims with hugs. When he arrived at the tent of the local *ishan* (priest) to begin arrangements for housing the foreign guests, disputes broke out for the honor of harboring them. Indeed, the native women became so passionate in claiming guests for their own tents that the local ruler finally had to intervene to restore order by assigning them to households. Vámbéry said the effusive reception emanated from the divine command to Muslims to respect travelers, especially those returning from pilgrimage to Mecca with the holy dust of Islam still clinging to their traveling clothes. The ruler claimed Vámbéry as his own personal guest, and installed him in a separate tent on the outskirts of Gomushtepe. Vámbéry was so worn out from the reception that he only wanted to go to sleep. He was sadly disappointed. No sooner had they performed the customary Turkmen ceremonial for taking possession of a new dwelling—circling the tent twice and peeping into the four corners—than the tent filled with visitors who stayed to the next morning asking thousands of questions. Vámbéry had heard of the hospitality of the nomads, but had never dreamed it could reach such a point. Like Vámbéry, I, too, am overwhelmed by this astonishing sense of hospitality.

Guvanch takes it as a matter of course. He fills our shot glasses full of vodka, then stands and says in broken English, "Talking, please." In his toast at lunch, he reminds us once again of the Turkmen proverb "The guest is higher than the father." Alla pushes delicacies onto our plates like a Jewish grandmother, urging us to eat. She asked how foreign guests would be treated in the United States. I couldn't bring myself to tell about our growing lack of ease with foreigners, the way Americans veer between acts of munificent generosity and alarming xenophobia.

In any case, before I could answer Guvanch was off on another subject, explaining to Moira the significance of Turkmen names. For their families as well as their children, especially their sons, they use names in a way that conveys as much information as possible. "Take my name," he said. "Guvanch Rosievich Djumaev. Guvanch means pride in Turkmen, but is a name used only for second sons. My older brother, Bigench, would never be called Guvanch. So my name tells a stranger where I fit in the order of birth of sons in my family. Rosievich is my patronymic, but what does it tell about my father? His name is Rosie-ye. That is the local term in this region for Ramadan, the Muslim Lent. So from my patronymic you know I come from a family of believers. Finally, my family name, Djumaev. 'Djuma' in Turkmen means Thursday, the Muslim holy day. Again, an indication of a religious family, so you see how much information is conveyed in a Turkmen name? Compare that to a Russian name; what does it tell you? The name of the father. What does that prove?"

The next week was spent learning on the job the profession of documentary filmmaker. Mindful of the harsh desert conditions I'd be working under—extremely high temperatures, lots of sand blowing, and no available electric power out in the field—I had tried to put together a durable camera kit worthy of the challenge. Fortunately for me, a new generation of compact, lightweight, affordable, broadcast-quality 8 mm. video cameras were just coming onto the market, developed to meet the demands of television journalists covering the Persian Gulf War. Knowing I would be filming outdoors around horses, with endless opportunities for dust to wreck the gear, I had taped heavyweight plastic film over every opening and seam: If the camera broke down in Turkmenistan, I was simply out of luck. Finally, I had fashioned a heavy canvas slipcase that could quickly cover the camera between takes, for moving to another position or for emergencies, as when a big truck drove by right next to where I was trying to film. Despite all my precautions, batteries suddenly went dead, tapes fried in the heat, and dust tormented the poor microchips in the camera. Once the rubber mount connecting the microphone to the camera body simply melted in the heat, and had to be repaired on the spot with chewing gum and duct tape. Nonetheless, I was aware that Guvanch Djumaev's patronage of the documentary provided me with unique access not only to the horses, but also to Turkmen life as well, and I was determined to keep my gear operational and make the most of the opportunity.

In this spirit, I set out to film the most important locations as soon as possible, figuring that if technical problems arose, at least I would have some footage of the Akhal-Tekes to show for the effort. Guvanch understood my concerns, and gave me carte blanche, the company car, and Donatar. Guvanch was with us whenever he could get away from business, made all our arrangements when he couldn't, entertained us most evenings, and yet never intruded when Moira and I were working in the field or tried to interfere with my program.

We filmed the first Sunday after arrival at the Ashkhabad racetrack, where I hooked up again with Yusup Anaklichev, the commercial director at the Komsomol stud, and the Akhal-Teke breeder, Geldi Kiarizov. Both men had been told by Guvanch that I was returning to Turkmenistan, and each was eager to help.

The following day, Moira and I went out to the Komsomol stud to begin filming with Yusup their stallions, mares, and especially their herd of yearlings. Traditionally, the Turkmen could not keep their horses in herds because of arid conditions and lack of pasturage, but under the Soviets, the Komsomol stud and Turkmen collective farms practiced something akin to the traditional open-range horse herding of the Eurasian nomads. The yearlings were let out to graze on unfenced pastures during the day, and led by one or two mounted herdsmen to a large enclosure at night.

It was impressive to spend several days following the herd, observing their behavior on the seemingly limitless plains under the blue-black mantle of the Kopet-Dag. Central Asian horse herding developed over several thousand years by the careful observation of how wild horses and their relatives—wild asses, ponies, Przewalski's horses, et cetera— behaved in the wild wherever grasses swayed in the winds. The Eurasian nomads came to understand the dynamics of the wild equid's social behavior and put that knowledge to work in their own herding practices.

Although more is known of early horses' anatomy than of their social behavior, we may construct a fairly accurate sketch of herd life prior to the domestication of equus. Russian officers describing the last true wild horses of Tartary, called Tarpans, to Colonel Hamilton Smith in Paris in 1814 reported herds of several hundred animals always proceeding slowly forward while grazing in lines or files with their heads to windward, and preferring wide-open elevated steppe. These large herds were subdivided into smaller troops of perhaps fifty, each led by a stallion, which would occasionally circle round his own troop. These smaller troops would likely include a dozen or so mature mares, each with a foal less than one year old, and assorted yearlings and older fillies. The lead stallion protected his troop from predators, defended the foals against wolves when escape was cut off, and fought rival stallions to the death. He would tolerate no competition within his own family, driving colts off as soon as they gave signs of attaining sexual maturity. The Russians told Colonel Smith that young Tarpan stallions moved singly at some distance from the main herd, expelled by the older stallions until they could form their own troop of mares. At maturity the young stallion would indeed have to go off on his own, looking for an opportunity either to knock off an older stallion and inherit his mares, or else start a new herd for himself. It is unlikely that unsuccessful stallions lived very long, not only dying from wounds attained in battles for dominance, but also for the simple reason that, deprived of mutual predator detection afforded by the herd, they were not able to keep their heads down long enough to obtain sufficient food.

As I watched and filmed the Komsomol stud's pampered young, I wondered whether the bachelor stallions of predomestication days might simply have lost heart, succumbing to diseases complicated by loneliness. It is worth pondering how impossible life would be for the young if all job openings and family formations depended on the death of the current job holder. In any case, the successful lead stallion also chased away his daughters when they came of age, following his instinctual aversion to in-breeding. Fillies, however, easily found acceptance into a herd ruled by another stallion as soon as they were old enough to stand with their legs spread and emit the proper concoction of sexual perfumes.

One evening after work, Guvanch and Yusup came by Donatar's palace to pick me up for an evening on the town (Moira was down for the count with a vicious, though thankfully brief, stomach virus). We had been invited to a banquet prepared in my honor by a friend and ally of Guvanch's—a member of the Yomut tribe, he said. As I understood Guvanch's explanation, my friends and contacts in Ashkhabad were all Tekes, and it was politic for Guvanch to share his foreign guest with another tribe. My presence at the banquet would both give honor to my Yomut host and strengthen Guvanch's relations with other Yomuts.

It interested me to discover how meticulously Guvanch handled tribal relations, especially since I knew from reading Vámbéry, O'Donovan, and others that a hundred years ago the Tekes and Yomuts had been enemies who carried out slave raids and depredations against each other whenever they had the chance. It was one link of evidence that the Soviet policy of settling the Turkmen nomadic tribes had been successful in removing pasture and water disputes as a principal cause of fratricidal warfare between them. It also reinforced my impression—it was only an impression—that somewhere down the line Guvanch might reenter politics. He was clearly capable, conscientious, and charismatic. Perhaps he was maintaining his tribal relations in order to keep his options open.

On the way across town, Yusup began talking horse talk, answering some of the questions I had brought from the Cases in Virginia. They were especially interested to find out what the Turkmen feed their horses, and how Komsomol's breeding program operated. Yusup said the breeding season at the Komsomol stud ran from April to May, with the foals born from December to January. Komsomol has one hundred "production mares," as they are called, which produce seventy-five to eighty foals per year. Each mare receives ten kilograms of *luzerna*, which the stud imports from southern Russia, and five to six kilograms of oats each day, to which is added half a bucket of finely cut carrots, a little honey, and from two to twelve raw eggs to help keep the horse's coat glossy. Before the revolution, Yusup said, "Turkmen always fed their horses bread soaked in mutton fat. This allowed the horse to go long distances without drinking water. The Russians always fed their horses up, in a raised trough attached to a wall. But Turkmen put *torbalyk* [feed bag] down in the ground, because they wanted a horse with a long neck for seeing far away across the desert."

As Yusup spoke, his voice lowered with gathering intensity. He was grateful that I had gone to visit the Akhal-Teke breeders in America and brought him a letter and photographs of their Akhal-Tekes. At the banquet I was planning to present him with a horseshoe from the Cases' stud farm. "You must tell Phil Case, Jon, that we Turkmen arose from Oguz tribe. They were nomads in this area at the time of the Arabian caliphate of Sultan Sandjar. His mother was an Oguz tribeswoman, his father Arab. From the time of Sultan Sandjar in the eleventh century, the Turkmen people began. Turkmen served the caravans as guides through the desert, providing camels, water, food. When asked by caravan traders, 'Who are your people?' one said, *'Turk-men.'* The word *'men'* means 'I am' in Turkic language, so he was saying, 'I am Turk,' but to the trader it came out 'Turkmen,' the name by which we have been known ever since.

"The Turkmen loves three things," Yusup went on. "His horse, his wife, and his hunting dog. The old Turkmen started out from his tent at four A.M., when the air was fresh and cool, and rode his Akhal-Teke hard, so they needed to breathe deeply and develop strong leg muscles for galloping through the desert. The Akhal-Teke was always used for hard work over long distances—perhaps across to Iran on a raid, then back down to the desert. Tell Phil Case that the foals have to go out with their mothers. *Only* with their mothers. You can't let other mares out with them. They need to run. That is the answer to the contracted heel problem. Here foals are generally hardy, but they could be stronger if they exercised the mares more when in foal. Here they are afraid of walking them. They do the same with pregnant women here; it's the Turkmen culture to confine pregnant females. But these mares have been birthing for many years. They are constantly confined. As a result, their muscles and uteruses have atrophied. If this continues, it will weaken the breed. Already our horses are not attaining the size of earlier generations; they are becoming smaller. The reason is weak feed and not running the mares. The Akhal-Teke must run."

Our host at the banquet, a Mr. Khodir, was a plain little man who only spoke Turkmen and drank his vodka neat from an eight-ounce waterglass. He welcomed me as his honored guest and told me through Guvanch, "A Turkmen has guests all the time if he can."

I decided there must be some sort of point system with Allah. Mr. Khodir showed us into his living room, which had carpets on the floor and walls but no furniture. The floor was lavishly and artfully set with perhaps a dozen prepared dishes, colorful bowls of fruit and nuts, and bottles of vodka, mineral water, and soda. It really looked ready for a photographer from a food magazine. He had us change into cotton pajama bottoms that he supplied, then invited us to stretch out on the floor and eat and drink ourselves into oblivion.

It wasn't difficult. A Turkmen banquet is less formal than an American dinner party. In Turkmenistan, you don't have to pay attention to your host, who makes no effort to manage the dinner except when offering a toast. Everyone present eats what he wants when he wants. No one would dream of rushing a guest through to the coffee and cake, then hustling him out the door. If you happen to get hung up on some particular dish—let's say fried pastries filled with spicy ground lamb and winter squash—you may simply continue to eat them until they are all gone, and soon a plate of new hot pastries will appear. You may eat them or not; no one will notice or care. If you grow too tired to continue stuffing yourself, you may lie back, close your eyes, and sleep for a few minutes. No one will think the worse of you as long as you're awake for the next round of vodka. Best of all, you may eat with your hands.

Women did not enter this room; Mr. Khodir seemed strict about this. They brought new dishes only as far as the door, where Mr. Khodir took over as long as he could still stand. When Guvanch and I had finished off the fried pastries, which were delicious as chasers for shots of vodka, a rather dry roast chicken was served. Then we ate pistachios, walnuts, almonds, grapes, pears, apples, and dried apricots for half an hour. Next the women brought soup bowls in which had been placed thin layers of soaked bread, shredded meat, cooked tomato and onion. A clear boullion was poured over this to make a scrumptious and filling soup, eaten with handsomely painted wooden spoons. It was a dish made for the Muslim holiday of Ramadan, but they were serving it to me out of season.

I was already stuffed, but Guvanch kept making me eat more meat pastries, which he thought were especially good. By now two or three hours had passed. We'd had a lot to drink, and things were loosening up. Guvanch and Yusup lay on their backs crooning Beatles songs. It turned out they had played in a rock 'n' roll band together in high school.

When it was my turn to toast, I presented Guvanch and Yusup with the cowboy hats I had brought for them, and Yusup with his horseshoe, and spoke about my idea of bringing a delegation of Turkmen riders to the States in the autumn to ride a short marathon on Akhal-Tekes from the Cases' farm in western Virginia to Washington, D.C. Yusup was bowled over, hugged me, and told me that I must come to the Komsomol stud to ride his own stallion. Guvanch gave his hat to Mr. Khodir, and expressed his concern about trying to bring Akhal-Tekes from Turkmenistan to the United States. I assured him there were Akhal-Tekes to ride in my country, but he responded only that my idea was "worthy of respect and attention." It struck me as a phrase he might have used in his previous career as a Komsomol apparatchik.

The banquet wasn't half over yet, although Mr. Khodir was having increasing trouble maneuvering the food platters. Unlike Guvanch, who was always careful to chase the vodka with something substantial to eat, like camel's milk yogurt or pickled eggplant, Mr. Khodir poured twice the normal dose of high-octane liquor down his gullet without flinching. The next course was *plov* made with lamb and rice and served on big common platters that were set down at either end of the floor. Guvanch taught me how to eat it properly, by shaping a ball of it with your right hand, then swiftly moving the hand to your mouth to take it in, deftly licking your fingers as they leave your lips.

We drank again and again. New guests arrived and joined the party. The drinking went on; the eating slowed down. It was a bit like being at a college fraternity house on a week night, though the food was much better. I was about ready to bow out while still conscious, but didn't know the correct procedure. Someone brought in a *dutar*, the fretless stringed instrument of Central Asia, and Mr. Khodir strummed while one of the new arrivals, a young Turkmen artist with dark good looks called Rachman, stood to recite poetry for us. He introduced a poem by the eighteenth-century Turkmen national poet Makhtymkuli, whose statue is in the central park I had been directed to a hundred times on my first visit.

"Makhtymkuli's poems," Rachman said, "recount the dreams and visions he experienced. He often had visions when he drank too much."

No wonder he's the Turkmen national poet, I thought to myself.

Guvanch said how stupid it was that the Soviets had shut off the road to Makhtymkuli's grave all these years simply because it is in Iran. "We could not even visit the grave of our national poet because it was across the border!"

Yusup said, "The *dutar* is the soul of the Turkmen, the Teke rug is the pride of the Turkmen, and the Akhal-Teke horse is the wings of the Turkmen!"

"Makhtymkuli wrote that?" I asked.

"That is what kept Turkmen culture alive under the Soviets," he answered vaguely.

I was confused, which was not surprising after a dozen shots of vodka. Rachman explained that Makhtymkuli composed his poems in Farsi, the language of Persia, which at that time was also the literary language of the Turkmen—the Turkmen having no written language of their own, and using the Arabic, Farsi, and Cyrillic alphabets over the course of their history. Then he began to recite from memory Makhtymkuli's long and extraordinary poem of spiritual epiphany called "The Revelation." I am able to reprint it here only because Rachman offered to translate it into English and deliver it to me via Guvanch:

> By night once, while I lay asleep,
> Four horsemen came. "Arise!" they said,
> "For you must know that they are come—
> The Enlightened Ones—and you shall see them!"
>
> When those four people I beheld,
> My brain did burn, my heart did tremble.
> Two holy madmen also there told me:
> "Don't tarry, son. Make haste, be gone!"
>
> We sat, then two young saints appeared
> With tearful eyes and praying.
> Six men on foot came, saying, "Hu,
> The man will come now: see him!"
>
> Came four more horsemen all in green,
> With rods of green and rearing stallions.
> They said, "The circle is too small,
> For we are many—set it wider!"

And in the distance sixty riders loomed.
"Muhammed," said they, and proceeded.
They greeted all, inquired their health in turn,
And said, "Wait not, proceed to yon great place."

Ali—for he it was, they said—he held me by the hand.
He dragged the pallet on which I sat;
I comprehended not; he poured a substance on me.
"The time is passing," said Ali. "Enjoy it."

I asked Haidar about them, one by one.
"That is the Prophet, be not alien to him.
That is Eslim Hoja, that one Baby Zuryat,
And that—Veys-al-Karani, you should know.

That Enlightened One is Bahauddin.
That one is Zengi Baba, such a famous man.
Those close together are the Four Companions.
Ask anything your heart desires to know."

Two young sheiks also present said:
"We ask that this young man be blest."
The thirty prophets and the companion thirty
Are here. This you must know, they said.

And now the Prophet makes his call: Oh, Ali,
Oh, Eslim Hoja, Oh, Baba Salman,
Oh, Abu Bakr Siddiq, Oh, Omar, Oh, Osman,
Fulfill the wishes of this fine young man."

Eslim and Baba Salman to the jar were called;
The glass was dipped into the drink.
I lay there swooning. I was told
To see all things in heaven and on earth.

Turned into wind, I hurtled to the very depths
Of earth; and then the vault of heaven did see.
"In this great world go and behold the Lord
And see Him for yourself," they said.

Whate'er I thought about was mine.
Whate'er I looked on, He was there.
In peaceful sleep I felt their spittle on my face
(This was their blessing.) "Now arise," they said.

The Prophet said, "Companions, pray go on,
And all give this young man your benediction."
He ordered the four horsemen, "Take him hence,
Return him to the place from whence you brought him."

Makhtymkuli awoke, and opened wide his eyes.
What thought had passed all through his head!
His mouth foamed like a lustful camel.
"Go, son," they said, "and may the Lord be with you."

The Turkmen did not applaud, but congratulated Rachman in bracing gales of Turkmen, a language that I now yearned to speak. When Donatar finally drove us home, it was almost dawn. Even then I had only been able to escape by insisting to Mr. Khodir that I had to look in on my sick assistant, Moira. He was not happy about my leaving; he didn't see the point of my worrying about a female. It was after we had put on our shoes in the foyer that the women brought yet one more dish of roasted lamb. Mr. Khodir was too drunk to get up and take the platter from them, but it was all right for them to serve it to us directly in the hall as we were leaving. They must have been cooking for at least twelve hours straight.

Every time we drove somewhere, Donatar tried to speak English.
"Noowww," he said. "It means *nyet*?"
"Right."
"Nooww. Nowwww. Nooowwwww!"

I tried to teach him, "Let's eat lunch."

He said, "Louze een lashh."

"I want to eat now."

"I xwha to neat nooowww!" He shook his lips as if it hurt.

I wasted little time in taking up Yusup's invitation to come out to the Komsomol stud for a ride. It had been more than two years since I had first heard about the Akhal-Teke breed and started conspiring to travel in Central Asia. A slow seduction is always more exciting than a quick one, and a successful campaign on challenging terrain is more satisfying than a lucky chance on home turf. Still, it seemed an awful lot of work to have endured to ride a damn horse, even if it *was* a direct descendant of the "horses of heaven" that the emperors of China had sent forth their armies to obtain.

Now that the long-awaited day had actually arrived, I did my usual stretching exercises and calmly put on my britches and boots, the same way I would have if I was going out to Ilona's barn to ride her school horse Flash. If I was thrilled, I must have fooled myself. Yet the long period of anticipation I had put myself through was not without personal significance. When had I ever waited two years for anything? Like most of my gender, I wanted everything fast: love, money, success, life, and, when necessary, death, too. Only two years before, "patience" was a word I despised. When people put me on hold to take another phone call, I immediately hung up. What, me wait? Never!

But now that I had made a serious start as a rider, I found my habits changing, and my attitudes with them. I could not look upon the horse merely as a tool of sport, a means of exercise, or a way of attaining gratification through domination of yet another object. For me the development of equestrian skills was corollary to the development of an inner commitment to higher human attributes like calm perseverance, steadiness, consistency, partnership, and patience—attitudes out of fashion, perhaps, but required of the accomplished horseman. I realized that the horse was carrying me down one road of enlightenment, even if I was only at the beginning of that journey and could not know what I would find at the end. Perhaps nothing more than the dry bones of Don Quixote.

Donatar drove me out to the stud farm, where Yusup awaited me. I don't think he really had much to do as commercial director because the several times I went there, he was usually hanging around the turnout of the stallion barn like a shopkeeper on a slow day. Yusup led out his own horse, Tarlan, a striking six-year-old golden chestnut stallion, and chose for me a five-year-old golden bay named Keledjar, about 15.2 hands high. When I looked him over in the sunlight, I was shocked. Although a ravishingly handsome animal with power rippling from his flanks and neck, and fire streaming from his nostrils, his hooves were completely neglected, unclipped to the point of curling. They desperately needed care.

Without grooming or cleaning their feet—there weren't any brushes or hoof picks in the barn—we threw pads and English saddles over their backs while one of the stable boys bridled my horse for me. Then he moved back beside the saddle to give me a leg up Russian style, clasping his hands together to make a place to put my knee. He gave a toss, I gave a leap, and the next thing I knew I was comfortably seated. It was a lot more enjoyable than using a mounting block, which I always avoid anyway.

As soon as we were both up, Yusup shouted, "Hahhh, Tarlan!" and his horse bolted forward into a lively high-stepping trot. My horse broke before I gave the command to trot, and we followed Yusup through the gates. I could feel Keledjar's high-actioned, short-stepping rhythm; it was as though he had been trained to trot on furrowed fields, as Vegetius said the Parthians had long ago trained their horses. Although quite fast, it was a smooth, comfortable trot that was easy to post to. I steadied him with my hands and seat as we rode down the paved road. None of the vehicles on it slowed down. It occurred to me when I tried to make a transition from a trot down to a walk that Keledjar didn't speak English and wouldn't recognize my voice commands. He probably didn't speak Russian, for that matter. How do you say "Walk!" in Turkmen? I decided to confine myself to judicious use of the legs, seat, and hands.

After half a mile, we came to the end of the access road to the stud and crossed the paved highway. On the other side was a three times life-size statue of the famous Akhal-Teke stallion Polotli, and then several thousand kilometers of open desert. I never knew whether Yusup gave Tarlan the command, but as soon as we got off the road onto the sand, Keledjar kicked his legs straight out behind him and took off across the Kara Kum at a completely uncontrolled and uncollected gallop. The last thing I remember Yusup shouting was, "Pull the reins back hard, Jon! You must use tight reins!"

Of course it was the exact wrong advice. The Akhal-Teke stallions in the barn at the Komsomol were all ex-racehorses. They had never been trained as saddle horses, and I'm sure hadn't been ridden, even infrequently, but were kept continually stabled, except for being taken out for breeding purposes or to be exhibited to visitors. Take a horse like that into open country, pull hard at the bit, and it can mean only thing: It's post time!

By the time I realized that the best thing to do would be to soften the reins, I was already streaking across Central Asia on the back of a thousand pounds of uncontrollable muscle and progesterone. It was at this very moment I happened to notice that the particular area of desert we were galloping through had but one type of vegetation, a kind of broad low-growing thistle plant with excruciatingly long, thick spines. To fall on top of one of these or to get dragged across several of them would hurt a lot for a really long time. It had been foolish of me to not bring my safety helmet.

Next thought: Let the stallion run it out of his system. There were no obstacles anywhere and nowhere to go. Ahead were the same flat sands as behind. Once I recovered from the initial shock of having the horse take off, my seat was actually fairly secure; the worst thing I could do was try to bring him up short. Eventually, if I didn't panic, he would start to tire and I could exert control. This thought relaxed me considerably, and the more I relaxed, the more confident I became.

Just as I thought, Keledjar did eventually slow down, until he was galloping at a somewhat more manageable pace. Then, of course, I didn't want him to stop, only to keep flying forward like a magic carpet. Before I knew it I was in a kind of trance, enchanted by my union with this wild horse of the desert. When Yusup finally came abreast of me, he shouted "This is the Akhal-Teke horse, Jon! How do you like him?"

"Otlichno!" I answered. "Excellent! Can we go on?"

We returned to the stables within two hours, put the horses away, and flopped down in the building's shade; further exertion was impossible after exposure to the direct sun. I was overcome with thirst; though Yusup said he didn't think the water from the stable hose was pure, I couldn't resist and swigged freely. I have no idea whether the fever, headaches, and nausea I suffered later came about as a result of this, but having traveled in a number of third world countries, I knew that I always went with the intention of not drinking bad water—and always ended up in situations where drinking seemed more urgent than healthy intentions. Thankfully, I either have a strong stomach or have been lucky.

Yusup was still overcome with appreciation for the horseshoe and photographs from the Cases that I had given him at Xodir's banquet, and was eager to get something off his chest. "You know, Jon," he took me gently by the arm, "you must tell Phil Case that things are very bad here now. It's already two years since Moscow stopped taking our horses for the Moscow auction, and that is good. But at the same time they have cut us off financially; all government subsidy has ended. No one here was prepared to run the Komsomol stud as a profitable business without any transition. The apparatchiki have no experience. They don't know breeding or marketing. Eighty percent of our horses are infected with the piroplasm. This is the great problem in our business. We can't sell our horses abroad. The virus is spread by insect bites and is carried in the blood. They could cure the horses in Moscow with special treatment, but here we have no facility for this and no money to set one up. We have no money for a veterinarian; there isn't one in all of Turkmenistan. There used to be farriers and blacksmiths, but now they have all died out or left. We have to buy shoes in Moscow and put them on ourselves. The man who is supposed to take care of the horses' feet drinks vodka and doesn't come to work. Still, no one will fire him. He was born on the farm and has worked here all his life, so how can he be fired? This is the problem: We don't have the old system, but we don't have a new system. You understand? When I say something to the managers, they say, 'You are the commercial director; you are not a specialist.' But they don't know anything about running a horse farm. I will give you an example. Last year a Polish businessman came here and signed a contract with Komsomol to take thirteen of our most promising young Akhal-Teke horses to train in Poland for the Barcelona Olympics. According to the agreement, he would work with them for one year, and they would compete for the Polish Olympics equestrian team. He took the horses overland to Poland. More than one year has gone by, and no one has heard from him again. We received no money, we have no horses back—nothing. He is somewhere near Kraków, but we have no way of finding him. He took off with thirteen of our best young horses. We will probably never see them again. If I ever find him, I will break his teeth!'"

Guvanch agreed that we should film more than Akhal-Tekes, since no Western film crew had shot documentary footage in Turkmenistan before. On a bright, hot Sunday, he took us to Ashkhabad's bazaar and flea market—the "Turkmenski supermarket," as Guvanch called it.

The bazaar was a peek into the Turkmen's mercantile soul. Old or new, big or small, alive or dead, the comrades in the brown fur hats at the bazaar sold it—and if they didn't have it, they'd buy it from you. From the latest Turkish pop cassettes to heirloom carpets, from one-humped camels to raw licorice roots, from fine silks spun in Firyuza to green tomatoes; all you had to do was wander around till you found the right area and establish a price. Everything was for sale, no questions asked. Money talks, nobody walks. A ton-and-a-half farm truck drove up, lowered its back gate, and sold about a hundred baby lambs in the space of ten minutes.

With so many consumer goods passing from private hands to private hands, the Communists were squeamish about the bazaar. Despite the danger of setting off an insurrection, security forces had been sent to close down the bazaar several times in the past, but since Gorbachev it had remained open and grown greatly. The bazaar was one gigantic hotbed of speculation and profiteering.

It was also a great desert spectacle. Thousands of people, mostly women (and mostly Teke, in their red-patterned dress yokes and head pieces) streamed from their cars, buses, and trucks that let them off directly in front of the entrance. Most had come to shop for food, which the Turkmenski supermarket supplied in abundance. Some merchants had wood stands, others nothing more than an old carpet or blanket to spread their goods on; one woman sat cross-legged surrounded by mounds of green pomegranates. The irrigated farmlands on both sides of the Kara Kum Canal produce everything but grains: grapes, tomatoes, melons, green onions, radishes, raisins, pistachios, carrots, potatoes, and apples.

There was an extensive animal market for lambs and goats, camels and poultry, but no slaughtering on the premises; everyone does that at home in Ashkhabad. Men carried live karakul sheep to their cars, tied them to the trunk with rope, and drove away. The camel market was alive with prospective buyers inspecting the animals' teeth and skin. It is common for Turkmen families to keep a female camel in back of the house for milking. Male camels no longer used for transport wander in the desert on their own, unfed and undersexed. The females at the market were hobbled together with their young, which are always sold with the females to keep them producing. How the buyers trucked their purchases home I don't know; perhaps there is a trucking service that delivers them, because I would see a truckload of camels on the streets of Ashkhabad now and then. There is nothing more stupid looking than a camel's head sticking over the tailgate of a truck, except perhaps turkeys with their heads out the windows as they rode in the backseat with the women.

We went to the clothing section, where both imported Western and traditional Central Asian styles were hawked. Turkmen like to say they are the only national ethnic group in the Soviet Union that have kept their traditional costume as it was before the revolution. For Turkmen women this means their solid-color tribal dresses with patterned hand-made yokes—thousands to choose from in a line of women merchants a football field long—and standard head pieces, which are simply patterned kerchiefs.

The male costume is more complicated. Starting from the head down, it consists of a fluffy lamb's wool *telpek* (hat)—brown for everyday wear, white for weddings and special occasions; a red-and-yellow striped silk *khalat* (robe) that comes down to the middle of the knee like a lady's housecoat, and is still worn mainly by elders; *Turkmenbalak,* which are gray, brown, or dark-blue pantaloons of wool or cotton; and high black boots, which have been traded in for cheap Soviet loafers or sandals. This is not, of course, the costume of an actuary or tractor driver, but of a horse-mounted desert warrior. For this reason, and perhaps for political considerations as well, more and more Turkmen men are turning to Western dress, though the majority still wear their brown fur hats on even the hottest day of the year. It would be unimaginable for Turkmen men to give up wearing their fur hats.

We crossed finally to the rug market, an even more extensive area, where carpets are unfolded on the ground, displayed on racks, or hung over walls to display them. Most of the rugs produced at the great rug factories of Turkmenistan today are Teke designs, known in the trade as Bukhara rugs; Bukhara was the main export market of the region. Without exception all Turkmen families possess carpets, often using them instead of furniture. Since Turkmen don't subscribe to the Western fetish for antiques, they try to buy new carpets for their homes. The secondhand, the worn-out, and the just plain old rugs wind up for sale in the bazaar, where there are few customers outside a trickle of foreigners. The women dealers jumped to their feet as Moira and I passed, shouting in competition with each other, "Look, it's old, very old, a hundred years old!" No one mentioned the standing government decree that made removing antiquities from Turkmenistan a crime against the state, though Guvanch said he could help us evade it.

Here is the way to purchase an Oriental rug in an Asian bazaar: First, forget everything you ever heard or read about Oriental rugs—in particular, that Oriental rugs are valuable investments and will gain or lose value according to how good they are. Think only that buying a rug should be like choosing a mate: You intend to live with it for the rest of your life. All you do, then, is stroll down the rows of rug merchants, not listening to them, concentrating only on the colors and designs until your eyes meet the one rug that really moves your soul. It must be love at first sight, second sight, and third sight. The rug must speak to you. It must tell you a beautiful story with a wise moral. You must love it spontaneously, but must always think about its future effect. It will help if it is tightly knotted and has no dry rot. Thereafter, all that remains is to capitulate to the rug merchant and pay the price. Only after you have paid does the merchant take your hands in his and pronounce the traditional Islamic Salaam Aleikham, to which the correct response is Aleikham Salaam.

I had long wanted to visit the archaeological site of Nisa, the first capital of the Parthians, predecessors of the Turkmen in raising large horses of quality on the dry steppes. The ruins are located twelve kilometers west of Ashkhabad off a paved road that today runs through shriveled clusters of crude mud-brick huts, then to open desert where camels graze. The site is less than a square mile, and appears to have been only partially excavated by Soviet archaeologists. Missing from view are the mighty walls of Nisa, which were nine feet thick in the second and first centuries B.C., when the Parthians were Oriental rivals of the Romans, ruling an empire that stretched from Syria to India. The walls of old Nisa have served as a windbreak for two thousand years, until they now appear as a great aureole of sand fifty feet high and running around the entire perimeter. This, and its isolated location in the desert, make the old Parthian center look more like a strange port for UFO landings than a city of ancient Central Asia.

From the top of this earthwork, which can easily be climbed at any point, I looked due west toward the jagged rock faces of the Kopet-Dag. From the point of view of an incoming UFO, the site of Nisa must look like a long line with a small circle next to it. Maybe it was meant as some kind of coded communication from the Parthians to the aliens.

Not much is known about the Parthians. They left few written records, and most students of Parthia study their coins to glean information. Apparently they were a group of exiled or breakaway Scythians, nomadic horsemen who migrated from the northern steppes around the shores of the Caspian Sea and established themselves on the plains of Central Asia in the first millennium B.C. The Roman historian Justinian points out that the word *parthi* actually means "exiles" in Scythian; he called the Parthians "the most obscure of all people of the East in the time of the Assyrians and Medes." When the Persians took control of Central Asia just before the time of Alexander, the Parthians were still, according to Justinian, "a herd without a name."

After the time of Alexander, however, the Parthians began to increase in population and power. Never a territorially stable empire with a strong monarchy, it was more a loose confederation of provinces ruled by a strongly assertive aristocracy, which contributed military forces in defense of the monarch or to expansionist efforts. It is thought that under Greek influence Parthia developed an imperial organization capable of planning, financing, and carrying out massive irrigation projects. These gravity-flow canals, the remnants of which have been located in former Parthia by aerial photography, made the agricultural exploitation of semiarid land possible, which in turn fostered maximum human settlement. Having come from the nomadic steppe, the Parthians may have been an example of a civilization that resettled the land with the aid of Greek-style administration and Greek technology. The perception of Parthia, then, is generally one of large cities with great populations set in a well-watered, fertile land.

The area within Nisa's sand-covered walls is an open bowl-shaped meadow, perhaps once the parade grounds for the famed Parthian cavalry. In fact, the whole site of Nisa appears to be little more than a fortress housing cavalry, a round temple, and a residence for the king. While Moira took some footage and Sasha waited in the shade afforded by the rustic roof of the site's entranceway, I sat on a portion of unmortared stone wall and made a sketch of the site in my notebook.

Nisa's situation, snuggled up under the Kopet-Dag, must have made it almost impossible for enemies to attack from the west. They would have had to lower themselves down on ropes, cross the open plains, and surmount the high walls. The cuts in the earthworks facing east and west are probably the gates of old Nisa. How stupendous and terrifying must have been the sight of thousands of Parthian horses—mailed lancers on mailed horses—emerging from the gates of Nisa ready to gallop across the broad plains.

It is Geldi Kiarizov's contention that the Parthians were the first to make cavalry warfare specialized; they deployed both heavy and light cavalry. Light cavalry archers, the prototypical mounted warrior of Central Asia over thousands of years, attacked and withdrew fast. The heavy

PLAN of NISA

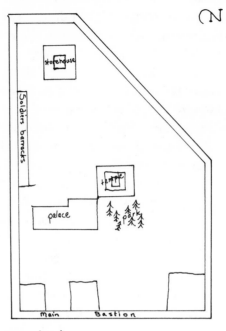

N

xpam = temple
Авореų = palace
казармы = soldiers barracks
хран илище = storehouse

cavalry carried long wooden spears on their armored mounts. Geldi thinks the light cavalry horse corresponds to the Akhal-Teke foundation stallion Boynou from which come more than 80 percent of contemporary Akhal-Teke blood lines. Its frame was like that of the 1960 Rome Olympics winner Absent, a horse of more than sixteen hands.

How many horses did Parthia have? Geldi said that initially, when they became part of the Persian Empire, the Parthians were required to send twenty thousand horses a year as tribute. Considering that mares would not have been acceptable, and that not every mare would produce a foal every year, he deduces that the Parthians must have had herds totaling almost one hundred thousand when their territory was still confined to their original homeland, the provinces adjoining the great desert of Chorasmia. Later, they scaled the mountains and carved themselves new grazing grounds for their horse herds on the plateau of eastern Iran. At their strongest, the Parthians could put an army of horses in the field all

266

by themselves, though no one is sure if this might include the nomadic allies who sometimes fought with them.

Such immense numbers of horses must, in any case, have required truly vast harvests of alfalfa and other grasses. Yet today, looking out from the eastern side of the earthworks, the view to the horizon in three directions is a flat, desiccated, monochrome yellow at the height of summer. Could these scabrous flatlands have once been green, lush, and bountifully watered? It is easier to believe this was a fortification at the end of the world, at a time when the world still had certifiable ends.

Classical sources agree that the Parthian army was a nasty piece of work. Aside from the small aristocracy that formed its elite, the military consisted of slaves captured in war and their offspring, whom the Parthians brought up as their own children, teaching them the arts of riding and shooting a bow from horseback. Justinian says that when Mark Antony faced an army of fifty thousand Parthians, only four hundred of them were free men.

Although the Parthians lived as settled agriculturalists, the Parthian military retained its nomadic roots. Never confronting an enemy army head on, the Parthians would instead appear suddenly, charging full tilt from every direction, cutting the enemy down with devastating volleys of arrows, then turning tail to speed away, firing the infamous "Parthian shot." This phrase, passed down through classical times, eventually was corrupted to become "parting shot." They often faked flight, luring the enemy into thinking they had run away. The Romans were suckers for this trick. Just when they thought themselves out of danger, the Parthians would charge afresh. As Justinian wrote, "When you feel most certain that you have conquered them, you have still to meet the greatest danger."

Using such cunning, the Parthians inflicted the most humiliating defeat the Roman legions ever suffered, at the battle of Carrhae in northern Syria in 53 B.C. Plutarch gave the most complete account of this black day in his life of Crassus. Crassus was sixty years old when he became consul and received the provinces of Syria as part of a power-sharing arrangement among him, Pompey, and Julius Caesar. At that time the Parthians ruled lands up to the Euphrates River bordering Roman Syria. Though they were a small threat to the Romans, Crassus decided he would launch a war against them, then extend Roman rule past Bactria and India to "the utmost ocean"—in other words, as far as Alexander had ventured. Many Romans objected that the Parthians lived in amity and posed no danger, but as Plutarch says, Crassus was "strangely puffed up and his head heated" for war. Caesar wrote from Gaul inciting him, and Pompey also supported the adventure, probably because he wanted Crassus out of Rome.

Crassus brought his army to Syria, where he built a bridge over the Euphrates and began occupying the cities of Mesopotamia on the Parthian side of the river. He spent an off-season in Syria "more like a usurer than a general," counting up treasures and computing revenues instead of training his troops. When his son joined him from Gaul with a thousand select horse soldiers sent by Caesar, and they were making ready to move against the enemy, a Parthian delegation came to Crassus. They told him it was one thing if the people of Rome sent an army to make mortal war, but another if Crassus had undertaken this military adventure against the consent of his countrymen purely for his own profit. In the latter case, they said he could be forgiven because of his age; the Parthian King Hyrodes would allow the Roman soldiers installed on the Parthian side of the river to retreat and let bygones be bygones.

Crassus boastfully told the delegation he would give his answer at Seleucia, at that time the main city of the Parthian Empire, deep inside Parthian territory. Upon which the eldest of the Parthian ambassadors laughed and showed Crassus the palm of his hand. "Hair will grow here before you ever see Seleucia," he told him.

So it was war. Up until that time, the Romans considered the Parthians a trifling enemy. The worst aspect of war with them would be the tedious marches to battle, and the difficulty of chasing down an enemy that only retreated and was afraid to fight. However, Roman soldiers who had been stationed in Mesopotamia escaped with scary stories of the Parthians' barbaric manner of fighting. Their horses were so fast that it was impossible to overtake them if they fled, and just as impossible to escape them if *you* fled.

With this new intelligence, some of his officers advised Crassus to reconsider the invasion. His soothsayers told him the signs were adverse. Preternatural thunderstorms fell on the Romans' camp, and a gale washed away part of the bridge they had built over the Euphrates. As if all this weren't bad enough, when the priest making the last sacrifice handed the entrails to Crassus, they slipped out of his hands and splattered on the ground.

Crassus laughed. "See what it is to be an old man," he said. "But I shall hold my sword fast enough."

Crassus marched seven legions, four thousand cavalry, and about the same number of lightly armed soldiers through the mountains along the Parthian side of the Euphrates River. The Roman scouts didn't see a single enemy soldier, only the tracks of many horses. From this the Romans began to despise the Parthians again as cowards, and Crassus "conceived great hopes" of taking the territory without a fight. In fact, Hyrodes had prudently split his army in two. One part he led north to waste the Romans' ally Armenia, preventing them from sending Crassus supplies or relief troops. The other part was put under the command of Surena, a thirty-year-old hotshot whom Plutarch praised as the first in prowess and courage among the Parthians. Surena's noble family had long held the honor of placing the crown on the king's head at Parthian coronations. Only half Crassus' age, Surena had twice his wisdom and ability.

Surena sent a fast-talking Arab chieftain with former ties to the Romans named Ariamnes, who convinced Crassus that the Parthians were in full flight toward the Iranian plateau. If the Romans were to engage them at all before they got away, Crassus would have to leave the river and hills and go onto the open plains. Ariamnes' cunning tongue worked its wiles, and Crassus was lured to the vast plains and desert of northern Syria. There the Romans found "not a bough, not a stream, not a hillock, not a green herb, but in fact a sea of sand, which encompassed the army with its waves." By the time the Romans realized Ariamnes' treachery, Surena's Parthians were on hand in full force.

Crassus drew his troops into squares of twelve cohorts each, with their fronts facing outward and a troop of cavalry assigned to each square, then rushed forward, convinced his army was facing "neither so many nor so magnificently armed" Parthians as the Romans expected. Surena had actually camouflaged the glittering armor of his heavy cavalry with cloaks and skins. It is tempting to think he had borrowed a leaf from nature's book, camouflaging his soldiers the way the Parthians' golden horses blended in with the sands of the desert. As soon as the Romans engaged, the Parthians sent up "a hideous noise and terrible clamour. For the Parthians do not encourage themselves to war with cornets and trumpets, but with a kind of kettle drum, which they strike all at once in various quarters." Again, perhaps, imitating the frightening din of horse hooves.

When the Romans were terrified by the noise, the Parthians threw off their camouflage and "shone like lightning in their breastplates and helmets of polished Margianian steel." (My friend Victor Fet raised the interesting question that if the Parthians made steel, how did they fuel their blacksmiths' fires? Animal dung, the common desert fuel, cannot be fired hot enough to make steel. The widespread use in Central Asia of charcoal must mean large supplies of trees, probably saxaul, juniper, and pistachio, the last two of which all but vanished in historical times.)

The Parthians showered arrows on the Romans from all sides. At first Crassus thought they would surely run out of them and have to stop the onslaught. Then came news that the Parthians had thousands of camels in the rear loaded with arrows to resupply them. There was nothing for Crassus to do but try to break the encirclement with a charge. He sent his son, Publius, with thirteen hundred horse, five hundred archers, and eight cohorts, but the Parthians suddenly fled. Young Publius pursued them, thinking the flight was the prelude to Rome's carrying the day.

It was the classic Parthian tactic. As soon as Publius and his troops were sufficiently distanced from the main Roman forces, the Parthians turned around and, aided by fresh troops, galloped around the Romans until the sands stirred up by their horses' hooves blinded them. The Romans could not see or speak to one another. The cavalry then drove the Romans inward upon one another and put them all to slow, painful deaths pierced by their arrows.

The Parthians put the son's head on a spear and rode back to taunt Crassus with it. In spite of being surrounded and losing his son, Crassus rallied himself and made a brave speech about the necessity of personal sacrifice if great deeds are to be accomplished. When he was finished with his oration, however, he saw it was no use; "when he ordered them to shout for battle, he could no longer mistake the despondency of his army." The Parthians began picking them off, and Plutarch describes how their heavy cavalry started forking two or three Romans at a time with their long, thick spears, as if they were french fries.

At this point, darkness fell, and Surena gave Crassus the night to mourn his son. The Roman soldiers gathered to hear what the old man, who had been the sole instigator of this debacle, would say. But Crassus only wrapped his cloak around his defeated carcass and lay down. Seeing he was past helping, his lieutenants ordered the army to drop their weapons, abandon the wounded, and flee for their lives—all very un-Roman. Next morning the Parthian light cavalry put the wounded to the sword and massacred the rest in flight.

Rome lost twenty-one thousand men at Carrhae. The Parthians made the defeat all the more humiliating by capturing the standards of the defeated Roman legions, the sacred symbols of Rome's power. As for Crassus, he somehow made it alive to the town of Carrhae, where Surena managed to capture him alive. He put old Crassus on a Parthian horse with a golden bit, but a fight broke out during which the Parthians cut off Crassus' right hand and head. They stuck it on a spear and carried it in a gay procession all the way to Armenia. In this mocking victory parade, they dressed a Roman prisoner who looked something like Crassus in a woman's robe, and displayed the bleeding heads of the slain Romans on the ends of Parthian axes and spears. The "Seleucian singing women" (apparently a popular group at the time) followed the parade singing "scurrilous and abusive songs upon the effeminacy and cowardliness of Crassus."

From that time on, the Romans never again directly confronted the Parthian cavalry. Instead, they conspired, connived, and intrigued to get what they wanted. For thirty years the Romans were haunted by the loss of their legions' standards, until Emperor Augustus engineered their return as part of a peace treaty with the Parthians. Grateful for ending the dishonor, Augustus presented the Parthian monarch Phraates IV with an Italian concubine named Musa. She persuaded the king to have their children educated in Rome, whereupon she murdered him and placed her son, Phraates V, whom she later married, on the Parthian throne. The two ruled Parthia together, issuing Roman-style coins with the heads of the happy couple.

Perhaps the Parthians should have stayed in the saddle and left the bed work to the Italians.

After ten days of intense filming and even more intense banqueting Guvanch had to go to Moscow on business, and decided that Moira and I should take a trip while he was gone. This decision was really based on his anxiety about what his treasured foreign guests would do in his absence. With the paternalism of the desert patriarch, Guvanch was concerned lest something happen to us while he was away. It might also have had to do with jealousy: As in a new and passionate sexual affair, our Turkmen host was afraid I might fall for someone else the minute he left town.

In any case, I wanted to try to film a traditional Central Asian saddle maker, if possible, and had been asking everyone I met in Ashkhabad where I might locate one. The nomads of Eurasia might have been the first equestrians to use a stiff saddle; the ancient Greeks and Persians were always portrayed without. I thought it would be interesting to see if anyone still kept up the ancient crafts of saddlery and harness making. I was also aware that the desert nomads "dressed" their horses according to ancient customs, and decorated them with jewelry and fine textiles. Yusup Anaklichev thought there was still one old Turkmen alive who was a famous maker of equestrian tack in the city of Tashauz, all the way across the Turkmen republic on the border with Uzbekistan. Though he couldn't come up with a name or address, I thought it worth the fourteen-hour train trip on the chance we might encounter something never seen before in the West. Guvanch arranged our tickets, and Sasha Skorokhodov was "volunteered" to accompany us; there would be no question of permits or trouble with the authorities in the company of this former national policeman and Komsomol deputy.

As usual, the Turkmenistan Express, with the blue camels still imprinted on its compartment curtains, pulled out at eight A.M. Since I had already been on this train on my first trip to Turkmenistan, there was only the different season to observe; what had been green in April was now brown.

At midday, I asked Sasha if we could get a meal in the dining car. Through a vestibule reeking of rotting cabbage, we entered a car full of people eating from tin plates with tin spoons. It looked more like a concentration camp mess hall than a railroad dining car. The pleasure of dining on a train had been transformed into a punishment. We sat down to the blue-plate special: a bowl of lukewarm cabbage soup and a small plate of burned macaroni with gristle. I gave up the idea of lunch and we returned to our compartment, where Sasha miraculously produced a whole boiled chicken and scrumptious smoked ham from his overnight bag.

Since I had traveled this route before, I ignored the monotonous desert landscape and spent the rest of the trip working on a short essay I had started in New Jersey at a time when it seemed I would never get to Turkmenistan. The essay went as follows:

Whenever I ride my amiable school horse Flash, and he reaches out to snatch a tree branch to eat, I am reminded, as I pull his fat head back into line, of the long evolutionary path that equus has traveled to become the magical, magnetic creature he is today. At times, when I peek down over Flash's shoulder to check that I'm posting on the correct diagonal at a trot, or that he is on the correct lead at a canter, it reminds me of the adaptations of design and flesh that have made horses such a wondrous mode of transport. And at the end of our sessions together, sweating if not sated by our far-from-perfect efforts, as I let the bit fall from Flash's mouth, stroke his neck, and feed him carrots, I think of how all the changes in horses through millions of years have come about only as innovative ways of getting something to eat without being eaten.

The fossil evidence of the modern horse's ancestors has led to the general view that the progenitors of *Equus caballus* were many and diverse: some jumpy little critters, others more svelte or saurian, or little mules that depended on one kind of food—between them more like the many leaves on a bush than a family tree. Some lived simultaneously, some shared characteristics, some not, and always there were many gradual intermediate forms. The bush metaphor for the descent of the horse from many species to only a handful (*Equus caballus,* zebras, Central Asian ass, et cetera) departs from the kind of mechanical Darwinism of the nineteenth century, when it was believed that one adaptation followed another in an orderly, uniform progression: like a family tree with straight branches.

Darwin himself was basically a tree man when it came to horses, writing in *The Variation of Animals and Plants Under Domestication* that "the seven or eight species of Equidae now existing are all descended from an ancestor of a dun colour more or less striped." It is said that when Darwin was a young man at university all he did was ride, hunt, and drink; if so, how could someone who knew horses well and was as good an observer as he was offer such a simplistic theory on the origin of domesticated horses? The answer is not enough fossil evidence.

The extensive collection of early equid fossils in North America found only in the last fifty years was a principal reason that naturalists began to refine Darwin's idea of evolution. Today we are more likely to conceive of evolution in general as neither making a purposeful beeline toward a finished product, nor as completely random, but some combination of chance and adaptation as endlessly varying among species as the outcome of a roulette game, although a lot more fascinating. Nevertheless, there was one watershed evolutionary event in the development of equus after which the modern horse became a practical possibility, but before which development of the modern horse was out of the question.

The American paleontologist George Gaylord Simpson referred to it as "the great transformation." It occurred entirely within the Miocene epoch, which began some twenty-five million years ago and lasted approximately fifteen million years. Until the Miocene, all early ancestors of the horse were browsers. Like most herbivores at the beginning of the age of mammals, they fed on the leafy plants that grew in the swamps and marshy forests surrounding the great epicontinental seas. In those times immediately preceding the Miocene, vegetation typical of today's moist subtropical lowlands ranged widely over Europe and the United States. Palm trees and alligators were common as far north as the Dakotas. Cycads and other plants we usually associate with the age of dinosaurs still ranged widely over the landscape. Even magnolias and figs could grow in Alaska, suggesting a uniform mild climate like Florida or Louisiana extending over the entire breadth of the northern hemisphere.

The earliest relative of the horse, known as *Eohippus* or dawn horse, must have been a handsome, wiry, athletic little animal in this lush, succulent world. It stood scarcely a foot high, with an arched back and long tail like a canine, so that fossil hunters at first named it *Hyracotherium*, placing it with the early ancestors of hyraxes and dogs. Indeed, it probably moved more like a combination of Fido and Puss than Seattle Slew. The dawn horses had to escape predators by pushing off mushy ground in order to make a short, bolting, weaving flight to safe haven in dense foliage. To get traction on such soft earth, dawn horses had hind feet with three toes and front feet with four. A flexible catlike spine provided the ability to make sharp turns at top speed.

When the Miocene era began and the great seas regressed, new lands emerged; rising mountains intercepted the winds, creating more varied and more arid regions on the lee side of mountainous uplifts. As the climate cooled and dried, the soil of swamps firmed into plains, which were receptive to the spread of grasses. This is evidenced by the widespread discovery of fossil grass seeds in Miocene rocks, as well as by the wholesale development at this time of herbivorous mammals with high-crowned grinding teeth adapted to the grazing habit. While the old lines of small browsing horselike animals dwindled, new, more widespread, and ultimately more successful forms of equids developed to exploit this new environment and its increasingly abundant food sources. The evolution of grasses has been called one of the great milestones in the history of life.

Grass is a tough food. Both the seeds and blades contain abrasive silicas, the compounds that give hardness to quartz and flint. Low-growing or cropped grasses also inevitably contain sand and grit. A successful grazing animal requires exceptionally hard, flat, high-crowned teeth, which will grow as slowly as they wear away in order to maintain a good grinding surface over a lifetime. The pointy, pitted teeth of the carefree browser simply won't do.

The *Merychippus* of the Miocene epoch, which had already attained the stature of a small pony, was a dentist's dream. It possessed the pattern of dentition that has stayed basically the same in horses to the present day. The pits of the incisors were filled in with hard dentine. The molars got bigger, the crowns higher. An entirely new bonelike dental substance known as cement developed, deposited on the outside of the tooth enamel like a cap to fill the valleys and pockets of the grinding surface, and also inside the enamel walls of the crown to prevent the teeth from shattering when they took on the hard casing of grass seed.

At the same time, the whole head and neck of *Merychippus* were becoming much more horsy to adapt to this new grazing way of life. Its deeper, more massive jaw accommodated both the longer tooth crowns and made possible the characteristic grinding of the lower jaws side to side against the upper—the action that always gives us such an impression of satisfaction in a chewing horse. The muzzle became longer relative to the cranium, and the eyes were set high. A longer head enabled *Merychippus* to reach low-growing grasses; the high-set eyes allowed it to keep a lookout for potential danger while grazing. A longer neck increased its field of vision over treeless flatlands. Binocular vision helped it to spot approaching enemies over a wide angle, improving the chances of escape and survival in a habitat where there was plenty of room to run, but no place to hide.

Let's get down off this higher horse for a moment and consider what other adaptations a grazer on open plains might require to succeed in the risky, eat-or-be-eaten game of life. For roaming and running, a design for speed would be an advantage of the first order— not simply a compact trunk and long legs, but legs with the heavy working muscles bunched high at the flanks and shoulders in order to give maximum leg motion with minimum muscle movement; legs extended in the lower part to achieve the longest stride; and legs poised on a single toe with the heel (hock) high. (Think of how flat-footed five-toed humans run by lifting their heels and running on the balls of their feet, essentially attempting to position themselves on tiptoe in the way the horse's foot is already structured.)

In Miocene horses, the forearm and shin bones fused and were no longer able to move separately. Rotating motion of the feet was eliminated, and the leg joints followed suit by becoming able to move only in the fore and aft plane. These developments turned *Merychippus'* legs into strong, stiff machines singularly designed for bearing weight and moving forward. The spine became rigid.

Merychippus retained the three toes of some earlier horselike animals, but as time went on the middle toe became more the weight bearer while the side toes and their hooves became progressively smaller and moved higher on the leg. The foot pad of the "primitive" mammals was lost. In advanced forms, the animal's weight was carried entirely on the large central toe, ending in a convex hoof and attached to a strong cannon bone like the modern horse. How to explain the two small dangling hooves on each foot? Simpson speculated that form followed function. The horse does not move its legs at a 90 degree angle to the ground. In its long running stride, the legs actually strike the ground at a sharp angle, perhaps as much as 45 degrees. This would have brought the elevated side toes close to the ground, where the shrunken side hooves could be planted to help stabilize Miocene horses when they galloped, and prevent injury due to the overextension of ligaments. These side toes were later relegated to the useless role of the modern horse's fetlocks.

By the end of the Miocene, the graceful grazers of the North American Plains would have been instantly recognizable to us as horses, though they might have had green zebra stripes. There would still be further developments of the horse's senses and nervous system—improvements in eyesight, faster connections between brain and legs—bringing its ability to detect predators into line with its talents for escaping them. But with the great transformation accomplished, nature was well on the way to creating an animal almost perfectly suited to a life of plains grazing and superb flight from lions, tigers, and wolves. Engineered to respond to fear, fashioned mainly for avoiding fights, the horse's supreme defense was to spot carnivorous enemies before they attacked and to run away with such astonishing reflexes, speed, and stamina that much later, when humans began to ride horses, we mistook their skittish personalities for intelligence, and have resolutely believed to this very day that their adaptations for swift escape demonstrate courage. In fact, the opposite is probably true; the horse is one of nature's more perfect cowards.

But please don't tell Flash.

It was 3:30 A.M. when the Turkmenistan Express pulled into Tashauz. The platform was in darkness except for the weak lights cast by the train itself. Two young men came up and introduced themselves as Polat and Yusup. Were we the Americans they were supposed to meet? "Do you see any other Americans?" I asked them, unnecessarily sarcastic because of the lateness of the hour.

In fact, no one else got off the train in Tashauz. Polat, impervious to my ill humor, was relieved to hear me respond in Russian; they had been worried because they didn't speak a word of English, and were afraid they wouldn't recognize us. I just wanted to go to sleep.

They spoke with Sasha; then we put our gear into their small sedan, and the five of us drove off through the dark, empty streets of Tashauz. The night air was cold and dusty. From the little I could make out of the city, it had a strange, ominous feeling. The streets were lined with boxy wooden houses, but there were no sidewalks, trees, or front yards, and the streets were not paved. It seemed like a crude place, built without planning or even thought, an outpost on the edge of an empire, or perhaps on the edge of the world itself. The desert wind whipped through the streets, and as we turned corners, the dust in our headlights danced in satanic swirls.

When I looked closer at the dwellings picked up in the beams of the car, I saw that none of the houses had windows. I'm sure they had practical reasons for this, but it supported my sense of an unfriendly place. I had gathered the impression from Sasha that Tashauz was a major victim of the drying up of the Aral Sea, a result of the Soviet Union's diversion of the Amu Darya River to make the Kara Kum Canal. Maybe this accounted for the lack of vegetation that made Tashauz seem stark and bald.

At length we stopped before a large dwelling much like the others: a two-story windowless box sided with raw wooden planks like a huge packing crate. Polat and Yusup rapped loudly on the door, and we were admitted to a cavernous lobby. In the spooky light of the single electric bulb, I could see that the walls were painted in exotic Central Asian patterns—like Donatar's house, but not so ornate, and certainly less festive. There were some sleepy children there, a low, round coffee table with metal chairs around it near the front door, and a washstand with a sink against the wall; these were the only furnishings in a hall thirty-five or forty feet long. It was hard to tell at that late hour if this was somebody's home, a lodge for travelers, or the beginning of a nightmare. I didn't really care as long as I could go to sleep.

Then a man came from the interior of the house and introduced himself as our host, Alabergem, an Uzbek and a business associate of Guvanch and BEVIKO. "And how are our friends in Ashkhabad?" he asked Sasha, whom he apparently did not know. There was something cold-blooded in the way he said "our friends in Ashkhabad." He was only about five feet tall, swarthy, with greasy hair, puffy eyes, and this unsavory, fast-talking manner.

"Very attractive," I said to Moira. "Maybe we could find a hotel."

"I think it would be taken as an insult," she answered.

"You're right. Let's do it."

Instead, out of politeness, we had to sit around a low table. Alabergem proceeded to bring out and show a bottle of Napoleon brandy. I was too tired to be impressed, but I did notice that it had already been opened; I asked for tea instead. At this, Alabergem clapped his hands and a woman appeared out of the kitchen in the back. She was pretty, humble, solemn, and black-haired, Oriental-looking, with a slightly puckered mouth full of gold teeth. From her neat black dress it was apparent that she had already been awake; probably they had been awaiting our arrival. She averted her eyes and said nothing while Alabergem, without introducing her, ordered her to set the table for their honored foreign guests. Moira rolled her eyes.

While the woman prepared, Alabergem began pouring shots of brandy to toast our arrival. Just the smell of it at that hour made Moira sick. She begged off, but Sasha said it would be better if I drank; it was expected, as their honored foreign guest. There was nothing to be done; anyway, I was so tired that a shot of brandy more or less would make no difference. Alabergem made a toast, but I didn't pay close attention. It was the standard effusive Central Asian rhetoric about welcoming guests, which, however true, seemed inappropriate. A hot bath and a soft bed would have been more hospitable. The table and chairs were near the front door, and suddenly I was aware of how hideously the wind moaned outside, like the screams of a thousand martyrs tortured by a thousand demons. The door banged furiously until it flew back, whipping the curtain about violently. Alabergem didn't get up to close it.

"This guy is really making me sick," said Moira in English. I didn't need a crystal ball to predict that this scene was only going to get worse. We should probably have insisted on leaving then and there; once you eat a meal in someone's home, it makes it much more difficult to leave.

We were now served flat bread, a platter of fruits, a freshly boiled chicken, bowls of walnuts and pistachios, a plate of tomatoes, two kinds of candied figs, mineral water, and black tea. The woman served us with downcast eyes, but instead of joining us retired to the kitchen.

"Why do you look so surprised?" asked Sasha. "Uzbeks in Tashauz eat and drink even more than Turkmen in Ashkhabad. It is the way of life here. They drink until they pass out or fall asleep at the table. When they wake up, fresh platters of food are brought and they start to drink again. It can go on for days."

"You misunderstand me. It's not the food that surprises me."

Sasha looked at me, and then realized that I disapproved of Alabergem for his not having introduced the woman. He gave me a superior look, and said, "Sometimes you sound like an American liberal."

"Whom should I sound like, an Uzbeki husband? We don't even know who she is."

"Nothing could be more clear," Sasha said. "She's his wife."

Alabergem grunted with satisfaction. "She is my woman," he said, "and you are my guests." What he meant was, "She is my slave, and you are my prisoners." He insisted, "Have another drink."

When the woman came back to clear some dishes, Alabergem finally introduced her. Her name was Kurbangul, a lovely name to pronounce, a product of the Central Asian custom of naming women after flowers (*gul* means flower). For the first time she lifted her eyes to meet ours and said we were the first Americans she had ever met in person, and that if we were tired, she had prepared our bedroom.

What luck! Without wasting a second, Moira and I stood, gathered our gear, bid our host good night, and left Sasha to keep him company on his drinking bout. Kurbangul led us down a wide hallway, where children were sleeping on mats placed atop trunks. It must have been her own room that she had readied for us because the colors of the wall hangings and bedding were shades of pinks and reds, and a woman's vanity table stood in the corner. She must have thought Moira and I were husband and wife, because there was only one bed for the two of us.

I stripped down to boxer shorts and lay down on one side, then noticed that Moira had rolled up a blanket lengthwise and was putting it down the middle of the double bed, as if to create "his" and "her" sides. I didn't care: I was already almost asleep.

Moira turned off the light, lay down on her side of the blanket in the dark, and said, "What are we going to do about this guy Alabergem?"

"I don't know," I told her. "Let's see how it goes in the morning. If worse comes to worst, I'll offer him sex with you and beat it the hell out of here."

"Very funny!" she said.

—

In the morning, it went much better than expected. The house had no bathing facility, but at least there was a flush toilet in the rear courtyard. It was also possible to brush one's teeth and take a stand-up bath at the washstand in the living room.

Sasha, waking up slowly on a bedroll in the large blue dining room off the living room, said they had finished off two bottles of brandy before Alabergem had let him sleep. The good news was that as a result, our host was dead to the world. The bad news, I figured, was that he had more Napoleon brandy. Had they stopped after one bottle, it would have meant that was probably all he had, but to knock off two bottles almost surely meant he had a bigger supply. I sat at the large dining-room table, where Moira joined me. Our best hope to avoid a day of drinking was to try to get out early to find the saddle maker before our host woke up.

Kurbangul entered to serve us green tea. She looked tired but was uncomplaining. While we sipped our tea, there was a small commotion outside, and the doors of the dining room suddenly burst open. In strode a burly old man in an ill-fitting suit jacket and a porkpie hat. He came right over to me, sat at the corner of the table, put his elbow up so his chin rested on his fist, scrutinized me for about twenty seconds, and finally said in a gruff truck-driver's voice, "I'm Alabergem's father, Ibrahim. Excuse me, your honor, but when I heard there was an American here, I just had to come over to see for myself. We've never had an American here before. Mind if I ask you some questions?"

"Why not?" I replied.

"Among your people," he began, "what does a bride cost?"

I explained to him that we didn't buy our women.

"Well, at what age do your women marry?"

"Oh, it could be anywhere from twenty to thirty, but often older than thirty, too."

He scratched his head and screwed up his eyes. "But your honor, twenty to thirty are the most fertile years for women. Isn't it dangerous for your women to give birth after thirty?"

"I suppose so."

"Then why do your women wait so long?"

"Because they work. They have jobs and professions."

"Ah, understood, your honor," he nodded his head vociferously.

"Since Gorbachev, we have seen this on television from American pro-grams. It's very interesting to me. I'm retired now. I was a truck driver. My wife never worked outside the home. It's Uzbeki system. But speaking of home, tell me, your honor, is it true that in America all the houses are on one floor?"

"No, not all. But there are many one-floor houses."

"I have been told that all Americans own their own homes."

"Often true. It's something Americans want. Many do, some don't."

"Ah-ha. What about you, your honor? You have your own house?"

"Yes."

"With land?"

"A little."

"How much land?"

"About half a hectare."

"You have a garden? What do you grow?"

"Yes, I have a garden in the summer. I have some fruit trees, and I grow vegetables. My favorite is melons."

"Melons? You don't say? You know about our delicious melons here? How do they compare to yours?"

"I haven't tried them here."

"What? My son, Alabergem, didn't serve you melons?"

"No."

"We have an unusual melon here, your honor. It is called *staraya babushka*—old woman. We call it that because it can stay fresh for as long as seven months after harvest. I will present you with such a melon."

"Very kind of you."

The old man wiggled his gray mustache and poked his nose in my direction. "You are tired of answering questions now?"

"Not at all. Please continue. Ask me anything you like."

Ibrahim nodded. "Now this house of yours. How many rooms does it have?"

I counted. "Six. But upstairs is my office. I work at home."

"And you have someone from your family to help you take care of your home?"

"No. My family lives in another state."

"Father? Mother?"

"Both. They live in Boston. It's about four hundred fifty kilometers from my home to theirs."

"I see. But tell me this, your honor, who will take care of them when they're old? Who will bathe them and feed them if you don't?"

It was an extraordinary conversation. Politely but firmly, the old man asked one question after another, listening intently to my replies, weighing and evaluating this firsthand news from the other side of the world that interested him so greatly. Many of the questions—about drugs, violence, cars, divorce, money, race relations—had to do with what he had heard on television about the United States, and he didn't want to quit. Even Alabergem's entrance after an hour didn't stop him. With barely an acknowledgment to his hung-over son, who neither looked nor spoke anything like his old man, Ibrahim continued to throw questions at me. Alabergem sat on the other side of the table, lighted a cigarette, and looked on passively, as if not wishing to put himself in the path of his father's unstoppable truck.

"But now may I ask *you* a question?" I said finally. "We have come to Tashauz on a mission. We hope to find a certain *shornik* [saddlemaker]. We do not have his name or address. All we know about this man is that he is a traditional maker of saddles and tack for Turkmen horses, and that he has worked for many years somewhere in or near Tashauz. Do you know of such a *shornik*, and could you help us find him?"

"Oh, yes, I think I know who you are talking about," said Ibrahim. "I drove a truck in this region for forty years, so I know almost everyone. This *shornik* is famous because he is one of the last to do this kind of work. His name is Emutbau Khalbaev. He lives outside of town on the Lenin collective farm. We can go there in my car this morning. Since it is on the way to the ancient city of Khiva, I will take you there in the afternoon. I've been meaning to take my grandchildren there anyway. Kurbangul will come with us also, to take care of the grandchildren, and we will take two cars, mine and my son's. Let's go now before it gets late."

Moira and I looked at each other, unable to believe our good luck. It had all happened so fast that Alabergem sat with his mouth open. Within thirty minutes, we took off in our two-car caravan, leaving him behind; his father had saved us, temporarily, from his son's hospitality.

We drove through the city, which looked different in daylight, but not necessarily better. At least many of the packing-crate houses had grape vines espaliered on wooden arbors in front for shade, but Father Ibrahim said nothing else could grow there, because so much salt had seeped into the groundwater as a result of the drying of the Aral Sea nearby. How sterile and inhuman a city becomes without flowers and trees to soften its edges! The very center of town was occupied by the new Communist party of Turkmenia headquarters, a massive octagonal brick building of about four or five stories, which seemed to me to be of the same architectural ilk as new Baptist churches. Directly behind it was a high-rise apartment house made out of the same dark-red brick, constructed for the party bosses and looking very much like a Lego construction. Every single other domicile was a cheap wooden hovel sitting under a sulfurous yellow sky. The smog cover made the place feel like a gigantic cement factory. One wondered at the comrades' gall.

From the edge of town, cotton fields ran unbroken for miles. As we sped by, women and children dressed in colorful, striped Turkmen and Uzbek robes and head pieces lifted their heads, making that heroic gesture—working their brows with their hands—that is favored in social realist films. For a moment I didn't know where I was. The workers were toting bags and picking cotton by hand, as in Mississippi circa 1929.

It was almost noon when Father Ibrahim and Sasha found our saddle maker. He lived in a disheveled compound of houses and stables surrounded by fences and separated by a few kilometers of cotton from the residential area of a gigantic collective farm. Mr. Khalbaev came out of the sprawling old house to meet us. He was a wiry old man with marked Mongolian features and wearing a funny little hat, still robust and animated, and still active in his craft. Behind him came his entire family: wives, sons, daughters, and grandchildren—and a handsome family it was. They were all curious and excited once they realized we weren't the authorities.

The *shornik* didn't speak Russian, but Kurbangul volunteered to act as interpreter into Russian, from which Moira helped me understand what the saddle maker was saying. At the outset he indicated that no one had ever come to speak with him about his work, much less film his wares, and that he was happy to spend as much time with us as we wanted, and to show us anything we liked.

We learned that Mr. Khalbaev had worked as a *shornik* all his life, just as his father and grandfather had before him. All his work was done by hand with rudimentary tools, which he showed us. He made not only saddles, but also felt blankets, leather harnesses, surcingles, woven saddlebags, and *ookrashaneya*—i.e., decorations akin to jewelry. Now he worked with his son, who would carry on the craft. He believed they were the last saddle-making family in Turkmenistan.

In earlier times, he told us, the Turkmen was a professional warrior, serving either the khans of Khiva as mercenary mounted troops or organizing raids on other tribes and settlements. As a result of this way of life, the Turkmen was entirely devoted to his horse, upon which he showered all his attention and much of his affection. Nowadays, the saddles Mr. Khalbaev makes are for weddings, during which horses are often "dressed" in the traditional Turkmen fashion. In the last few years, he said, horse racing had also returned as part of the Turkmen wedding celebration. Now he had a backlog of a year's worth of orders.

I asked if it would be possible for Mr. Khalbaev to show us how a Turkmen traditionally outfitted his horse, and he was happy to oblige. A Yomut palomino of about fourteen hands was brought out and and dressed while we filmed. Once we started, Kurbangul interpreted our directions to the *shornik*. Then an amazing thing happened: She started moving Mr. Khalbaev around by herself. Go to the other side of the horse! Lift your face this way! Take off your hat! Turn around! Don't block the camera! She was a born film director, and got a wonderful performance out of the old man.

Mr. Khalbaev dressed the palomino first for winter, then for summer, explaining as he went along. Turkmen horses were kept tethered to a stake with a long rope outside the yurt, and were always kept covered head to tail with heavy felt blankets, which protected the horse from cold in winter, and in summer from flies and the sun. Blankets were fastened with a single surcingle. You could always tell a Turkmen horse because traces of this surcingle remained throughout life as a depression on the chest.

When the Turkmen saddled his horse, he first removed the felt blanket and brushed off every particle of dust. Then two thick saddle blankets were put on, one of lamb's wool and one of felt. Over them went a third, very thick blanket, felt inside, cotton outside. Mr. Khalbaev now put his saddle on the Yomut's back. It consisted of a wooden tree with a leather covering, and stirrup leathers coming out of slits set well forward on the tree. The saddle itself had no padding. Instead, he put a cushion on top of the saddle. Then came a riding cover over all—felt for winter, light cotton or silk for summer. All this was covered with a second, embroidered blanket, and everything tightly fastened with a surcingle. The final touch was twin necklaces embedded with the turquoise and carmine with which Turkmen liked to adorn their mounts. When Mr. Khalbaev was done, he lifted his grandson into the saddle. Dressed in a red silk *khalat* and a fluffy white *telpek,* the boy looked like a miniature Turkmen warrior of one hundred years ago.

The horse looked beautiful enough to take to the prom, and I couldn't help thinking that no Turkmen ever dressed his wives so well.

Khiva is a walled Islamic city built in the seventh through twelfth centuries, miraculously preserved considering the successive waves of warfare and destruction that swirled again and again across Central Asia. In its final incarnation it was the seat of the last Central Asian khan who traced his ancestry directly back to Genghis Khan. Along with his harem of 350 wives, he was deposed by the Bolsheviks in 1921. His poster bed is still there for tourists to photograph, though the comrades removed the bedding and bricked up the cell doors of the seraglio long ago.

In its earlier lives, Khiva was rebuilt, moved, and renamed several times—the city was far more interesting as part of Khwarizm, the site of one of the most important and ancient markets along the network of caravan routes later named the Great Silk Road. Its geographic position near the Amu Darya also put it along the rough line dividing settled agricultural peoples from the nomadic steppes, and at one fateful point, it was also the immediate western neighbor of Genghis Khan's empire, which spread all the way from the Syr Darya River to China.

An idea of what the city was like when caravans bearing goods for China to trade for silk stopped here is provided by the fourteenth-century Arab traveler Ibn Battutah, who called it "the largest, most considerable, beautiful, and majestic city of Turks, with fine bazaars, wide streets, numerous buildings, and impressive views. In the city life is in full swing, and seems like the perturbing sea because of the great number of citizens." Crossing this city, Ibn Battutah came to a market, and suddenly found himself so stuck in a swarm of humanity that he "could move neither forward nor backwards." Such a great population presupposes a highly productive farming system, one that depended on large-scale irrigation from the canalization of the Amu Darya River.

Driving to Khiva, my first impression was of a magical sand castle; enormously high, smooth, yellow mud-brick walls form perfectly geometrical angles of shadow and sunlight, behind which rise turquoise-blue towers of mausoleums, mosques, minarets, and the university.

We parked and walked in. The city is a national historical treasure with no vehicles allowed. In the days of the Khwarizm shahs, said our guide, who had little tusks like a wild boar stuck into a Mongolian face with crossed eyes and a triple chin, the muezzins climbed the stairs of the minaret five times a day to call the faithful to prayer. They were religious athletes, and each kept a special wife whose sole responsibility was to rub his legs between trips up the steep steps of the 250-foot tower. "It kept their hearts in such good shape that the muezzins often lived to be one hundred," said the guide.

It was not until Moira, Kurbangul, and I climbed one minaret and looked out over the flat plains that I had some idea of what it must have been like to live on this frail perch of civilization at a time when a cloud of dust in the distance meant either a caravan or an attack by marauding nomads. The geographic fact that these pastoral peoples, in their ignorance and contempt of settled agriculture as tantamount to slavery, and their view of trade caravans as easy and legitimate prey, moved at no great distance from cities like Khiva, probably made conflict inevitable. There is no way of really knowing what envy or hatred the affluence and culture of cities like Khiva aroused in the nomads, condemned to live on the fringes of civilization while caliphs pleasured themselves in their watered gardens. In many respects they were like today's third world people standing hungry and sullen outside the charmed circle of the industrialized nations.

But it is wrong to read too much into the motives of a people who purposely left no written records—in fact, did not write at all, and thought of the invention only as a contemptible way of keeping tax accounts. In any case, the nomads were unlike the third world in at least one respect because they possessed the ultimate weapon of their day, the itinerant horse-mounted bowman. The Mongols, who took the field against Khwarizm in 1219 under Genghis Khan, traveled with a herd of twenty-five or thirty reserve horses following each soldier. These spares followed the bell mare the soldier usually rode, which was intended to eventually be eaten. It was the nomads' understanding of the horse's herd instincts, not superior training or military strategy, that gave them the ability to expand their empires so quickly and widely. A Mongol army could move tremendous distances rapidly because supply wasn't its business; each soldier was responsible for his own kit and provisions. Life on the march was not markedly different from during peacetime.

The Mongols were the last wave of nomads to overwhelm Khwarizm. To this day the people of the area retain their Mongolian looks; every guide and schoolchild knows the story of how Genghis Khan "killed the land" that had been Khwarizm, devising for the first time in history what has since become known as the scorched earth policy. It began peacefully enough with an exchange of embassies between the Mongol Khan, who had just conquered China, and the Khwarizmshah Mohammed. Genghis Khan's gifts included a famous piece of gold said to be the size of a camel's hump, so weighty that it required a cart of its own. The Mongol Khan suggested a peace agreement, and was ready to consider Mohammed as "equal with my dear sons." Probably, the khan meant this as a high compliment, but Mohammed thought that "son" was a demeaning term for dependence. The Khwarizmshah took umbrage and laid plans to lower the Mongol's pretensions.

Thinking the trade route through Khwarizm safeguarded by his friendly diplomacy, Genghis Khan sent a caravan of four hundred Muslim merchants and five hundred camels loaded with gold, silver, silk, and sables. But when it tried to cross the Syr Darya River at Otrar and enter the Khwarizmshah's lands, Mohammed's deputy Inalchik detained the caravan, accused the merchants of spying, and beheaded everyone. Even so, Genghis Khan only demanded that Inalchik be delivered to him. Mohammed refused, so it was he himself who brought the Mongols down on his people's heads.

Genghis Khan split up his forces three ways, placing his sons at the head of two of the armies, and moved with terrible effect against Khwarizm. At that time Khwarizm consisted of a number of walled cities set in fertile valleys connected across arid plains by caravan roads—what Charles Lamb called "a kind of chain of human life and dwellings extending through the barrens." The cities included Bukhara and Samarkand, "the citadels of Islam," as well as Merv, Khiva, Urgench, and Otrar. Before his campaign against Khwarizm, the Mongol chieftain was not well known in the Near East or Western Europe; afterward, he was called the "scourge of God" for what he did to these garden spots of Asia.

At Otrar on the Syr Darya River, the two sons laid siege for five months, and succeeded in killing all Mohammed's soldiers and capturing Inalchik. He was sent to Genghis Khan, who ordered molten silver poured into his eyes and ears, the traditional death of Mongol retribution. The walls of Otrar were razed and the population driven away.

Genghis Khan himself headed for Bukhara, hoping to find the shah, who had already fled. When the garrison of twenty thousand Turkic troops tried to follow Mohammed out, the Mongols caught them at the Amu Darya and put them to the sword. With the city left undefended, Mongol horsemen surged in, broke into the granaries, stabled their horses in the libraries, ravished women in front of their husbands and fathers, and trampled the Koran underfoot. According to legend, Genghis Khan is supposed to have ridden his horse up the steps of the mosque, dismounted at the reader's lectern, and ordered the mullahs to find provender for his army. The Mongols plundered Bukhara at leisure and set it to the torch; then the population was driven toward Samarkand before their army as a human shield.

On reaching Samarkand, with its orchards and groves, flower gardens and ponds, the Mongols drove the population of Bukhara straight into the arrows of the Turk defenders, let the bodies mount up as high as the walls, and then simply marched over them into the city. The Kankali Turk garrison, thirty thousand strong, immediately surrendered; the Mongols received them amiably, gave them Mongol military dress, and two nights later massacred every one of them.

Perhaps the worst was saved for the city of Urgench, the shah's seat. Having recently conquered China, Genghis Khan brought with him to Khwarizm Chinese engineers with siege machines and naphtha bombs. For the first time he had the technology not to simply vanquish, but to annihilate his enemies. He was a very methodical person who believed that any job, including destruction, was worth doing thoroughly. The

Mongols settled in for a long siege in front of Urgench, but lacking stones for their Chinese casting machines, they cut down all the big trees, hewed them into blocks, and soaked the wood in flammable materials. You wouldn't want to be standing underneath when one of these flaming blocks fell out of the sky.

Though the Mongols burned and trampled the standing crops, it still took months to starve the city out. To repay its citizens for the time it had taken, the conquerors went to the considerable trouble of having their Chinese engineers dam the Amu to alter its course so that it flowed directly over the debris of wasted houses and walls.

The Khwarizm campaign left the garden cities of Islam a desert. Nothing was left; a once-fertile kingdom was made barren. The French historian Grousset has pointed out that this wasn't evil or even savagery as much as that the nomads simply had no idea what to do with captured cities, no administrative experience in running them, and no ambition to rule them or live in them. Genghis Khan's idea was to create an uninhabitable buffer between the Mongol grazing lands and the Turkic or Arabian empires to the west. In the countryside, the Mongols targeted dams, waterworks, and irrigation canals. Destruction of the great dam at Merv was one of Genghis Khan's lasting achievements in Central Asia. Soviet historians long maintained that the Mongol Tatars unleashed such destruction during the Khwarizm campaign that they succeeded in "killing" a part of the Earth. In this restricted sense, the Kara Kum Desert is manmade.

—

But on the way back from Khiva, Father Ibrahim made us stop by the side of the road to look at the white dust on top of the soil. He picked up a handful, put his tongue to it, scrunched his face in disgust, and blew it away.

"It's salt," he said. "It's blown from the Aral Sea, which is drying up. The soil has become too saline to grow anything around here. The water is polluted with the pesticides they've used on cotton. We have the highest infant mortality rate in the USSR right here in Tashauz Oblast. You can't blame all that on Genghis Khan!"

The sun was going down slowly as we drove back to the city. There were sheep in the road, and Alabergem's teenage son, who was driving, was going much too fast. We almost ran down a herd as it tried to cross. When I turned my head to look back, the little girl herding the flock had run to the middle of the road and started beating the lead sheep out of fright. The fields were still full of children picking cotton.

Alabergem's son turned on the radio. It was Uzbeki music because to get to Khiva we had actually crossed into Uzbekistan. The singer sounded like a lonely figure in a pitiless universe whining in a falsetto voice. It reminded me again of the Mississippi Delta blues. We lapsed into silence, feeling our own sundowns till the singer finished. Then Sasha said, "This music comes out of the depth of the centuries."

When we got back to Tashauz, Alabergem had already started partying without us. Tired as we were, Moira and I dutifully sat down in the dining room with the blue curtains, glumly prepared to humor our host. After all, the day had been an unmitigated success. We had located the *shornik*, videotaped him dressing horses in traditional Turkmen nomadic fashion, and visited an extraordinary medieval walled city. I had especially enjoyed the way Kurbangul had bloomed as a member of our little film crew, and the unexpected delight of Father Ibrahim's befriending us left me ready to tolerate almost anything his son did.

Alabergem's first toast was actually quite sweet. Lifting our glasses, filled again with brandy (I would eventually learn he was working his way through an entire case he had somehow obtained in a business deal having to do with some relative's wedding), he commented on the friendly relations that had so quickly formed between his father and me. "Little would I have thought," he began, but changed his mind. "I am pleased about this friendship. A son's first duty is to his father. I love my father, and I hope that meeting him has given you, my guests, as much pleasure as I'm sure meeting you has given him."

Father Ibrahim sat there in his little porkpie hat, glass in hand, waiting to drink with an expression that said, "Get it over with, son, I'm thirsty." When Alabergem finished, his father nodded curtly in acknowledgment and tossed back a healthy shot. Sasha and I did the same; Moira sipped hers. As soon as we had drunk, Father Ibrahim got up to go. Shaking hands, he said, "Listen, one more question—"

"Enough questions!" Alabergem interrupted.

"It's okay," I told him. "Please continue."

"You have divorce, right? I have heard that if a man and his wife divorce in America, he must pay her to care for the children."

"Right."

"But I have also heard that even if she remarries and he remarries, he must continue to pay for the children. Is this true?" He scratched his head in dismay. Perhaps he had been watching *Divorce Court* on television.

—

As soon as Ibrahim left, the scene started to slide downhill. The more Alabergem drank and smoked, the more sinister he got. His hands started jerking like a puppet on strings, and he ordered his wife around in a voice you would use on a dog that had stolen the Sunday roast. It was clear to me he wasn't happy about having been left at home during the day. He hadn't snared a couple of prestigious foreign guests only to have them run off with his wife and old man.

"Put your videotape of Khiva on my VCR," he ordered. "I want to see it."

I should have told him that our tapes wouldn't play on his VCR. Instead, I told him the truth: I hadn't shot any video footage at Khiva, but had taken color slides instead.

"What?" Alabergem jumped to his feet as if he'd been personally insulted. "What? You didn't film Khiva? I did not know this. This was a serious mistake. You have missed a chance to record something that can never be repeated."

"Never repeated? What are you talking about?"

"If you had only told me, I would have arranged everything for you."

"Arranged what? I didn't want to tape Khiva. I wanted slides." This did not deter him, and he started ranting at me in a voice that resembled a mouse caught in a glue trap. Didn't I realize how unique Khiva was? How could I go home to tell my people about the wonders of Central Asia without a videotape of Khiva?

Kurbangul began serving dinner. Her demeanor had completely regressed. She was no longer the forceful, amusingly bossy director she had been earlier that day. She was a meek, cowering instrument of her husband's will. She dared not lift her eyes or show any expression other than the misery so clearly written on her face. She put down the platter of chicken and was on her way back to the kitchen when Alabergem stopped her.

"Woman, play music. Dance. I want to see you dance."

Without replying, Kurbangul immediately headed to the console in the corner, where a large screen Japanese color television and stereo unit stood. She put on some Uzbek music, much like what we had listened to in the car, with haunting melodies and sad, falsetto voices. Then she came out to the center of the room and started to dance by herself, with her eyes closed. It was a slow, simple dance, sexually restrained. She raised her arms above her head and circled the floor, clapping in time to the music. It cost her little in pride; perhaps she enjoyed it. I would have found her dance engaging had Alabergem not been sitting there like a slave owner with a drunken, salacious sneer across his hideous shrunken face. It changed the meaning of Kurbangul's dance into a naked demonstration of his domination, a perversion of the sensual art of dance. I could no more watch this with pleasure than watch a man beat a horse.

That evening seemed to drag on forever, like a pounding headache when you still have two hundred miles to drive. After a few more rounds of brandy, Sasha Skorokhodov got up and began to dance in his stocking feet. Back in Ashkhabad, he had warned us of his penchant for Uzbeki dancing. At his fiftieth birthday celebration, he had gotten drunk and started to dance by himself. As I watched him circle, I reflected on his increasing argumentativeness in our company. On my first trip to Turkmenistan he had proved himself a knowledgeable and interesting companion, eager to steer me right and help me to understand Central Asia. I had felt slightly guilty that our friendship had stood in the shadow of my relations with Guvanch, and was glad when it turned out that he would come with Moira and me to Tashauz. But as I got to know him better, I found a rigid, doctrinaire personality. At dinner in an Ashkhabad restaurant one evening, he announced his belief that only a spiritual revolution which returned the czar and the Russian Orthodox Church to power could save Russia from the twin curses of Soviet communism and Western materialism. "Democracy," he had said, "is the forerunner of Fascism."

Aside from such alarming pronouncements, and perhaps worse from a practical point of view, Sasha and Moira had almost instantly struck up an adversarial relation. The subject was always women. Sasha believed men were superior in intelligence and ability, and must always maintain unquestioned authority in all matters. This is not an unusual attitude among Russian men. At first Sasha had not taken Moira seriously. Then he resorted to an air of superiority. When he saw that this didn't work, he switched to sniping and belittling, which made being with him increasingly uncomfortable. I'm sure he took my refusal to engage as another sign of my fuzzy-headed weakness.

Still, it was Alabergem who took the prize that night. The beginning of the end was when he ordered Moira and me to do the Uzbeki dance, too. By now he was so drunk and hostile that I sensed the only alternatives were to give in or hit him. I gave in, following Moira and Sasha onto the floor and making a pretense of a few indifferent steps so as not to rile him any further. Shortly afterward, I complained of a terrible headache, which was not far from the truth, excused myself, and walked out. It was the one thing you never do in Central Asia.

I heard his unbearable high rasping voice trailing after me, a mixture of angry invective and orders to stay. I no longer cared; if he wanted to throw us out, we would find somewhere else to stay. I went into the bedroom and lay down on my side of the bed. Thirty or forty minutes later, just as I had drifted off to sleep, I was awakened by shouting, then a woman wailing. An upset and shaken Moira ran into the bedroom. She said that after I left Alabergem had really gone out of control and had blamed Kurbangul for my leaving, berating her again and again for insulting his foreign guests. He had grabbed her by the arm and struck her across the face. It was she who had cried out. During the night, I awoke to the sounds of her whimpering as she slept on the floor in the hall.

—

Early the next morning, intending to settle the situation by leaving as soon as possible, I went out to the living room and bathed at the washstand while Kurbangul, already dressed in the same black dress, swept the floor with a grass-stalk broom. She seemed unmarked from the fray. Her children played on the floor under her feet. There were three little ones, two boys and a tiny girl, perhaps two years old, with a shaved head and eyes that stared right through you. I had noticed before that Central Asian kids' eyes don't sparkle, but set on you to assess you solemnly. I enjoyed watching one of the boys race across the

294

floor on his tricycle while his brother roughhoused with a tiger-striped kitten.

With Alabergem asleep, the house had an air of normalcy about it. The older son, who had driven the car the day before, dressed and went to school without washing or eating breakfast—another Soviet habit. Kurbangul finished sweeping with her half-sized broom and served me breakfast: green tea with cherry preserves, *baranki* (a kind of dry, unsalted pretzel), and cold meat patties left over from the night before. I could tell she was nervous. As I began to pour the tea, she whispered urgently, "Look, about last night. I know you are a writer. Please don't write about what happened. Alabergem isn't a bad man. It's only when he's drunk he gets like that."

So when isn't he like that? I wondered. He had been drunk, or on the way there, or sleeping it off every minute since our arrival at 4:00 A.M. the previous day. Undoubtedly it was all in our honor; he was probably a teetotaling workaholic when we weren't there. I made Kurbangul no promises, but tried to explain in my broken Russian how ashamed I felt that our visit had been the occasion of her husband's lifting his hand against her. Because of it, I didn't feel we could stay with them any longer. I would explain this to Alabergem.

It proved almost more difficult to explain to Sasha. According to his plan, we weren't scheduled to return to Ashkhabad for another two days, when reservations had been made for us to return by air. He disclaimed responsibility, and said there was nothing to be done about it because tickets had already been arranged. There followed an unpleasant test of wills in which I insisted that this trip to Tashauz was wasting valuable time that would be better spent filming the documentary. I refused to be delayed because no one would change our plane reservations to an earlier flight—a simple matter, I argued, that I would be willing to facilitate by paying for in hard currency.

"You get the idea? I will not stay in this house any longer than necessary. That's final."

For an hour or more, Sasha hemmed and hawed, but when I remained adamant he suddenly remembered a friend who worked for something called the Special Service at the airport and who might be able to help. I put on all the heat I could until Sasha agreed to make the phone call. "You are the guest," he said finally. "I will do whatever you want."

"Good. Call your friend."

I felt slightly guilty about pressuring Sasha to pull strings. He was hung over—admittedly on our behalf since his keeping Alabergem company had reduced our burden—and limping from a knee injury suffered the day before when he tried to jump a ditch in a cotton field and fell short. On the other hand, I could not face another thirty-six hours *chez* Alabergem the Barbarian. I told Sasha I would rest, and he should wake me immediately if he had any news. I went back into the bedroom and lay down in a nervous state; though it was still morning, I felt as if I hadn't slept at all. I was tired of arguing, tired of the heat and dust, and especially tired of fending off brandy and trying to get away from Alabergem. Our little sojourn in Tashauz had shown me a dark side of Central Asian hospitality that would remain one of those unpleasant memories of travel not soon forgotten.

I had dozed for an hour or so when Valeri Davidov, Sasha's friend in the Special Service, arrived. I was never clear what this *Spetzviaz* was, only that Valeri Davidov had it within his power to help us out with our ticket problem. He was a tall, athletic Russian with a trim black beard, militarily erect posture, and a black belt in karate. Wonder of wonders, he hadn't touched liquor in nine years. At the moment, this made him something of a miracle man in my eyes.

We sat at the dining-room table to get acquainted, and I was immediately taken by him. He understood that he had been called in to solve a problem, because when Alabergem, who was once more drinking brandy in a stupor, asked Valeri to make a toast according to custom, he raised a goblet of plain water and offered the following anecdote:

"A son went to his father and said, 'I have killed someone. Help me.' The father told his son first to go ask his own friends for help. So he went to the house of his first friend, sat down to eat something, and then said, 'My friend, I have killed someone. I need your help.' The friend said he would be glad to help, but just at this moment his own legal situation was difficult, and he simply couldn't. So the son went to another friend, sat down at his table, ate, drank, and finally said, 'I have killed someone. Help me.' The friend said he would, but right now his wife was being nasty and he couldn't do so. And so it went. One friend was strapped for money and couldn't help; another had a sick relative. Every friend turned him down.

"Finally, the son returned to his father, and told him, 'My friends won't help me.' The father took his son to the house of his oldest friend, and knocked on the door. Even before they entered the house, the father told his friend, 'Look, my son here has killed a man and needs help. Will you help him?' The man grabbed his saber and came running out of the house, crying, 'What other enemies have you got?' "

At first Valeri Davidov seemed so refreshingly straightforward that it was almost possible to believe he had somehow created a life for himself separate from the maddeningly complex system of cross allegiances and hidden agendas. What was Alabergem's relationship, for example, to "our friends" in Ashkhabad? (I never found out.) But as we talked, it became clear that there was no escape from the system within the system. If anyone ever projected the image of a young, vibrant, ambitious, competent Russian—just the type the country needed to become a democratic society—it was Valeri Davidov. Since the advent of Gorbachev and economic reform, he had consigned his duties at the Special Service to what the Russians call *khaltura*—hack work for money—and devoted his energy to launching a private enterprise—though, unlike Guvanch Djumaev, without extensive party contacts or foreign partners. Davidov had decided to launch a cable-television company in the Tashauz market of about 150,000 people, where cable-ready Japanese sets had flooded the market, but there was nothing to watch except the same old state channels and pirated foreign-language videos.

Valeri had gone to Moscow to take a course in cable technology, business economics, programming, and marketing. Unfortunately, the course's shotgun approach had failed to address a major difficulty, particularly in relation to Tashauz. Tashauz is a low-density residential city of detached houses with almost no high-rise apartments, and it simply is not economic to install cable in such a one-story market. Valeri and his partners realized this only after they had spent several years and most of their capital making the required payoffs to obtain the legal franchise. But at this point, with so much time, energy, and money sunk into the enterprise, there was no turning back. The franchise was only good for three years, and without a private banking system or a functioning stock market Valeri was in danger of losing everything he had been working for. As a result, he had begun a desperate search for side ventures to bring in the profits he needed. Like many business ventures launched on Western technology and naïve hopes in the old Soviet Union, Valeri Davidov's company had turned to trading. They were selling the same pirated videos they had started the cable company to improve on. Even these videos were hard to sell because there was so much competition from those whose ambition was more limited. It seemed that whatever business was attempted, in the end one was reduced to buying cheap and selling dear, the most primitive form of capitalism. Yet incredibly, the reversals had not daunted Valeri's optimism. In this, too, he was a far cry from the usual Russian; he was an individualist waiting for the slimmest opening.

Valeri Davidov proved as good as his word. Later that day he called to say he had us on the first plane out in the morning. Moira and I were told to be at the Tashauz airport at 7 A.M. for an 8 A.M. flight. When Alabergem found out we were leaving, he tried to patch things up as best he could. As we were drinking the green tea that Kurbangul had prepared for us, and taking our leave of her, he entered the living room.

"Wherever you want to go, I can arrange it. If you want to go out of the city, I will fix it. If you wish to go for a walk, I can organize it."

He could do everything but understand. "Listen," he said, dumping himself into a chair, "what would it cost for me and my woman to travel in America?"

We were packing up our gear and ignored him.

"What would a ten-day trip cost? Would ten thousand dollars buy ten days?"

I started for the door.

"You could be my host," he went on in the same grating voice. "We are friends. You have been my guests here. What would the invitation cost?"

I was already out the door. It was at this moment that Moira, a Wellesley College graduate with Seven Sisters manners, for the first and only time, turned around and let him have it right between the legs. "Alabergem," she said, "if Kurbangul wants to come to the United States, we will invite her with great pleasure. I will pay for her whole trip. If Father Ibrahim wants to come, we will send an invitation and be his host. But we will never, *ever* . . ."

Sasha dropped us off at the airport; he was still sticking to the former plan and was apparently in no rush to leave Tashauz. We arrived on time and set our gear down to wait. Moira went off somewhere, and I was writing in my journal when a uniformed policeman suddenly appeared.

"You," he said, "what are you measuring there?"

He was looking at the tripod, which was standing next to where I was seated.

"Measuring? I'm not measuring anything. It's a tripod."

"What are you doing there?" he repeated.

"Waiting for a flight. I'm a passenger. This is an airport, correct?"

"It is illegal to measure in an airport in the Soviet Union. Airports are strategic objects. You will please come with me."

"Go yourself."

The policeman went off to get the airport's director.

Not again, I thought. Did I have to get taken into custody on every trip to the Soviet Union? This could be a lot more serious than my previous arrest for crossing a regional boundary without a permit. We were talking "strategic objects" here, whatever that meant.

Luckily, Valeri Davidov arrived with our tickets before the police returned. Instead of arrest and interrogation, Moira and I were shown into the diplomatic lounge and treated to a free breakfast of fried eggs and toast. The director of the airport came in to apologize for the policeman's error. He was an obsequious man in an ugly brown suit with slicked-down hair and rheumy eyes.

"Allow me to offer you a glass of brandy," he said, though it was only 7:30 in the morning.

I couldn't help noticing that the bottle was Napoleon.

We flew straight over the Kara Kum in a small twin-engine prop plane that held about forty passengers and was ripe with the stink of rotting vegetation and unwashed bodies. The flight was a little less than one hour. It looked like the surface of the moon down below. We passed over an amazing sinkhole, where the desert floor had collapsed. Then for maybe two minutes there was some sort of road or trail that began nowhere and ended in nothing. Whereas the railroad had hugged the mountains until the desert was at its narrowest, then darted across to the Amu Darya River like a migrating bird, the plane flew arrogantly straight across the Kara Kum's midriff. This was actually my fourth trip across, counting the quick round-trip I'd made to Repetek on my first trip to Turkmenistan. Looking down on the desert, it seemed to me that flying was far more terrifying than traveling overland; from several thousand feet there was no sign of life. The rivers had died long before they reached here. Even any evidence of the irrigation works made in ancient times was absent. The earth looked dead. What if the plane had to make an emergency landing? We'd be desiccated ducks in a day.

The desert ran right up to the edge of Ashkhabad. Even as we landed, the sand was still below us until our wheels touched the landing strip. I didn't think I'd ever be so glad to see the Turkmen capital. Donatar was there to meet us with the car, and had a box of chocolates for Moira. We hugged him. "How there?" he wanted to know, hefting all of Moira's gear and most of mine.

On the way into town, we told him a little about our misadventures in Tashauz, and how glad we were to be back in his care; it was as if we had lost our genie for several days. I asked Donatar if he'd ever been to Tashauz.

"What? What do you mean? I can't go anywhere!" He waved his arms violently and launched into a familiar refrain. "I have to pay so much for my wedding, I can't afford to go anywhere. Fifty thousand rubles for the bride. The house cost a hundred thousand rubles, you know. I borrowed twenty-five thousand rubles from a friend yesterday. I have to make money—money!" He rubbed his fingers together. "Money, money, money, money to me necessary. The car will be seventy thousand rubles. The wife costs almost as much as the car, so how can I go anywhere?"

Then he stopped complaining and produced his most beatific, genie-like smile. "I had the house cleaned while you were gone. I put in Pepsi, soda, melons, meat. We'll stop for fresh bread on the way. You will eat when you get there. You will rest. Guvanch is in Moscow. I'm glad you're back. I missed you!"

The next day I asked Donatar to drive Moira and me out to Geldi Kiarizov's stud farm to arrange to film his horses. At dusk, the comrades were driving their camels and sheep home for the night in the streets of Ashkhabad. Women stood outside their houses, shaking the dust from carpets. Everyone had something, it seemed, to contribute to the dust blanketing the Turkmen capital. Donatar mashed his foot to the pedal, and in a few minutes the city lay behind us.

It had been ten years since Geldi had jumped the gun on perestroika and staked a claim to some unused desert acreage north of the city. It was located near an artificial lake created from the overflow of the Kara Kum Canal, where he could obtain sufficient water for his horses. Ten years ago he had been ignored by the authorities and scorned by his family. They all thought he must be out of his mind to move into the open desert. But now Geldi has the first privately owned herd of Akhal-Tekes in Turkmenistan since the Bolshevik Revolution. He had almost finished the construction of his open-air stables, with cement stalls for about fifty mares, and two cruder but stronger wooden stalls for his stallions. The complex was secured by a new stone wall with locked gates.

While Geldi was building his stud farm, the desert around him was becoming a smart new suburb as other people claimed lots and built dwellings. It lacked paved roads and city services, but at least there was plenty of space for large family houses, yards, and compounds. To the

Western eye it looked like a desert Scarsdale; all that was missing were green lawns and the hum of mowers.

Donatar rolled down his windows. "Up till two years ago, you could not build a home here. You would fear arrest for profiteering. Now the government sells the lot to you. It's capitalism. Everything is going up."

Geldi met us outside, and showed us around the homestead, which he calls "Akhal," before dark. Once again, I had a strong impression of Geldi as a man on a mission for Turkmenistan's golden horses. As the mares were put in for the night with their foals in the same stall, he went from stall to stall to show us the different strains and characteristics of the breed. He said the most typical and ancient form of Akhal-Teke was a horse with a very "dry" anatomy: a long, narrow, dished face, little mass on the bones, long ears for hearing over desert distances, a long neck, and long, lean legs. And, of course, an exotic color: golden, silver-gray, or lustrous black.

"These are the physical factors Turkmen have always favored. The Arabs who took Turkmen horses to Arabia to make the Arabian breed took a different path. Those are also strong horses with great endurance, but they are rounder, more 'wet.' The English Thoroughbred is also more wet—heavier, fuller. The Turkmen warrior wanted this dry type for strength over long distances. He needed to cross the desert to Persia and back, carrying hundreds of pounds of weight." (Geldi didn't mention that this weight often consisted of captives the Tekes carried back from slave raids, or of bags full of the heads of enemies, which the Turkmen delivered to the khan's keeper of accounts for money.)

When it got too dark to see, Geldi took us into the rudimentary house he had built for his family, where assorted ragamuffins played on the floor and his plain wife served us delicious homemade *kefir*, a yogurt from sheep's milk. He took down a photograph from the wall, showing the desired conformation in a stallion from the 1950s.

"Why does the Akhal-Teke win marathons?" he asked rhetorically. "Because of the heart. It must pump blood to every muscle in the body. A Thoroughbred will run the first ten kilometers of a five-hundred-kilometer race faster than any horse in the world, but then, because of all the weight it carries in its muscle mass, the heart has to work hard, and the horse begins to tire. The dry anatomy of the Akhal-Teke means the heart has to work less hard to circulate the blood."

———

Geldi picked up his thought almost precisely where he had left off the next day when we came with tripod and camera to film his horses. At first light, around 6:30 A.M., the desert air was cool, gray, and soothing, and the horses were still waking up. We took shots of the mares and foals; then Geldi and his herders let them out to forage on the green alfalfa spread on the sand in front of the stable compound. After less than an hour, the boys drove the herd down to the pond while we remained at the stables to shoot footage of the stallions. Despite their powerful movements and fiery personalities, which give the impression of large horses, they had surprisingly short barrels and narrow chests.

I asked Geldi about this. "The English began to build up the mass of chest and flank muscles in the Thoroughbred in the eighteenth century," he answered. "They have been breeding for certain traits in England for three hundred years. The Akhal-Teke was not bred to run in a short burst. But in the last seventy-five years, we have accomplished nothing in breeding. That is why we are so far behind in bloodstock and selection. I am certain the Akhal-Teke will eventually prove itself as an endurance horse. Nothing can touch it when it is bred to a Thorough-bred for steeplechase racing, for example. As for long-distance events, I want to tell you about one Akhal-Teke stallion I know about. It belongs to a ranger at the Badkhyz Nature Refuge in the southern part of Turkmenistan. The park ranger goes into the refuge to look for onagers, and every day he collects two heavy sacks of pistachio nuts, which grow there, to bring home. The onagers can run up to a hundred kilometers in two hours. This Akhal-Teke stallion, weighed down with rider and sacks, chases down the onagers, takes a drink of water, rests three or four minutes, and is refreshed and ready to ride back a hundred kilometers. Any other breed would drop dead from such a regimen."

We moved the heavy tripod and camera in Geldi's car down to the canal-fed pond, where I spent several hours making shots of the herd. The foals hadn't been weaned, so stayed close to their dams, nuzzling, milking, and finally resting in the shade of their mothers' bodies—the only shade present—when the sun climbed. The young herders disappeared into the bushes, and were probably napping, when Geldi later came down to join us. He whistled sharply, and the two boys staggered out into the open like soldiers caught with their pants down.

Geldi wanted to know what would be done with the video we were making; was there any chance it might attract partners from Western Europe or the United States? I told him it was hard to say. He had hoped that the auction Guvanch had set up with Alex in Bulgaria would open up a market, but it had turned out to be a fiasco. "I was told I would sell some of my horses at this auction. I sent eleven horses, and Komsomol did the same. It was a difficult journey overland, and one of Komsomol's horses died on the way. But there were no buyers. The town of Kavarna was trying to promote itself as a horse-trading center, but it didn't do any advertising and nobody bought. You could hardly call it an auction; only two or three Bulgarians showed up. Now my horses are stuck there. I can't export horses out of the Soviet Union, and then import them back again. I will try to move them to Essen, Germany. *That* is the place to sell horses, not Bulgaria. Who knows Bulgaria? It's not even in Europe. Alex was trying to make a sharp deal for himself. He wanted to buy our Turkmen stallion Yalkimli, but no Turkmen would sell that horse to a foreigner. He is a national treasure."

I remembered the look of greed and desire in Alex's eyes the day he first took me to the stables at the hippodrome to see the great golden bay stallion with the amazing neck and the one blue eye. All his schemes had collapsed around him. Now I realized why Guvanch had failed to mention anything about Alex or the Bulgarian auction since my arrival. Also why once, when Alex's name came up in conversation, and I described him to Moira as Guvanch's Bulgarian friend, Guvanch quickly broke in to correct me: "Not a friend, really, just a business acquaintance."

While I had been in Tashauz, the president of Turkmenistan, Saparmurad Niyazov, went on television and announced that he would bring all horse breeding and sales of the Akhal-Teke in the Turkmen republic under his power, creating a new ministry. In an instant, the future of the breed was thrown into doubt, and the work Guvanch and his allies were doing was jeopardized.

Niyazov, who would become the first president of independent

Turkmenistan after the breakup of the USSR, was a Gorbachev appointee who had been elected in a one-man race. A career apparatchik, he was a smooth Turkmen operator who knew how to play his hand. He had skillfully manipulated traditional Turkmen fears of Iran in the referendum, asking the comrades whether Turkmenistan should remain part of the USSR. While every other Central Asian republic voted for independence, the Turkmen voted by more than 90 percent to remain in the Union. More recently, Niyazov had managed to withhold news of the coup against Gorbachev for several days until he saw which way the wind was blowing.

It seemed to an American observer that Niyazov saw the handwriting on the wall for the future economy of Turkmenistan and wanted to move swiftly to keep his grip on it. The desert republic was rich in export products. It shared geography with Iran and oil-field geology with Azerbaijan, giving rise to the certainty there are large deposits of oil and gas sitting under Turkmen sands. Irrigation water from the Kara Kum Canal and a warm climate guaranteed strong fruit and vegetable crops, including grapes. Rugs were another item Niyazov could turn to his profit; already draconian laws had been issued forbidding anyone from taking a single rug out of the republic without permits and licenses. Undoubtedly the fees paid would find their way into the pockets of Niyazov's henchmen—just as would happen with his new ministry regulating horse breeding.

Not all my friends agreed with my cynical analysis; everyone had his own crystal ball. When I went out to the Komsomol stud again to shoot some more footage, Yusup Anaklichev said he had received an invitation from the Turkmen president's office to attend a kind of horse summit meeting with Niyazov. It was clear that Yusup thought he was under consideration for the job of minister, so he viewed Niyazov's decree as a way of halting the ruination of Akhal-Tekes by racing them, and of reforming the breeding program at Komsomol.

I had also become friendly at the hippodrome with a grandfatherly Russian named Sitnikov, a former circus roustabout who now treated and shoed the racers at the track in the absence of a legitimate veterinarian and trained farrier. He, too, had been called to attend Niyazov's summit meeting, and he, too, saw some potential good in the new ministry, even if it fostered some high-level corruption. "The current situation is untenable," he said. "On the one hand, without Moscow there are no funds available. How even to keep buying feed? Alfalfa is only grown in southern Russia now, but every stud farm in the Union demands it."

At the Ashkhabad track the crisis had gotten so bad that they were reduced to a total budget of 350 rubles for medicines—about 2 rubles per horse per year. On the other hand, Sitnikov continued, as more Western Europeans learned about Akhal-Tekes and the collapse of the Soviet Union, they were coming at a fast canter to strip Turkmenistan of its finest bloodstock. Italians, English, Germans, and French had all begun probing, some buying, and some robbing the Turkmen blind. "If this continues without regulation," he warned, "there will soon be nothing left here but second-rate Akhal-Tekes." If payoffs to Niyazov's associates were the price of reform, he thought it might be worth it.

When Guvanch returned to Ashkhabad, however, he kept his distance from the whole affair. He distrusted anything Niyazov did—"Gorbachev's rubber stamp," he called him—yet for the present it was clear he wished only to forget politics and concentrate on building his business. He was a born entrepreneur with energy to spare. In Moscow he had just been elected editor of a new national newspaper, the official organ of the union of cooperative business enterprises. In Ashkhabad he was buying farms and planning to open a restaurant. He had also returned from Moscow with a heady new idea. Since there was little food and a miserable climate in Russia, and lots of food and a sunny climate in Turkmenistan, he had decided to sell two-week package vacations to Russian tourists. He would fly them down to Ashkhabad, put them in a hotel, and feed them three or four Turkmen-sized meals a day in his new restaurant.

I concluded that the Bulgarian auction had soured Guvanch on horse trading for the time being, though Akhal-Tekes were never far from his thoughts. Guvanch always kept his saddle—the one he had used to lead the marathon ride to Moscow—in the trunk of his car, the way some people keep spare candles and canned goods in case a storm knocks out their electricity. With his saddle in his trunk, Guvanch was prepared for some unimaginable calamity that would necessitate a return to nomadism.

—

Guvanch took off from work the Saturday following his return, and we went with his twelve-year-old son, Timur, into the desert to visit a pig farm that BEVIKO had bought to produce pork for the non-Muslim population. On the way back, we stopped at a place alongside the road where they brewed beer in two yellow-plastic tank trucks and sold it fresh from the tap. Guvanch drew a liter into a plastic soda bottle he had brought for the purpose. The brew had a lovely amber color, and although not chilled, a heavy, yeasty, sweet, but highly drinkable taste. We finished off one bottle standing on the road, then bought two more and took them back to his apartment, where we spent a merry afternoon reclining on the living-room carpet, drinking homebrew, and eating the sweetmeats delivered by Alla and his daughters. Guvanch sat cross-legged, alternately guzzling and smacking his lips with deep satisfaction.

"Ahhhh," he burped. "I love to drink beer!"

I couldn't help thinking in the back of my mind how Niyazov's decree, which included a ban on the export of Akhal-Teke horses, made Guvanch's shipment of eleven of them to his "business acquaintance" in Bulgaria suddenly look like a very prescient move indeed.

The one who stood to lose most from Niyazov's edict was, of course, Geldi Kiarizov. His independent stud farm and breeding program could compete successfully against Komsomol for all the same reasons that capitalism proved superior to bureaucratic socialism in economic production: better information, less red tape, an all-consuming vision, and, most important, Geldi's personal stake in the outcome. But if Niyazov's new ministry meant a continuation of the command economy, only under another name and at the republican level, private enterprises like Geldi's would be unwelcome and vulnerable. He would be the first one they would come after.

"It all depends on what Niyazov has in mind," Geldi told me. He, too, had been summoned to the big meeting at the president's office. "If this new agency fosters better standards and improved breeding practices at the Komsomol stud, it might have some benefit. To me it doesn't seem likely. At worst, it could be like another 1937, when they took all horses out of private hands and shot any Turkmen who tried to keep one. Probably Niyazov will take his cut and appoint some party person whom he can control to oversee the industry. Like Yusup Anaklichev, for example."

"*Our* Yusup?" I was shocked he would criticize his friend to me by name.

Geldi became steely-eyed. "He's a party worker. He's been active with horses only two or three years. He's not a specialist. Niyazov would be able to control him."

It was an example of the intense politicking in the horse trade of Turkmenistan that no outsider can really grasp. Geldi's anxiety shed light on what makes Central Asia so difficult for foreigners to fathom. But all I saw was just a second layer of the deep, dark, Oriental mind. It wasn't until a few nights later that I found out the results of the Turkmen president's horse summit.

—

Geldi had invited Moira and me to be his guests at an evening banquet, and Donatar drove us to it. When we got there, it was already dark. Geldi led us up a ladder climbing a wooden lookout about fifteen feet off the ground, which he used as his dining veranda. You didn't need to get very high off the desert floor to command a wide view. There was a bright crescent moon, and all the lights of Ashkhabad twinkled in the clear desert air. Beyond the city the Kopet-Dag's black summits towered crisply against the navy-blue sky. The stars were coming out one by one. It was in this sky that the Indo-Parthian king Caspar saw the star he followed to Bethlehem. Tonight the desert's mood was airy, expansive, revealing a rare beauty.

We removed our shoes and lay down on the carpet along with Geldi's other guest, a roly-poly former movie stuntman now breeding horses on a farm near Moscow. Before the first toast, I pressed our host to tell us what had taken place at the horse summit.

"I am satisfied for now with the outcome," Geldi declared. The president had appointed a professional administrator to head the new ministry. He portrayed Niyazov's choice as a colorless figure with no experience in the horse trade, but a man in his fifties with much managerial experience, who knew how to organize a staff, gather information, and make decisions. "I will remain open-minded until I see what results." Clearly Geldi was relieved; they hadn't shot or even arrested him.

A dinner banquet in Turkmenistan is always an occasion for storytelling and emotional toasts, but I had never seen Geldi so relaxed. When the first drink was poured, he lifted his glass and offered this toast in the lovely night air: "The Turkmen have many sayings, good and bad. When the Turkmen wants to curse someone, he says, 'May the wind blow the door of your tent open and shut.' It means that your tent is empty—a very bad curse. If a Turkmen wants to please someone, he says, 'May your tent be full of guests.' To the Turkmen, guests mean prosperity. We could not be generous if we had nothing ourselves. We believe that each guest brings his own angel into a home. The Turkmen wants his home full of angels; then it will be like heaven. So I would like to offer this toast to my guests. I want to thank you, Jon, for the interest you show in us and in our horses, and I hope that some day I can do something very small for America!"

A small boy of four or five climbed the ladder to bring a kerosene lamp. Behind him came another, only slightly bigger, carrying a round watermelon under his arm. Geldi gathered his sons onto the carpet with him, and as he cut the melon in the flickering lamplight he spoke about his life.

"My father is a devoted Communist. He is a Marxist scholar, and teaches in the faculty of philosophy at the university here. He teaches courses in Marx, Engels, dialectical materialism, and atheism. He wished me to finish my university education, then become a party member. But even as I was going through school, I felt something wrong inside me. It seemed to me a system based on deception and lies. I got my degree in economics, and shortly after I graduated I was called to Communist party headquarters. I knew they would offer me my party card. I went into the room, and there was a party official. I sat down while he looked over my dossier. First he asked me a few ordinary questions. 'You practice sports? Do you get good grades in school? That's fine.' Then he said, 'Comrade Geldi, the proposal has been made to invite you to join Communist party of Turkmenia.'

"I looked around and thought to myself, who made such a proposal? There wasn't anyone else there. In that moment I knew it was all a big lie. Even the invitation to join the party was one more deception. I refused. My father wouldn't talk to me. That is when I came out here to build this farm ten years ago. There was nothing at all here. The state did not give land to people then, nor did the state sell it. There was no water—nothing. But I said to myself that a system built on lies and deception cannot last. So I built everything here myself. Now, sure enough, the system is falling apart. My wife sometimes asks me, 'How did you know ten years ago that all this would come to be?' "

"Falling apart, you say?" harrumphed the stuntman. He hauled himself up on one elbow, and screwed up his eyes against his own cigarette smoke. "I could tell you something about falling apart. Look at me, comrades! You're looking at a broken man. Yes, broken by the Soviet system. I don't mean my soul or my spirit or any of that crap. I was a stuntman for the Soviet film industry for twenty years. For a hundred rubles and a bottle of vodka, I crashed cars, jumped from cliffs—it didn't matter what. On one movie the stuntmen were playing the cavalry, and in this scene we were supposed to gallop through an artillery attack. The bastards were too cheap to practice the scene even once. They said, 'What for? You're the stuntmen. Don't you know what you're doing?'

"We were galloping across a field when they fired a live round, and the shell exploded at our horses' feet. Several stuntmen were killed and five horses were destroyed. I was thrown thirty feet in the air. When I woke up in the hospital, I had broken bones everywhere and burns over much of my body. Before I was even awake, they came to me and told me I must sign some routine papers. I signed. After I got out of the hospital, I found out that what they made me sign was a statement absolving the studio of all responsibility for the accident. Of course, my career as a stuntman was over. I couldn't bend my knees for three years. The studio denied me my pension. It said I was well enough to work."

For several minutes there were only the sounds of eating and of bugs roasting themselves in the lamp. We were having noodles with lamb sauce and tomato salad. Then Geldi said, "I will tell you a story about the Akhal-Teke Absent. You may know this was the stallion that won the Olympics dressage gold medal in Rome in 1960, with Sergei Filatov riding. Absent never won again, even though he was entered in the next three Olympics, because the Soviet team assigned different riders to him. According to their ideology, a horse is nothing more than a machine, so anyone can operate it. They put their riders on any of their horses, not on those the riders have trained themselves. Filatov was different. He trained with Absent before the Olympics. When he went to the stables and the horse followed him willingly, Filatov knew he could work with him that day. But if Absent didn't want to go, Filatov didn't force him. He won Absent's loyalty. Anyone who finds the key to an Akhal-Teke can win. But no one can jump on a strange Akhal-Teke and expect to find that key."

I reflected on how similar Geldi's story was to what Margot Case had said about Akhal-Tekes back in Virginia.

"That's right," agreed Potokin, the stuntman, after some thought. "The Akhal-Teke is a one-man horse. And another thing, have you ever seen this breed jump? I rode all breeds of horses as a stuntman, but I never saw another horse jump the way they do. Other horses canter up to the jump and take off smoothly, to get speed and spring. The Akhal-Teke runs up to the jump, stops, rears up, and vaults over on the strength of its hind quarters alone. Yet an Akhal-Teke was the champion in jumping in the Soviet Union. It's the damnedest thing!"

Another one of Geldi's children arrived with a large bowl of *kefir* for dessert. Geldi swigged it and passed the bowl around, and we all drank. Then green tea was served as the last course. Geldi's wife took no part in the dinner and never put in an appearance, though I assumed she was doing the cooking in the house below the lookout. We had drunk no vodka—a first in my Turkmen experience. The moonlit evening grew cooler as a breeze kicked up, but no one was in a hurry to leave. Late into the evening, Geldi held forth on his horses and their breed; he never spoke about anything else, and I believe there was nothing else for this horseman of the Turkmen steppes—not family, not love, not money or fame. If the knights of medieval Europe had used the horse to achieve a higher way of life for themselves through chivalry, the horse itself was that higher way to him.

In the end, Geldi Kiarizov also revealed his key when he said, "For seventy-five years, the Soviets took horses and horsemanship away from the Turkmen. Whatever traditions survived did so only out in the desert, where the *aksakals* [white beards] passed them along by word of mouth. The lore of our people was almost lost, and if there had been one more generation under Soviet rule, it would have disappeared forever. I knew it would die out completely if someone did not collect the traditions, so before coming here to start my farm I went into the desert to speak with the *aksakals*. I gathered information wherever I could. I spent many nights around tent fires listening at the feet of those old men. What I learned is what formed my knowledge of the Akhal-Teke horse. If those traditions had died, soon there would be no more Akhal-Teke breed, and without the breed there would be no more Turkmen people."

Donatar yawned. I think he was working at night to raise the fearsome bride price. "What time tomorrow?" he wanted to know.

"Two-thirty," I told him.

"*Too fruitee?*"

"*Nyet*, Donatar. *Dva tritsat.* Two-thirty."

"Wan, two, free, four, fishki, shishki, shevski, gravy—ayyyy!" Then he folded his arms across his chest, and said, "Geldi Kiarizov two."

"Two what?"

He winked. "Two wives."

"Really?"

"Yes. One at the Akhal farm; the other on Prospect Marx with his family."

Now I recalled that on my first trip to Turkmenistan, when I had attended the wedding of his brother, Kakysh, Geldi had danced with a woman of high bearing I had assumed was his wife, while their children spun dizzily around them. I asked Donatar, "Is it a secret?"

"They know each other but don't speak. He keeps them in separate houses. They are very different. The wife on Prospect Marx is from an important Teke family with plenty of connections. The wife at 'Akhal' you saw. She is a desert woman. She works hard."

Polygamy was approved of by Islam, but the Soviets tried to put an end to it. Apparently they weren't completely successful.

"And children?" I asked Donatar.

"I don't know exactly. Maybe six or seven."

"Altogether?"

"Together? *Nyet!* Each wife. Thirteen or fourteen children altogether. Geldi Kiarizov is a real Turkmen!"

We were filming a parade of Akhal-Teke stallions in front of the Komsomol stud stables when suddenly a great roar of engines was heard and
a convoy of military vehicles stormed through the gates. It was the Red
Army. Oh, no, I thought, not another coup.

The lead Jeep came to a halt in a spume of dust. Out of the passenger
side climbed an officer of truly monumental proportions—at least seven
foot six, and 290, maybe 300 pounds—and wearing dark aviator glasses
and camouflage fatigues. His crew cut rippled with power, and he had
pectorals the size of the Ritz. Some lackey must have polished his
sparkling black combat boots; no one that tall could have got so close
to the ground.

Flanked by unshaven subordinates in scratchy old wool uniforms
buttoned to the top in the piercing heat, this prodigious Soviet Man
marched right over to where Moira and I had the camera set up on the
tripod. There he put his hands behind his back, spread his tree-log legs,
and stood at parade rest, watching me work with a great stone face that
could have killed babies at fifty paces.

"Moira," I said, "find out what that big clunk wants. His shadow's
in frame. Tell him he's ruining the shot. If he's going to liquidate us,
could he move out of the way for ten minutes so we can wrap up this
sequence?"

Such considerations, however, proved entirely unnecessary, for General Luminosov had no ill intentions toward us. On the contrary, he was
fascinated to know who we were and what we were doing. Despite his
size, information reached his brain surprisingly quickly. Since the coup
attempt, he told Moira, there had been a military shakeup; he had just
arrived in Turkmenistan to take over as regional commander, and had
come right over to the stud to see the famous Akhal-Teke horses. "To
me pleasing to learn to ride while here," he said. I tried to picture this,
but the image wouldn't come. His feet would have dragged on the
ground even if he rode a seventeen-hand war charger.

Moira explained that we were Americans making a documentary
about the famous Turkmen horses. As soon as he realized this, General
Luminosov brought his Adam's apple into speaking position and fired

off a round of rambling incoherence in which he expressed the "sincerest hope that the cultural cooperation between the great Soviet and American peoples demonstrated by your project may someday also come to pass in military affairs, so that our two great peoples might come to know one another, and by friendship avoid the road to war," et cetera.

"God, where's this guy been for the last few years?" I asked Moira.

"Up in the ozone layer," she answered. "He's tall enough. Maybe it was his head that made the hole."

We were lucky: apparently, General Luminosov spoke no English. By this time Yusup, who had been preparing the horses before the stable boys brought them out for us, had gotten wind of General Luminosov's presence and came scampering out. It was distressing to see how servile he became in front of the Russian general. After all, despite his intimidating appearance, a man like General Luminosov could do no worse to you than other men in authority: He could have you arrested, liquidated, or put his sidearm to your head and blow you away right there, but nothing worse.

While Yusup showed the general around, we took a break. I went across the wide sand yard to the stables where the mares were kept and ran into ex-Comrade Potokin, whom we'd met at Geldi's banquet. He was carrying a battered old attaché case, the kind you put cash in.

"Now it holds only documents." He shook his head wearily. "The money was last time . . . what, I failed to tell you just why I am here in Ashkhabad? It's not a nice story. It's a terrible story, really. You see, I came here in June seeking to purchase several Akhal-Tekes for my own farm near Moscow. So I saw them, picked out eleven, and sat down with the Komsomol officials to make a contract. I paid them for the horses, but as it was summer and already very hot, I could not transport them to Moscow in the summer heat. So we agreed as part of the price that they would keep them for me until I returned in September.

"So now I come with the big *mashina*, which can carry twelve horses. It's three days and nights' drive from Moscow, and what do you think these shits tell me when I arrive? Nothing. *Nothing!* They won't talk to me. I waited three days, and no one at Komsomol found time to speak with me. But I cannot stay here forever. Each day I am paying for that *mashina*, and it's very expensive.

"Finally, they confessed to me: They sold my horses to someone else.

" 'How could you do such a thing?' I cried. 'We made a contract for those horses. I've already paid for them. What do you mean you sold them?'

" 'Oh, Comrade Potokin, please understand how very sorry we are. There has been a terrible mistake, a gross injustice! We are as upset about this as you are. How can we rectify this situation? Would you like to choose eleven other horses from the herd? Please, we invite you, Comrade Potokin, take any you want.'

" 'No,' I told them. 'I won't accept any other horses. You broke the contract. Now you must return my money and I will decide what to do. Can you imagine anything more corrupt? And these, mind you, are the same managers who agreed to send Akhal-Teke horses to the sausage factory in order to meet the meat-production quotas in the state five-year plan. Yes, they did, why look surprised? Geldi Kiarizov told me about this; you can ask him. As for me, the situation is difficult, but I must do something. Perhaps I will take some of the broodmares. I have instructed my lawyer by telephone to Moscow that he should write a letter to the United Nations. Maybe you've heard that Turkmenistan asked to be admitted as a member of United Nations. How could anyone even contemplate admitting such people to the UN? They are not a nation, they have no laws, they are little better than horse thieves.' "

Poor ex-Comrade Potokin. First his accident, then being screwed out of a pension, now this. What was incredible was that he continued to be quite jolly as he told his story. At the same time, I couldn't help wondering whether Yusup, the stud's commercial director, was somehow involved in this fiasco. I never got the chance to ask, because just then Moira came looking for me; we were wanted at the stallion barn. News of the general's arrival had apparently reached the Komsomol stud farm headquarters, where, as it happened, the minister of the new Ministry of Horse Husbandry (as President Niyazov's new agency would be called) was working that day. He had driven over to the stables to glad-hand General Luminosov, and Yusup thought it an opportune moment for me to meet the new minister, and for him to present my idea of a cultural exchange of riders between the United States and Turkmenistan.

As it turned out, Yusup had chosen the precise wrong moment. I found myself shaking hands in the hot sun with the minister, who, true to Geldi's impression, was so bland and impersonal that I forgot his name before we stopped shaking hands, and to this day I cannot remember a single detail of what he looked like. I do remember that Yusup mentioned to him in a soft, low, reverential voice that we were making a promotional documentary about Akhal-Tekes, and wanted to invite a delegation of Turkmen to ride a marathon in the United States. "An interesting proposal," the minister said without enthusiasm. "Put it down in writing and we will give it serious consideration. How do you propose to pay for this exchange?" Then he walked away without waiting for Yusup's reply.

Poor Yusup was mortified. He said, "I will mention this exchange to President Niyazov the next time I see him." He was trying to save face, but when he saw that I remained silent, he shrugged his shoulders. "I am sorry, Jon. No money, you see?"

At last the evening arrived when Donatar brought us to meet his future bride, Gulya, at her parents' home. When we arrived, however, she was nowhere in sight, so we sat in the kitchen with her mother happily eating caviar on buttered bread. The mother was a portly garrulous woman in Teke costume who kept the neatest home we had seen in Turkmenistan. Moira complimented her; I complimented her. She served tea with homemade raspberry preserves to go with the caviar. Dinner would still be a while, she said, since she had only just returned home from her job at the Ashkhabad library.

"You work?" asked Moira. "Is it common for Turkmen women to work?"

"It is not common. My husband is a modern man, so I was able to finish my education after I married. Many here are not so progressive or open-minded. Donatar's family is very traditional. His mother said to me, 'I'm giving you my son,' implying that Gulya wasn't up to her level. Perhaps it is because Gulya works in a sewing factory. I don't mind. We have decided not to demand a bride price from Donatar. We understand that his family won't help him."

At this young Donatar gave a big smile, smacked his lips, and downed more caviar.

"Donatar has been living at our house ever since he met Gulya," the mother went on. "The way I see it, the marriage means we can finally get rid of him."

Donatar mockingly shook his fist at his future mother-in-law. "I lo'zz she," he crooned in fractured English. Then he shouted, "Gulichka!" loud enough to hear in the back of the house. A giggle could be heard, but she didn't emerge.

"She's shy," he said, and called again, "Gulichka, come out."

Still nothing.

"Gulichka, come out here now. Come, Gulichka!"

Still nothing but giggling.

Donatar was tired and wanted to lie down. He led me outside and across the yard under the grape arbor to the men's quarters in a separate building, which consisted essentially of a dining room furnished by a single Teke rug. The rug was huge, tightly knotted, and unusually colored. Instead of the usual white *guls* (flowers) on a wine-red background, this rug had wine-red *guls* on a white background. The *kilim*, or edging, was wide, bright white, and finished at both ends in long tassels. It was a beautiful rug, and I have never felt such covetousness. Gulya's mother came in with food as well as with Moira and two daughters, but still no Gulya. One daughter was a petite, henna-haired woman who spoke no Russian and had a baby boy of her own. The other daughter was twelve or thirteen years old. They had decided that since Gulya's father wasn't home this evening and the women outnumbered the men in any case, we would eat together. But first Donatar sent Gulya's little sister to fetch his bride, who finally came out of hiding— probably because of hunger.

"Gulichka!" Donatar said proudly. He nibbled her ear and crooned again, "I lo'zz you! I *looo'zzz* you!"

Donatar's bride stood before us in a dark-blue dress. She looked big and strong enough to sing opera. Most humans resemble some animal—physically, temperamentally, in the soul. From the moment I set eyes on her, there could be no doubt at all: Gulya was a horse. She was robust, square-shouldered, tall and big-boned, with a lanky black mane flowing over her shoulders and a pale, round, flattish face. Not pretty to look at, but ample where it counted. She didn't have much to say, but she had something in her dark eyes besides bashfulness, something strong, stolid, and steady. It was obvious that Donatar was crazy about her. I thought how fitting it was that a young heady Turkmen would marry a horse.

I reclined on the Teke carpet with two pillows, and let Moira do the talking because I thought the women would feel freer if they talked among themselves. It was my first opportunity to listen to Turkmen women speak candidly—a sharp contrast with our experiences in Tashauz. Once more I felt lucky to have Moira there because I would have never heard Turkmen women speak so freely without her. Gulya's mother had heard we had gone to Tashauz—actually, she had washed our laundry while we were away—and asked about our trip there. Moira told her about our uncouth host, Alabergem, and the conversation quickly turned to men, the one subject a lot of women apparently never tire of discussing.

"A Turkmen woman is given one chance of escape from a bad husband," said the mother, whose name was Kariva Guzil. "This occurs forty days after a woman marries, when she returns to her parents' home for the first time to visit. At this time, if she doesn't love her husband, she may run away with someone else, especially if the husband has not yet paid the bride price. Nowadays, the engaged couple mostly agree between themselves on the price, and the family of the husband helps him out. Parents receive money from the marriage of their daughters, but they generally use it to buy wives for their sons, so it is the same."

The mother served us what I had come to recognize as the standard Turkmen dinner: meat soup and lamb *plov* plus cooked greens, all delicious. "In the old days before the Soviet revolution," she went on, "the khans who ruled the Turkmen tribes did not allocate water for women. They had to collect rainwater or find hidden springs. They did not count for much with the nomadic desert Turkmen. At weddings the bride stayed in the yurt with a few friends while the fathers and male friends of the bride and groom celebrated. The old men and women watched horse racing and wrestling and listened to poetry readings and music, but the bride took no part until she was taken home by her new husband after the wedding. She might never have met her husband before the wedding. When relatives visited, she was always required to wear a veil. Family dominates everything else here, and the father is still the patriarch of the family. There is absolute respect for elders. Among men, the attitude toward women is that they should not be allowed any freedom; in return, the men care for them and give them protection and security. Mostly, though, men want their wives to have children and to cook for them. Food is extremely important to the Turkmen man. It is the main way of evaluating a woman before marriage. A Turkmen will eat three kilograms of meat a week by himself. It must be cooked fresh every day. A Turkmen won't eat leftovers. Meat is the basis of life here. When a Turkmen goes abroad, he takes his own meat with him in a jar filled with fat to preserve it, in case he cannot get enough where he is going. Meat preserved like this can keep for years. Once when my husband and I went to Yugoslavia on holiday, we took our own meat. At that time they let us bring only thirty rubles out of the USSR for a fifteen-day holiday. One bottle of beer was ten rubles. I had to sell my gold earrings there just to eat."

Small meat pies and exquisite green melons were served. Then the mother brought out a bottle of vodka and offered her guests a simple toast of welcome to her home. She was a thoroughly modern Turkmen, but it was hard not to think that her life would have been a lot harder without the Soviets. In turn, Moira offered our hosts a toast, not forgetting best wishes to the happy couple.

"We will know about Donatar soon enough," cackled Kariva Guzil. "In Turkmen culture the new wife should become pregnant within one year of the wedding; otherwise the marriage agreement is annulled. Do you hear that, Donatar?"

Our virile genie grabbed the other daughter's baby son by the sweater behind his neck, swung him around in the air, and pretended to throttle him. The women yelled for Donatar to put him down before he dropped him, but he took glee in scaring them. Of course the baby loved the roughhouse, and I found myself envying Donatar for the way Gulya's family admired him, and the way he took just the right advantage of it.

The women's banquet was over. They began to clear the dishes and to herd Moira out to the kitchen with them for some more intimate talk: It was, as always, a once-in-a-lifetime opportunity for them to host an American, and the mother was not one to waste it. As they headed for the kitchen, I heard her say to Moira, "The number of children a Turkmen couple has is never determined by how many they want, or how many they can afford to feed. Turkmen believe that Allah will provide bread. Every child is wanted. Turkmen believe men can have up to twelve wives . . ."

Their voices petered out in the cool night, and Donatar and I were left alone to digest and reflect. I lay down on the deep pile of that gorgeous carpet and watched Donatar pull thick wads of rubles from his pockets. He started spreading them in piles around him like at the beginning of a Monopoly game. I heard him counting aloud feverishly: "Ten new dresses at two hundred rubles each. That's two thousand rubles. Three thousand rubles for vodka. Two thousand for cognac. Four sheep at a thousand each, that's four thousand. Two thousand for the band . . ." But he soon grew tired of such figuring, rolled onto his back, and fell asleep, snoring, surrounded by a flimsy wall of paper money.

On Sunday Donatar arrived to take Moira and me to Guvanch's for lunch, then out to the racetrack. He had something that he couldn't wait to show us: his fiancée's wedding shoes. They were candy-apple red patent leather and looked like gondolas from Venice. He had picked them out himself. "Two thousand they cost! From Austria. That's in Europe, right?"

"Right."

"I promised them to her. Nice?"

"Very nice, but, Donatar, where do you get this kind of money?" The average monthly salary in the Soviet Union was two hundred rubles at the time.

"Money, money," Donatar chortled. "I'm free with money. When I have it, I spend it. I throw it away, burn it. I don't care. Money isn't important to me; I'm not tight. Some people are stingy, but not me. Look, yesterday I bought some apparatus for twenty thousand and sold it today for twenty-five thousand. That's five thousand in profit! I bought the shoes, keep a little spending money, give the rest to Gulya." He was weaving through traffic like a dervish, one hand on the wheel, the other wildly illustrating his lesson in Turkmen Business Management 101. "Tell me what Turkmen thing you desire; I will present it to you."

"Donatar, all I want is your friendship."

He hugged my neck in a half nelson with his big hairy arm. He was probably happy because his friendship wouldn't cost money.

I said, "But there is one thing."

"Name it, just name anything!"

"Do yourself a favor, Donatar: Don't marry more than once. Gulichka is all the wife you'll ever need."

He gave his patented sly wink and nod, rolled down the window, and whistled at some girls we were passing. "Not to worry," he said. "I see how Guvanch does. He is a clever man. One wife, three kids, now he lives the good life. I will do the same. Did you know that while you were gone in Tashauz I found out that my family wouldn't give me money for the wedding?"

"No? Why not?"

"Aaacchhh!" This time he took both hands from the wheel; the car hit a pothole and nearly crashed into a group of women waiting for a bus by the roadside. Donatar laughed, honked, and sped off. "My brothers won't help me. I loaned them money for *their* weddings. Now I'm the last one, but will they help me? *Nooow!* After the wedding I won't need them anymore."

He wiped his hands clean of them, but when he returned them to the wheel, he grasped it so tightly that you would have thought it was a brother's neck. Poor Donatar. His frantic attempts to establish himself in high Turkmen style were running smack into inflation, fears, and the economic fragmentation of the USSR. Even a crazed twenty-five-year-old Turkmen yuppie couldn't reach back to the old world to pay for life in the new. There was only one solution. "I will get the money by myself. I don't care how. I dealt in contraband before I worked for Guvanch. If I have to, I'll trade contraband again, but don't tell the boss I said that. I'm lucky her family told me not to worry about the bride price and to just pay for the wedding."

"You *are* lucky," I told him. "Very lucky. You're marrying into a good family."

He made kissing noises. "Her mama loves me!"

—

At lunch Guvanch and Alla were boisterous and talkative. She took down the family picture album and showed us a photo of them in 1971, when Guvanch was going through his Beatles phase—big, floppy shirt collar, tinted granny glasses, hair cut round and long. When I saw this picture,

I knew for certain that for better or worse Turkmenistan was already part of the global culture, distant though it might be and perhaps a few years late. There was no doubt that Guvanch Djumaev had been touched by the spirit of romantic rebellion of the 1960s.

With my plans for a Turkmen equestrian delegation to the United States scotched by President Niyazov's shakeup, I had decided to invite the Djumaevs to visit the United States as my guests. Guvanch, who had clearly been cool to the idea of coming as part of a delegation, responded warmly to my invitation. "It's better now to come for a holiday as a private citizen," he said. "We don't know what will happen five days from now. Besides, it is very difficult to make arrangements to travel abroad with the USSR in such chaos."

I asked the question on everyone's mind: What would happen if the Soviet Union fell apart?

"It would be a disaster for Turkmenistan," Guvanch said bluntly. "We would do much better with a loose confederation. We have no experience here as a nation, no experience of democracy, little of modern capitalism. An independent Turkmenistan would be weak and vulnerable to a powerful Iran next door. We will become, I think, a dictatorship under the same men as now, only they won't have to accept any reforms that Moscow might order. However, I am afraid this is inevitable. On his return to Moscow, Gorbachev should have realized that it was the people who stood up for democracy and saved him from the party. He still could have saved the Union by allying himself with the people the moment he got off the plane; instead, he acted as if nothing had changed. He said he still believes in the Communist party. He is immobilized by his past; he cannot imagine another future. This was a big mistake that Gorbachev and the whole Soviet Union will pay for."

But on our last Sunday together we didn't dwell long on politics. Would it be possible when they came to the States, Guvanch asked, to meet with some American importers interested in Turkmen products? He was especially eager to find someone to import a kind of sweet chewy confection made only in Turkmenistan by drying melons in the sun. Because it contained no sugar, he felt that this traditional Turkmen candy would be an excellent product for diabetics. He presented Moira with a sample, which came in a handsome flower-patterned container about twice the size of a standard candy box. Of course it no longer surprised me that my Turkmen friend mixed business with pleasure. By this time I knew his mind worked twenty-four hours a day, and like the *divan* at BEVIKO, he could be absorbed in a political discussion one moment, just as deeply absorbed in a new commercial idea the next, and strumming Beatles songs on his guitar in yet another.

Lunch was superb. Alla served fresh-slaughtered boiled mutton with stuffed peppers and large meat-filled pelmeni. She sat down with us to eat, and offered this unusual toast: "One is for God. Two is for love, a man and a woman. Three is for family, the parents and child. Four is for home, which has four corners. Five is the number of times a Muslim prays each day. On the sixth day, God created the world. Seven is the Turkmen's lucky number. Eight is for grandchildren—two houses, and so for middle age. On the ninth day, the soul rises. And ten is woman's power, for if she, the zero, stands on the right side of the one man in her life, it will be full and he will succeed, but if she stands on the left side, he will be the less and will fail."

We ate and talked and drank some more, and Guvanch again played the videotape of his triumphant marathon ride to Moscow. He must have seen it a million times, but still jumped up to put up the volume when the Turkmen riders entered Moscow, as if he were seeing himself on television for the first time. As in Dr. Shikhmurad's house on the other side of Ashkhabad, the set at Guvanch's was always turned on when I was there, another sign of Turkmenistan's connection with the rest of the world, and one that, all things considered, must be viewed as positive compared with the isolation of Central Asia in earlier times.

It was time to go to the hippodrome. Guvanch stood and repeated one of his few English phrases, "Talking, please." By now we knew that this meant to *stop* talking; the moment had come when we would offer our last toasts, trying to wrestle into words the emotions of our friendship.

Guvanch began. "When you first came to Ashkhabad last April and said you would return in August, I did not know whether to believe you. Now I see you with my own eyes. We have met for the second time, and I hope these meetings will go on as long as life."

We bolted down our vodka, and I watched Guvanch wince and reach quickly for something salty to dampen the fire. Then he refilled our glasses and it was my turn. I got to my feet and kept it simple so I could say it in Russian.

"The word 'home' has several meanings in English. First, a house, a place to live. Second, one's native soil. And third, a place where the heart can feel at rest. We say we feel 'at home.' You have changed Turkmeni-stan for me from an unknown land to a place my heart can feel at home. I will always be grateful to you, and I offer this toast to you, your family, and your homeland."

Guvanch nodded with eyes shut and a wide smile, happy despite my grammatical mistakes. I think he would have been satisfied to stay home and watch the races on television, but I wanted one more chance to film at the track to wind up a sequence we had started several weeks earlier.

By the time we got there it was already the fifth race on a fourteen-race card. We went over to our usual place among the cognoscenti near the starter's wagon, where I immediately saw a sight that tickled my soul: Geldi Kiarizov and Yusup Anaklichev strolling arm in arm along the hedges at the inside of the track as if nothing had happened, no doubt debating an arcane point of Akhal-Teke lore. With the crisis of Niyazov's decrees passed for the moment, they must have patched up their differences. Perhaps they had realized that they needed each other, for both of them put the Akhal-Teke breed above personal ambition, and there are few enough in any society who put anything above their own interests. Both greeted me with warm handshakes and pats on the back.

The featured race of the afternoon was the seventh, a six-kilometer test that everyone was waiting for because it pitted the top Akhal-Tekes from the two leading state collective farms against each other. Moira and I set up our camera for hand-held shots of the finish line and crowd reactions, but just before the start, clouds covered Ashkhabad, the light changed drastically, and the rain started sprinkling. I kept rolling with Moira holding a piece of plastic over the camera to keep the water off, but suddenly the clouds burst and it really started pouring. The crowd scattered from the grandstand as if someone had fired a gun; no one ever carries umbrellas in Ashkhabad, which receives only a few inches of rain a year, and never in September. In thirty seconds, the grandstand had emptied, just as the race started. Kids ran toward the track and stood in the downpour behind the bushes, which were the only obstacle between them and the track. When the mounted cops gave chase, the kids started flooding across the track; it was as if the rain had freed them of inhibi-tion. They became even wilder than when they were in the grandstand, baiting the cops to catch them, dancing recklessly in front of their horses with all the dirty gestures they knew.

We sheltered under the platform used by the local television crew and kept the camera rolling. Somehow the jockeys managed to finish the race, at which point the kids coalesced into a mob and simply ran amok. There was nothing the cops could do, so they stopped trying. The mob circled the winning horse, a fleet gray, foaming at the mouth and wild-eyed at all the confusion. The kids pulled off the jockey, a boy about the same age as they, tossed him high into the air, and ran screaming and waving their fists beside the gray Akhal-Teke as he took his victory gallop, a purple sash draped around his proud, arched neck.

While packing the next day for the first flight out the following morning, I felt a certain dissatisfaction with my travels in Turkmenistan, but I couldn't put my finger on the reason. I had made wonderful friendships in a totalitarian society, stepped inside an ex-nomadic culture effectively unknown in the West, and captured unique images of one of the world's rarest and most beautiful breeds of horse. I had seen a land as rich in stories as it was poor in life. Now, like a latter-day Marco Polo, I was starting for home laden with fine carpets and silk robes, fur hats, and more than fifteen hours of videotape of Akhal-Tekes and Turkmen life. But some flea had gotten inside my breeches.

Perhaps I was still disappointed with myself for failing to have ridden across the Eurasian steppes. Once I met Guvanch, Geldi, and the others, a long journey overland seemed less important. A traveler ought to remain flexible, going with the flow and following opportunities as they present themselves. Besides, on reflection I had to admit that every time I had made a foray of any appreciable distance into the Kara Kum Desert, it had ended in tears. I hadn't found any way to ride into the baked lilac horizon. Instead, I remembered Madame Commissar with the golden fangs, pounding her desk like Khrushchev at the UN. I remembered my nights *chez* Alabergem. Considering my experiences, I was certain that if I had actually found a horse and trotted off into the burning sands,

I would have only proven the old proverb correct: "If you go to the Kara Kum, you will not return." Besides, now that I had ridden an Akhal-Teke, I could say without doubt that I wasn't a good enough rider to make a solo journey through such an implacably hostile environment. I could be well satisfied that Central Asia had taught me to recognize personal limits and accept them. This is a hard lesson for a male.

As on my first trip, we had brought a supply of gifts, and while packing I noticed I had overlooked a bag of fifty toy balloons. I interrupted Moira's packing, and we went out in front of Donatar's palace. It was late afternoon, and the street was practically empty. When one kid wandered out, I blew up a balloon and handed it to him. He looked at it strangely for a few seconds, and then, deciding it wasn't something to eat and wouldn't eat him, ran to get his sister. We gave her a balloon, too. Another child arrived, and another. Word spread. Soon they were coming in twos and threes, on foot and on bicycles, to get in on the fun. We couldn't blow up the balloons fast enough. The kids hugged them, tossed them, kicked them, popped them, screamed, laughed, and rioted. This went on until the balloons were all broken or had been taken home. When the last kid had raced around the corner chasing the last red balloon blown by the hot wind, we went back inside.

It grew dark. Dogs started barking all over the neighborhood. An hour later, someone knocked at Donatar's front door. When I opened it, there was a man with a small boy there. The man was dead drunk, rocking back and forth in pajama bottoms and a flannel shirt, his eyes red and drowsy. I recognized him as one of the family from next door, whose yard comprised the biblical tableau I had been watching from the windows of Donatar's house since our arrival. I had seen him chopping fodder for the sheep, sitting with his male kin on the ground swigging beer from a jar, and toting hay on his shoulders, as the sinking sun burnished his changeless world.

But the little boy was new to me. Perhaps they kept him inside where he couldn't be seen. He was dressed in a pinstriped sweat suit that read SPORT vertically on the breast; a matching pinstriped beanie covered his head. He looked up at me with an expression of accusation, as if he were being forced to do something he disliked intensely on account of me. The drunken father mumbled some words. I had no idea whether it was slurred Russian or slurred Turkmen, so I called Moira out. She couldn't understand him either, so we decided it must be Turkmen. But it was clear to us that he had brought the boy to receive a balloon like the other kids. Regrettably, I had to gesture that they were all gone.

At this point, the father reached down and took the boy's beanie off, revealing a wound a quarter inch thick that went from the top of the forehead right over the top of the head to the base of the skull. It was as if someone had taken an ax and cleft the boy's head in two, so that it was like a cracked egg. The wound seemed to have been sewn, but was not healed. Some scar tissue was there, some scab, some red edges, and some blood. There was no way of knowing what had happened. Had he fallen off a wall like Humpty Dumpty? Or had the father somehow been responsible? The little boy stood there and said nothing, his eyes pinned to me.

"He's shy," the father said; that much was intelligible in Russian. I felt sick to my stomach. I had to run away. I went inside and came back with a pack of chewing gum and a blue bandanna, all I could find. The boy took the gum. The two stared at the bandanna. They didn't know what it was. Moira told him in Russian it was "cowboy" style.

The boy's mouth turned down, as if to say, "Wear it yourself, Turkmen cowboy." He kept staring at me. He had intelligent eyes, not retarded, and studied the foreigner like other Central Asian kids. The father took his son's left arm and moved it up and down. It seemed paralyzed: The boy didn't flinch or register any sensation. He held the pack of gum tightly in his other hand. The father seemed in no hurry to go. He passed his hand over the terrible gash again and again and sighed heavily.

"I think he wants us to help him," Moira said.

I sent the drunken man home; there was nothing we could do for the boy. Any money we gave him would go immediately for vodka. He took the little boy by the hand and reeled off toward the front gates. I stood and watched their backs. What had they really come for? I didn't know. Maybe the father didn't know, either. Perhaps he had only brought the boy around for the small treat he had missed, and then improvised to see if he could get something else. Or maybe, without really being conscious of it, he wanted to share with us the grief Allah had visited upon him. Perhaps it was all he had to share with these foreign guests. I felt his drunken misery, and in its aftertaste a hopeless sense of the enigmas of Central Asia.

The rivers had dried up, and the meadows turned to salt. The cities had been razed, and empires had disappeared under the sands. One people after another had swept through on horseback, only to vanish utterly. Soon it would be the Russians' turn to vanish. In a few years, perhaps when the boy with the cracked head grew up, the Russians and their system would be only another piece of old string in this hopeless tangle of history, geology, and climate. But so it must be, for humanity is not entering an era of simple solutions to our planet's problems, and there will be more deserts made before the world ends. I could only hope the coming cataclysms produce something as beautiful as the Akhal-Teke. Then I went back inside to finish packing.

PART IV

Afterword

Shortly after my second trip to Turkmenistan, the hammer and sickle came down from the Kremlin flagpole and the Soviet Union ceased to exist. For the first time in history, Turkmenistan became an independent nation under the same government as prior to the Union's collapse, only no longer proclaimed Communist. It joined the Commonwealth of Independent States, though what that meant was unclear at the time, and the commonwealth was effectively and predictably defunct a year later.

In Central Asia, the breakup of the old Union was not followed by the construction, as I had hoped, of a country called the United Stans of Asia (U.S.A.): Turkmenistan, Kazakhstan, Uzbekistan, Kirghizstan, and Tadzhikistan. The golden opportunity of being mistaken for the American delegation at international diplomatic functions was tragically wasted. However, with financial help from Pakistan, they were able to make some progress toward a Central Asian common market.

The United States recognized Turkmenistan's sovereignty along with the other former Soviet republics of Central Asia; an American ambassador was appointed and an American embassy established in Ashkhabad. The newly independent Turkmen moved boldly onto the world stage in 1992 by presenting Boris Yeltsin with an Akhal-Teke, although it is doubtful that he rides it. They also tried to present a horse to Bill Clinton for his inauguration, but he had left his saddle in Little Rock and could not trot to the White House. These publicity stunts are apparently the Turkmen government's idea of promoting the Akhal-Teke breed. Meanwhile, Turkmenistan's President Saparmurad Niyazov, who flies to meetings like a real world leader, extended his ban on the export of horses from Turkmenistan through 1994. This might have left Geldi Kiarizov twisting slowly in the wind.

At least in the short run, Turkmen independence was not followed by a reversion to pre-Soviet tribal hostilities. The Tekes don't seem to be massacring the Yomuts, or "ethnically cleansing" the Geoklen areas. They must be too busy trying to make money. For one thing, the Saudis made a billion-dollar loan to Central Asia for oil exploration. Turkish, Arabic, and Iranian capital are competing for Central Asian markets and investments. Turkmenistan Airlines has supposedly established regular direct service between Istanbul and Ashkhabad, though I don't know anyone who has actually flown it, and it doesn't appear on the computers of American travel agents. I can't imagine that someone isn't growing opium poppies and hashish in the Turkmen hinterlands, both the poppy and hemp being native to Turkmenistan.

Strangely, independence seems not to have made any difference in easing communications between Turkmenistan and the United States. Travel still depends on the cumbersome system of formal written invitations and visas, made even more cumbersome now because it is handled by a special section of the notoriously ineffective Russian embassy in Washington. There are still no direct telephone connections. The postal agreement supposed to have been made by the commonwealth states was dead before the ink was dry; the old Soviet postal system no longer functions, and nothing has taken its place. Russian immigrants living in the United States give letters for visitors to hand carry.

After failing to get my invitation to visit the United States to Guvanch Djumaev by post, I, too, reverted to a personal messenger, for it turned out that my old fellow delegation member Professor Gleason was making another trip to Ashkhabad. I got the document into his hands typed out in Russian and English, and he was good enough to deliver it to Guvanch in Ashkhabad. Unfortunately, the invitation lacked a notary's stamp, without which the Turkmen government wouldn't issue travel visas. I got the invitations notarized and tried again: one copy by mail, one by fax to Leonid Kordonski in Moscow. But as the summer of 1992 began I had received no reply. Then a fax came from a London trader who had been to Ashkhabad, done some business with Guvanch, and offered to act as an intermediary through his company's office in Moscow. I immediately sent out another invitation to London for transmission to Moscow and thence to Ashkhabad. Again there was no answer.

Then in December, just as I was finishing this book, another New Mexican called to say that he would be going to Ashkhabad, and could I recommend someone who knew about Akhal-Teke horses? At last, I thought, a way to reach my Turkmen friend. My new messenger was a church worker visiting Turkmenistan to arrange for developmental and charity projects. He was more than willing to carry my letter, so I sat down and wrote the following:

My Dear and Respected Brother Guvanch Rosievich:

More than a year has gone by since I left Turkmenistan and returned to the United States. I have tried so many times to correspond by mail, to reach you by fax, or through an intermediary that I began to think you were lost to me forever and that we would never see or speak to each other again. I hoped that you and Alla Borisovna would come to me as guests last summer; it passed slowly and more slowly without you. Every day I wanted you here, till I began to wonder why God wanted us to meet and become friends if only then to deny us the chance to continue and develop our brotherhood?

Then, by chance, Mr. Brian Holtz of Albuquerque, New Mexico, called me to say he was traveling to Ashkhabad. Moreover, he is very interested in learning about Akhal-Teke horses, with a view toward creating Turkmen–American cultural exchanges. I have not met him in person, but we have held several telephone conversations, and I feel that I can recommend him to you as a serious person, a colleague, and perhaps a friend. He is carrying my letter to you in his hands, and I very much hope you will send a letter for me with him when he returns to the United States. You can hardly imagine how much I want to hear from you, to know how you and your family are, and what you, Alla Borisovna, and all my friends in Ashkhabad are doing.

Since I left you last year in September, of course, great and historical changes have taken place; in particular, the Soviet Union is no more and Turkmenistan is now an independent republic. This must have caused both great hardship and also great opportunities for as the American proverb goes, "When God closes one door, He opens many new ones." I think the end of the Union must have made our communications so difficult. Here in the United States, we have no news at all about what is taking place in Turkmenistan. For us it is as if Central Asia left the Earth, and only Russia now exists.

I want to tell you the news about the documentary film I shot when I visited you last year. The film is not yet completed. Progress has been steady but slow, mainly because I have had to pay for all the work myself. The quality of the film is wonderful. The horses look splendid. Those professionals who have seen it are very enthusiastic. Of course, I still remember my promise to finish this film for you. It will certainly be completed within a year, and then we will decide how you can receive a copy, and how to distribute it. From the point of view of both culture and business, I know you will be satisfied. I am only sorry it is taking so long to complete.

When will we meet again? Can't we try for next August or September? I will invite you and Alla Borisovna to come to me for two weeks' vacation just as we tried to do last year. You must send word with Brian Holtz to inform me exactly how to prepare the invitations, and how to get them to you without fail. I sent the invitation last March by fax to Mr. Don Selby in London, but received no reply. Are you still in communication with him? I am willing to try to send the invitations to him for transmission again if you think that is best.

Meanwhile, know that I am thinking of you every day, and looking forward to the moment when we meet again. I send my greetings, respects, and best wishes to you, your family, and everyone at BEVIKO. I wish you good health and prosperity in the New Year.

Sincerely,

Jonathan Maslow

I waited for a reply. Then Brian Holtz called from Albuquerque to say he had been unable to deliver my letter in Ashkhabad. He had called the BEVIKO office number I had given him, but it wasn't functioning. He had gone with his driver to the address on Universitetskaya Street, but could find neither the correct number nor BEVIKO headquarters.

Yet I am sure I was in Turkmenistan, rode sacred horses in the Kara Kum Desert, and swore eternal friendship with a desert chieftain.

Pretty sure, anyway.

Selected Bibliography

BOOKS

Adcock, F.E. *The Greek and Macedonian Art of War.* Berkeley: University of California Press, 1957.

Anderson, J.K. *Ancient Greek Horsemanship.* Berkeley: University of California Press, 1961.

Arrian. *The Campaign of Alexander,* trans. Aubrey de Selincourt. London: Penguin Classics, 1971.

Atagaryev, E., and T. Khodzhaniyazov. *Turkmenistan on the Great Silk Road.* Ashkhabad: Academy of Sciences of the Turkmen SSR, 1990.

Bosurliere, Francois, and the editors of *Life. The Land and Wildlife of Eurasia.* New York: Time Incorporated, 1964.

Breeds of Horses in Middle Asia, ed. W. O. Witt. Moscow: All-Union Research Institute of Horse Breeding, Lenin Academy of Agricultural Sciences, 1937.

Bunbury, E.H. *A History of Ancient Geography.* New York: Dover Publications, 1979.

The Cambridge Encyclopedia of Archaeology, ed. Andrew Sherratt. New York: Crown Publishers/Cambridge University Press, 1980.

Chekhov, Anton. *The Steppe,* trans. Constance Garnett. New York: Hippocrene Books, 1987.

Custine, Marquis de. *Journey for Our Time: The Russian Journals of the Marquis de Custine.* Washington, D.C.: Gateway Editions, 1987.

Dent, A.A. *The Horse Through Fifty Centuries of Civilization.* New York: Holt, Rinehart, Winston, 1974.

Ecology and Empire: Nomads in the Cultural Evolution of the Old World, ed. Gary Seaman. Los Angeles: University of Southern California, 1989.

Edwards, Elwyn Hartley. *The Saddle in Theory and Practice.* London: J. A. Allen, 1990.

Encyclopedia of the Horse, ed. Elwyn Hartley Edwards. New York: Octopus Books, 1977.

Esenov, Rakhim. *Turkmenia.* Moscow: Novosti Press Agency, 1982.

Faegre, Torvald. *Tents: Architecture of the Nomads.* New York: Anchor Books, 1979.

Fairley, John. *Great Racehorses in Art.* Lexington: University Press of Kentucky, 1984.

Falls, C.B. *The First 3000 Years.* New York: Viking Press, 1960.

Fax, Elton C. *Hashar.* Moscow: Progress Publishers, 1980.

Frankfort, Henri. *The Birth of Civilization in the Near East.* New York: Doubleday/Anchor, 1950.

Frye, Richard N. *The Heritage of Persia.* Cleveland: World Publishing Company, 1963.

Grousset, René. *The Empire of the Steppes: A History of Central Asia,* trans. Naomi Walford. New Brunswick, N.J.: Rutgers University Press, 1970.

Hamlyn, Paul. *Horses.* London: Westbrook House, 1962.

Heisler, Charles B., Jr. *Seed to Civilization: The Story of Man's Food.* San Francisco: W. H. Freeman and Co., 1973.

Herodotus. *The Histories,* trans. Harry Carter. New York: The Heritage Press, 1958.

Herzfeld, Ernst. *Zoroaster and His World,* Vol. I. Princeton, N.J.: Princeton University Press, 1947.

The History of Civilization: Travel and Travellers of the Middle Ages, ed. C. K. Ogden and Arthur Newton. New York: Alfred A. Knopf, 1930.

Hostler, Charles Warren. *Turkism and the Soviets.* New York: Frederick A. Praeger, 1957.

Jankovich, Miklos. *They Rode into Europe: The Fruitful Exchange in the Arts of Horsemanship Between East and West.* New York: Charles Scribner's Sons, 1971.

Kahn, Paul. *The Secret History of the Mongols: The Origin of Chingis Khan.* San Francisco: North Point Press, 1984.

Knystautas, Algirdas. *The Natural History of the USSR.* London: Swallow Editions, 1987.

Konnevodstvo v USSR. Moscow: Kalos Publishers, 1983.

Lamb, Harold. *Genghis Khan: The Emperor of All Men.* NA: Robert McBride and Company, 1927.

Lansdell, Henry. *Russian Central Asia.* Boston: Houghton Mifflin, 1885.

Legg, Stuart. *The Barbarians of Asia.* New York: Dorset Press, 1970.

Lessar, P.M. "P. M. Lessar's Journey from Askabad to Sarakhs," in *The Country of the Turkomans: An Anthology of Exploration*, taken from Journals and Proceedings of the Royal Geographic Society of London, Oguz Press Limited, 1977.

Littauer, Vladimir. *Horseman's Progress: The Development of Modern Riding.* New York: Van Nostrand, 1962.

MacLean, Fitzroy. *Eastern Approaches.* New York: Time-Life Books, 1964.

Meakin, Annette M.B. *In Russian Turkestan.* New York: Charles Scribner's Sons, 1915.

Moscow, Henry. *Russia Under the Czars.* New York: Harper and Row, 1965.

Nomads of Eurasia, ed. Vladmir N. Basilov. Los Angeles: Natural History Museum of Los Angeles County, 1989.

O'Donovan, Edmund. *The Merv Oasis.* London: NA, 1882.

Pahlen, Count K.K. *Mission to Turkestan*, ed. Richard A. Pierce. London: Oxford University Press, 1964.

Pasevyev, I. *Ashkhabad, A Guide.* Moscow: Progress Publishers, 1986.

Plutarch. *The Lives of Illustrious Men.* The Spencer Press, n.d.

Polo, Marco. *The Travels of Marco Polo*, trans. Robert Latham. London: Penguin Books, 1958.

Quintus Curtius Rufus. *Life of Alexander*, trans. John C. Rolfe. Cambridge: Harvard University Press, 1946, two volumes.

Ridgeway, William. *The Origin and Influence of the Thoroughbred Horse.* London: Cambridge University Press, 1905.

Rosenberg, James N. *On the Steppes: A Russian Diary.* New York: Alfred A. Knopf, 1927.

Rudenko, Sergei I. *Frozen Tombs of Siberia.* Berkeley: University of California Press, 1970.

Russia and Asia, ed. Wayne S. Vucunich. Palo Alto, CA: Hoover Institution, Pub. 107, 1972.

Schurmann, Ulrich. *Central Asian Rugs.* Frankfurt: Verlag Osterrieth, n.d.

Schuyler, Eugene. *Turkestan.* New York and Washington, D.C.: Frederick A. Praeger, 1873.

Simpson, George Gaylord. *Horses.* London: Oxford University Press, 1951.

Stubbs, George. *The Anatomy of the Horse.* New York: Dover Publications, 1976.

Tarn, W.W. *Alexander the Great*, Volume II, *Sources and Studies*. London: Cambridge University Press, 1950.

————. *The Greeks in Bactria and India.* London: Cambridge University Press, 1951.

Vámbéry, Ármin. *Travels in Central Asia.* London: John Murray, 1864.

Vernadsky, George. *A History of Russia.* New Haven, CT: Yale University Press, 1951.

Warry, John. *Warfare in the Classical World.* New York: St. Martin's Press, 1980.

Wilcken, Ulrich. *Alexander the Great.* New York: W. W. Norton, 1967.

Xenophon. *The Art of Horsemanship,* trans. M. H. Morgan. London: J. A. Allen & Co., Ltd., 1962.

Zaehner, R.C. *The Dawn and Twilight of Zoroastrianism.* New York: G. P. Putnam's Sons, 1961.

PERIODICALS

Anthony, David, Dimitri Y. Telegin, and Dorcas Brown. "The Origin of Horseback Riding." *Scientific American,* December 1991.

Cunningham, Patrick. "The Genetics of Thoroughbred Horses." *Scientific American,* May 1991.

Fet, Victor. "According to the Red Book of Turkmenistan." *Cape May Geographic Society Bulletin,* No. 44, 1991.

Gleason, Gregory. "The Political Elite in the Muslim Republics of Soviet Central Asia: The Dual Criterion of Power." *Journal of the Institute of Muslim Minority Affairs,* Vol. X, No. 1, 1989.

————. "Marketization and Migration: The Politics of Cotton in Central Asia." *Journal of Soviet Nationalities,* Vol. 1, No. 2, 1990.

Index

Absent (horse), 196, 266, 310
Adcock, F. E., 142
Akhal-Teke Association of
    Turkmenistan, 199
Akhal-Teke horse, 14, 24, 40, 56,
    106–107, 110, 211, 229, 231,
    251
    appearance of, 77–78, 106, 108,
        302–303
    in Ashkhabad–Moscow marathon,
        71–74, 105–106
    care and training of, 111–112,
        220–222, 250–251, 311
    endurance of, 72, 208, 302–303
    history of, 63–64, 112–114, 306
    racing of, 76–77
Alexander the Great, 3, 14, 17–18,
    86–87, 98–102
Amu Darya River, 14, 138
Anaklichev, Yusup, 199–201,
    208–209, 248, 250–251,
    258–261
Aristotle, 102

Ashkhabad, 14, 31
    bazaar of, 261–263
    description of, 35–36, 191
    1948 earthquake of, 36, 38–39,
        223–224

Badkhyz Nature Refuge, 62–63,
    303
Basilov, Dr. Vladimir, 51
Battutah, Ibn, 17, 287
BEVIKO, 24, 70, 86, 105
Boynou (horse), 266
Bucephalus (horse), 98, 99–102
Budyonny, Marshal Semyon, 112,
    231
Byerly Turk (horse), 227, 229

Carrhae, battle of, 267–271
Case, Phil and Margot, 200–201,
    219–222, 253
chappows (plundering raids), 48,
    49
Chorasmia, 17–18, 231

climatic change, 85
Crassus, 268–269, 271

Darley Arabian (horse), 230, 231
Darwin, Charles, 273–274
Davidov, Valeri, 296–298
desertification, 83–84
divan (Central Asian business
    meeting), 69–71, 105
Djumaev, Guvanch, 25, 33–34,
    69–74, 105, 150–151,
    194–197, 209–212, 242,
    246–247, 250, 253, 272,
    306–307, 321–324
Djumaeva, Ala Borisovna, 245–246
Domodedovo Airport, 8–10,
    240–242
dutar (instrument), 253

falconry, 63
Fet, Victor, 58, 234
Firyuza, 201–202

Galishiklee (horse), 114
Geok Tepe, battle of, 45, 46,
    47–50
Gleason, Prof. Greg, 7, 65, 96–97,
    134–135, 213
Godolphin Arabian (horse), 229
Gorbachev, Mikhail, coup attempt
    against, 232–234
Great Wall of China, 84, 143
*Greek and Macedonian Art of War,
    The* (Adcock), 142
Guzil, Gulya, 317–318
Guzil, Kariva, 316–319

Hammer, Armand, 196
Herodotus, 13, 139–141
hippodrome, Ashkhabad municipal,
    75–78, 206–209, 248,
    324–325

horses:
    ancestors of, 273–277
    behavior of, 248–249
    Central Asian style of riding,
        52–54
    domestication of, 13, 51
    Eohippus, 274–275
    Merychippus, 275–276
    "Nisaean," 140
    training of, 188
    Turkoman, 13, 14, 17, 106, 111
Huns, 84

International Sister Cities program
    (Albuquerque–Ashkhabad), 23,
    54–56

Kalinin Institute of Agriculture, 60,
    123
Kaplan (horse), 108
Kara Kala, 58, 62
Kara Kum Canal, 14, 31, 80–81,
    138
Kara Kum Desert, 14, 58, 71–74,
    114, 138–139, 161, 176
Keledjar (horse), 258–259
khalat (robe), 263
Khalbaev, Emutbau, 283, 284–286
Khan, Genghis, 3, 17, 144,
    288–290
Khan, Makdum Kuli, 47
Khiva, 286–287, 290
Khogyshev, Dr. Shikhmurad, 37–38,
    103–104, 154
    Gulya or Yedesh, 36–37, 41–42
    Yenye, 68, 91–93, 102–103,
        154–155
Khwarizm, 288–289
Kiarizov, Geldi, 105–107, 110, 248,
    302–304, 307–308, 312
    father of, 148

house of, 109–110
stud farm of, 301–303
Komsomol stud farm, 56–57,
    199–200, 248–249, 257
Kopet-Dag Mountains, 31, 83, 87,
    137, 162
Kordonski, Leonid, 213–214, 236
Kou-Ata cave, 88–89
Kozlov, Andrei, 127–129, 138

Lenin, Vladimir Ilyich, 80, 123
lucerne (alfalfa), 137–138

Makhtymkuli, 35, 253–256
Marco Polo, 17, 82
Mary, 164
Merv, 164–165
Miocene epoch, 274–277
Mongols, 288–290

Nisa, 264–265
Niyazov, Saparmurad, 304–305
nomads, 10, 50–54, 84–85, 144
    as herders, 51
    in migrations, 52
"Nomads of the Eurasian Steppes"
    (1989 U.S.–Soviet exhibition),
    51

O'Donovan, Edmund, 47–50
offitsialnoye litso ("official face"), 46
*Origin and Influence of the
    Thoroughbred Horse, The*
    (Ridgeway), 224

Parthians, 17, 86–87, 231,
    264–265, 267–271
phalanx (Macedonian infantry), 86,
    99, 142–143
Philip, King of Macedonia, 99–102
Plutarch, 268–269
Polotli (horse), 199

Railroad, Central Asian, 50
Ratchford, Moira, 219, 245, 279,
    293–294, 299
Reebok, Sasha, 39, 54–55, 123–127
reindeer, 82
Repetek:
    Institute of the Desert, 58, 62,
        166–167, 168–169
    settlement, 180–181
Ridgeway, William, 224
rugs, Oriental, 263–264

Sandjar, Sultan of Seljuq, 165,
    251
Sarmatians, 84
Scythians, 13, 53, 84, 211
Semedov, Djura, 32, 44, 54, 65,
    67–69, 94–95, 120–122,
    173–174, 203–206, 210
Shambarant, Vladimir Petrovich,
    114
Shammakov, Professor, 130, 146,
    156–161, 162–164, 167,
    177–178, 182–184
shornik (saddlemaker), 283
Skorokhodov, Sasha, 86, 197–199,
    202–203, 272, 293–296
Sopiev, Prof. Ovez, 60–64,
    131–132, 138
steppes:
    description of, 10–11, 13, 84,
        143–144
    Neolithic agricultural settlements
        on, 52–53, 83
Surena, 269, 271

Tamerlane, 47
Tarlan (horse), 258
Tashauz, 277–278
telpek (hat), 262
Thompson, Sally Alice, 6, 7, 23,
    54–55, 213

Thoroughbred, history of the
English, 225–231
traditional cultures, 12–13
turkmenbalak (pantaloons),
263
Turkmen culture:
cavalry practices, 49
horses, way of outfitting,
285–286
Oguz (tribe), 251
saddlery and harness making,
272, 284–285
Teke (tribe), 35, 111, 250,
262
traditional banquet, 251–253,
309–311
weddings, 147–150
Yomut (tribe), 250
Turkmen Friendship Society, 27,
32, 43–44, 54
Turkmenistan, 6, 15–17, 47
Turkmenistan Express, 155,
272

Turkmen Society for the
Conservation of Nature, 60
turtle, Central Asian (*Testudo
horsfieldi*), 157–158

Ujhelyi, Ilona, 22
Urugan, 116

Vambery, Armin, 246
Vavilov, Nikolai, 137
Ve-De-En-Kha (Exhibition Hall of
the Accomplishments of the
Turkmen People), 192–194

Witt, Dr. W. O., 230–231
woodpecker, scaled, 129

Xenophon, 99
Xerxes, 140–142

Yengi Sheher, 49

Zhukov, Marshal Georgi, 113

A writer, naturalist, and filmmaker, JONATHAN MASLOW is the author of two other highly acclaimed books. His first, *The Owl Papers*, took him on a year-long nocturnal journey in quest of these wise birds of prey. *Bird of Life, Bird of Death: A Political Ornithology of Central America* is the fascinating, often chilling account of the author's daring odyssey into the highlands of Guatemala in search of the rare and beautiful quetzal, a spectacular bird that symbolizes the unfulfilled dreams of the Mayan Indians.

In his documentary film *A Tramp in the Darien*, Mr. Maslow became the first to record a congress of Kuna Indians, the grandmother of democratic parliaments going back to before Columbus. His current documentary video is *Geldi: A Horseman of the Turkmen Steppes*, which was shot in Turkmenistan and tells the story of a Turkmen breeder of Akhal-Teke horses.

Mr. Maslow lives in Cape May County, New Jersey.